ENCYCLOPEDIA OF DISASTERS

ENCYCLOPEDIA OF DISASTERS

Environmental Catastrophes and Human Tragedies

VOLUME 1

ANGUS M. GUNN

GREENWOOD PRESS
Westport, Connecticut • London

Library of Congress Cataloging-in-Publication Data

Gunn, Angus M. (Angus Macleod), 1920–
Encyclopedia of disasters : environmental catastrophes and human tragedies / Angus M. Gunn.
p. cm.
Includes bibliographical references and index.
ISBN-13: 978–0–313–34002–4 ((set) : alk. paper)
ISBN-13: 978–0–313–34003–1 ((vol 1) : alk. paper)
ISBN-13: 978–0–313–34004–8 ((vol 2) : alk. paper)
1. Natural disasters—Encyclopedias. I. Title.
GB5014.G86 2008
904—dc22 2007031001

British Library Cataloguing in Publication Data is available.

Library of Congress Catalog Card Number: 2007031001
ISBN-13: 978–0–313–34002–4 (set)
978–0–313–34003–1 (vol 1)
978–0–313–34004–8 (vol 2)

First published in 2008

Greenwood Press, 88 Post Road West, Westport, CT 06881
An imprint of Greenwood Publishing Group, Inc.
www.greenwood.com

Printed in the United States of America

The paper used in this book complies with the Permanent Paper Standard issued by the National Information Standards Organization (Z39.48–1984).

10 9 8 7 6 5 4 3 2 1

Contents

Volume 2

Credits for Illustrations

Figure 1 Artist: Paul Giesbrecht.
Figure 2 Artist: Paul Giesbrecht.
Figure 3 Artist: Paul Giesbrecht.
Figure 4 Artist: Paul Giesbrecht.
Figure 5 Artist: Paul Giesbrecht.
Figure 6 Artist: Paul Giesbrecht.
Figure 7 Artist: Paul Giesbrecht.
Figure 8 Artist: Paul Giesbrecht.
Figure 9 Courtesy National Library of Medicine.
Figure 10 Courtesy Prints & Photographs Division, Library of Congress, LC-USZ62–54977.
Figure 11 Artist: Paul Giesbrecht.
Figure 12 Artist: Paul Giesbrecht.
Figure 13 Courtesy U.S. Geological Survey Photo Library.
Figure 14 Courtesy U.S. Geological Survey Photo Library.
Figure 15 Artist: Paul Giesbrect.
Figure 16 Courtesy Prints and Photographs Division, Library of Congress, LC-USZ62–3066.
Figure 17 Artist: Paul Giesbrecht.
Figure 18 Photo: P. Hedervari. Courtesy National Geophysical Data Center.
Figure 19 Courtesy U.S. Geological Survey Photo Library.
Figure 20 Photo: J. K. Hillers. Courtesy U.S. Geological Survey Photo Library.
Figure 21 Archival Photograph by Steve Nicklas, NOS, NGS. Courtesy National Oceanic and Atmospheric Administration/ Department of Commerce.
Figure 22 Courtesy Prints and Photographs Department, Library of Congress, LC-USZ62–46831.

Figure 23	Geo. Barker, photographer, Niagara Falls, N.Y. Courtesy Prints and Photographs Division, Library of Congress, LC-USZ62–96085.
Figure 24	Courtesy National Oceanic and Atmospheric Administration/Department of Commerce.
Figure 25	Courtesy National Oceanic and Atmospheric Administration/Department of Commerce.
Figure 26	Courtesy of Panoramic Photographs, Prints and Photographs Division, Library of Congress, pan.6a13048.
Figure 27	Courtesy, Prints and Photographs Division, Library of Congress, LC-USZ62–123884.
Figure 28	Artist: Paul Giesbrecht.
Figure 29	Courtesy Prints and Photographs Division, Library of Congress, C-USZ62–47617.
Figure 30	Courtesy Prints and Photographs Division, Library of Congress, LC-USZ62–75513.
Figure 31	Courtesy: NOAA/NGDC/B. Bradley, University of Colorado.
Figure 32	Chicago (Ill), 1904, Photographer—*Chicago Daily News*. Chicago History Museum.
Figure 33	Chicago History Museum.
Figure 34	Courtesy Prints and Photographs Division, Library of Congress, LC-USZ62–95042.
Figure 35	Photograph by Ralph O. Hotz. April 1906. Courtesy U.S. Geological Survey Photo Library.
Figure 36	Courtesy U.S. Geological Survey Photo Library.
Figure 37	Courtesy U.S. Geological Survey Photo Library.
Figure 38	Courtesy U.S. Geological Survey Photo Library.
Figure 39	Courtesy of the *Charleston Gazette*.
Figure 40	Courtesy Prints and Photographs Division, Library of Congress, LC-USZ62–56585.
Figure 41	Courtesy Prints and Photographs Division, Library of Congress, LC-DIG-ggbain-11212.
Figure 42	Courtesy Prints and Photographs Division, Library of Congress, LC-DIG-ppmsc-01940.
Figure 43	Courtesy Prints and Photographs Division, Library of Congress, LC-B2–2571–8.
Figure 44	Photograph by R.E. Wallace. Courtesy U.S. Geological Survey Photo Library.
Figure 45	Courtesy Prints and Photographs Division, Library of Congress, LC-DIG-ggbain-25894.
Figure 46	Courtesy Prints and Photographs Division, Library of Congress, LC-USZ62–126995.
Figure 47	Courtesy of the National Museum of Health and Medicine, Armed Forces Institute of Pathology, Washington, D.C. NCP 1603.

Figure 48	Courtesy National Oceanic and Atmospheric Administration/Department of Commerce.
Figure 49	Courtesy U.S. Geological Survey Photo Library.
Figure 50	Courtesy Prints and Photographs Division, Library of Congress, LC-USZ62–126498.
Figure 51	Courtesy U.S. Geological Survey Photo Library/Los Angeles Bureau of Power and Light.
Figure 52	Courtesy U.S. Geological Survey Photo Library.
Figure 53	Courtesy Prints and Photographs Division, Library of Congress, LC-USZ62–123429.
Figure 54	Courtesy Prints and Photographs Division, Library of Congress, LC-USZ62–70085.
Figure 55	Courtesy AP Images.
Figure 56	Photo: Archival Photography by Steve Nicklas, NOS, NGS. Courtesy National Oceanic and Atmospheric Administration/Department of Commerce.
Figure 57	Courtesy National Oceanic and Atmospheric Administration/Department of Commerce.
Figure 58	Photo by R. Morrow. Courtesy U.S. Geological Survey Photo Library.
Figure 59	Courtesy U.S. Geological Survey Photo Library.
Figure 60	Courtesy The Cleveland Press Collection, Special Collections, Cleveland State University Library.
Figure 61	Courtesy Prints and Photographs Division, Library of Congress, LC-USZ62–134192.
Figure 62	Courtesy Prints and Photographs Department, Library of Congress, LC-USZ62–53609.
Figure 63	Photo credit: NGDC/NOAA/U.S. Coast Guard.
Figure 64	Photo credit: NGDC/NOAA/U.S. Coast Guard.
Figure 65	Courtesy City of Texas City and Moore Memorial Public Library.
Figure 66	Courtesy NOAA/NGDC.
Figure 67	Courtesy U.S. Geological Survey Photo Library.
Figure 68	Photo credit: U.S. Navy.
Figure 69	Courtesy Prints and Photographs Division, Library of Congress, LC-USZ62–114381.
Figure 70	Photo courtesy of The Texas Collection, Baylor University, Waco, Texas.
Figure 71	Courtesy National Oceanic and Atmospheric Administration/Department of Commerce.
Figure 72	Photo: D. J. Miller. Courtesy U.S. Geological Survey Photo Library.
Figure 73	Photo by J. R. Stacy. Courtesy U.S. Geological Survey Photo Library.
Figure 74	Photo: I. J. Witkind. Courtesy U.S. Geological Survey Photo Library.

Figure 75 Courtesy U.S. Geological Survey Photo Library.
Figure 76 Courtesy NOAA/NGDC/Pierre St. Amand.
Figure 77 Courtesy AP Images/stf
Figure 78 Artist: Paul Giesbrecht.
Figure 79 Photo by Emanuele Paolini, Wikipedia commons.
Figure 80 Courtesy U.S. Geological Survey Photo Library.
Figure 81 Photo: R. Vetter of the American Red Cross. Courtesy National Oceanic and Atmospheric Administration/ Department of Commerce.
Figure 82 Courtesy AP Images.
Figure 83 Courtesy National Oceanic and Atmospheric Administration/Department of Commerce.
Figure 84 Courtesy Angus Gunn
Figure 85 Photo Credit: University of Colorado.
Figure 86 Courtesy NOAA/NGDC/University of Colorado.
Figure 87 Courtesy U.S. Geological Survey Photo Library.
Figure 88 Courtesy AP Images/Kurt Strumpf.
Figure 89 Photo by R.D. Brown Jr. Courtesy U.S. Geological Survey Photo Library.
Figure 90 Courtesy U.S. Geological Survey Photo Library.
Figure 91 Courtesy Angus Gunn.
Figure 92 Courtesy NOAA/NGDC/National Park Service.
Figure 93 Figure 55, U.S. Geological Survey Professional paper 1002. Courtesy U.S. Geological Survey Photo Library.
Figure 94 Figure 46-C, U.S. Geological Survey Professional paper 1002. Courtesy U.S. Geological Survey Photo Library.
Figure 95 Courtesy Angus Gunn.
Figure 96 Courtesy NOAA/NGDC/J.M. Gere, Stanford University.
Figure 97 Courtesy AP Images/Paul Vathis.
Figure 98 Courtesy U.S. Geological Survey Photo Library.
Figure 99 Courtesy Angus Gunn.
Figure 100 Courtesy U.S. Geological Survey Photo Library.
Figure 101 Photo: M.G. Hopper. Courtesy U.S. Geological Survey Photo Library.
Figure 102 Courtesy AP Images/Sondeep.
Figure 103 Courtesy NOAA/NGDC/U.S. Geological Survey.
Figure 104 Courtesy NASA
Figure 105 Courtesy NOAA/NGDC/C.J. Langer, U.S. Geological Survey.
Figure 106 Courtesy AP Images.
Figure 107 Photo: C. E. Meyer. Courtesy U.S. Geological Survey Photo Library.
Figure 108 Photo by G. Plafker. Courtesy U.S. Geological Survey Photo Library.
Figure 109 Courtesy Defense Visual Information Center.
Figure 110 Courtesy NOAA/NGDC/R. Batalon, U.S. Air Force.

Figure 111	Courtesy National Oceanic and Atmospheric Administration/Department of Commerce.
Figure 112	FEMA News Photo.
Figure 113	Credit NASA GSFC Visualization Analysis Laboratory.
Figure 114	Courtesy AP Images/Richard Drew.
Figure 115	FEMA News Photo.
Figure 116	FEMA News Photo.
Figure 117	Courtesy NOAA/NGDC/Dr. Roger Hutchison.
Figure 118	Courtesy NOAA/NGDC/Dr. Roger Hutchison.
Figure 119	FEMA News Photo.
Figure 120	Photo by Michael Rieger/ FEMA News Photo.
Figure 121	Courtesy Angus Gunn.
Figure 122	Photo by Dave Gatley/ FEMA News Photo.
Figure 123	Courtesy NASA Visible Earth.
Figure 124	Courtesy U.S. Navy. Photo by Photographer's Mate 2nd Class Philip A. McDaniel.
Figure 125	Courtesy Angus Gunn.
Figure 126	Courtesy Jeff Schmaltz, MODIS Rapid Response Team, NASA/GSFC.
Figure 127	Courtesy Jocelyn Augustino/ FEMA News Photo.
Figure 128	D.K. Demcheck. Courtesy U.S. Geological Survey Photo Library.
Figure 129	Courtesy Lieut. Commander Mark Moran, NOAA Corps, NMAO/AOC.
Figure 130	Photo by Michael Raphael/ FEMA News Photo.

Guide to Thematic Entries

EARTHQUAKES AND TSUNAMIS

Kamchatka, Russia, earthquake, 1923
Tokyo, Japan, earthquake, 1923
Charlevoix, Quebec, earthquake, 1925
Clarkston Valley, Montana, earthquake, 1925
Santa Barbara, California, earthquake, 1925
Lompoc, California, earthquake, 1927
Grand Banks, Nova Scotia, earthquake, 1929
Nevada earthquake, 1932
Sanriku, Japan, earthquake, 1933
Baffin Bay, Canada, earthquake, 1933
Bihar, India, earthquake, 1934
Quetta earthquake, 1935
Imperial Valley, California, earthquake, 1940
San Juan, Argentina, earthquake, 1944
Unimak, Alaska, tsunami, 1946
Vancouver Island, Canada, earthquake, 1946
Nankaido, Japan, earthquake, 1946
Puget Sound, Washington, earthquake, 1949
Queen Charlotte Islands, Canada, earthquake, 1949
Assam, India, earthquake, 1950
Kern County, California, earthquake, 1952
Kamchatka, Russia, earthquake, 1952
Fallon-Stillwater, Nevada, earthquake, 1954
Lituya Bay, Alaska, earthquake, 1958
West Yellowstone, Montana, earthquake, 1959
Chile earthquake, 1960
Prince William Sound, Alaska, earthquake, 1964
Peru earthquake, 1970
Managua, Nicaragua, earthquake, 1972
Kalapana, Hawaii, earthquake, 1975
Guatemala earthquake, 1976
Tangshan, China, earthquake, 1976
Coalinga, California, earthquake, 1983
Mexico earthquake, 1985
Armenia earthquake, 1988
Loma Prieta, California, earthquake, 1989
Northridge, California, earthquake, 1994
Kobe, Japan, earthquake, 1995
Peru offshore earthquake, 2001
Sumatra, Indonesia, earthquake and tsunami, 2004
Northern California offshore earthquake, 2005
Pakistan earthquake, 2005
Taiwan earthquake, 2006

CONFLICTS

St. Petersburg, Russia, revolution, 1905
Ukraine catastrophe, 1932
Nanking massacre, 1937
Hiroshima, Japan, nuclear bomb, 1945
Bikini Atoll, Marshall Islands, nuclear tests, 1946
Tiananmen Square, China, massacre, 1989
Rwanda genocide, 1994
Srebrenica, Bosnia-Herzegovina, genocide, 1995

FLOODS

Yellow River, China, flood, 1887
Johnstown, Pennsylvania, flood, 1889
Netherlands (Holland) flood, 1953
Brisbane, Australia, flood, 1974
Red River flood, 1997

HUMAN ERRORS

Rome, Italy, fire, 64
London, England, fire, 1666
Bengal, India, famine, 1770
Chicago, Illinois, fire, 1871
Turtle Mountain, Alberta, Canada, landslide, 1903
Theater, Chicago, Illinois, fire, 1903
Monongah, Pennsylvania, explosion, 1907
Titanic iceburg tragedy, 1912
Halifax, Nova Scotia, Canada, explosion, 1917
St. Francis Dam failure, 1928
Stock Market Collapse, 1929
Hindenburg crash, 1937
Cleveland, Ohio, gas explosion, 1944
Texas City, Texas, explosion, 1947
London, England, suffocating smog, 1952
Thalidomide drug tragedy, 1957
New York City, New York, midair collision, 1960
Vaiont Dam, Italy, collapse, 1963
Aberfan, SouthWales, Britain, landslide, 1966
Iraq mercury poisoning, 1971
Teton Dam, Idaho, collapse, 1976
Seveso, Italy, dioxin spill, 1976
France oil spill, 1978
Love Canal, New York, contamination, 1978
Three Mile Island, Pennsylvania, nuclear accident, 1979
Canada, sinking of oil platform, 1982
Bhopal, India, gas poisoning, 1984
Challenger (space shuttle), Florida, fire/explosion, 1986
Chernobyl, Ukraine, nuclear accident, 1986
Alaska oil spill, 1989

HURRICANES AND OTHER TROPICAL CYCLONES

Calcutta, India, cyclone, 1864
Bangladesh cyclone, 1876
Georgia/South Carolina hurricane, 1881
Haiphong, Vietnam, typhoon, 1881
Georgia/South Carolina hurricane, 1893
Louisiana hurricane, 1893
Galveston, Texas, hurricane, 1900
Louisiana hurricane, 1909
Texas hurricane, 1915
Florida/Gulf of Mexico hurricane, 1919
Florida hurricane, 1926
Lake Okeechobee hurricane, 1928
Labor Day hurricane 1935
New England hurricane, 1938
Northeast United States hurricane, 1944
Japan typhoon, 1959

Hurricane Betsy, 1965
Hurricane Camille, 1969
Bangladesh cyclone, 1970
Hurricane Agnes, 1972
Hurricane Andrew, 1992
Hurricane Floyd, 1999
Hurricane Katrina, 2005

PANDEMICS

Constantinople, Byzantine Empire, Black Death plague, 542
London, England, Black Death plague, 1665
World-wide flu pandemic, 1918–1919

TERRORISM

Munich, Germany, terrorism, 1972
Air terrorism, 1985
Persian Gulf oil inferno, 1991
New York City, New York, terrorism, 1993
Oklahoma City, Oklahoma, terrorism, 1995
Nine Eleven, New York City, New York, terrorism, 2001
United States anthrax terrorism, 2001

TORNADOES

Natchez, Mississippi, tornado, 1840
Marshfield, Missouri, tornado, 1880
Louisville, Kentucky, tornado, 1890
St. Louis, Missouri, tornado, 1896
New Richmond, Wisconsin, tornado, 1899
Goliad, Texas, tornado, 1902
Amite, Louisiana, tornado, 1908
Omaha, Nebraska, tornado, 1913
Mattoon, Illinois, tornado, 1917
Illinois/Indiana/Missouri tornado, 1925
Gainesville tornado, 1936
Shinnston, West Virginia, tornado, 1944
Woodward, Oklahoma, tornado, 1947
Waco, Texas, tornado, 1953
Flint, Michigan, tornado, 1953
Greensburg, Kansas, tornado, 2007

VOLCANIC ERUPTIONS

Supervolcano Toba, Indonesia, 74,000 BC
Pompeii, Italy, volcanic eruption, 79
Arequipa, Peru, volcanic eruption, 1600
Tambora, Indonesia, volcanic eruption, 1815
Krakatau, Indonesia, volcanic eruption, 1883
Mount Pelee volcanic eruption, 1902

Santa Maria, Guatemala, volcanic eruption, 1902
Katmai, Alaska, volcanic eruption, 1912
Kelud, Indonesia, volcanic eruption, 1919
Paricutin, Mexico, volcanic eruption, 1943
Tristan da Cunha volcanic eruption, 1961
Iceland volcanic eruption, 1973
Mount St. Helens, Washington, volcanic eruption, 1980
Nevado del Ruiz, Colombia, volcanic eruption, 1985
Mount Pinatubo, Philippines, volcanic eruption, 1991

Preface

This encyclopedia is a descriptive, illustrated account of disasters, both natural and human-induced, that have occurred throughout the world at different times over the past two thousand years. They include experiences of earthquakes, tsunamis, volcanic eruptions, floods, extremes of weather, droughts, pandemic illnesses, land subsidence and landslides. Most troubling of all is a newcomer to the world of disasters, the terrorist attack. While terrorists have, from time to time in the past, wrought havoc on human environments, the expanded volume and brutality of their activities over the past thirty years has gone beyond all previous acts of violence. Terrorism is the type of disaster that may become increasingly destructive in the future.

Sometimes disasters are so named if a large number of people are killed. At other times, the criteria is the amount of damage done to homes and other structures. A third identifying characteristic is the long-term consequences of the event. In this encyclopedia, disaster events have been selected on the bases of all three of these characteristics. A calamitous event that occurred at a given point in time is selected if it caused great damage, significant loss of life, and carried important consequences for subsequent years. The majority of the events included are natural disasters such as earthquakes, floods, and volcanic eruptions because, for the better part of the past two thousand years, catastrophes of this kind were the costliest and deadliest in human experience. Natural disasters were also, and still are, highly unpredictable, so there are good reasons to study them and so continue the search for answers to their predictability.

Human tragedies, events that involve human choices, though fewer in number over the course of the two thousand years that this encyclopedia covers, must also be included in any study of disasters because they, unlike natural tragedies, will continue to increase in both frequency of occurrence and extent of damage. Furthermore, the understanding, prevention, or minimization of the destruction of any disaster anywhere in the world is vital to the preservation of our global environment. The enormous power and influence that can be wielded by one person raises the need for a better understanding of human behavior. A single error by one person, as happened in the Chernobyl nuclear power station in the Soviet Union in 1986, can cause extensive damage to a whole continent. In the Bhopal Chemical Factory in India in 1984, the mistakes of one or two workers led to the deaths of 8,000 and the injury of 250,000.

Human-induced disasters appear to be fundamentally different from natural ones. They are regarded as the results of human error or malicious intent, and whatever happens when they occur leaves us with the feeling that we can prevent a recurrence. In fact, the difference between these human-induced and natural disasters is not clear. More and more we find that human activity affects our natural environment to such an extent that we often have to reassess the causes of so-called natural disasters, recognizing that preventable human error might have contributed to the damage. Take, for example, the San Francisco earthquake of 1906. The firestorm that swept over the city immediately after the quake, causing far more damage than the direct impact of the earthquake, could have been less destructive if the city's fire prevention plans had been better organized.

The intended audience for this encyclopedia ranges in age from the beginning of elementary school to senior citizens. I have always found that if a topic is sufficiently important and interesting to gain space in newspapers and popular magazines, almost everyone wants to know about it. There is still stronger evidence for the popular interest in disasters in the large number of movies that have been made about them. Disasters initiated by terrorists have recently begun to appear; one is based on the murder of Israeli athletes at the Munich Olympics in 1972; the terrorist assault on New York and Washington in 2001 was the basis for two others. Movie directors in China produced a movie based on the atrocities committed by Japanese soldiers in China's old capital, Nanking, in 1937. Some disaster movies have hit the highest levels of financial success.

The problem with this kind of movie is that accuracy of detail is a victim. Hollywood takes liberties with historical events, shaping them to fit the goals of the producer. All of this poses a special problem for me because I made every effort to stick to historical accuracy. It is important that readers recognize this disparity between the facts of the event and the additions and subtractions included by the film producer. I recommend that you read about a disaster in this book before you see a movie about it. In this way you can tell what is true and what is fiction. In addition to the information about the disaster that you can read in this encyclopedia, references are provided for further study. A reader can also go the many web sites for descriptions and photos of an event.

The complete list of disasters is arranged chronologically, beginning with one from pre-history and followed by two from the times of the Roman Empire. Many countries are represented in the whole collection and each one constitutes a single event occurring within a short span of time.

Wartime events are excluded except for the bombing of Hiroshima in 1945, which was included because of the vast environmental consequences that followed from it in later years. Alternative ways of categorizing the various disasters are provided and these, along with the index, simplify searches. In each description of a disaster there is first a summary overview of the event with details of its location, time of occurrence, and type of disaster. A detailed description with explanations of causes follows next, and the account then deals with remedial actions, where possible, together with recommendations to ameliorate damage in the event of similar disasters occurring in the future.

Acknowledgments

I am indebted to very many people who helped me in researching, selecting content, and writing this encyclopedia. Everybody seems interested in stories of disasters. I found colleagues at my university, friends, and especially my family members, always ready to talk about disastrous events from the past, and to focus on the ones that impacted them most—tragedies such as the assault on the Twin Towers in 2001 or the tsunami of Boxing Day, 2004, that swept across the Indian Ocean, killing over 200,000 people. In addition to help from the rich literature on both natural and human-induced catastrophes from the past, I was greatly assisted by journal articles and e-mail replies from scholars in The U.S. Geological Survey, The Geological Society of America, The Seismological Society of America, and the Smithsonian Institution. Last, but certainly not least, I am very appreciative of my editor at Greenwood Press, Kevin Downing, whose quick and helpful responses, and courteous treatment of problems, enabled me to complete the manuscript far ahead of my expectations.

Introduction

These two volumes on disasters deal mainly with environmental catastrophes, earthquakes, volcanic eruptions and extremes of weather, because they are the causes of the costliest and deadliest events throughout history. They are also the least predictable among the many kinds of disasters, so there are good reasons to study them and to continue the search for answers to their predictability. Human tragedies, events that frequently involve human choices, must also be included in the study of disasters because they, unlike the environmental disasters, will continue to increase in the future in both frequency of occurrence and extent of damage. Understanding of disasters anywhere in the world is vital to the preservation of our global environment. Unfortunately, all too often, as will be evident in the events that are documented in these books, we fail to learn from past disasters and so we encounter them again at a later time, augmented expressions of tragedies that could have been avoided.

We tend to think of the environment as the natural world around us—the physical ground beneath our feet, the rocks, water, vegetation, and life forms, together with the atmosphere above. This outlook probably comes from earlier times when humanity was greatly influenced by the vagaries of weather and the quality of crops grown. We are still very dependent on these things, but our dependence is greatly reduced to the point where we become serious players in the shaping of our natural environment. Global warming is one example of this. While climatic shifts take place over long periods of time, these shifts are now being accelerated by our widespread use of materials that raise average temperatures faster than would occur naturally.

Our independence from the controlling influence of the natural world is largely related to technology. The traditional necessity of having to travel considerable distances for almost every activity has been enormously reduced by computers, television, and the Internet. University degrees can be earned at home and the most intricate items of clothing or furniture can be manufactured at a distance using computer technology.

Our rate of consumption of almost all natural resources has dropped greatly because of the efficiency of new methods and new materials. In some instances we create the new materials we need from the fundamental elements of matter. Cars run faster and farther on less fuel and other machines use less electricity to do the same work they formerly did. As a result, we consume less of irreplaceable oil and gas supplies.

While the more obvious benefits of technology are easily identified the dark side must also be acknowledged. Chemical industries worldwide are causing havoc in our air and water, greatly endangering our health. Several case studies in these books address the problem. They are not isolated events. The enormous power and influence that can be wielded by one person raises human behavior to a new level of concern. A single error by one person in a major chemical factory can kill thousands of people. In a nuclear installation such as Chernobyl, one person's mistake can and did damage a continent. A terrorist can blackmail a whole city by threatening to contaminate its water supply. Relationships and the social life of humans are now key elements of our environment because they may determine errant individual behavior. Are we going to see more and more natural as well as human disasters as population and human activity of all kinds continue to increase? For disasters involving human activity, yes. For those caused by volcanoes, earthquakes, and extremes of weather, maybe. Before examining that last statement further, the word "disaster" needs to be defined.

MEANING OF DISASTER

The titles of both books, *Encyclopedia of Disasters: Environmental Catastrophes and Human Tragedies*, need to be defined because there are many reasons behind the usage of the word "disaster." Sometimes a disaster is defined by the number of people killed, sometimes by the damage done to homes and other structures, and at other times we call an event a disaster if there are long-term negative consequences. The definition followed in these books is this: a calamitous event at one point of time causing great damage, loss, and destruction. The majority of the events will be natural disasters such as earthquakes and volcanic eruptions because of the time frame chosen, the past two thousand years. Throughout that period of time, most disasters were caused by natural happenings. There are large gaps in the history of such disasters because the details of many events that in all likelihood happened are just not available in any of the documentary records. Occasionally field research will unearth a famous disaster and it is then added to the records we have. The massive earthquake in the Pacific Northwest in 1700, described in this book, is a good example of this kind of finding.

The research regarding the 1700 earthquake is also an example of a new and intriguing branch of geology, determining the recurrent rates of major earthquakes and volcanic eruptions. Through examination of past surface deposits, as well as underground evidences of past disruptions of bedded layers, it is possible to date the approximate times of past events. Thus, for some powerful earthquakes like the one in 1700, the technologies available can identify when the most recent event before 1700 occurred and often several of the ones from still farther back. Once a series of times are found, our ability to predict similar disasters in the future is greatly enhanced. In the case of the 1700 earthquake, identifying the time of its occurrence, a time that was before the arrival of people from Eastern United States, was greatly aided by accurate Japanese records and both the year and the date of the event became known. Additionally, the dates for past eruptions of Yellowstone Volcano are known for two or three past eruptions. The last eruption was over 600,000 years ago. Because of the great time periods involved and the few past records available it is impossible to predict when the next one will come. More will be said later in this introduction regarding predicting earthquakes.

Natural disasters—earthquakes, hurricanes, floods, droughts—are familiar events, and we feel that we have little control over them. All we think we can do is minimize damage to people and property. Human-induced disasters, however, appear to be fundamentally different. They are regarded as the results of human error or malicious intent and whatever happens when they occur leaves us with the feeling that we can prevent a recurrence. In fact, the difference between these two types of disasters is not at all crystal clear. More and more we find that human activity is affecting our natural environment to such an extent that we often have to reassess the causes of so-called natural disasters, recognizing that preventable human error might have contributed to some of the damage. Take, for example, the great San Francisco earthquake of 1906. The firestorm that swept over the city immediately after the quake, causing far more damage than the direct impact of the earthquake, could have been minimized had alternatives to the city's water mains been in place.

The story was similar when the Loma Prieta earthquake struck in 1989. The Marina District of San Francisco that was known to be unstable and had been severely damaged in 1906 was subsequently developed and built up. When Loma Prieta struck, the area collapsed due to liquefaction. The shaking of the relatively loose soil changed the land into a liquid and buildings sank into the ground. These secondary effects of human action or inaction are increasingly important considerations in the study of disasters. However, they were not the primary elements in the two examples quoted. The main causes were still the unpredictable and uncontrollable forces of nature and these will be examined in some detail before looking at human-induced disasters. Worldwide, earthquakes both in the past and today, along with their associated events, tsunamis and volcanic eruptions, are the most costly of all natural hazards and so they will be given first place in the following descriptions. Floods are second in importance in terms of costs but first in relation to loss of life. Other major natural hazards are hurricanes, tornadoes, fires, drought, and landslides.

CITIES AT RISK

Earlier I mentioned that there is a question, a 'maybe' about whether purely natural disasters will get worse with time. In general, there is little doubt that there have been disasters as bad as or worse than current disasters all through time and pre-history and the processes, like the plate tectonics that cause them, will continue in the future to affect the same places as they have always done. Worldwide there are at the present time, on average, two or more earthquakes of magnitude 8 per year, twenty of magnitude 7, one hundred of magnitude 6, and three thousand of magnitude 5. Below magnitude 5 there can be fifteen thousand or more earthquakes every year. The reason for the 'maybe' in future rates of natural disasters is related to a major human activity, the growth of large cities.

Throughout most of human history, the total number of people increased very slowly. Birth rates were high and death rates were also high. Famine, disease, and wars prevented substantial population increases. From about 1 AD to the year 1700 the world's population doubled and reached one billion. Even after 1700, growth rate remained slow. The death of one in every four children in the first year of life was common. In spite of these challenges and with a life expectancy of only thirty-five years, the world's population doubled again by 1950. The benefits of the industrial revolution, especially the ability to control some diseases, contributed to this growth. However, the very big increases in the world's population and the constant increases in its rate of growth—the development that we called the "Population Explosion" in the 1950s and 1960s—all relate to events from 1950 onwards.

Improvement in medical services throughout the world in the aftermath of World War II caused a dramatic cut in death rates. Birth rates, however, remained high. Thus, from 1950 to 2000 the world's population jumped from 2.5 billion to 6 billion. Alongside these rapid changes came urbanization, the movement of people away from rural settings into cities; a movement that became so big by the 1970s that the majority of a nation's population in many developed countries would be found in cities. Some cities, because of their locations or their local resources, were more attractive than others and, before long, there began to emerge the super cities, the ones with extremely large numbers of people. In 1950, New York was the first to have a population of more than ten million. By 1970 there were three cities with more than ten million each, and by 1990 there were ten. Any disaster in one of these super cities, whether caused by natural or unnatural events, would inevitably be a terrible tragedy.

The following table will illustrate the nature of this new problem.

The world's ten biggest urban centers at different times.
Population data are all in millions.

1950	1970	1990	2010
New York, 12	Tokyo, 16	Tokyo, 25	Tokyo, 29
London, 9	New York, 16	Sao Paulo, 18	Sao Paulo, 25
Tokyo, 7	Shanghai, 11	New York, 16	Bombay, 24
Paris, 5	Mexico City, 9	Mexico City, 15	Shanghai, 22
Moscow, 5	London, 9	Shanghai, 13	Lagos, 21
Shanghai, 5	Paris, 8	Bombay, 12	Mexico City, 18
Essen, 5	Buenos Aires, 8	Los Angeles, 11	Beijing, 18
Buenos Aires, 5	Bombay, 8	Buenos Aires, 11	Dacca, 18
Chicago, 5	Los Angeles, 8	Seoul, 11	New York 17
Calcutta, 4	Beijing, 8	Rio de Janeiro, 11	Jakarta, 17

What has happened is this: over the sixty-year period from 1950 to 2010, the big urban areas that are in the locations of greatest risk of earthquakes have increased their populations much more than those that face a lesser risk. In 1950, sixteen million people lived in high-risk urban centers, Tokyo, Shanghai, and Calcutta. In 2010 there are 122 million people at risk in six vulnerable urban centers, Tokyo, Shanghai, Mexico City, Beijing, Dacca, and Jakarta, an increase of more than 600 percent. In 2010, the other four of the top ten cities that are located in less vulnerable locations only add up to eighty-seven million, a much smaller percentage growth. The augmented destruction that can occur in these more vulnerable cities was vividly portrayed in Mexico City's earthquake in 1985. Although the epicenter was hundreds of miles away from Mexico City, about 9,500 people were killed and 30,000 injured. The cost of all the damage reached three billion dollars.

Even in cities much smaller than the above groups of ten, the high concentrations of people and buildings can lead to devastating costs when an earthquake strikes. The following illustrations from Kobe and Los Angeles (Northridge) show how the destruction is greatly increased when an earthquake strikes any urban area. Kobe has a population of 1.5 million. It is a seaport, the main economic center for western Japan, and it has a high concentration of transportation systems and high-rise buildings. When it was hit with an earthquake in 1995, about 5,400 were killed, another 26,800 injured, and 300,000 left homeless. In addition, over 100,000 buildings were destroyed beyond repair. Costs amounted to 150 billion in U.S. dollars. In Northridge, on the northern outskirts of Los Angeles, when the city was hit with an earthquake one year before Kobe, 57 were killed, 9,000 injured, and 20,000 left homeless. Damages amounted to $20 billion, one of the costliest in U.S. history. These two examples are far from being super cities so we can imagine the increase in damage if today a large earthquake struck Tokyo.

EARTHQUAKES

To understand earthquakes and volcanic eruptions the fundamental role of tectonic plates needs to be examined. At their points of collision with a neighbor, or when tension or pressure builds up through encounters with obstructions, earthquakes occur and the area affected by the interference is shaken. Waves of different types and strengths are radiated from the shaken location, referred to as the epicenter. The fastest and most widely distributed of these waves are known as "P" waves. They transmit shock waves of alternating compression and dilation that can pass through gases, liquids, and solids and so reach most of the earth at all levels of depth depending on their strengths. There are other, slower types of waves that emanate from the epicenter. One of them, known as an "L" wave, moves rapidly in and out of the outermost layer of the earth and is responsible for much of the physical damage caused by earthquakes.

The Alaskan earthquake of 1964 was one of the strongest to be recorded since seismograph records began. Its "L" or long waves lasted for five minutes and, since their strength was very high, they were felt in places all over the world. Their strength was so high that the instruments at that time were unable to measure the maximum shocks. Later, as evidences of its destructive power were examined in detail, its strength according to the Richter Scale was known to be 9.2. See Appendix 4 for explanations of the measures in use for different types of disaster. Because of the strength of its long waves, the Alaskan quake made the surface of the earth shake up and down like the ringing of a bell. Three thousand miles away, in the Great Lakes on the U.S./Canada border, the same long waves set up several series of surface waves known as seiches and, on the other side of the globe in South Africa, there were seiches in lakes and on the ocean. The same long waves lifted up the surface of the surrounding earth surface by more than forty feet and pulled it down ten feet below its normal level. This is still regarded as the greatest deformation ever known from an earthquake.

A powerful tsunami emanated from the Alaskan earthquake. This is a phenomenon commonly associated with earthquakes and will be described in more detail in the next section of this introduction. The tsunami resulting from the 1964 earthquake carried wave heights greater than thirty feet and they swept down the west coasts of Canada and the United States all the way to San Diego, causing damage wherever they went. In Crescent City, California, a location that always experiences some destruction whenever a tsunami reaches northern California, over thirty city blocks were flooded. In Canada, at the head of an ocean inlet leading to the city of Port Alberni, eighty miles from the sea, a small subdivision was destroyed. All along the coastal area of southern Alaska, landslides and land subsidence occurred in places where the underlying soil happened to be clay. Additionally, liquefaction happened in areas close to the epicenter. All three of these surface disruptions—landslides, land subsidence, and liquefaction—are common concomitants of earthquakes and they will be found as parts of the records of some earthquakes in this book.

The first two of these three disruptions, landslides and land subsidence, are familiar because they occur in small ways wherever there are steep slopes and the danger of their recurrence can be anticipated by putting up protective barriers. Liquefaction is not so easy to anticipate because it occurs on flat ground and most frequently on shorelines that are presently above the elevation of high water. During an earthquake, the long waves vibrate the surface, create spaces among the particles of hardened soil, and allow water to seep in and change the surface to a muddy surface that cannot hold up buildings. Again and again, as will be found in accounts of earthquakes in this book, developers of land for residential or industrial uses discovered that these shorelines are low cost flat land that needs no clearing and so they have built on them, often in violation of building regulations. Such developments are low-cost because they are built on dangerous locations. Sometimes, as in the case of the San Francisco earthquake of 1906, in which liquefaction destroyed areas that were close to the water, those same areas were rebuilt in later years, only to be destroyed again by liquefaction in a subsequent earthquake.

In certain earthquakes, landslides have proved to be extraordinarily destructive forces. In the case of the greatest earthquake of all time, as far as loss of human life is concerned, the Shaanxi Province earthquake of 1556 in China, the long waves of the earthquake encountered one of the lightest types of soil found anywhere on earth, those of the loess regions of northwest China. They were deep deposits, often hundreds of feet thick, easy to demolish and, in modern times, their destruction would never have led to the death toll of 1556—more that 800,000. But, in that time, loess soil, because it was dry and easy to excavate, provided low cost homes for the people who lived and farmed there. People dug out loess caves and they proved to be warm in the cold winters and cool in the hot summers. When the long waves created high, massive landslides of loess, hundreds of thousands of Chinese were smothered or crushed before they could escape. A similar story of landslide power related to an underwater earthquake in Unimak, Alaska, in 1946, from which a massive landslide was triggered. The amount of seawater displaced by the landslide gave rise to one of the biggest tsunamis ever experienced in the Pacific Ocean. It destroyed local areas of Alaska and swept across the Pacific to do enormous damage in Hawaii. The details of the event are included in this book.

The vast majority of the half-million earthquakes that occur every year are located at the margins of tectonic plates. However, as will be seen from two events that are described in this book, one in the interior of the United States and the other in Siberia, some very powerful earthquakes occur in the middle of continents, far from the margins of any tectonic plate. The causes of these interior earthquakes relate to the fault lines that develop at weak places underground as continents and ocean floors together continue to move across the surface of the earth. Tensions build up over time and, since the rate of movement in the interior of a continent is slower than on the ocean floor, it takes a long time for stresses to build up to a crisis. Something finally gives way at the place of tension and there is an earthquake. The quake is strong because it has built up for a long time and the local population is unprepared for it because they have lived through a long quiescent period with no evidence to indicate an impending quake.

Every year, on average, earthquakes kill thousands of people and cause damage that adds up to hundreds of millions of dollars. In one fifteen-year period toward the end of the twentieth century, half a billion people lost their lives from earthquakes. Most of these deaths occurred in countries that are less developed than North America or Northwest Europe. Why is this? One explanation may be the type of surface layers of rock beneath the cities or rural areas hit. If there are numerous faults as was the case in the Guatemala City earthquake of 1976 the long waves will and they did shatter the surface rocks, with the result that a very large number of people died and damage was enormous and widespread. Additionally, in Guatemala City, and this was also true in many other places in Latin American earthquakes, the typical adobe-type homes collapse easily and people are killed by falling buildings. Engineers who work in earthquake zones repeatedly point out that buildings, not earthquakes, kill people, and they urge authorities to push for safer building codes.

TSUNAMIS

The word "tsunami" comes from Japan where it has always been a frequent visitor and where it originally meant a wave in harbor. Before there was a clear understanding of the tsunami phenomenon, Japanese fishermen would frequently return home from sea and observe their whole harbor area devastated by water. Nothing had been experienced while they were in deeper water so they were very puzzled about the event and described it as a wave in harbor. In Japanese usage, the plural of the word is also tsunami but in English it is tsunamis. Because it is a wave formed when water is displaced in an area of ocean from events such as earthquakes, mass movements above or below the ocean's surface, volcanic eruptions, or landslides, there is little evidence of a tsunami in deep water. Even if a wave is forty feet high it makes little difference in water that is a thousand feet deep but, as it comes into shallow water, the wave rises higher and higher and finally strikes the shore area with devastating force.

A tsunami can be generated when tectonic plate boundaries at subduction sites abruptly deform and vertically displace the overlying water. This happens in most places as tension builds up between two plates due to some obstruction preventing the natural movement of the plates. The tension builds up until something finally snaps, pushing one of the plates up or down and, by doing so, displacing a quantity of ocean water. Around the Pacific Rim, known as the Ring of Fire because of the many massive earthquakes of this type that occur, these displacements are greater than anywhere else. This is because the main subduction sites are located at the edge of continental areas like Alaska, California, South America, and Indonesia, in all of which the resistance to plate movement is particularly strong. As a result, a build up of tension persists for a long time between the two very big plates and a powerful earthquake then ensues. The displaced mass of water moves under the influence of *gravity* and radiates across the ocean like ripples on a pond.

Although there have been many examples of huge destructive tsunamis from subduction earthquakes around the Pacific Rim, there is nothing in the historical record like the one that originated in an Indonesian earthquake offshore from the Island of Sumatra on Boxing Day, 2004. The displacement of one of the plates and, therefore, the extent of the seabed that was moved upwards, was more than seven hundred miles. Indonesian fishermen who were at sea at the time, true to Japanese experience, felt nothing and had they stayed at sea for a time their lives could have been saved. Unfortunately, even today, tsunamis are not well understood; both in Indonesia and all over the stretch of ocean from Indonesia to Africa where the tsunami went, few people took advantage of what is known about tsunamis to run to higher ground. The tsunami, traveling at 500 mph as is common for such, devastated shore areas and even whole nations that were generally low in elevation, all the way from Indonesia to Eastern Africa. The earthquake was so powerful and the tsunami so big that the speed of the earth's rotation was slowed down for a fraction of a second.

Just as this one was part of the Ring of Fire, so were most of the other big tsunamis that occurred globally over the previous century. Krakatau was a volcanic eruption in another part of Indonesia. The tsunami that accompanied it killed 36,000 in the two major islands of Indonesia on either side of the eruption—Java and Sumatra. Japan, thirteen years after Krakatau, experienced a monster tsunami from an offshore earthquake that took the lives of 26,000. In many other places across the Pacific since that time, lethal tsunamis took away many other people and did major damage in Hawaii, Alaska, and Papua New Guinea. While the Rim of Fire was the setting for most tsunamis from the past, Europe and the Eastern Mediterranean Sea have also seen powerful tsunamis in past times when, because of their lack of knowledge of tsunamis, many thousands were killed. The Lisbon tsunami of 1755 that followed an offshore earthquake killed many thousands and, much earlier in time, in Alexandria in the year 365, a tsunami generated by a distant earthquake in Greece killed thousands of Egyptians.

A tsunami wave generated by an earthquake and carried from the epicenter of the quake by gravity is like waves generated by dropping a stone in a pond. More than one wave results from the impact of the stone and its displacement of some water. Similarly, in the greater setting of a tsunami, many waves are generated and they can be close together or widely spaced depending on the volume of water displaced and the shape of the seabed around the epicenter. As the first wave nears shore it encounters friction from the seabed as water depth decreases and the shape of the wave is distorted. It may rise as high as thirty, forty, or more feet at this point. The first wave often retreats back out to sea leaving the seabed dry for great distances from shore. This aspect of tsunamis gave rise to the observation that they are far more dangerous than the earthquakes that generate them. A tsunami might be as long as sixty miles and, since it is not pushing water ahead of it but rather carrying water along with it, strange things like the retreat back out to sea happen when the sixty miles of water hits a small shore.

A tsunami is really a crashing wall of water, a bit like the giant waves off the coast of Hawaii that are so loved by surf riders; however, tsunamis are far more dangerous and not to be played with by these surfers because the tsunami is really a mass of water carried along in a series of waves. It is not just a local wave created by wind or the displacement caused by passing ships. A more accurate picture of tsunamis might be a river overflowing its banks because a high volume of water was added to the river upstream and it can no longer carry it. Some tsunamis come ashore and move huge volumes of water, along with the masses of debris that it collected along the way, far inland. Later, sometimes hours later, it retreats far from shore. As has already been noted, thousands of people were killed, both in the past and in the recent Indonesian tsunami, when they ventured out on to the newly-dried seafloor and were drowned in the next phase of the tsunami. In Thailand, as the Indonesian tsunami of 2004 reached its shores, a young girl was close to the shore when the first wave arrived and then retreated far out to sea. She and her family were on holiday in Thailand. This girl attended a school in Edmonton, Canada, and she had learned about tsunamis in a geography lesson. Immediately she saw the wave retreating she shouted, "run for higher ground" and then ran in that direction. Only a few followed her.

Tragically there was no tsunami warning systems in the Indian Ocean when the Indonesian earthquake and tsunami struck. It had been such a long time since the previous big tsunami had affected the area that authorities became complacent about this danger. Attitudes were still somewhat indifferent even when the earthquake happened as became evident in the responses from some countries in the region. Thus it was the Pacific Tsunami Warning Center in Hawaii that gave the quickest information to the rest of the world. This center along with its associated seismic stations and tidal gauges in places all over the Pacific Ocean, including Chile, New Zealand, Japan, Alaska, and all places in between, was established in the late 1940s after Hawaii experienced severe damage from several tsunamis. It is expected that there will be a similar system in place in the Indian

Ocean in the future. Huge tsunamis have struck many places around the Pacific and Indian oceans in the past but little is known about these where historical records go back for only two or three hundred years. The west coast of North America is one of these places and Australia is a second. Research work is needed on the evidences of these past tsunamis, including the oral records of native peoples, so that there is a greater awareness of the possibilities of future mega-tsunamis.

PREDICTING EARTHQUAKES

In spite of the fact that we know now exactly what causes earthquakes, their sudden, repetative appearance is as disturbing as the former ignorance of causes, so the quest to be able to predict their arrival has become a central interest of geologists. In fact, from earliest times, alongside the fanciful reasons for the occurrence of earthquakes, there were theories that pointed in the direction of predictions. Aristotle, for example, tried to explain the existence of earthquakes by theorizing that air was trapped in cavities below the surface of the earth and the rumbling of earthquakes was the result of that as the blocked cavities sought to free themselves. Pliny the Elder of Roman times, the man who died at the time of the eruption of Vesuvius, thought similarly to Aristotle, that there was a blockage of air inside the earth and caves and wells were necessary to release this trapped air. Often he would propose a solution that would involve drilling holes to allow the trapped air to escape.

A variety of attempts have been made over the years to predict earthquakes by looking at the minor seismic events that always occur around the time of an earthquake, hoping that the way these appear and their strength might indicate when the earthquake would occur. These have been successful to a point. For example, at the time of the Mount St. Helen's earthquake and volcanic eruption in 1980, the small shakings that preceded the earthquake and the major eruption were an accurate forecast of what was going to happen. But the exact time of the explosion was not predictable and so the nearest that experts could come to a prediction was to say that there would be an explosion within a few weeks. That level of accuracy has been proved successful, not only in the case of Mount St. Helen's, but also in the many earthquakes that recur in Alaska, where patterns are frequently repeated over long periods of time. The Tangshan earthquake of 1976 was kept secret for three years because the Chinese felt they had developed similar methods for predicting earthquakes but, unfortunately, they were totally wrong in regard to the Tangshan quake.

Many reports, some dating back hundreds of years, have pointed out that animals of all sizes and kinds seem to detect earthquakes hours or even days before humans. At the time of the tsunami that followed the Indonesian quake of 2004 it was observed that almost no animals were caught in the event. It seems that they moved away from danger areas in good time. This behavior of animals was also noted and recorded in 1755 at the time of the Lisbon earthquake and tsunami. In the year 2004, a book by a Japanese geologist, Motoji Ikeye, was published in Singapore by World Scientific Publishing Company and titled *Earthquakes and Animals*. In this book he describes in detail one possible explanation for animals being able to sense an oncoming earthquake. Ikeye was aware that, in recent years, in major earthquakes in Japan, China, and India, there were numerous reports of animals fleeing from the scene twelve to twenty-four hours before the earthquakes struck. Ikeye also knew, from his own experiments, that flashes of lightning or lights of some kind accompany earthquakes, perhaps due to collisions or friction among rocks as they are shaken. The thesis that he developed related to these lights. He concluded that they frightened animals and so they moved away from them. It seems to be a very persuasive argument, one that is likely to be investigated further in the future.

Ikeye's book included list of animals that were seen to be running away from a place that later experienced an earthquake. This list is more detailed than any other similar record. His list includes reports of avoidance of earthquakes by dogs, cats, sea lions, hippopotamai, squirrels, rats, seagulls, snakes, turtles, fish, dolphins, octopus, crocodiles, and rabbits. Each had its own pattern of behavior and the following details concerning dog and cat activities will indicate the varieties within each category of animal. Some dogs howled like wolves while others refused to be separated from their owners, either insisting on staying inside or trying to get the owner outside. Some dogs left their homes before the earthquake and returned several days later while others barked continually up to thirty minutes before the earthquake. With cats, some tried to get into bed with their owners, waking them up and even biting them. Forty-five minutes before an earthquake other cats meowed to be let out of the house. The places selected by Ikeye for the collection of his data about animal behavior prior to earthquakes were taken from Japan, Turkey, Taiwan, and India.

Most research on prediction still remains focused on the characteristics of rocks and terrain in areas that have a history of earthquakes. Tilting of the ground, changes in elevation, even rising water levels in wells can all be indicators of stresses deeper down. Appearance of small cracks may be the surface manifestation of a fault hundreds of miles below ground. In places that were hit by very powerful earthquakes in the past, it is possible to predict the frequency of recurrence by examining soil and rock layers below ground and calculating the likelihood of another quake. This is a very rough method of prediction, making it possible to say no more than that an earthquake of such and such magnitude will recur sometime within the next so many years. In California, at Pallet Creek on the San Andreas Fault a little over fifty miles north of Los Angeles, a location where slippages on the San Andreas Fault have been repeatedly noted in the form of disrupted sedimentary layers, an expert from the California Institute of Technology decided to dig down at this location and make accurate assessments of the soil layers to discover when past quakes had occurred. His purpose was earthquake prediction. He thought that if he could date older slippages he might be able to draw up a timetable of recurrences and thus an average frequency of earthquakes for this part of the San Andreas Fault. It was already well known that most California earthquakes occur on or near this fault. A history of 1,400 years of earthquakes was identified and from these the average recurrence interval was calculated at about 150 years. Since the last great earthquake on the San Andreas near Pallet Creek was in 1857, the finding from this investigation and prediction came uncomfortably close to the year 2007.

Earthquake prediction is always an inexact science. No one can claim certainty about the future, yet scientists are always at work seeking to gain as much predictability as possible. Occasionally a successful forecast occurs and then efforts are redoubled to capitalize on the event. In China, in 1969 on a particular morning, zookeepers noticed unusual animal behavior—swans avoided water, pandas screamed, and snakes refused to go into their holes. About noon on that same day a 7.4 magnitude earthquake struck the city. Ever since then, and especially now in the light of Ikeye's 2004 report, scientists take careful note of any relevant animal behavior. Although probability seems to be a very weak method of prediction at first glance, it is turning out to be the best of all. When dealing with a very large number of variables in a situation where most of the variables operate independently of one another, the ordinary predictive methods of science do not apply. Scientific prediction requires stability in several variables so that the behavior of one can be evaluated.

Weather forecasters were among the first to recognize the value of probability prediction but the idea did not originate with them. It came from scientists working with very small things, like cells or atoms, where all the common laws of physics give way to random behaviors. Only probability is predictable in those domains. Meteorologists trying to cope with increases in the frequency and power of both hurricanes and tornadoes decided to settle for probability methods in giving storm warnings. It is now the same in geology. The basis of the method is the record of past events. If there are extensive records of say earthquakes in a given region, including magnitudes and dates, it can be said with a stated degree of probability that an earthquake of a certain size will hit within a given time period. This approach has become standard practice over the past twenty or thirty years with the Global Seismograph Network (GSN) that was set up in the early 1960s. In 1990 it rated the probability as high, of a magnitude 6 quake striking the eastern United States before 2010.

FLOODS

Floods are not as costly nor are they as destructive, on average, as earthquakes. At the same time, they are the deadliest of all environmental hazards. In the course of the twentieth century, worldwide, close to seven million died as a result of floods, one million were injured and over one hundred million were rendered homeless. The majority of the deaths occurred in China, almost all of them from the Yellow River, or Huanghe as it is known today, often and appropriately named the "River of Sorrow." In its long journey from the high ground of Northwest China the Yellow River flows through territory bordered by hundreds of miles of deep deposits of loess, a very light soil that is easily eroded and added to the river. By the time the Yellow River reaches the lowland areas near its mouth and slows down, its water level is high because of the load of yellow loess deposits. All it takes at that stage to create a crisis is an unexpected heavy rainfall. Such an event can raise the river level above the levees, making it overtop the banks and flood the farmland below.

Again and again, in the more than 2,000 years since levees were first built on the banks of the Yellow River, overtopping has happened and hundreds of thousands of the farmers who lived and worked on the fertile land beside the river were drowned. In response to each of these tragedies, the levees were built up a bit higher than they had been in order to forestall another flood. As a result, over time, the river flows along high above the villages below. When rainfall triggers another overtopping the destruction is greater than that of previous similar occasions because of acceleration in the flow of water from the higher elevation of the river. Additionally, because it is a slow-moving river as it reaches its mouth, alternative channels are carved out in the delta area. On one occasion, late in the nineteenth century, the river carved out a channel farther south than it had ever done before, linking it with the other great river of China, the Yangtze, so that both rivers flowed together into the East China Sea.

The Mississippi River drainage basin is the largest in the world and certainly the largest in North America. Flood risks are annual threats and, historically, flood events were left to states to resolve. There was an assumption that nothing could be done on a collective, national, basis to anticipate and prevent flood damage. All of that kind of thinking changed after the massive flood of 1927 when 246 lost their lives, about 137,000 buildings were flooded, and 700,000 lost their homes. Pressure on the national government led to the Flood Control Act in the year following the big flood. Levees, two thousand miles of them, together with a number of floodwalls and floodways, were installed by joint state and federal authorities. In 1993 there was a much worse flood than the one in 1927. The 1993 flood affected more than half of the total area of the river basin. A rare combination of highs and lows raised rainfall levels from the Dakotas to the upper areas of Mississippi. The loss of life from this event was considerably lower than in 1927, thanks to the precautions taken after 1927. Nevertheless, about 74,000 people were left homeless and 1,000 levees collapsed.

The tragedy of Hurricane Katrina and the flooding that ensued may have led to new concerns about the relationships between hurricanes and floods. Whether it was because of Katrina or otherwise, the National Oceanic and Atmospheric Administration (NOAA) decided in 2005 to document the details of hurricanes that made landfall in the contiguous United States and, in the course of their first two or three days, caused nine or more inches of rainfall in their landfall areas. There is another aspect of Katrina that should be noted because they have national implications—the insurance claims. Residents in New Orleans who had taken out insurance policies against damage from hurricanes were refused benefits from their insurance companies because, in the opinion of the insurance companies, the damage elements that residents suffered and that had been caused by flooding was not covered. Far away from the United States, on the other side of the earth, in Australia, there are new concerns and many public protests over the failure of the national government to protect people from floods. On this normally very dry continent major floods in 1973 and 1990 did extensive destruction and state and federal authorities were totally unprepared to deal with them.

VOLCANIC ERUPTIONS

Somewhere on earth, a volcanic eruption is either happening or about to happen. About 1,500 of them have erupted at different times within the last 10,000 years and, because we never know when one becomes extinct, it is possible that any one of the 1,500 could spring into life again. Over five hundred have erupted within the past four hundred years. A volcanic eruption can occur at times because of a nearby earthquake triggering it but, in general, volcanic eruptions occur for a variety of reasons, all of which distinguish them from the world of earthquakes and tsunamis. From the times of Rome when Mount Vesuvius erupted and the entire town of Pompeii was smothered with lethal ash, volcanic eruptions have created intense interest. Pompeii's ruins are still being studied at the present time, especially the findings of the outlines of the bodies of those who died because they were preserved by a special technique. Even the name of Pliny the Elder, a Roman leader who died in Pompeii's destruction, has been taken to define the eruptions that are like the Vesuvius one. They are known as Plinian eruptions, continuous flows of pumice, ash, and volcanic gases forming a deadly cloud.

One of the easiest volcanic eruptions to study can be found in Hawaii. Mount Kilauea on the Island of Hawaii, often referred to as the Big Island, is an intra-plate volcano, that is to say it is erupting from inside a tectonic plate rather than at the junction of two plates. It is erupting almost daily at the present time and at such a low level of violence that its activity can be easily observed. Molten magma just oozes out. The entire island group that constitutes the state of Hawaii is formed from volcanic action and the Big Island, the island of Hawaii, is the principal actor at the present time. Other islands of the state were active in the past and this condition is a reminder of another feature of Hawaii—it is a hot spot. There are more than thirty of these hot spots around the world and some of them will feature in the events of this book. What is a hot spot? They are places deep in the earth below the level of mountains and ocean crust from which magma is escaping to the surface. In sharp contrast to everything we see on the surface of the earth these hot spots do not move with respect to the surface of the earth. Instead the tectonic plates pass over them as they move.

The huge volume of molten rock that reaches the surface in the island of Hawaii over time from the hot spot is evident in the thousands of feet to which a volcano such as Kilauea has risen above sea level and its height is achieved after it has already risen many thousands of feet from the ocean floor up to sea level. Over a period of a few million years, Kilauea will move way from the hot spot as the Pacific Tectonic Plate on which it sits continues its westward movement. A new mountain will take shape over the hot spot and Mount Kilauea will gradually cool down to become inactive like the rest of the state of Hawaii. The long history of this process, over a period of more than seventy million years, can be observed today in the islands above and below sea level that stretch from Kilauea to the other islands of the state of Hawaii, and then across the Pacific all the way to the Kamchatka Peninsula of Russia. These islands form the Hawaiian-Emperor Chain and identification of their age, that is to say, the lapse of time since they were magma rising from the hot spot, tells the story of the movement of the Pacific Tectonic Plate over time.

The two tallest volcanic mountains on the chain lie on the Big Island of Hawaii. They are Mauna Kea and Mauna Loa. Each is more than 12,000 feet high but if their total individual heights, counting from the ocean floor, is calculated, they each stand more than 30,000 feet high, higher than that of Mount Everest in the Himalayas. The gentle rate at which magma flows upward into the mountains of Hawaii is common in intraplate volcanic eruptions. Yellowstone National Park stands on the remnants of an ancient volcano and it, like Kilauea, stands today on a hot spot on an intra-plate site. Furthermore, its activity is quite benign and so thousands of tourists visit it every year. But Yellowstone was not always so quiet. Three extremely large explosive eruptions have occurred there in the past 2.1 million years and scientists have estimated Yellowstone's recurrence interval as about 600,000 to 800,000 years. It is difficult to be more precise with such long intervals. The most recent of these explosive eruptions was about 640,000 years ago. Given the estimates for recurrence rates it is possible, despite assurances from USGS experts that there are no indications now of the likelihood of such an event, that another explosive eruption could come within the next one or two hundred years.

The consequences of such an event are unimaginable. The eruption of about 640,000 years ago, among other things, covered most of what is now North America with six feet of hot ash. Thus the USGS, from time to time, issues reminders of the kinds of things that need to be considered so that the area is as prepared as possible for the future. There are potential future hazards that could affect as many as 70,000 people even though the area is sparsely populated and this fact has to be kept in mind by all who are responsible for the care of the park. The plateau on which the park sits was built by one of the earth's youngest, but largest, volcanic systems. It has been the scene of eruptions for more than two million years. The three largest of these eruptions sent out ash that was so hot that it welded into sheets of rock. Each of the three produced a crater-like depression, a caldera, tens of miles wide, formed by the collapse of the ground surface into the partly emptied magma chamber beneath. Faults within the present caldera are small and they produce small earthquakes from time to time that reflect strains in the earth's crust. The active hydrothermal system of Yellowstone is one of the largest on earth and, although accidents involving hot water occasionally injure visitors, these can be avoided if park regulations are followed.

At the places where tectonic plates interact, especially at subduction zones, most of the most violent eruptions of the twentieth century have occurred. The interaction of the Nazca and South American plates is one general location that experienced catastrophic eruptions, particularly because the coastal area is high in elevation and lahars rush down from eruptions to overwhelm the towns and cities below. The 1985 eruption of Colombia's Nevado del Ruiz volcanic mountain carried plenty of warnings of the coming event, both in the minor eruptions that were observed for days before the main explosion and in the opinions given by local authorities. Despite these warnings, there seems to be little understanding of when one must escape to some protected place. In the case of Nevado del Ruiz, the lahars rushed down from the mountain, from 17,500 feet above sea level, devastating everything in their path. About 21,000 people lost their lives in one town, Armero, which only had a population of 28,000. The USGS scientists, particularly horrified by the things that happen to people at volcanic sites, decided to do something to alert people to the dangers and to inform them about how to avoid an imminent event. They devised a three-part action plan.

First, they produced a video depicting the typical phases of volcanic eruptions and what happens to people, buildings, and environment when they erupt. It was quite a scary video, deliberately so, not suitable for younger people. Second, they selected fifteen volcano sites from around the world to study intensely and to examine along with the various local authorities in order to have the details of a collection of representative case studies. The third element was instrumental usage for predicting when a volcano would blow given that the advance signals were evident. In 1991 the video was rushed to the Philippines when Mount Pinatubo was threatening to erupt. The day after it was shown on television, about 50,000 chose to evacuate voluntarily. A few days later the volcano erupted. Tens of thousands of lives had been saved. Convincing people to evacuate as they had done in the Philippines was the biggest challenge everywhere it was attempted but it was the key to survival. What also was secured by Mount Pinatubo's eruption was a dramatic lowering of temperature worldwide for two years, more than countering the amounts that would have risen in that time as part of global warming.

Just as earthquakes pose enormous risks for big cities if their epicenters are nearby, so the proximity of cities to volcanic sites is an equally great risk and there are many cities in that kind of setting. Historically there are good reasons for such a condition. We tend to think of the destructive aspect of eruptions, and rightly so, but we need to remember that volcanic soils are among the most fertile anywhere. People were drawn to those great farming locations in earlier times and cities grew up there over the years. At least 500 million people live today under the shadow of a potential volcanic eruption and many big cities are included in that number—Tokyo, Manila, Jakarta, Mexico City, and Quito are examples of these. Mount St. Helens that erupted in 1980 was a good example of how to do the right thing. Advance indicators in the form of small vibrations alerted local officials to move access to the mountain farther back that had been customary. A day before the violent eruption a general clearance was ordered for everyone to move far away from the mountain and people did as they were told. The only casualties close to the mountain was a reporter and a man who had lived for much of his life near the mountain and refused to leave.

To compare the magnitude of volcanic eruptions geologists have developed a Volcanic Explosivity Index (VEI), similar in principle to the Richter Scale for measuring earthquake magnitudes. This index is based on the volume of explosive products and the height of the eruption cloud. Each category in the index represents a ten-fold increase in power over the previous one. Eruptions with magnitudes of 0 or 1, common patterns in Hawaii, ooze lava with little or no violent activity. Tristan da Cunha, 1961, was a 2; Iceland, 1973, was 3; Martinique, 1902, was 4; and Mount St. Helens, 1980, was 5. Mount Vesuvius, 79, and Krakatau, 1883, had VEIs of 6, and Tambora had 7. Tambora erupted in 1815 in Indonesia, presenting us with the greatest eruption known in history and giving us a glimpse into the incredible power and potential of such events. Their destructive power is frightening when we examine one like Tambora. Details of these scales for measuring different types of disasters are assembled in Appendix 4 at the end of the book. Toba was a supervolcano of VEI 8 and it is the only one from ancient times for which we have a large volume of data, a valuable reference if our planet ever experiences a supervolcano.

TROPICAL CYCLONES

Cyclonic storms are centers of low pressure with inward-spiraling winds that form where warm and cold air masses meet. Hurricanes develop over water about 10 degrees north or south of the equator in a manner similar to cyclonic storms elsewhere in the world, then move westward through the trade wind belt. Sea surface temperatures in these latitudes are close to 80 degrees, enough to stimulate high-speed inward-spiraling winds of 65–125 mph. The shape of the storm is circular with a diameter averaging 100–300 miles. As the hurricane moves toward the eastern seaboard of the United States, or into the Gulf of Mexico, the National Weather Service begins its warning and forecasting activities. As the storm approaches land, the biggest concerns relate as much to the expected rainfall as they do to any physical damage.

Attempts were made in the 1960s to reduce the severity of hurricanes by cloud seeding. The theory was that by seeding the clouds closest to the point of lowest pressure, latent heat would be released, raising the temperature and therefore decreasing the pressure. As a result the pressure gradient would be reduced and the maximum wind speeds as well because energy is redistributed around the storm center. Four of these storms were seeded on eight different days and results showed a 30 percent drop in wind speed on four of these days. Subsequently the experiment was dropped because additional research revealed that hurricane clouds carry a large volume of natural ice! Reliance is now placed on accurate forecasting and protective measures on shore.

Occasionally a hurricane takes an unexpected path because of cold air masses over the continent's interior. This can greatly increase the rainfall. Hurricane Agnes, in 1972, was one of these. It originated in the Caribbean and moved northward across the Florida panhandle through the Carolinas to New York State. In some places eighteen inches of rain fell in two days. Many streams experienced peak flows several times greater than the previous maxima on record. One hundred and seventeen lives were lost in the twelve states affected. Hurricane Hugo struck the United States mainland in mid-September 1989 just north of Charleston, South Carolina, with winds of 140 mph and a storm surge reaching nineteen feet. The barrier islands were completely inundated by the storm and their beaches severely eroded with sand being either washed landward or carried offshore. Altogether twenty-nine people from South Carolina lost their lives in the course of the storm and damage to buildings and property amounted to $6 billion.

Where there was a wide high beach and sand dunes, damage was greatly reduced and those buildings that had been built to withstand high winds and flooding survived. By contrast, where beaches had been severely narrowed through long-term erosion, as in Folly Beach, south of Charleston, there was substantial destruction. Homeowners had tried to compensate by dumping boulders and concrete rubble on the beach, hoping they might serve as a retaining wall. They failed. It is good that the USGS and other agencies have become more and more active in preparing for future hurricanes. While the probability that any one of these storms will hit land at a given point in a given year is low, and still less likely in the case of a category 4 or 5 hurricane, there is the danger that a false sense of security may develop. It can be said, for instance, that for any one building within the general zone of historic hurricanes, a category 3, 4, or 5 storm will strike it sometime in its lifetime. It also needs to be said that, given the many uncertainties associated with predicting hurricanes, there is no assurance that a second powerful storm will not hit again one year later in the same spot as the previous year.

North Carolina was struck by two hurricanes in 1996. The same rare sequence of two storms happened again in 1999. Hurricane Dennis struck the coast for several days early in September and Floyd made landfall later in that same month, causing record floods across eastern parts of the state and damaging shoreline structures. Bonnie, a fifth storm, just as big as the other four, reached North Carolina in 1998. Experts described the first of these five storms in 1996 as a fifty-year storm, that is to say one that would be expected to recur once every fifty years, yet all five of these storms were of equal strength. Obviously, concepts of fifty-year storms need to be reconsidered. Long-term forecasting at the present time must, therefore, remain as a difficult if not impossible task. The damage from Hurricane Katrina that devastated New Orleans in 2005 was mainly flood damage, not unlike the many floods that hit this city from high water on the Mississippi or one of its tributaries. This event was described as a hurricane, Hurricane Katrina, and all preparations for its impact were based on the city's understanding of hurricanes.

In all of the twentieth century there were only three category 5 hurricanes that made landfall in the contiguous United States. They provide a valuable historical perspective on the impact of hurricanes. The first was the Labor Day Hurricane of 1938. It earned the name "Storm of the Century" on account of three characteristics: 200 mph wind gusts, storm surge of fifteen feet, and a record low pressure. The year 1938 was still early days in the expertise of the weather bureau people. On the day before the storm hit the Florida Keys, the Bureau decided it would pass through the Keys and enter the Gulf. The Bureau was off by about three hundred miles on the storm's location on Labor Day morning. By the middle of the day, the administrator of a veteran's project involved in road construction, linking the Keys to mainland Florida, received the news that a direct hit on the keys was now certain. He decided to get all the veterans out of the area and requested that a train be backed down to the work site on the one-track line as soon as possible. Delays in delivery held up the train until 8 P.M. and by that time the full force of the storm was battering the track. Cars were tossed off the train as if they were toys. More than four hundred lost their lives.

Camille was the second of the three most powerful hurricanes. It entered U.S. waters via Cuba and moved into the Gulf where the warm waters increased its strength. It reached Bay St. Louis late in the evening of August 1969 with sustained winds of 190 mph and, in the course of the following ten hours, the entire Mississippi coast was devastated. As it moved inland, homes, motels, apartments, restaurants, even trees were swept away. The next morning the bewildered survivors searched among the wreckage for anything that might still be there. There was no semblance of normal life in the region around New Orleans for days, but fortunately the levees around the city were not affected because the storm was centered a few miles way to the east. About 15,000 people were homeless. There was no water, food, or fuel. The storm had wiped out all means of communication, and roads, bridges, airports, and even railways were impassable or destroyed. Added to the devastated landscape there was a serious vermin problem. There were thousands of dead animals of all kinds, and insects and rodents had quickly overrun the stricken area to feed on these and on rotting food. Rattlesnakes, fire ants, and rats bit dozens of victims who were sifting through the rubble. Before it left mainland United States, Camille had caused the deaths of more than 250 people and injured 8,900, destroyed 6,000 homes and damaged 14,000. The total costs of the destruction it caused were in excess of a billion dollars.

The third and by far the most expensive of the three category 5 hurricanes was Andrew. Hurricane Andrew reached the built up area of South Florida in August of 1992 with peak wind gusts of 164 mph. Before it moved on it had caused damages amounting to more than $26 billion. In the forty years from 1926 to 1966, Miami was hit with hurricanes about thirteen times, but from the quarter century 1966 to 1992 there were none and during that period of time people flocked to Miami, doubling its population. New subdivisions sprung up but supervision of building codes and other regulations was lax. There were fewer than twenty building inspectors for a population of one million. The sudden arrival of Andrew was a great shock. Its fierce winds caused most of the damage. Houses were torn apart, cars lifted off the streets, and trees uprooted. Boarding up their windows proved useless as a protection in the face of the wind and very few homes had basements where people could shelter. It was an almost total destruction of whole subdivisions. Reports from private barometers helped establish that Andrew's central pressure at landfall was 27.23 inches, which made it the third most intense U.S. hurricane of record. Andrew's peak winds in south Florida were not directly measured due to the official measuring instruments having been destroyed. A storm surge of seventeen feet was recorded.

TORNADOES

Tornadoes, like hurricanes, form in warm climates, but the tornado is the most intense cyclone of all. Its most frequent and violent occurrences are found in the United States, mainly in the Great Plains Region and to a lesser extent in the Central Lowlands. April, May, and June seem to be the favorite times for strikes with an average of more than four hundred in the United States as a whole in these months. The famous "Wizard of

Oz" movie was one of the first media events to raise awareness of a tornado's destructive power. The tornado is a small dark funnel cloud, a few hundred feet in diameter at its base with a cumulonimbus cloud above it. Its dark color comes from the dust it picks up by its powerful inward-spiraling winds. These wind speeds can reach 250 mph as the storm twists and turns and races along the surface of the ground. It can devastate almost everything in its path, yet at other times it can rise in the air and leave the ground below completely unscathed.

The National Weather Service maintains a tornado forecasting and warning system similar to the one for hurricanes. Whenever weather conditions seem to favor tornado development, places at risk are warned and arrangements for observing and reporting conditions are set in motion. Western Ohio is not a high risk area compared with states in the Great Plains but, on April 4, 1974, at Xenia, near Dayton, this state was hit with one of the worst tornadoes of the century. Ohio was not alone. Over the two days, April 4 and 5, a rash of 148 tornadoes attacked twelve states, killing 300 people and injuring 6,000. At Xenia some 3,000 structures were demolished. Elsewhere, entire towns were wiped out and $600 million worth of property devastated. The atmospheric conditions were ideal for triggering tornadoes: a cool mass of humid air lay over Chicago while farther west dry air was encountering a cold air mass from the northwest. Against both of these came a moist warm air mass from the south. The combination of all three created an explosive series of thunderstorms extending more than seven hundred miles from Texas to Illinois.

An earlier tornado swept through three states in 1925. It touched down first in Annapolis, Missouri, with a base at times as wide as one mile. Main Street's buildings were flattened in a few seconds and the twister then swept on into Murphysboro, Illinois, tossing trees, buildings, and even underground pipes as if they were toys. Over 230 people died in Murphysboro. The tornado moved next to DeSoto, a town of about six hundred, where it knocked down every structure more than one story high. Sixty-nine people lost their lives. The twister finally vanished in southern Indiana. Fortunately, storms like this one or those of 1974 are rare but, sadly, not unique. On the evening of May 3, 1999, the worst tornado of the century, as far as costs are concerned, touched down on Oklahoma City. It was the nation's first billion-dollar tornado. It was not alone. Other parts of Oklahoma, the state that gets more tornadoes per square mile than anywhere else on earth, were hit with sixty of these storms on that same evening, all of them in areas close to Oklahoma City. Within a period of five hours 8,000 buildings were in partial or total ruin as the rash of storms swept from southwest Oklahoma diagonally across the state toward Wichita, Kansas.

The difficulties involved in forecasting were evident on that fateful evening in May. The Storm Prediction Center (SPC) based at Norman, Oklahoma, issues bulletins every day and on that morning's statement announced it as unlikely that any tornado would appear during the day.

By early afternoon SPC raised its estimate to moderate. Not until close to 4:00 in the afternoon did SPC change its prediction to high risk, and then only because a powerful computer had shown that storms were charging across the state. One hour later, across a 150 mile swath that included Oklahoma City, the swarm of storms struck. The greatest damage was caused in Oklahoma City and one or two of its suburbs. On the F-scale of tornado strength, the one that hit the city was at 5, the top of the scale. Any F5 tornado is unusual and one that hits a major city even more rare. Street and after street was devastated. A typical sequence in a single family home would be: windows shattered, roof lifted off, walls caved in. Even homes that were carefully built to withstand 75 mph winds were unable to withstand this tornado.

Mobile homes fared very poorly as they usually do. An F1 tornado is usually enough to knock them over. With an F5 at speeds of 300 mph they were completely shattered. While the overall death toll was low for a storm of this size most of the fatalities occurred in the mobile home areas. Almost every one of the tornadoes that hit over the six hours from 5:00 to 11:00 in the evening was an F5 or close to that strength. They were super cells, sustained severe thunderstorms, and experts were left with the problem of how such a powerful series of storms could be sustained at that level of strength for so long. Most tornadoes develop within very large storms called super cells. These storms are found in unstable environments in which wind speeds vary with height and where cool, dry air rests on top of warm, moist air with a thin stable layer separating the two air masses, a condition similar to temperature inversion in other settings. If a weather system reaches this unstable mass, the status quo is disrupted, the low level air is forced upward and a vertical vortex gradually takes shape as the warm air ascends, cools to the point of condensation, and then is triggered into faster ascent as the latest heat of condensation warms the surroundings.

PANDEMICS

A pandemic is an outbreak of an infectious disease that spreads across a large region, a continent, or even the world. According to the World Health Organization (WHO), a pandemic can start when three conditions have been met: the emergence of a disease new to the population, a disease that infects humans, causing serious illness, and one that spreads easily and persists among humans. A disease is not a pandemic because it is widespread or kills a large number of people. It must also be infectious. For example, cancer is responsible for a large number of deaths but is not considered a pandemic. The plague of Justinian in the sixth century that devastated the eastern capital of the Roman Empire in Constantinople was the first well-known pandemic in Europe. It also marks the first detailed record of the bubonic plague that later would be known in London as the

Black Death. In Constantinople, while Justinian was the Roman Emperor, large quantities of grain were shipped from Egypt and it is thought that the disease was brought into Europe via rat and flea populations in the grain.

The bubonic plague came to be known in London, England, as the Black Death of 1664 because of the black boils in the armpits, neck, and groin of infected people, which were caused by dried blood accumulating under the skin after internal bleeding. People first experienced the bacterium of Black Death as chills, fever, vomiting, and diarrhea. Frequently the disease spread to the lungs and, almost always in these cases, the victims died soon afterward. For reasons unknown at the time some people never caught the disease even though they were in close contact with those who had. In 2005 Dr. Stephen O'Brien of the National Institutes of Health in Washington D.C. searched for descendants of those seventeenth century survivors. He was able to locate a number of them and from those people he took blood samples and recorded their DNA. Dr. O'Brien had been working with HIV patients and to his great surprise he discovered that the critical gene that saved the lives of Black Death survivors was the same gene that today enables people infected with the HIV virus to survive. It is known by the common name Delta 32.

In the twenty-first century two well-known experiences of pandemics, one closely related to terrorism and one accidental, illustrate the nature of this problem in contemporary society. The anthrax series of events that hit the United States in the same year as the terrorist attacks of September 11 was clearly an attempt to terrify the leadership of the nation because it was directed at government, media, and communications in general. In mid October, a few weeks after the devastation of 9/11 when the World Trade Center towers were destroyed and the Pentagon hit, letters containing anthrax spores began to arrive at various United States media centers and government offices in Washington, D.C. A photo editor in a Florida news agency was the first to be affected. He opened an envelope that arrived on October 15 and unknowingly inhaled some of the anthrax that fell out. Several days passed before the contents of the envelope were tested and identified. By then it was too late to do anything for the photo editor. He died two weeks later. By the end of October 2001, five people were dead from anthrax. The White House mail was quarantined and several government offices locked in order to check for spores while their staffs met elsewhere. For the first time in its history the Supreme Court convened away from its own chambers. The State Department cut off all mail to its 240 embassies and consulates worldwide.

The other pandemic, first known as "The Scars Epidemic," appeared toward the end of the year 2002. It was a deadly form of pneumonia that appeared in southern China and quietly spread, ignored for a long time, and during that period of time spread within China and to various places around the world. As its deadly nature became clear to public authorities, it was given the name "Severe Acute Respiratory Syndrome (SCARS)" and fears arose that it might be a repeat of the 1918 flu pandemic. When the World Health Organization investigated the disease they found that the majority of cases occurred in food handlers and chefs in the Guangdong Province of Southern China who were engaged in a particular kind of food preparation and delivery. These workers were always in close contact with exotic snakes and birds that were kept alive and killed immediately before being served to customers. Once the nature and characteristics of the disease was defined and isolation of patients became standard practice around the world SCARS slowly disappeared.

The present fear of a human pandemic stems from the appearance of a new virus in birds that quickly causes death. As soon as it is observed in flocks of poultry the whole flock is killed. This virus has already mutated so that a few humans have caught it. The mutated strain has been analyzed and found to be without any parallel to previous viruses. That means humans have no immunity to use against it and this is why the few who have contracted it died quickly. In 2005 the United Nations General Assembly called for immediate international mobilization against this new avian flu because of the possibility of a mutation appearing that would spread easily from human to human. The present mutation does not do that. So far, the number of humans that have died from the disease is less than a hundred and they are almost all in Asia. There are fears that this virus might become a pandemic like the one of 1918. That flu pandemic originated from birds just as this one has. Fortunately, to date, it has not yet mutated into the form that the 1918 one took and which led to the deaths of tens of millions of people all over he world. This present virus could be worse than that of 1918 because, while there is much greater knowledge on how to cope with it, there is at the same time far greater and more frequent travel around the world.

TERRORISM

The role of terrorists in the history of disasters is different from all others in that it is a sustained activity over time, a deliberate destruction of people or buildings in order to raise awareness of a political problem and use the publicity generated to gain some political result. The destruction of the Twin Towers of New York's World Trade Center (WTC) in 2001 and parallel atrocities represent the worst disasters of this kind ever experienced in the United States. They illustrate the worst features of terrorists' methods and define in quite a new way the nature of those disasters we label as terrorism. The beginning of the attack on the Twin Towers was a pair of flights from Boston. Of course, this was not really the beginning. Such attacks actually begin in the ghastly, inhuman mindsets of the people who conduct acts of terrorism. They plan for years ahead of action, sometimes for decades and, as part of their preparations for this particular series of acts, they exploit the good natures of the U.S. citizens who assisted them as they took flight training in the United States. On September 11, 2001, American Airlines Flight 11 left Boston for Los Angeles with ninety-two passengers and crew aboard. Sometime shortly afterward, the plane was taken over by five passengers who were hijackers. Just before 9 A.M. the plane crashed into the upper floors of the North WTC Tower. Fifteen minutes later a second plane, United Airlines Flight 175, also bound from Boston to Los Angeles, hit the upper part of the South Tower. It too had been taken over by hijackers.

The planes were flown into the buildings at full speed in what can only be compared to the kamikaze tactics used by Japan in World War II when young pilots crashed their bomb-laden planes into American ships. Flames engulfed the upper floors of both towers within moments and every branch of New York's fire and rescue organizations sprang into action. It was a chaotic situation and they knew they faced a daunting task. The places where rescuers were needed most were above floor eighty and they knew that both electricity and elevators would soon be cut off there. Fortunately, there were only 14,000 people in both towers at the time of the explosions, far fewer than in an earlier 1993 attack. Later in the day there would have been three times that number. Those inside first experienced a gigantic blast and felt the towers swaying backwards and forwards. Sprinklers came on as electricity and lights went off. For a time, the elevators below the eightieth floor continued to operate and many were able to get into them. Fires started in different places, many of them triggered by aviation fuel, then sustained by the flammable materials in the offices. Thousands of pieces of glass, papers, debris, soot and ash, even clothing and body parts from the passengers who were in the planes, rained down on the streets below. Temperatures reached thousands of degrees in parts of the towers.

For about an hour the main supports of the towers held firm, allowing many to escape. Fires, sustained by chairs, desks, and other flammables, raced up from the level at which the planes struck to the twenty or more floors above, steadily weakening the main steel supports. At these heights steel is thinner as the total weight to be supported is much less than at lower down. Finally there came a general collapse as the upper floors buckled and sides caved in. Like battering rams in ancient warfare, successive masses of thousands of tons of steel stomped on the floors below until they could no longer absorb the pressure. Both towers gave way in a cloud of dust. The noise of hundreds of thousands of tons of steel crashing down could be heard all over southern New York City as people ran from the scene as fast as they could. All public transportation had stopped. Among the most horrific of all the things that had to be endured was the sight of people jumping to their deaths from the top floors rather than be incinerated. The scale of destruction and the reckless indifference to civilian life rightly identified the event as war, a new kind of war, and subsequent actions in Afghanistan and elsewhere were in keeping with that analysis.

First response by the U.S. government was to stop all flights at U.S.

airports in case further attacks might be in process. Incoming planes from other countries were routed to neighboring countries. Canada, because of its proximity to the United States received most of these flights and for a time its airports were filled to overflowing. The pilots were not informed of the changes and were only told where to go. It was felt that unnecessary panic would be avoided by maintaining silence until the planes were on the ground. The towers had been designed to withstand an impact from a modern jet plane but not an impact that involved maximum speed and maximum amount of fuel. The flights that were hijacked were meant to fly to Los Angeles so they were fully loaded with fuel. Modern steel skyscrapers had never previously collapsed because none had ever been subjected to the levels of stress imposed on the WTC. It was feared at first that as many as 6,000 might have died within the towers. Later it became clear that the count was close to 3,000. Among them were 350 firemen who had climbed up into the towers to help. More than a million tons of debris had to be removed at a rate of 10,000 tons a day, so it took several months just to clear the site. Some of the individual pieces of steel weighed twenty-five tons. Excavators with a reach of 100 feet and cranes that could pick up as much as 1,000 tons were needed for the work.

All of this debris had to be hauled by barge or truck to a landfill location on Staten Island. Nothing at this scale had ever previously been tackled and costs for the whole project soared beyond a billion dollars. The dangers from toxic materials at the time of the attack were largely ignored because more urgent matters commanded attention. All who were near the towers as they came down were covered with dust that came from fibrous glass, computer screens, asbestos, and a host of products that had been made from different chemicals. Spills of mercury, dioxin, and lead were all around. Some initial testing was done after a week and it showed levels of toxic chemicals as being below danger standards. Few of the local residents were satisfied with these results. They continued to wear masks and protective clothing. Before the full impact of the destruction of the Twin Towers was known across the country a third plane had hit the Pentagon in Washington D.C., and a fourth that many believe was headed for the White House, crashed in Pennsylvania when passengers, at the cost of their lives, fought the hijackers but were unable to take control of the plane. The type of terrorism represented by the destruction of the Twin Towers is the one we have seen again and again over the past forty years. The future may introduce the more terrifying types represented by biological elements and nuclear material.

PREVENTING BIOTERRORISM

The American Society for Microbiology (ASM) discusses with the U.S. Congress issues related to the adequacy of federal law relating to dangerous biological agents. It is the largest single life science society in the world with a membership of 42,000, and represents a broad spectrum of sub-disciplines, including medical microbiology, applied and environmental microbiology, virology, immunology, and clinical and public health microbiology. The Society's mission is to enhance microbiology worldwide to gain a better understanding of basic life processes and to promote the application of this knowledge for improved health, economic and environmental well being.

It has a long history of bringing scientific, educational and technical expertise to bear on the safe study, handling and exchange of pathogenic microorganisms. The exchange of scientific information, including microbial strains and cultures, among scientists is absolutely essential to progress in all areas of research in microbiology.

It understands the unique nature of microbiology laboratories, the need for safety precautions in research with infectious agents and the absolute necessity for maintaining the highest qualifications for trained laboratory personnel. It conducts education and training programs, as well as publication of material related to shipping and handling of human pathogens. Through its Public and Scientific Affairs Board, it provides advice to government agencies and to Congress concerning technical and policy issues arising from control of biological weapons. The Society's Task Force on Biological Weapons Control assists the government on scientific issues related to the verification of the Biological Weapons Convention (BWC).

It is acutely aware of the threat posed by the possible misuse of microbial agents as weapons of terror. Concerns that bioterrorists will acquire and misuse microorganisms as weapons have resulted in stricter controls on the possession, transfer, and use of biological agents to restrict access to only legitimate and qualified institutions, laboratories, and scientists. Over the past ten years, the ASM has worked with the Department of Health and Human Services (DHHS), the Centers for Disease Control and Prevention (CDC), the Department of Agriculture (USDA), and Congress to develop and establish legislation and regulations that are based on the key principle of ensuring protection of public safety without encumbering legitimate scientific and medical research or clinical and diagnostic medicine for the diagnosis and treatment of infectious diseases. The ASM has been an advocate of placing responsibility for the safe transfer of select agents at the level of individual institutions supported by government oversight and monitoring to minimize risks without inhibiting scientific research.

It notes that national security efforts to control biological weapons require that the United States increase biodefense and public health capabilities at the same time that it tries to develop safeguards to prevent the misuse of biological agents to harm the public health. Limiting the threat of bioterrorism includes reducing access to biological agents that might be used as weapons; however, combating infectious diseases and increasing medical preparedness against bioterrorism necessitates increasing biodefense, biomedical, and other life sciences research, including work on the same "threat" agents that could be used as biological weapons. As safeguards are developed, we must ensure that biomedical research, public health, and clinical diagnostic activities are not inhibited or we risk jeopardizing the public's health and welfare.

Congress already has established a legal and regulatory framework to prevent the illegitimate use of toxins and infectious agents, outlawing virtually every step that would be necessary for the production and use of biological weapons. In doing so it has balanced assuring the availability of materials to the scientific and medical community for legitimate research purposes with preventing access to these agents for bioterrorism. For instance, the 1989 Biological Weapons Act authorizes the government to apply for a warrant to seize any biological agent, toxin, or delivery system that has no apparent justification for peaceful purposes, but exempts agents used for prophylactic, protective, or other peaceful purposes. Prosecution under this statute requires the government to prove that an individual did not intend to use the biological agents or toxins in a peaceful manner. The law also enables federal officials to intervene rapidly in cases of suspected violations, thereby decreasing the likelihood of bioterrorism while protecting legitimate scientific endeavors, such as biomedical research and diagnosis of infectious diseases.

The Antiterrorism and Effective Death Penalty Act of 1996 (the Act) broadens penalties for development of biological weapons and illegitimate uses of microorganisms to spread disease. ASM testified before the 104th Congress with respect to the control of the transfer of select agents that "have the potential to pose a severe threat to public health and safety" and contributed to the passage of Section 511(d) of the Act. The Act was intended to protect dual public interests of safety and free and open scientific research through promulgation of rules that would implement a program of registration of institutions engaging in the transfer of select agents. The transport of clinical specimens for diagnostic and verification purposes are exempt, although isolates of agents from clinical specimens must be destroyed or sent to an approved repository after diagnostic procedures are completed. The CDC is responsible for controlling shipment of those pathogens and toxins that are determined to be most likely for potential misuse as biological weapons. The ASM believes the CDC regulatory controls provide a sound approach to safeguard select agents from inappropriate use and should serve as a worldwide model for regulating shipment of these agents.

In her April 22, 1998, testimony before the Senate Subcommittee on Technology, Terrorism and Government Information Committee on the Judiciary and Select Committee on Intelligence, Attorney General Janet Reno stated that "mere possession of a biological agent is not a crime under federal law unless there is proof of its intended use as a weapon, notwithstanding the existence of factors, such as lack of scientific training, felony record, or mental instability, which raise significant questions concerning the individual's ultimate reason for possessing the agent." She, like other law enforcement officials, are troubled by the fact that someone can possess a biological agent that could be used as a weapon and not be in violation of a law unless one can establish intent. It is our understanding that the Department of Justice and other federal agencies have reviewed federal criminal statutes that could be expanded to make possession of certain biological agents illegal.

The ASM agrees that enhancing security and safety is a critical necessity when bioterrorism poses a credible threat to society. However, proposals intended to promote safety should not pose a threat to biomedical or other life sciences research and clinical diagnostic activities that are essential for public health. Unintended consequences could stifle the free exchange of microbial cultures among members of the scientific community and could even drive some microbiologists away from important areas of research. Ironically, extreme control measures to prevent bioterrorism, instead of enhancing global security, could prove detrimental to that goal if scientists can no longer obtain authenticated cultures. A key point is that natural infectious diseases are a greater threat than bioterrorism. Infectious diseases remain the major cause of death in the world, responsible for seventeen million deaths each year. Microbiologists and other researchers depend upon obtaining authenticated reference cultures as they work to reduce the incidence of and deaths due to infectious diseases. Dealing with the threatened misuse of microorganisms, therefore, will require thoughtful consideration and careful balancing of three compelling public policy interests.

We must acknowledge the terrible reality of terrorism within the United States and abroad from both foreign and United States origins. We cannot discount the possibility that, as unfathomable as it may be to the civilized mind, terrorism may take the form of bioterrorism. Most certainly, therefore, the government and scientific communities are duty bound to take every reasonable precaution to minimize any risk of terrorist use of microorganisms. The ASM is taking a proactive role in this regard.

Even as we strive to prevent bioterrorism, we must candidly recognize that no set of regulations can provide absolute assurance that no act of bioterrorism will ever occur. Therefore, as we strive to prevent such acts, we also have a duty to pursue research and public health improvements aimed at developing the most effective possible responses to acts of biological terror. Research and public health responses related to effectively combating an act of terror are a critical component of the public policy response to the threat that exists.

While the possibility of a future act of biological terrorism is a terrible threat with which we must and will deal, the scourge of infectious diseases is a terrible reality that daily takes the lives of thousands of Americans and tens of thousands around the world. Infectious diseases are now the third leading cause of death in the United States. Research on the prevention and treatment of such diseases is critical to the well being of our entire population. In responding to the threat of terror, therefore, we must minimize any adverse impact upon vital clinical and diagnostic research related to infectious diseases.

Congress and federal agencies have appreciated these competing considerations and have sought to minimize interference with research through such measures as recognizing appropriate exemptions in regulating the handling of pathogenic microorganisms. As we have stated, past legislation has recognized the need for balancing these concerns. We know that such balancing will continue, and the ASM is committed to providing all available assistance in achieving balanced and effective responses to the threat to the public welfare.

It supports making it more difficult for bioterrorists to acquire agents that could be used as biological weapons and to make it easier for law enforcement officials to apprehend and to prosecute those who would misuse microorganisms and the science of microbiology. Its code of conduct specifies that microorganisms and the science of microbiology should be used only for purposes that benefit humankind and bioterrorism certainly is inimical to the aims of it and its members. The ASM established its Task Force on Biological Weapons to assist the government and the scientific and biomedical communities in taking responsible actions that would lower the risks of biological warfare and bioterrorism.

It supports measures to prohibit possession of listed biological agents or listed toxins unless they are held for legitimate purposes and maintained under appropriate biosafety conditions. Accordingly, it supports extending the current regulations implemented by the CDC to oversee the shipment of listed agents to include possession of cultures of those agents.

Although the ASM will not offer specific proposals today, we do think it will be useful to outline certain basic principles that we believe should be considered. Governmental responsibility for establishing, implementing, and monitoring programs related to biosafety should remain with the DHHS and CDC for human health and the USDA for animal and plant health. The CDC possesses institutional knowledge and expertise related to issues of biosafety and the designation, transportation, storage, and use of select agents. The CDC is well qualified to balance the real need for biosafety regulation with the critical need for scientific research, especially clinical and diagnostic research for the prevention, treatment, and cure of infectious diseases.

The CDC's responsibilities should include duties to continue to establish and periodically revise the list of select agents; and in accord with proper administrative procedures, promulgate any additional regulatory measures related to registration of facilities, establishment of biosafety requirements, institution of requirements for safe transportation, handling, storage, usage, and disposal of select agents, and the auditing, monitoring, and inspection of registered facilities. The CDC should notify the Department of Justice about any concerns that it may have about institutions that possess select agents. Congress and the Administration must recognize that any expansion of existing regulations will require additional financial and other resources by the CDC. Based on surveys that ASM has performed, it is estimated that approximately 300 institutions possess select agents. Approximately half of those institutions are currently registered with the CDC pursuant to existing law. Registration of an additional 150 institutions, therefore, would impose additional expense and resource burdens upon the CDC that should be recognized and funded to ensure the timely and complete fulfillment of the CDC's critical mission.

Congress, the CDC, and any other relevant governmental agencies must maintain their focus on the legitimate, important, and fundamental issues related to biosafety. In this regard, biosafety initiatives should be directed toward, and focused on institutions that utilize select agents for scientific purposes, regardless whether such institutions are in the academic, commercial, or governmental sectors. As in other areas concerning biological, chemical, and radiological safety, the focus for ensuring safety should be on the institution. The institution rather than any individual scientist should be responsible for registering possession and maintaining the proper biosafety conditions for storage and usage of the agent.

In this context, ASM supports registration with the CDC of every institution that possesses and retains viable cultures (preserved and actively growing) of select agents along with the concomitant duty to follow all regulatory requirements related to such possession and usage. Institutions and individuals, thus, would be prohibited from possessing cultures of select agents unless the agents are maintained under appropriate biosafety conditions.

The DHHS/CDC, acting in cooperation with the scientific and biomedical communities and with public notice and input, should establish the rules and provide for governmental monitoring. However, the registered institution must be responsible for assuring compliance with mandatory procedures and for assuring fully appropriate biosafety mechanisms, including appointment of a responsible official to oversee institutional compliance with biosafety requirements.

These institutional responsibilities include assuring safety through proper procedures and equipment and through training of personnel. Thus, the institution would bear the responsibility for training employees regarding the biosafety requirements, including the absolute necessity for following those requirements, and such duties as reporting isolation of select agents or any breach in a biosafety protocol.

As institutions comply with appropriate safeguards, scientists may undertake their research with knowledge of clear procedures and with assurance that compliance with such procedures will fulfill all governmental requirements related to select agents. The institutions would be required to maintain records of authorized users and to ensure that they are properly trained as is currently the case for work with radioisotopes. Intentional removal of select agents from a registered facility would subject the individual to criminal sanctions.

Congress and the CDC must balance the public interests of minimizing the threat of bioterrorism and assuring vigorous scientific research, especially research relating to clinical and diagnostic methods and to protecting the nation's food supply. We must recognize that we are dealing with naturally occurring organisms that cause natural diseases. The focus should be on cultures of biological agents and quantities of toxins on the CDC select agent list in order to address any problem arising from an individual who may unknowingly pick up a dead deer mouse with Hantavirus, a handful of soil with Bacillus anthracis, a jar of honey with Clostridium botulinum, or contract an infectious disease with one of the select agents, and who could be in technical violation of a law prohibiting possession. Because microorganisms, including listed agents, are invisible and widely distributed, there is no way of knowing what you might possess unless you culture the organisms or use sophisticated molecular diagnostic procedures.

The CDC, working with the scientific community, should develop a comprehensive definition of a culture of a biological agent that would include microorganisms growing in artificial media, animal cells, and preserved viable materials from such cultures, which are the materials of concern.

Congress should recognize that the need to deal with the threat of biological terrorism will be an ongoing duty for the indefinite future and will continually require balancing competing considerations as discussed in our earlier testimony. Therefore, Congress, acting through the DHHS and CDC, should provide for continuing consultation with the scientific and biomedical communities regarding the substance and procedures of regulations governing select agents. The CDC should be empowered to act swiftly to adjust definitions, substantive duties, and procedural requirements to the inevitable changes resulting from scientific research. ASM is committed to working with Congress and the DHHS and CDC to protect against threats of terrorism while engaging in vigorous research for the betterment of humankind.

PREVENTING NUCLEAR TERRORISM

In 1986, the Nuclear Control Institute, in cooperation with the Institute for Studies in International Terrorism of the State University of New York, convened the International Task Force on Prevention of Nuclear Terrorism, comprised of twenty-six nuclear scientists and industrialists, current and former government officials, and experts on terrorism from nine countries. The report issued by the Task Force, along with more than twenty commissioned studies, remains the most definitive examination of nuclear terrorism in the unclassified literature. The Task Force warned that the "probability of nuclear terrorism is increasing" because of a number of factors including "the growing incidence, sophistication and lethality of conventional forms of terrorism," as well as the vulnerability of nuclear power and research reactors to sabotage and of weapons-usable nuclear materials to theft. The Task Force's warnings and its recommendations for reducing vulnerabilities, many of which went unheeded, are all the more relevant in today's threat environment of sophisticated and suicidal terrorists dedicated to mass killing and destruction.

There is now intense national and international attention to the risks of nuclear terrorism. The possibilities that al Qaeda might acquire the materials and the knowledge for building nuclear weapons or "dirty bombs" or might attack commercial nuclear-power facilities to trigger a nuclear meltdown, are of particular concern. The Nuclear Control Institute has been alerting the public and policymakers to these risks, seeking emergency measures to reduce the vulnerabilities, and monitoring and assessing the responses of industry, governments and international agencies.

DISASTER MOVIES

Fascination with disasters seems to be widespread as evidenced by the rapidity with which Hollywood picks up on so many, in many cases finding them extremely lucrative with a few hitting the top levels of popularity and income. One book listed more than a hundred successful disaster movies. Disasters engineered by terrorists have recently hit the screen. Munich is one, based on the murder of Israeli athletes at the 1972 Olympics in Munich, and now come two from the disasters of 2001, *The World Trade Center* and *Flight 93*. Even China has decided to get into movies of this kind by reliving the horrors of Nanking in the 1930s. The problem with this kind of movie is that accuracy of detail is a victim. Hollywood takes liberties with historical events, shaping them to fit the goals of the producer. For a book of this kind it is a particular problem. Many of the events documented in these two books have been the subjects of disaster movies and many people have seen them. It is important that readers recognize this disparity between the facts of the event and the additions and subtractions included by the film producer.

PLAN OF THESE TWO BOOKS

The disasters described in these books deal mainly with natural ones since they have been the dominant ones throughout history. Records of human tragedies become more frequent in modern times as our involvement in the total environment becomes more frequent and more pervasive. Sometimes a human-induced disaster is the result of ignorance, and at other times it is either error or poor judgment. There are also instances, fortunately few, where those responsible deliberately intended to destroy people and property. The terrorists who bombed Air India and Pan American flights are examples of these. All the events in the two books are scattered in terms of time throughout the past two millennia and are drawn from many countries. The United States has the biggest number from a single country because it tends to acknowledge publicly and in detail all of its disasters. Few other countries are as willing or as able as the U.S. to publicize disasters. As a result, there are fewer documented records of disasters from some parts of the world.

I selected each disaster on the basis of its impact on the social or physical environments of humans, both immediately and over longer periods of time. Oil spills are included because they are a continuing threat to our physical environment and we need to learn from the past. Coalmine deaths were far too numerous in the past and even today there are too many. They are an affront to human values. The unique nature of disasters creates its own rare responses. Emotions are triggered in new ways. There is a sense of isolation felt by both individuals and communities and this can sometimes lead to passivity or even paralysis if the event is catastrophic. For these people the human body is in shock, like recovering from major surgery, feeling that it cannot absorb any more change. Some react in other ways. There are individual acts of extraordinary bravery as when the captain of the Hindenburg ran back into the flaming wreckage to search for survivors. There are also the opposites of these selfless behaviors: looting and assault occur as people react to what they see as the total breakdown of their social order.

Each study is a single event, not a process, and so the disasters of wars and epidemics that are not pandemics are excluded. The nuclear bombing of Hiroshima, although a war event, is included because of the vast environmental consequences that followed from it in later years. In these books, in order to avoid having a catalogue of thousands of low intensity events, only earthquakes with strengths of magnitude 7 or more on the Richter Scale are included. Occasionally, some of lesser strengths are added when their impact is significant elsewhere. Events are arranged in chronological order, and lists of alternative ways of categorizing are provided at the ends of the books in appendixes. After a summary overview of the event there is a detailed description of what happened. Causes of the disaster and remedial actions to ameliorate damage or prevent recurrence are described and references are added for further study. Additional information on twentieth and twenty-first century events can usually be obtained in the archives of local or national newspapers for the day after each event.

References for Further Study

Ackroyd, Peter. 2001. *London: The Biography*. London: Random House.

Bolt, Bruce A. 1993. *Earthquakes and Geological Discovery*. New York: Scientific American Library.

Dudley, Walter C., and Lee, M. 1998. *Tsunamis*. Honolulu: University of Hawaii Press.

McGuire, Bill. 1999. *Apocalypse*. London: Cassell.

1

Supervolcano Toba, Indonesia

ca. 74,000 BC

Sumatra Island, Indonesia

The greatest volcanic eruption about which we know quite a lot

Lake Toba is in the middle of Northern Sumatra. It lies about two hundred miles from the epicenter of the magnitude 9.3 earthquake that devastated Asia in late December 2004, as its tsunami swept across the Indian Ocean. This lake is known as a caldera, the technical term for the crater formed by a volcanic eruption. It is a big lake, eighteen by sixty miles in extent and as deep as five thousand feet in places. The size of the lake can be attributed to Toba's eruption, which was the largest that has occurred, anywhere on earth, within the past two million years. About 74,000 years ago a high volcanic mountain that stood on the area, now occupied by Lake Toba, erupted and blew skyward a mass of ash and volcanic debris that was three thousand times as big as the total amount that erupted from Mount St. Helens in 1980. The entire subcontinent of India was covered with ash. All around the globe sunshine was reduced and temperatures dropped by about 3 degrees, and stayed at that level for years. During that time, throughout the world, millions of all forms of life died. Thousands of species vanished.

The naysayers of our time are busy telling us that increases of carbon dioxide in the atmosphere will destroy human life and our cities before the end of this century unless we change our ways and reduce the present levels of carbon dioxide. Yet, beneath our feet are forces of change far more destructive for the earth's environment and all of its occupants than anything that human activity has done or can ever do. Ordinary volcanic activity is familiar to us because we see it frequently. It is no surprise to visitors in Hawaii when magma pours on to the surface from deep volcanic vents. It is a common occurrence. Occasionally, however, a super volcanic eruption occurs—one that affects the entire globe. Fortunately, they appear rarely in human history but their destructive power is enormous and, unfortunately, their timing is not predictable. We give the name supervolcanoes to them. Toba was one of these, the biggest of all of them within the last two million years with a Volcanic Explosivity Index (VEI) of 8. It is now the model by which geologists assess worst-case scenarios for the future.

There are only about half a dozen locations around the world where geologists have identified supervolcanoes. One location is in New Zealand, one in Japan, and one in Russia. In the United States there is one in Yellowstone National Park where there was an eruption of strength 8 on the VEI, about 640,000 years ago. That strength represents a tenth of Toba's and a hundred times the strength of Krakatau. The past geological history of Yellowstone reveals that it builds up to the level of a super volcanic eruption approximately every 600,000 years so it is reasonable to say, as some geologists have already said, that another terrible explosion is overdue. Geological specialists have been checking the movement of magma deep below Yellowstone Park. The presence of this magma is well known by the surface manifestations of boiling hot springs and mud pots. Precise measurements over time show that the land within the caldera that is now Yellowstone rose thirty-five inches between 1923 and 1984. Later in the 1980s it subsided slightly.

A Yellowstone eruption on the scale of the previous one is a terrifying

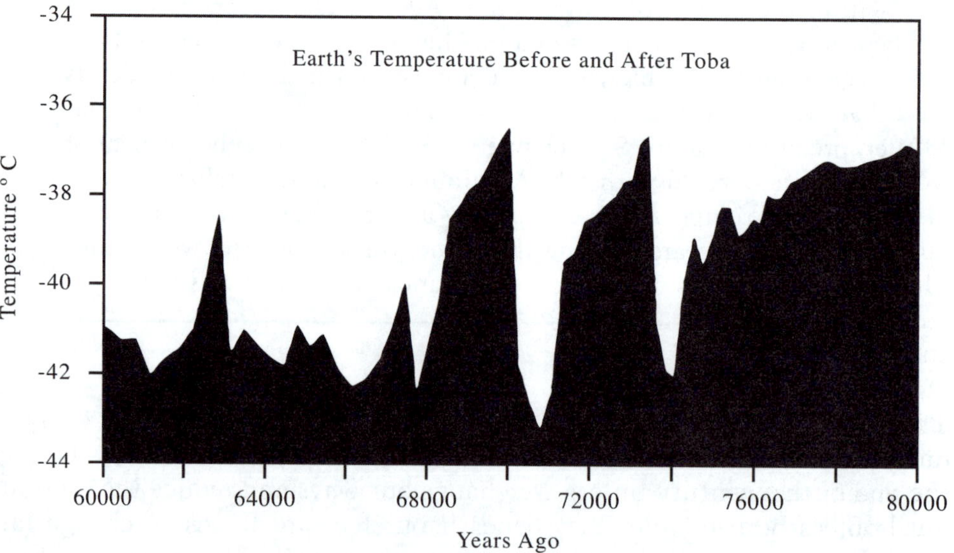

Figure 1 Impact of Toba on global temperature.

concept. It would transform all aspects of human life worldwide. The death toll would be huge. Although its VEI would only be one-tenth that of Toba, it would be disastrous. Tambora, an Indonesian volcanic eruption of 1815, was ten times stronger than Krakatau and only a tenth as strong as the ancient Yellowstone one yet it caused widespread destruction of life and agriculture all over the world. If no one wants to see a repeat of the ancient Yellowstone eruption, then it is even more certain that we do not want to see another Toba, especially since the scale of its destructive activity is now known through seafloor cores and ice cores from Greenland. From both of these data banks we can define climatic conditions around the time of Toba's eruption. Overall it is clear that the dust cloud from the explosion, one that reached high into the atmosphere because it happened near the equator, reduced the amount of sunshine that could reach the earth. Thus, temperatures worldwide were lowered by as much as seven degrees Fahrenheit and this condition remained for more than seven years. Had the eruption occurred near the North Pole the atmospheric dust would have stayed at a lower level within the atmosphere.

It is tempting to think that once the seven or more years had passed everything would come back to its former state. The reality was quite different. To begin with, the eruption coincided with one of the last phases of the last Ice Age, the Wisconsin Ice Age. The years of lower temperatures were an addition to the influences that ice was already exerting on the environment. Overall, geologists concluded that the damage caused by Toba was similar to the scenario drawn up by scientists for the effects of a nuclear war, generally described as nuclear winter. The aftermath of this global environmental disaster was most severe in tropical areas where vegetation is unprepared for coldness. In these tropical areas all the plant tissues above ground would die. Even temperate forests would suffer from the relatively sudden drop in temperatures and 50 percent of them would die. Large amounts of dead wood, aided by drought, typical of ice age regimes, would likely lead to an increase in forest fires. The story would be similarly destructive for life in the oceans but the elements involved would be different.

Geneticists believe that Toba had a particularly catastrophic effect on humans who, 74,000 years ago, were still at an early stage of development. The population on Earth may have been reduced to a few thousand people, pushing humanity to the edge of extinction. Homo sapiens had become an endangered species. The evidence for the catastrophic reduction of numbers around the time of Toba comes from an analysis of mitochondrial DNA that revealed a limited genetic diversity, far lower than the known age of humans would indicate. The total numbers of humans in the years following Toba seemed to be no more than ten thousand. Not until 50,000 years ago, 20,000 years after Toba, was there evidence of a rapid and widespread increase in the numbers of humans. In order to test the validity of their calculations regarding humans, geneticists examined the mitochondrial DNA of chimpanzees to find out if they too had been victims of the same environmental disaster. The results were conclusive. They had experienced a bottleneck similar to human DNA.

References for Further Study

Bar-Yosef, O. 1994. "The Contribution of Southwest Asia to the Study of Modern Human Origins." In Nitecki, M.H., and Nitecki, D.V., eds. *Origins of Anatomically Modern Humans*, New York: Plenum Press.

Clark, G. 1977. *World Prehistory in New Perspective.* Cambridge, UK: Cambridge University Press.

Jones, S., Martin, R., and Pilbeam, D. 1992. *The Cambridge Encyclopaedia of Human Evolution.* Cambridge, UK: Cambridge University Press.

Rampino, M. R., and Self, S. 1993. "Bottleneck in Human Evolution and the Toba Eruption." *Science* 262: 1955.

Simkin, T., and Siebert, L. 1994. *Volcanoes of the World.* Tucson, AZ: Geoscience Press.

2

Rome, Italy, fire

July 19, 64
Rome, Italy

Most of Rome, the Capital of the Roman Empire, was destroyed by fire in 64

On July 19, 64, the same date four and a half centuries earlier when the Gauls set fire to Rome, a fire broke out near the Circus Maximus and quickly spread all over the city of Rome. Large numbers of people lived in timber-framed tenements and, in the warmer weather of July, these readily provided the needed fuel for a fire. Over a period of six days, and then after a short lull, bursting into flames again for a further three days, the flames destroyed 70 percent of the city. Many of the most important buildings were destroyed and thousands lost their lives. One archeologist, examining the ground twenty feet below present levels, found nails that were partly melted by the heat before they fell from burning timber. Coins too were found in the same area, remnants of the possessions of the hapless victims that could not escape the fire.

The aristocrats lived on the higher ground of Rome and once a few tenements were ablaze, firestorms swept upward to higher and higher ground and burned their mansions. Experiments by archeologists trying to reconstruct the scene from 64 discovered that temperatures quickly rose beyond a thousand degrees Fahrenheit. This level of heat readily creates a vortex of swirling flames that reach higher and higher in order to find oxygen, to places like Capitoline Hill where the larger homes were. Attempts to put out the fire were hampered by the terrified cries of the many people who had nowhere to go. The speed of the flames soon caught up with them as they ran away from burning buildings. The emperor, Nero, was away in the eastern part of the empire at this time and he quickly returned as soon as news of the tragedy reached him.

Figure 2 Extent of destruction during Rome's fire.

Emperor Nero opened the Field of Mars and the Vatican Gardens to refugees and arranged food and shelter for them. Supplies were brought in from neighboring towns and the price of corn was cut back for a time to a small fraction of its normal price. Roman society attached great importance to anniversaries of any kind and on this occasion, because it was such a vivid reminder of the earlier malicious attack by the Gauls, the people wondered if this, the worst fire in the history of the city, was an omen of good or a harbinger of evil. In spite of his generosity to survivors, it was not long before rumors began to circulate that Nero was responsible for all that had happened. Had he started the fire, people asked, in order to make space for another building he wanted to erect? This kind of thinking was typical of the times. When news was good the ruler is praised. When a disaster occurs, the ruler is blamed. Furthermore, it was generally known that Nero had grandiose ideas about the city, wanting to demolish the older tenements in favor of elegant buildings that fitted the greatness of Rome.

Nevertheless, historians were doubtful about Nero's involvement because his palace was a victim of the fire. This building, the Domus Transitoria was a magnificent structure that stretched from the Palatine Hill to the Esquiline. It was also noted that Nero was in the eastern Mediterranean at the time of the fire. Fires were commonplace in Rome. Dozens broke out every day. Roman historian Tacitus was one person who was convinced that Nero was responsible but many Romans thought it had been triggered accidentally. In the course of the conflagration some people were seen to be spreading the fire while others prevented attempts to extinguish it. Was this the work of people acting under orders or were they just looters taking advantage of the chaotic situation? They were neither but rather were gangs of irresponsible people wandering the streets looking for anything they could steal. When the fire finally burned out only four of the city's fourteen districts had been untouched by the fire. Lost in the flames were all kinds of art works, both Greek and Roman, and many of the temples were also destroyed including Vesta and Jupiter Stator.

Fire fighting at the time of Nero was sharply contrasted to everything we know today about fighting fires. The people involved were slaves. They were the losers in the military campaigns that Roman generals waged around the empire and they were brought back to Rome to serve the city by doing the jobs that no one else wanted. These fire-fighting slaves had been organized into seven groups, each responsible for two of Rome's districts. Each group was given buckets for use in case of fire. Whenever they were called to deal with a fire they formed bucket lines through which water was passed by hand to the fire where it was squirted on to the flames with a hand-held device that served this purpose. As soon as the fire stopped, Nero closed off the devastated places so that the debris could be removed. Even those who were owners of homes or renters were prevented from returning. They had to fend for themselves in areas outside the city, finding food and shelter as best they could, wondering if and where they might ever again have a place within the city. All of this added to Nero's already poor reputation among the lower classes.

As soon as the old sites were cleared, Nero began the reconstruction. He had a number of triumphal arches erected throughout the city and he rebuilt the temples of Vesta and Jupiter Stator and other places of importance that had been destroyed. His tendency to be extravagant soon became evident in these new buildings as the new Rome took shape. Each building was bigger and more ornate than the one that had been lost in the fire. Nero added a huge arena close to the site of the present Vatican City. When he came to rebuild his former palace, Domus Transitoria, Nero's megalomania became obvious. In the new palace, which he named the Golden House because of all the gold, precious stones, and ivory that it contained, he envisioned an imperial residence, something far beyond the former palace. He added numerous pavilions, each linked to another with covered walkways, forming a small city within the larger one. Additionally, there were temples, baths, gardens, fountains, and a large artificial lake covering 200 acres that later became the site of the Roman Coliseum. To top off all this madness Nero had a bronze statue of himself erected close to the palace's entrance. It stood more than a hundred feet high and could be seen from any part of Rome.

Whether arson or accident was the explanation for the fire, Nero continued to be suspected so he felt he had to take action to clear his name from all suspicion of culpability. He singled out the Christians of Rome as the public scapegoats and, in a style very familiar to us today, was able to secure a few traitors among this group who were willing to confess to the crime. Tacitus described Nero's choice as choosing the notoriously depraved Christians, a phrase that was frequently used in Rome to identify them. They were considered cannibals because they spoke of eating the flesh and drinking the blood of their leader and they were described as incestuous because of their love for one another. To Tacitus, because the Christians' leader Christ had been executed in Tiberius' reign by the governor of Judea, Pontus Pilate, thirty years earlier, it was unthinkable that people would continue to be followers of such a criminal. He called their belief a deadly superstition, one that had broken out in Judea in spite of the death of their leader and had now spread to Rome. Tacitus concluded that all degraded and shameful practices seem to collect and even flourish in Rome.

In spite of the explanation proposed by Tacitus for selecting the Christians, it is unlikely that Nero was thinking of their beliefs when he blamed them. He just needed to find an unpopular and defenseless group, which he could blame, and his choice of the Christians was a popular one. They were seen as enemies of the human race because they were strange and, therefore, in the popular mind, always liable to behave in strange ways, perhaps stirring up civil strife or causing violent outbreaks. Strangeness is the term that Romans used to define every foreign cult. There was a strong feeling that only the ancestral gods of Rome ought to be worshipped and the only way to do that was by following traditional procedures. Any adherence to non-Roman religion was superstition, a label that could at any time imply crimes. Many of these superstitions successfully survived in Rome, especially when they happened to be in favor with the authorities, but safety and survival were never assured things.

The Jews too were considered strange and there were about several thousand of them in Rome. They were no more popular than the Christians. Why then were they not the scapegoats selected by Nero? There were two reasons for this: first, some Jews had helped the Roman army on one occasion so they inherited a sort of protected status for a long time. The second reason related to their attempts at revolution in Palestine, which began to appear during Nero's reign. The Emperor was anxious to avoid any action that would make it difficult for the Roman army in Palestine to stamp out these revolts. There was another development that made it easy for Nero to pick on the Christians. For the thirty years following the execution of their leader, Christians in Rome formed part of the Jewish community and attended their synagogues. A few years before the fire, a letter arrived from Paul, the Apostle, in which he defined the sharp differences between the Jewish ancient religion and the new Christian faith. As a result of this letter, Christians in Rome left the synagogues and met in their own communities. They had become an identifiable group completely separate from the Jewish ones.

Thus began the persecution of Christians in Rome, soon to spread throughout the empire. Hundreds of Roman Christians were arrested and put to death by Nero in the most cruel and farcical ways imaginable. Many were dressed in wild animal skins and torn to pieces by dogs. Others were crucified or made into torches to be lit after dark to illuminate Nero's gardens. It is probable that the two great Christian leaders, Peter and Paul, both of whom were in Rome at the time of the fire, met their deaths at this time. Tradition indicates that Peter was crucified while Paul was beheaded. So brutal was the treatment of the Christians that people began to feel sorry for them. Romans became convinced that they had nothing to do with the fire and that they were being sacrificed for one man's mania. Within four years of the fire Nero would be dead. Following rejection by the army and the Roman Senate he took his own life. His fourteen years of rule had ended but the persecutions he had inaugurated went on.

Nero's extremes seemed to spur the growth of Christianity rather than impede it. Late in the first century, the large numbers of Christians he encountered everywhere made Emperor Domitian decide to send a team of people to Galilee to find out who Jesus was and how he had attained such influence among his followers. Domitian's period of rule was marked with a series of violent persecutions against any individual or group that was different from the norms of Roman life as he understood it and his thoroughness in attacking Christians is a good example of his treatment of enemies. He discovered that Christians consistently refused to adhere to the imperial cult of Caesar worship and this gave him a rationale for launching a mass execution of Christians wherever he found them. Like Nero before him, his hatred of Christians was not based on any particular aspect of their beliefs but solely because they did not conform to Roman norms. For this reason they, along with other divisive groups, met terrible fates at the hands of Domitian.

A few years after the death of Domitian, when Trajan was emperor, some correspondence about Christians between a regional governor and the emperor, gives a good picture of the status of Christians around the year 100. Trajan, in sharp contrast to Domitian, tended to be sympathetic toward dissident groups but he forbade meetings of secret societies because he thought they might be subversive. This edict, inevitably, clashed with the behavior of Christians. They were different from all others around them and they knew it. Their leader had been crucified because he did not conform to the society within which he grew up. Their only opportunity for social life was to meet privately. They knew that they would get into trouble if they were seen meeting publicly. They posed no threat whatever to Roman authority. Their apostle Paul had made that very clear in his letters of instruction. Nevertheless, in the mind of Trajan, with the empire's history of rebellions and revolutionaries, secret meetings were dangerous. It was during Trajan's reign that a letter came to him from Pliny, a governor of one of the regions, asking for clarity about his edict concerning secret societies.

Pliny explained in his letter that he had never been present when

Christians were being examined about their loyalty to the Roman Empire but he now was faced with making a decision about some Christians who had been accused of opposing Roman laws. He went on in his letter to outline the procedure he took in these cases but he felt he needed assurance or correction about it because of his inexperience. The procedure he had followed in these particular cases was as follows: he asked each individual whether he or she was a Christian. If the answer was yes he repeated the question two more times, adding at each repetition of the question that serious punishment would follow if the answer continued to be yes. Anyone who persisted with yes three times he punished by sending him or her to Rome. In Pliny's mind, the Christian's stubbornness and unshakable obstinacy was something that ought to be punished. He added that he had dismissed those who denied that that they were Christians or who had left the Christian community provided they repeated after him a formula of invocation to the gods, made offerings of wine and incense to your statue, and cursed the name of Christ. Pliny knew that real Christians would never do these things. To make sure that the statements from those who cursed Christ were accurate Pliny investigated what he called the truth, from two slave women, using torture, but found nothing other than a degenerative cult.

The reply from Trajan was a firm endorsement of what he had done and it included an interesting double addition: first, Christians must not be hunted down but only questioned when specific charges are brought before a ruler; second, accusations must not be laid against Christians on the basis of pamphlets that criticize them and are circulated anonymously. This was an interesting recognition of the many conflicts and disagreements about Christianity that circulated at that time. Trajan's successor, Hadrian, seemed indifferent to Christians although, in all probability, they became involved in the massive purges that he enacted on Jews. If we look farther ahead to the second half of the third century, when Marcus Aurelius was emperor, we find a recurrence of the earlier hatreds. His persecutions of Christians were particularly bloody. Under Emperor Diocletian, at the beginning of the fourth century, violence against Christians began again and lasted for a number of years until, with the conversion of the Emperor Constantine, Christianity became the official religion of the Roman Empire. Perhaps Constantine had learned that persecution always adds more Christians rather than diminishes their numbers.

References for Further Study

Grant, Michael. 1989. *Nero*. New York: Dorset Press.

Griffin, Miriam T. 1985. *Nero: The End of a Dynasty*. New Haven, CT: Yale University Press.

Warmington, Brian Herbert. 1969. *Nero: Reality and Legend (Ancient Culture and Society)*. London: Chatto & Windus.

3

Pompeii, Italy, volcanic eruption

August 25, 79

On the Bay of Naples in southern Italy

Eruption of Mount Vesuvius destroyed Pompeii and killed its residents

In the early morning of August 25, 79, a mass of pyroclastic material erupted from Mount Vesuvius and, traveling at more than 60 mph, collapsed over the town of Pompeii. Hot ash, lava fragments, and poisonous gases were blasted into homes through tiny openings in windows, doors and roofs. Every one in the town was killed, but not instantaneously. As people inhaled the hot gases their lungs quickly filled with fluid. It was just like swallowing fire. With subsequent breathing the victims found themselves gradually suffocating in a painful death as their windpipes became clogged and their lungs stopped working. It was all over in a short time and, before the end of the day, Pompeii had been covered and destroyed by a twenty-foot blanket of volcanic debris. For more than 1,500 years the town lay buried and forgotten. All that remained was the memory until, after a long time, it was discovered by accident.

Mount Vesuvius is one of a chain of volcanoes stretching northward along the length of Italy. These volcanoes lie at the junction of the African Tectonic Plate and the Eurasian one, a location where there is always a zone of either pressure or tension. For millions of years the African Plate has been pushing against the Eurasian one along a line of action that stretches from Gibraltar to Turkey. From time to time, in the short term, a weak area gives way and either an earthquake or a volcanic eruption is the result. Over a much longer period, the influence of the African Plate gave rise to the Alps. The peak of Mount Vesuvius is about four thousand feet above sea level and six miles from Pompeii.

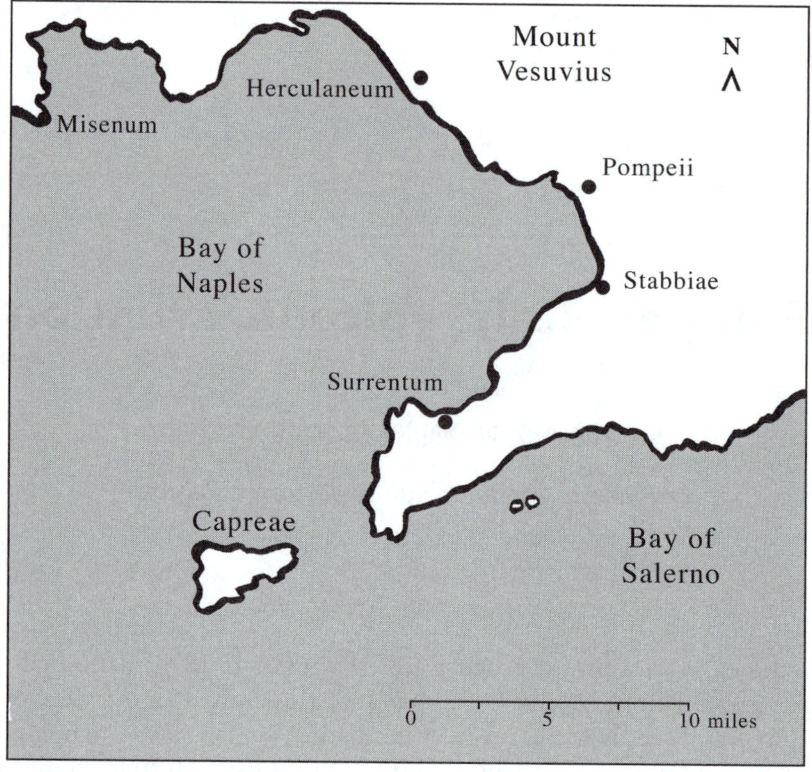

Figure 3 Location of Pompeii.

The accidental discovery of Pompeii's ruins happened in the sixteenth century when an underground irrigation canal was being dug and the workers found themselves cutting through old buildings. An inscription "Pompeii" was found on one wall and people thought it was the name of a house belonging to a wealthy person. Nothing was done about this discovery and two more centuries elapsed before further attention was paid to the buried buildings and even then the focus of interest lay in a search for any valuable objects that might be there. Many people visited the ruins in the eighteenth century but it was only after Italy became a united nation in 1860 that serious study was devoted to it. King Emmanuel II commissioned Giuseppe Fiorelli, a well-known archeologist, to conduct a thorough excavation of the ancient city of Pompeii. He worked on the project with great precision, creating a series of zones in which each one represented a number of houses. He arranged an identifying number for each building.

Fiorelli kept a meticulous record and also made sure that buildings would remain intact by excavating from the roof down. His plan was to leave as much as possible of the site in its original form and location. He did something else that was his own idea. It turned out to be the unique contribution that enables us today to see in three dimensions exactly what happened within individual homes as the volcanic ash arrived. In 1863 he noticed as debris was being cleared away that cavities resembling bodies began to appear in the volcanic material, so he found a kind of plaster that he could force into these cavities under pressure to prevent them collapsing. The result was extraordinary. The volcanic ash had solidified around human and animal bodies to such a degree that the smallest detail could be identified. The addition of the plaster meant that Fiorelli now had complete three-dimensional models of people and animals exactly as they had been in their last moments of life. Victims frequently died in agony as the ash smothered them and the pain of their experiences was clearly etched in their faces.

No one in living memory ever expected to see Mount Vesuvius erupt. It had been quiescent for many centuries and generation after generation had worked the land up the slopes of the mountain. Volcanic ash from time past had provided an ideal foundation for good soil so all kinds of crops were grown, often as many as two crops from a single field in a year. Wine, wheat, and a variety of sauces were shipped regularly to France, Greece, and Egypt. The warm Mediterranean climate, proximity to the ocean, and the advantage of being part of the Roman Empire all gave Pompeii a huge advantage for trade. It is not clear how many people lived in the town at the time of the eruption because Pompeii had been hit with an earthquake, a common occurrence in that area, seventeen years earlier and it had destroyed much of the town. At that time the population was more than ten thousand. Every effort was made to restore the town in the

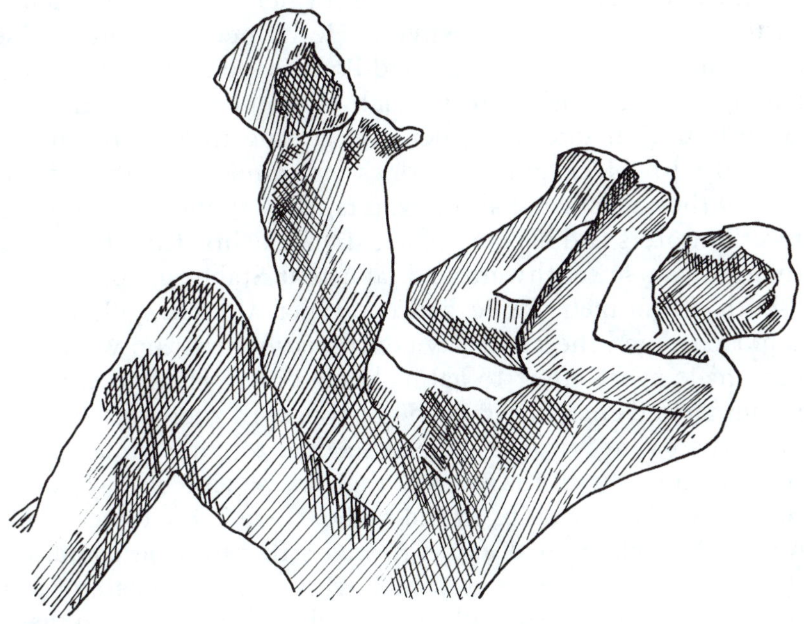

Figure 4 Drawing of reconstructed human body.

wake of the earthquake because it was such an agricultural paradise and every person benefited from its success. We may not know the exact population in 79 but we do know that thousands died instantly when the eruption occurred.

Fortunately for us today there were many historians in Italy and we have first-hand accounts from some of them. Pliny the Elder was a much-respected historian and he happened to be near Pompeii at the time of the eruption of Mount Vesuvius. He was fifty-six years of age, old for that time, a bit overweight, and suffering from asthma, so Emperor Titus decided to give him an easy responsibility, looking after the Roman fleet at Misenum, twenty miles northwest of Pompeii in the Bay of Naples. It seemed like a very comfortable position for him but he arrived at the wrong time for any ease, in the early part of August of 79. On the morning of the twenty-fourth of that month a servant came to him to report the appearance of a strange cloud hovering over the Bay of Naples. Pliny's description of the cloud and his experiences throughout the remainder of that day were recorded carefully by those who were with him, especially by his nephew, later known as Pliny the Younger. They provide a vivid picture of the impact of the eruption on individuals. In the case of Pliny senior, despite all the efforts by him and his staff to safeguard their lives, the twenty-fifth of August proved to be Pliny's, as well as Pompeii's, last day.

Pliny the Elder described the cloud as an immense tree trunk rising high into the air and opening out into many branches. He realized at once that he was witnessing a major natural event so he ordered his staff to make ready a small galley to take him closer to the cloud. Just as he was about to leave he received an urgent call for help from some friends who lived on the slopes of Mount Vesuvius. He immediately ordered several additional boats to go with him toward Pompeii to help in the rescue. As the boats approached the nearest beach to Pompeii, Pliny noticed that ashes were falling in increasing density, getting thicker and hotter and accompanied with black pumice stones and cinders, as they got closer. Suddenly, as they reached shallow waters, they found they could not go further as the waters had become blocked with debris from the mountain. They changed course southward and landed at Stabbiae, about five miles to the south of Pompeii. Panic had overtaken the crew of the ships as night approached and the night sky continued to be lit up with flashes of fire. Pliny made every effort to calm things down. He took a bath and a leisurely dinner and encouraged everyone to have a good night's sleep. The morning of the twenty-fifth of August seemed to come suddenly as they awoke to loud noises with the walls of their house violently swaying backwards and forwards. The ships in the harbor were being tossed about like toys. Although daylight had come it was still pitch-dark and as Pliny stepped outside the house he was met with sulfur fumes and a hail of pumice particles and ash. He collapsed, unable to breathe, and died.

The beginning of the eruption of Mount Vesuvius began on the afternoon of the previous day, the twenty-fourth of August, in the form of the cloud of ash and smoke that Pliny had observed from Misenum. Molten ash and pumice was being ejected from the volcano at a rate equivalent to 600 mph. Ten thousand tons of it left Mount Vesuvius every second. Much of the pumice consisted of pieces larger than a baseball. Within minutes, of the start of the eruption, the cloud of debris had risen nine miles into the sky, a height well beyond that of Mount Everest. Normally, in August, the wind direction over the Bay of Naples is from the northeast. On this occasion, however, it came from the northwest so the fallout was carried over Pompeii. The sky was dark and all over Pompeii people were lighting lamps in the middle of what would normally be bright daylight. Layers of pumice and ash were accumulating on roofs and buildings were shaking constantly from the earth tremors. From time to time a large piece of volcanic rock would crash through the roof of a building. By late afternoon the column of material from the mountain had risen to a height of ten miles, a hundred million tons of ash and pumice had been ejected and Pompeii's streets were twenty inches deep in volcanic debris.

Early in the morning of August twenty-fifth a series of pyroclastic surges emerged from Mount Vesuvius. The volcano's mouth had collapsed and volcanic material was being ejected at fifteen times the earlier rate. This column of ash and pumice was now so dense that it began to collapse and flow down the mountain slope as a glowing red cloud. Its temperature exceeded 1,500 degrees Fahrenheit and, as it rushed toward Pompeii at sixty miles an hour, the town was smothered. Pliny the Younger, the nephew of the Pliny who died at Sabbiae on the twenty-fifth of August, was still at Misenum when the final destruction of Pompeii occurred. He took time to write an account of it all and he sent it to the historian Tacitus a few years later. His descriptions are the best records we have of Pompeii's final day. So widespread was the destructive power of these final pyroclastic surges from Mount Vesuvius that places like Misenum, twenty miles away from the mountain, were so badly shaken and so heavily covered with volcanic material that people felt they had to get as far away as they could. Pliny persuaded his mother to follow him out of Misenum and together they managed to get to a place that was beyond the reach of the falling debris.

From his vantage point north of Misenum, Pliny saw the entire area between him and Pompeii covered with one black cloud. The sea was like the land and we know now that pumice fragments, the main part of the material that flowed from Vesuvius, is lighter than water so it formed a new surface on the ocean. He felt like a person who had been locked in a sealed room without light because in every direction he saw darkness all through the next day. All around him the cries of people and children went on throughout that day. Occasionally there was a flash of light, not from the sun but from the fire that accompanied the cloud and fortunately never reached Pliny's location. All around him ashes were falling steadily and to avoid being buried and crushed beneath them he had to get up periodically and shake them off. Finally, Pliny saw some glimmers of light and then he saw the sun. It was very faint, as if an eclipse was occurring. He and his mother began the journey back to Misenum. Everything and every place were different because of the thick layer of ashes that looked like a giant snowfall.

Mount Vesuvius has erupted dozens of times since that fateful day in 79, including ten times between 200 and 1100. Then, for five hundred years from 1100 to 1600, just as it had been in the period before 79, it was quiescent. No doubt people were lulled into a false sense of security in those times too because their knowledge of geological activities was as inadequate as it was in Roman times. In 1631 Vesuvius burst into action once again and continued frequently until its final eruption in 1944. It seems to an onlooker now that the crater is sealed shut with not even a sign of smoke emerging from it. The one thing we do know, and this was not known even as recently as 1944, is that the underground motions of the great tectonic plates that cover the earth are constantly in motion and always will be. In particular the two plates that meet in Italy are today pressing against each other, building up pressures that some day will give rise to new earthquakes and fresh volcanic eruptions.

References for Further Study

Andrews, Ian. 1978. *Pompeii*. Cambridge, UK: Cambridge University Press.
Connolly, Peter. 1979. *Pompeii*. London: Macdonald Educational.
Giovanni, Casell. 1999. *In Search of Pompeii: Uncovering a Buried Roman City*. New York: P. Bedrick Books.
Harris, Robert. 2003. *Pompeii*. London: Hutchison.
Wilkinson, Paul. 2003. *Pompeii*. London: BBC Books.

4

Alexandria, Egypt, tsunami

365 AD

Harbor of Alexandria, Egypt

A tsunami generated by an earthquake in Greece destroyed Alexandria

In the summer of 365, the port of Alexandria in Egypt was hit with a powerful tsunami that traveled across the eastern Mediterranean from a sea-floor earthquake near Turkey. Italy, Greece, and other places were also hit but the heaviest blow fell on Alexandria. It was in direct line with the direction that the wave took and it was one of the first places to feel the impact of this wall of water traveling at more than 500 miles an hour. As is always the case with large tsunamis, when the wave reaches shallow water, as it would in the harbor of Alexandria, it first rises to a great height, then recedes back out to sea before coming back a second time with renewed force. The people of Alexandria, unaware of the nature of tsunamis, walked out on to the new beach to collect fish. The seabed had been laid bare and all kinds of sea life could be seen. People wandered freely far out from land gathering fish and they were caught in the returning wave. As many as 50,000 people were killed either from the returning wave or in the destruction that followed on shore.

Ships were picked up by the wave as it reached the harbor and they were thrown some distance on to land. In some cases they landed on roofs. The strength of the tsunami was evidence that the earthquake that caused it was a major one, probable at least 8 on the Richter Scale. Sediment cores taken from the harbor in recent years enabled geologists both to date the event and to establish the probable location of the earthquake that caused it. Alexandria does not lie on a geologic fault like so many other places

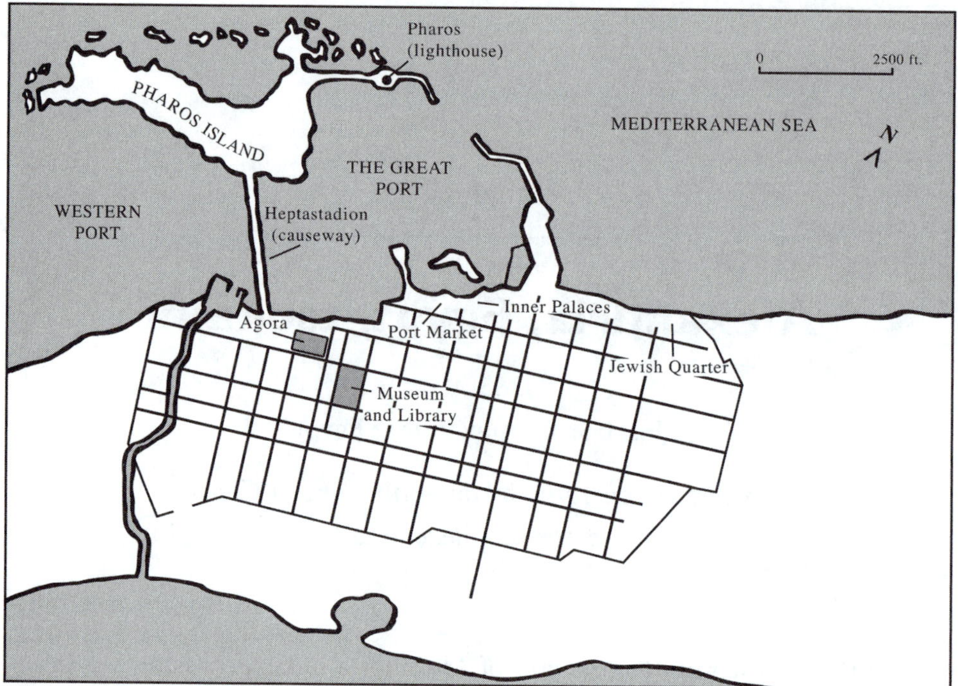

Figure 5 Alexandria at the time of the destructive tsunami.

in the eastern Mediterranean so it has no record of earthquakes and the occurrence of a tsunami is so unlikely that the port authorities of Alexandria gave no thought to it. Royal palaces and the obelisks that were known as Cleopatra's Needles were built along the shore and one of the ancient wonders of the world, Pharos Lighthouse, stood on the outermost extremity of land around the port. Alexandria, founded by Alexander the Great more than 300 years BC, was the biggest commercial and cultural center of the whole Greco-Roman world in 365. It was from here that the Roman Empire's main supply of wheat was shipped. The Nile Valley was the best wheat-growing region in the empire. It had also been the seat of the world's oldest university, located next door to the biggest if not also the oldest library of antiquity.

Powerful earthquakes are known to have occurred previously in the same location that originated Alexandria's tsunami. One of these earlier quakes was so powerful that it created a hole, deep into the sea floor. Not every earthquake gives rise to a tsunami but, whenever the level of the seabed is changed over a significant distance, the displacement of water that it causes creates a special wave, a tsunami. That was what happened when the level of the seabed was changed in the 2004 Indonesian earthquake. The power of the initial release of energy sends the tsunami across the ocean at more than 500 miles an hour. In the deeper parts of the ocean the huge displacement of water is barely visible on the surface and it has little effect on ships in the same place. Once it approaches land, however, it changes dramatically. The lower part of the wave slows down as it encounters the friction of the seabed in shallower waters while the upper part increases in height as the same volume of water enters shallow water. As it rises in height it creates a vacuum that sucks water away from the shoreline, leaving as much as two miles of the seabed exposed. This was the condition that caught Alexandrians off guard. They had never before encountered a tsunami. Today we know that the withdrawal of water is the prelude to a sudden and fast destructive wave crashing on to the shore.

Saint Jerome, whose original work led to the famous Latin Vulgate Bible, was so moved by the destruction of Alexandria in 365 that he thought the world was returning to its original chaos. Like other great scholars, both of that time and from earlier years, he knew that Alexandria was one of the greatest cultural and literary centers of the world and he hoped that its famous library would be preserved. Hundreds of thousands of manuscripts were stored there. Euclid's work in mathematics was there as was also the work of another famous Greek mathematician, Eratosthenes, the man who was the first to calculate the length of the earth's circumference. The Greek version of the Old Testament, known as the Septuagint because it was assumed that seventy Jewish writers wrote it, was compiled in Alexandria. It was the version widely used by Paul and others in the first century of Christendom before other translations of the Old Testament were available. Unfortunately, Jerome's wish was not to be, not because of the tsunami but rather on account of the many conflicts that were centered on Alexandria as different religious and military powers fought for ascendancy there. The library dated from the times of the Ptolemaic rulers of Egypt. Over the years it suffered major damage from accidental fires. In 47 BC, during his military campaign in Egypt, Caesar set fire to ships in the Port of Alexandria and the fires spread to the library.

In 391 riots were instigated by fanatical Christians because of the collections of heretical documents that were stored in the library. Their actions caused serious damage. Over the two hundred years that followed, the library was restored to a condition close to its former greatness as manuscripts were added and lost ones replaced with copies. Then, in 641, the Caliph of Baghdad, in another moment of religious fanaticism, ordered the burning of the entire library. Archaeologists have found what they believe to be the former site of this library. A Polish-Egyptian team excavated parts of Alexandria and discovered what looked like lecture halls or auditoria. They found thirteen of these lecture halls, sufficient space to accommodate five thousand students. The question most-frequently asked is, how did this, the greatest collection of books in the ancient world, came to an end? In fact, as archeological research has revealed, there were two libraries in Alexandria, the royal one and a daughter library. Both were within the city of Alexandria. The Royal Library was destroyed in the aftermath of Christianity becoming the official religion of the Roman Empire. The daughter library survived a bit longer but it too was destroyed before the year 400. One thing about this library's demise is known: when Arabs conquered Egypt in 642, there was no library there.

In the thousand and more years that followed this event, the underlying threat of another tsunami never disappeared because the tectonic forces that caused the tsunami in 365 continued to operate as they had always done. The people of Alexandria had no understanding of these forces and so the memory of what had happened remained as an inexplicable event. Fortunately, in relation to this risk of another tsunami, Alexandria ceased to exist as a seaport and important city in the centuries that followed the conquest of Egypt. The new authorities had little interest in a major seaport and decided to make their capital on a site that is now the city of Cairo. The waterways that connected Alexandria to the Nile gradually silted up and maritime trade dropped off. People who were connected with the sea trade left and, by the time that Napoleon's ships arrived there around the year 1800, Alexandria was little more than a small fishing village. Napoleon's visit created a new interest in the sea on the part of Egypt's rulers. Within twenty-five years, the city was once more a busy seaport as new canals were dug, linking the port with the Nile. With French assistance, warehouses, docks, and homes were built. By 1840, Alexandria's population had risen to 250,000. Today it is a city of more than six million and the danger of another tsunami like the one that arrived in 365 still remains.

References for Further Reading

Canfora, Luciano. 1989. *The Vanished Library: A Wonder of the Ancient World*. Berkeley: University of California Press.

El-Abbadi, Mostafa. 1992. *Life and Fate of the Ancient Library of Alexandria*. Paris: UNESCO.

Macleod, Roy. 2004. *The Library of Alexandria: Centre of Learning in the Ancient World*. New York: I.B. Tauris.

Orosius, Paulus. 1964. *The Seven Books of History Against the Pagans*. Washington, DC: Catholic University of America.

Vrettos, Theodore. 2001. *City of the Western Mind*. New York: The Free Press.

5

Antioch, Syria (now Antakya, Turkey), earthquake

526 AD

Antioch was located in what was called Syria, at the time of the earthquake

Deadly earthquake with hundreds of thousands killed

Antioch, like several other locations in the eastern Mediterranean, had a history of repeated damage from earthquakes. It was probably damaged to a greater extent than most of its neighbors because of the multiple actions of four tectonic plates. The Anatolian Tectonic Plate beneath Antioch was moving north-westward under pressure from the Arabian Plate. These two were then influenced by the African Tectonic Plate as it subducted under the Eurasian Plate. In May of 526, in the early evening while people were in their homes, the worst of many earthquakes hit the city, demolishing it completely. Every building was destroyed. There were many aftershocks that added to the terror of the event, but the greatest devastation came the next day when a fire engulfed the entire city. A quarter of a million people perished in the course of all that took place.

Antioch was a critical frontier in the political and military world of the sixth century. Conflict between the Byzantine Roman Empire and Persia had frequently exploded into warfare and Antioch, at that time part of Syria, was the place that defined the boundary between the two. The earthquake of 526 was followed by aftershocks and, in the course of one of these, the Great Church was demolished. Thousands of lives were lost, largely those of the Christians who were there for a church assembly. Several major earthquakes hit again in later times. The 526 earthquake is singled out partly because of the enormous damage it caused, but also because of its significance for the Byzantine Roman Empire. Emperor Justin was about to hand over his authority to Justinian who had made it clear to all that he intended to extend the boundaries of the empire to what they were in the heyday of Roman power. Antioch was a key location for this purpose because of threats from Persia, so the emperor in Constantinople spent two thousand pounds of gold to rebuild it. Some years later, Emperor Justinian was reminded of the value of Antioch when the Persian King Khosran I sacked the city in 540.

The significance of Antioch to Rome dates from the Roman army's conquest of it in 64 BC. At that time, the city received all kinds of attention from Rome. Great temples, a forum, a theater, aqueducts, and baths were added. Constantine, after he became emperor in 305, added the golden-domed Great Church. The church was so much admired by the people that, when it finally caught fire and disintegrated, everyone decided that the earthquake was a punishment from God. The few survivors of the earthquake and fire described the catastrophe as the destruction of every building and every other thing that was standing. When the fire finally ended there was nothing left but the rubble and ashes on the ground. Not only in ancient times, as was the case here, but in the twentieth century too, great earthquakes were often followed by fires because the materials used for building and the open fires used for cooking made it easy for fires to spread as houses were toppled over. San Francisco in 1906 and Tokyo in 1923 both experienced far greater destruction from the fires that were triggered than happened from the earthquake alone. Saddest of all the survivors' experiences was the sight of looters who arrived from neighboring communities to steal what they could from bodies or buildings, using violence whenever any person tried to stop them.

Seleucia was the port of Antioch in Roman times and sometimes the capital of Syria. This port, less than twenty miles from Antioch, is mentioned in the Bible as the place from which Paul sailed on his missionary journeys. It carried the name of its founder, Seleucius and was the commercial port for Roman Antioch. Seleucia had a strong fortress and a naval shipyard. During the early stages of Christianity, Seleucia had the privileges of a free city. Its harbor was enlarged several times under different Roman emperors. Seleucius must have had a passion for building cities because there were eight other cities in Roman times named after him. Antioch had a population of about 500,000 in Roman times. Its great Greek buildings and theater along with the sacred grove of laurel and cypress earned for it a reputation of being devoted to pleasure. The city was often referred to as Antioch the Golden but, because of the frequency of its earthquakes, it often had to be rebuilt. One such earthquake, in 37, caused the Emperor Caligula to send two senators to report on the condition of the city. Another earthquake followed in the next reign and, in 115, during Trajan's sojourn there with his army, the whole site was convulsed in an earthquake, the landscape altered, and the emperor was forced to take shelter in the circus for several days.

The empire, following the acceptance of Christianity in the time of

Constantine, had a special interest in Antioch because of its ties to historic Christianity. By the end of the third century, estimates of the numbers of Christians were more than 100,000 and Antioch had become the seat of one of the four great Christian centers, the others being Rome, Constantinople, and Alexandria. One of the canonical Eastern Orthodox churches is still called the Antiochian Orthodox Church, even though it had moved its headquarters from Antioch to Damascus many centuries ago. Arrangements of this kind were not unusual; some popes of the Roman Catholic Church retained the title "Bishop of Rome" when they happened to reside in Avignon, France.

From the viewpoint of the beginnings of Christianity and its spread all across the Roman Empire in spite of severe persecution, Antioch was by far the most important location. For some time after the crucifixion of Jesus, his followers were dominantly Jewish converts and their life as a community was centered in Jerusalem. At one point, their teaching angered the non-Jewish authorities and a widespread murderous assault was launched against them. Surprisingly, the leader of these attacks was the same person who, later, would be their main advocate and teacher. His name was Paul. Large numbers of Christians left Jerusalem to escape the persecution and many of them reached Antioch. Paul pursued them and it was while he did so that he had an extraordinary experience of Jesus near Damascus. As a result of this experience Paul became an ardent Christian. He joined the Christians of Antioch and from there began his life work of traveling throughout the Roman Empire to share the Christian news about Jesus.

The name Christian had not been in use as a definition of Jesus' followers until they came to Antioch. It is an indication of the importance of this city that it gave posterity the name by which the followers of Christ would be known for all time. Paul traveled from one end of the Mediterranean to the other and finally ended his life in Rome. The final triumph of Christianity came with the conversion of Emperor Constantine in the fourth century and the adoption of Christianity as the official religion of the Roman Empire. Antioch, because of its strong relationship with the early spread of Christianity throughout the Roman Empire, became a key source of Christian beliefs, especially beliefs about interpreting the Bible. Other centers of theology had a variety of views, mainly symbolic or philosophical. Antioch, by contract, based its views on the historical context within which biblical narratives and teachings were recorded. The historical context then became its key to interpretation, a key that has become a norm in modern times.

Today Antioch, or Antakya as it is known, has a population of 125,000 and is a key trading center for the rich agricultural region in which it is situated on the southeastern coast of Turkey. For centuries it had been little more than a village and its present good health and popularity with tourists is due to French rule in the years between World War I and II. Remnants of the ancient city, mainly blocks of old marble on walls of streets, stand nearby on ancient ruins. France's main legacy from its years of occupation is a film palace and the outstanding contribution from earlier centuries is a seventeenth-century mosque. Some of the ancient walls on the higher ground above the present city have been preserved but they are not very accessible to tourists. A key attraction for every visitor is the collection of Roman mosaics that come from the heyday of the Roman Empire and are preserved in the Archeology Museum. Their color and detail are so clear that experts refer to them as the best available anywhere.

The plain around Antakya is littered with historical mementoes, mounds that cover buildings and people that were destroyed by warfare or earthquakes, and ruins of places that survived assaults. The old seaport of Seleucia, long abandoned because the harbor filled up with silt in the long stretches of time that saw no shipping activity of any kind, still holds fascinating artifacts. During Emperor Vespasian's reign, a tunnel was dug out of rock at sea level to provide water for Seleucia. Today a visitor can see this tunnel with its series of thirty-foot-high great halls. Even though a small irrigation canal was built through these halls in modern times, a visitor can still easily walk through them and see at first hand some of Rome's renowned construction handiwork. Antakya claims to have the oldest church in the world, the one named St. Peter's, not to be confused with the bigger church of the same name in Rome. The apostle Peter is said to have preached in this church. If true, that would date it back to a time before 100. This church is a cave complete with a reservoir of water and a tunnel to ensure escape during the period of Christian persecutions.

A thousand years later, soldiers of the Crusades, people from the Roman Catholic Church who took vows to restore to Christian ownership the lands that had been captured by Muslims, decorated this cave in Antioch in honor of its history. A small Catholic community still lives in Antakya. It celebrates mass in a nineteenth-century church on the city's main street. A famous temple of Apollo also stands in this place, surrounded by villas and gardens that were added by wealthy people. Additionally, there is a legend that Antony and Cleopatra spent time here. The Antioch games, a major event of Roman times, were held in Antioch for many years and they surpassed in popularity and importance their counterparts in Olympus. The ruins of several monasteries can be seen today on the hills surrounding the old city of Antioch, including Saint Simeon's, named after the saint who, in the fourth century, initiated the strange rite of people sitting on the tops of high pillars, often for long periods of time. At its later stages of popularity more than a hundred of these pillars were occupied.

The Roman Emperor Julian, who had grown up in Antioch, was particularly fond of returning to the city to spend time there. Late in the fourth century, when he went back once again to Antioch, he found Christians busy at work tearing down the Temple of Apollo in order to use its stones to build churches. He was furious and immediately arranged to have it rebuilt. Julian had come to the throne after Constantine, the man who restored freedom of worship to Christians and made Christianity the official religion of the empire, so he could not outwardly attack or criticize Christian activities. He was, however, opposed to Christian faith and always looked for opportunities to strengthen the older forms of Roman religions. On the day after he left Antioch and with the rebuilt Temple of Apollo in place, the Christians again demolished it. There is no record of Julian returning again to Antioch or confronting the Christians. There is, however, a record of the Crusaders arriving in Antioch a thousand years after Julian and, like Julian, leaving evidence of their sojourn.

The main destination of the Crusaders was Jerusalem, seen as the most sacred site of Christianity, one that they felt must, at all costs, be restored to Christian ownership. To reach that destination, they had to traverse a lot of territory, all of it occupied by Muslim enemies, so they found they had to build fortified centers along the way, places where they could rest and recuperate from the journey without fear of being attacked. The Crusaders had reason to fear, not because the Muslims were particularly ferocious, but because they had behaved so cruelly as they traveled. They plundered homes and mosques, killing everyone they encountered at these places. Even Constantinople, with all of its treasures from Roman times, was raided and everything thought to be of value was stolen. Many remnants of the castles and fortified sites that they established in Turkey and Syria can be seen today. Among them are the old walls of Antioch. To Crusaders, Antioch represented a site of enormous strategic advantage. It guarded access to the rich plain of what is now southern Turkey. The Crusaders attacked and conquered it in the eleventh century.

References for Further Study

Downey, Glanville. 1963. *Ancient Antioch*. Princeton: Princeton University Press.

Eisen, Gustavus A. 1923. *The Great Chalice of Antioch*. NewYork: Kouchakji Freres.

Kousoulas, D. G. 1997. *The Life and Times of Constantine the Great*. Danbury: Rutledge Books, Inc.

Palmer, Andrew. 1993. *The Seventh Century in the West-Syrian Chronicles*. Liverpool: Liverpool University Press.

Scavone, Daniel C. 1989. *The Shroud of Turin*. San Diego: Greenhaven Press.

6

Constantinople, Byzantine Empire, Black Death plague

542 AD

Constantinople, now Istanbul, Turkey

Bubonic Plague from Asia arrived via Africa at Constantinople in 542

In 542, Roman Emperor Justinian was actively rebuilding the empire from its new headquarters in Constantinople, often referred to as the Byzantine Empire since there was so much Greek influence there. The old western part with its center in Rome had been taken over by barbarians, vandals, and others. Through a series of military victories, Justinian's forces had been able to recapture much of Italy and had also been successful on other fronts. It was in the midst of these successes that Constantinople was ravaged by the first case of a Black Death pandemic. It reached Justinian's capital from Egypt, probably carried by rats in ships. Historians have estimated that close to half the population of Constantinople died from the plague during its four or five months of active infections. The number of soldiers left for Justinian's campaigns was completely inadequate so he had to step back from defending or further extending the historic frontiers.

Procopius, a historian living in Constantinople at the time, vividly described the plague and its effects. He pointed out that often, in the first day of infection, nothing very serious was evident but, on the second day, a bubonic swelling developed in the groin, armpits, or on the thighs and mental problems began to appear. Some went into a deep coma while others became delirious. Death came quickly to many while others lived for several days. When small black pustules appeared in the skin, the infected individual usually died within a day. Another symptom, vomiting blood, almost always led to death within a few hours. The physicians of that time tried a variety of cures but the results were always the same: again and again the cases that they fully expected to live died and the ones who seemed to the physicians to be hopeless lived on far beyond the period of the pandemic.

In the sixth century there was no significant understanding of bacteria and their role in the spread of diseases, and nothing was yet known anywhere about genes and their critical influence in determining who survived and who did not. These are the reasons for the perplexity experienced by the physicians when they tried their best to save the sick and the results were disappointing. It was the same centuries later when the same Black Death that overtook Constantinople in 542 swept over London in 1665. Many people in London, such as gravediggers, who were constantly exposed to infected bodies, stayed quite healthy while those who had just a single exposure to the infection died within two days. U.S. researchers who investigated this problem in the late 1990s solved the problem: those who had a particular gene, commonly known as Delta 32, did not catch the disease if they inherited this gene from both parents. If they received the gene from only one parent, they got sick but they recovered. The same gene in HIV patients is now known to be the reason for them escaping the consequences of that particular infection.

Procopius went on to describe the disease in Constantinople by showing how it affected pregnant women. Here, as in the general population, death came to both mother and baby but, in a few instances, either a mother died at the time of childbirth while the child survived or else a child died and the mother survived. It seems likely that in these rare cases the Delta 32 gene had been inherited from one parent. One common cause of death that seemed to have escaped the attention of Procopius was inflammation of the lungs, usually followed by spitting blood. Death followed quickly in these cases. Overall, the 542 pandemic ran its course over a time period of four or five months, a common sequence in other places at different times. At its peak, 10,000 died daily. The disposal of dead bodies overwhelmed the whole city. At first, friends and relatives attended to burials but very soon, with bodies being left unattended in streets and homes, huge pits were dug for mass disposal of the dead. Even these arrangements were inadequate so, with more and more bodies piling up, men removed the tops of the towers on the city walls and threw bodies into the spaces inside the wall.

The great leaders of the Roman Empire saw the whole inhabited world as their domain of responsibility, yet when Justinian became emperor there had not been any additions to the empire's traditional territory since its acme in the second and third centuries. A glance at a map of the empire in second century and then one in the sixth reveals the enormous amount of shrinking that had taken place in the intervening four hundred years.

Justinian was determined to change this condition and push back the existing frontiers to encompass as much as possible of the known world. The Greek city of Byzantium became the new Rome in the year 330. It was named Constantinople in honor of Emperor Constantine who established Christianity as the official religion of the Roman Empire. Justinian ruled this eastern empire from 527 to 565 and, in the first half of that period, he set about restoring the size and prestige of the former empire. In many ways his reign therefore represented a preservation of the Roman past.

There was an unbroken tradition in Roman law that had continued from the earliest days of the empire into the sixth century. Justinian felt that the preservation and renewal of these laws was as important as the recovery of former territory and he set about getting the work done. It was an immense task, one that was to last far beyond the life of the Byzantine Empire and serve in later centuries as the basis of European jurisprudence. The work was begun in 528 when Justinian appointed ten jurists to compile a new codification of the statute law and it was completed a year later. The next task was even bigger, the preparation of a summary of jurisprudence from the great Roman lawyers of the second and third centuries. This involved the reading of two thousand manuscript books, assessing the key matters of content, and reducing the total amount of material to one fifth of the original. All this took three years of hard work. Justinian had a reputation of being a very hard worker and he inspired these writers by his own example. His staff often used to find him busy at work in the middle of the night.

Once the work of codification and summary of jurisprudence had been completed, no further commentary on the law was permitted. The code and the summary, or digest as it was called, now represented the whole of the law. Any new legislative acts were referred to as novels; they usually dealt with issues in ecclesiastical and public affairs. One very long novel dealt with Christian marriage law. It was a sign of the times, particularly the changed times that accompanied the move of the empire's capital from Rome to Constantinople, that all of these novels were written in Greek, not Latin. Furthermore, Justinian knew that many Roman laws had never been popular in the Greek east so local preferences frequently replaced old Roman laws. Hellenic traditions affecting family, inheritance, and dowry, for example, appeared in the new legislation. In addition, the power of the father, traditional in old Roman thought, was now considerably weakened. Christian influences too appeared in much of the newer legislation. There was a desire to make law more humane, an emphasis that came from Justinian's interest in including the idea of a love of humanity, and it was expressed in laws protecting the weak against the strong, favoring the slave against the master, debtor against creditor, and wife against husband. These improvements may seem small today but they represented a huge advance from the days of the old Roman Empire.

Justinian's role in the Black Death pandemic needs to be examined because it was he who greatly extended the activities of the empire into Africa, the place that was the source of the Black Death. His first moves were directed at recapturing some of the lost lands of the west. His armies invaded the Vandal and other kingdoms, one after another, in a series of bitter wars from 540 onward, and in all of these he achieved considerable success. He made the Germanic kings servants of the eastern empire but there remained the difficult problem of religious purity. Justinian was devoted to the Nicene Creed, brought in by Constantine as the official religion of the empire, but the Germanic kings were practicing and preaching a form of Christianity considered heretical by the established church. The Vandals were most zealous and quick to seize orthodox churches in order to convert them into different places of worship. The Vandals were so few in number that they resorted to terror in order to control their subjects so their kingdom became a police state in which orthodox Christians were stripped of property rights, and frequently of freedom and even of life. When a delegation of orthodox Christians from Africa appealed to Justinian to fulfill his role as defender of the faith, he decided that the time had come to bring Africa back under the control of the empire.

The immediate incentive for attacking the hundred-year-old Vandal kingdom in Africa was soundly based. Their king, Hilderic, had fostered good relations with the orthodox Christians. Exiled bishops had been recalled and churches reopened, but in 530 he was deposed by his cousin Gelimer and, from his prison, Hilderic appealed to Justinian. Even so, Justinian was uncertain about taking action because an earlier expedition had led to disaster. Finally, after much deliberation, Justinian went ahead with the invasion of Africa, convinced that the restoration of true Christianity justified it. The expedition set sail in 533 under the command of Belisarius. The field army numbered 18,000 men, 10,000 of them infantry and 5,000 cavalry. There were also some others. In Sicily, Belisarius got the welcome news that Gelimer was unaware of the offensive and had sent 5,000 men and 120 ships under his brother Tata to put down a rebellion in Sardinia. The expedition from Constantinople landed in Tunisia, and the army marched along the coast toward Carthage while the fleet accompanied it offshore. Gelimer's reaction was to put Hilderic to death and then march out to resist the invasion. His tactics were poor, perhaps due to inadequate planning, and he was routed. Belisarius marched on and took possession of Carthage. Gelimer fled westward and joined his troops who had been recalled from Sardinia, but within a few months suffered another defeat near Carthage. Gerlimer hid for a time with local tribesmen but finally surrendered. Belisarius went back to Constantinople with his captives and booty and Justinian arranged a victory celebration for him when he arrived, somewhat like the old Roman celebrations that followed successful military campaigns. About two thousand of the captives were conscripted into the army of Justinian.

Quite apart from his military successes and defense of traditional Christianity, Justinian achieved fame because of his extensive building program. The outstanding illustration of his work, one that still survives in the Istanbul of today, is the Hagia Sophia. There was an earlier church on the site that would become Hagia Sophia's, built by Constantius in 360. He was the son of Emperor Constantine who had liberated the Christian faith from centuries of persecution. The earlier church was known as the Great Church. In 404, this church was destroyed by mobs and, later, in 415, rebuilt. It too fell victim to a rampaging mob of heretics in 532. The new emperor, Justinian, firm defender of orthodoxy, made short work of the howling heretics and ordered that construction begin on a brand new basilica. Construction work lasted from 532 to 537 and the new church was consecrated in 537. Architecturally the grand basilica represented a major revolution in church construction. It had a huge dome and this demanded new skills and new materials in order to support the weight of the dome. No one had ever previously attempted this. There were no steel beams available at this time so the dome had to be supported by massive pillars and walls. The church itself measured 260 by 270 feet, the dome rose 210 feet above the floor, and the overall diameter of the dome was 110 feet.

Some awareness of the danger of earthquakes was known at the time but everyone was convinced that the huge structures employed would meet any threat. They were wrong. Parts of the church and dome were destroyed subsequently in an earthquake and large buttresses had to be added to the supports. In 1204, Roman Catholic crusaders attacked and sacked Constantinople and Hagia Sophia, leaving behind a lasting legacy of bitterness among Eastern Christians. For more that 1,000 years Holy Wisdom had served as the cathedral church of the Patriarch of Constantinople as well as the church of the Byzantine court, but that function came to an end in 1453, when the Ottoman Turkish Sultan seized the Imperial City and converted Hagia Sophia into his mosque. Today, Justinian's dreams of restoring the greatness of the old Roman Empire are long forgotten but the magnificent Church of the Holy Wisdom, which is the interpretation of the words Hagia Sophia, is still admired. It is a tourist attraction because it dominates the skyline of the modern city. Such was its stability over the centuries that, during an earthquake in Constantinople in 1999, the safest place for people was considered to be the Hagia Sophia. It is the mother church of all Eastern Christians of the Byzantine liturgical tradition both the Orthodox and the Greek Catholic.

The reign of Justinian proved to be a major factor in all of the history of late antiquity. Paganism finally lost out and the Nicene Creed that Constantine had established in the fourth century was almost universally recognized. From a military viewpoint, it marked the last time that the Roman Empire could go on the offensive with any hope of success. Africa and many other areas had been recovered. When Justinian died, the frontiers he had secured were still intact but it was the degree of restoration of the old empire that he had won back and the accompanying greatly expanded trade with the rest of the known world that led to the pandemic which destroyed so much of Constantinople and cut short all further military campaigns. Justinian had not created the disease, but he created the pandemic, which followed the movements of men and goods in Justinian's greatly expanded empire. Without the empire and its huge shipments of grain and cloth from Africa, it is difficult to imagine how the First Pandemic could ever have hit Constantinople at such an early date.

Istanbul (Turkish: İstanbul) is Turkey's largest city, and its cultural and economic center. It is located on the Bosphorus Strait, and encompasses the natural harbor known as the Golden Horn (Turkish: Haliç) in the northwest of the country. Istanbul extends both on the European (Thrace) and on the Asian (Anatolia) side of the Bosphorus and is, thereby, the only metropolis in the world which is on two continents. Its 2000 Census population was 8,803,468 (city proper) and 10,018,735 (province), making it, by some counts, one of the largest cities in Europe. The census bureau estimate for July 20, 2005, is 11,322,000 for Istanbul province, which is generally considered as the metropolitan area, making it one of the twenty largest metropolitan areas in the world. Istanbul is located at 41° N 28° E, and is the capital of Istanbul Province. Istanbul, formerly known as Constantinople, had been the popular name of the city for five centuries already, a name which became official in 1930. Due to its three-thousand-year old history, it is considered as one of the oldest still existing cities of the world. Istanbul has been chosen as the European Capital of Culture for 2010. Istanbul is sometimes called the "City on Seven Hills" because the historic peninsula, the oldest part, was built on seven hills, and is also represented with seven mosques at the top of each hill.

References for Further Study

Evans, J. A. S. 1996. *The Age of Justinian.* London: Routledge.

Evans, J. A. S. 1998. *Rome and Persia at War, 502– 532* Leeds, UK: Francis Cairns.

McNeill, William L. 1976. *Plagues and Peoples.* New York: Bantam Doubleday Dell Publishing Group.

Orent, Wendy. 2004. *Plague, The Mysterious Past and Terrifying Future of the World' s Most Dangerous Disease* New York: Simon & Schuster.

7

Corinth, Greece, earthquake

856 AD

Corinth, Greece

Corinth, a city well acquainted with earthquakes because of its many underground geological fault lines, experienced an earthquake of magnitude 8 or more that almost totally destroyed the city in 856

Corinth, a busy and successful seaport in Greece and once part of the Byzantine Roman Empire, was no stranger to earthquakes. It stood amid a series of fault lines and the conjunctions of several tectonic plates or platelets so, like Iran and several other eastern Mediterranean places, Corinth frequently experienced earthquakes. The speed with which these tectonic plates moved far beneath its surface was greater that almost anywhere else. One subducting plate moved at three quarters of an inch per year. In geological terms that is very fast. Today that movement still continues at the same rate and we have the advantage of GPS technology to confirm the rate. In 856, Corinth experienced its worst of many earthquakes, one that is now recognized as having a strength greater than 8 on the Richter Scale. The city was almost totally destroyed and 45,000 people lost their lives.

Ancient Corinth, the original Corinth, founded more than three thousand years ago, was the richest port and the largest city in ancient Greece. Strategically located guarding the narrow isthmus that connects the Peloponnesus (as southern Greece is called) to the mainland, it was a powerful commercial center. The four-mile-wide Isthmus of Corinth was always a problem because Corinth was on the west side of it. Thus ships arriving through the Gulf of Corinth from Italy and other places west had to turn back through the Gulf and take the long journey around Peloponnesus in order to reach Athens. Yet Athens was less than fifty miles from Corinth. If only they had a canal across the isthmus the journey would be so much easier. Ships could continue their voyage past Corinth for the short journey to Athens. Some sailors were so anxious to overcome the hazard of the isthmus that they would drag their ships across it rather than contend with the long sea voyage. Ships were very much smaller in these times so they could do this. In addition there were the dangers of encountering pirates at sea and every sailor wanted to avoid that type of encounter.

As early as 67, Emperor Nero saw the advantages of having a canal dug across the isthmus. He lifted the first sod with a golden trowel, then instructed six thousand Jewish slaves he had brought from Palestine to get on with the work. There is no record of anything significant having been done by Nero's slaves. It was not until 1893 that the canal was finally dug and the ship voyage from Corinth to Athens was shortened by two hundred miles. The present site of Corinth (Korinthos on maps) with a population of 50,000 is quite close to the site of the ancient one. It is a port and a major transportation center on the Gulf of Corinth trading in olives, tobacco, raisins, and wine. Founded in 1858 after the destruction of Old Corinth by an earthquake, it was rebuilt after another earthquake in 1928 and was formerly known as New Corinth. Old Corinth, just southwest of modern Corinth, is now a village. It is strategically situated on the Isthmus of Corinth and protected by the fortifications on a two-thousand-foot-high limestone mountain above the city. Almost all of the pillars that held up the temples of ancient Corinth have collapsed under successive earthquakes over the past two thousand years.

References for Further Study

Carpenter, Rhys, and American School of Classical Studies at Athens. 1936. *A Guide to the Excavations*. Athens: Hestia Press.

Engels, Donald W. 1990. *Roman Corinth*. Chicago: University of Chicago Press.

Yeats, R. S., Sieh, K., and Allen, C. R. 1997. *The Geology of Earthquakes*. New York: Oxford University Press.

8

Damghan, Persia, earthquake

December 22, 856

Damghan in the north central part of what is now Iran

An earthquake of magnitude 8 hit and destroyed the city of Damghan, Iran, in 856 AD. Both the city of Damghan and many areas around it were destroyed

On December 22, 856, an earthquake of magnitude 8 struck the city of Damghan, at that time the capital of the area we now know as Iran. While the earthquake was centered on Damghan and destroyed most of that city, damage to neighboring areas extended east and west over a two hundred mile stretch of countryside. Every village in this area was destroyed. One third of the town of Bustam, about fifty miles east of Damghan, collapsed. In mountain areas close to the center of the earthquake the surface of the ground parted in several places. Overall, 200,000 people lost their lives. The memory of the event was so vivid that, two generations later, detailed memories of all that had happened were still being recounted.

Iran has always been known as a place of earthquakes because of its location along fault lines and between two major tectonic plates that are always colliding. In earlier times, news of earthquakes in this remote region east of Mesopotamia was almost nonexistent. Not until the early Islamic Period, after 622, was it possible to locate reliable records of events. Of the significant earthquakes reported after 622 and before 922, Damghan was the most powerful. There were about forty others within this period with magnitudes ranging from 5 to 7. At this early stage of scientific thinking, explanations for earthquakes among the more educated Muslims were based on Aristotle's thinking, a sort of philosophy of nature based on mathematics or on orderly patterns observed in nature. Unfortunately, earthquakes are anything but orderly. We know their causes but not their timing. For the vast majority of people in 856, earthquakes were viewed with awe and their origins attributed to the actions of a supernatural power.

Even in modern times, this theological interpretation of earthquakes is a common view. One group regards them as punishment from their god for bad behavior. Another sees them as omens of contemporary political events; that is, they indicate what is about to happen in a particular country. This view is so common in China today that the government of that country delayed for three years the detailed reporting on an earthquake that came in 1976. In the case of Iran, there was a fairly large earthquake in that country on the sixteenth of January 1979, in which several hundred people were killed. That particular day happened to be the one on which Shaw Pahlavi departed from Iran, leaving the government of the country in the hands of the theological leaders who replaced him. To many people in the country, the earthquake was evidence of the behavior of their god in rearranging the nation's government. With our present knowledge of the causes and outcomes of earthquakes, Iranian patterns can be identified across time and space, some because of local records and traditions seen to be repeating every thousand or even every five thousand years.

The Eurasian and Arabian tectonic plates converge at an average rate of a little over one and a half inches every year. Iran is in the middle all of this activity and its numerous fault lines bear the evidence. Across a line that stretches east and west for more than six hundred miles strike-slip and reverse faults are the places where plate movements are expressed. In earlier times, as in the Damghan earthquake, most of the country consisted of small farming settlements in which homes were built of simple mud-walls, a type of construction that easily collapses when an earthquake strikes. Some commentators have suggested that people built simple inexpensive homes because they knew that there would be new earthquakes and they would lose whatever they built. In places like these ancient Iranian ones, most of the deaths in an earthquake are caused by the collapse of homes. As a result, it often happens that huge numbers of deaths are reported from developing countries, where buildings are incapable of withstanding even low magnitude earthquakes; while developed countries report fewer deaths when hit with similar magnitude earthquakes.

Much of the history of homes in Iran is typical of conditions in other developing nations, so a closer examination of how single homes and clusters of buildings are constructed in Iran is worthwhile. In addition, their failure until very recent times to make buildings earthquake resistant is also typical of many other countries. In December of 2003, the ancient Iranian city of Bam was destroyed in an earthquake. It was clear in reports from the British Broadcasting Corporation (BBC) that failed buildings were the main cause of the large number of deaths. According to the BBC, Bam experienced a strong earthquake at four in the morning when most of the residents were in bed. One-third of its population of 200,000 was either killed or seriously injured. Most of the buildings, including two of the city's hospitals, were destroyed. The BBC's reporter told of intense scenes of grief as survivors stood beside corpses wrapped in blankets or buried beneath rubble. This story in all probability was very much like the one that was recounted in Damghan twelve and a half centuries ago.

Homes built a thousand years ago and those built today in most rural areas are built of dried mud or adobe bricks, rarely with a type of clay that gives significant strength to the building. Where timber is available, beams can be installed for the support of flat roofs in spite of the fact that the kind of timber available is often warped or weak from repeated use in previous constructions. Typically, a flat roof is very heavy. It consists of some kind of boarding on which two feet of earth is laid. A flat roof is always preferred because it provides a cool place in which to sleep during the hot summer months and can also be used for drying crops. In mountain villages, a common sight in a country that has one third of its land area higher than ten thousand feet above sea level, houses are built with stones and held in place with a clay mortar. Where slopes are steep the roof of one house becomes the ground floor and outdoors of the next home above it. On lower elevations homes are built close together with very little space between them. When a home is damaged, the repair work rarely tries to make the place stronger and, therefore, better able to withstand the next earthquake.

The concept of making buildings as earthquake resistant as possible was unknown until recently. Heavy rainfall still destroys hundreds of homes in the course of a few hours. The idea of changing both the appear-

Figure 6 An Asian yurt, the safest type of dwelling in Iran during ancient earthquakes.

ance and shape of a home to make it better able to resist an earthquake began to appear for the first time in the second half of the twentieth century. There is one group of Iranians who have no need to make their homes earthquake resistant—the nomadic tribes who need homes that can be dismantled and remounted in a short time as they move from place to place. Their homes are yurts and they are perfect examples of earthquake resistant homes. These structures are dome-shaped, circular, tents made of collapsible walls of willow poles, known as yurts. The roof of a yurt is domed and both roof and walls are covered with a kind of felt made from animal wool. Dried grass and strips of leather are used for holding the structure together. In summer, the felt sides are rolled up to admit air and, in winter, extra sheets of felt are added to the outside for warmth. The whole structure can be taken apart and reassembled in an hour, a vital feature for nomadic life. A yurt can provide a comfortable home for at least fifty years.

References for Further Study

Ambreseys, N. N., and Melville, C. P. 1982. *A History of Earthquakes in Persia*. Cambridge, UK: Cambridge University Press.

Andrews, Peter A. 1997. *Nomad Tent Types in the Middle East*. Wiesbaden: L. Reichert.

Arberry, A. T. 1953. *The Legacy of Persia*. Oxford: Oxford University Press.

Barth, Frederik. 1961. *Nomads of South Persia*. Oslo: University of Oslo.

de Boer, Jelle Zeilinga, and Sanders, Donald T. 2005. *Earthquakes in Human History*. Princeton: Princeton University Press.

9

Aleppo, Syria, earthquake

1138 AD

Aleppo (modern name Halab)

The earthquake destroyed a vast area around Aleppo and killed 230,000

In 1138, a deadly earthquake destroyed the city of Aleppo and the area around it. This city is set in a nest of fault lines and earthquakes have always been a feature of life. A large earthquake of intensity greater than 7 hit the coastal area immediately south of Aleppo five hundred years earlier. Its impact was felt over a large part of the eastern Mediterranean and it was accompanied by a tsunami. The East Anatolian Fault line passes through Aleppo and, as it moves, it gives rise to a series of earthquakes over time. Additional disruptions come from the westward movement of the area as a whole under pressure from the Arabian Tectonic Plate. The earthquake of 1138 completely destroyed a vast area in and around Aleppo, now called Halab, and jolted places two hundred miles from the city. The death toll was 230,000, making it one of the five deadliest earthquakes in recorded history. There were several small aftershocks and, twenty years later, another very strong earthquake.

Aleppo has been settled for more than three thousand years. Initially it was the territory of the Hittites, then the land of the Assyrian and Persian empires for almost a thousand years until the Greek Empire of Alexander the Great captured it. The Romans were the next owners of this part of the Middle East and, after them, Arab and Ottoman masters until the fall of the latter in 1923. The key location of Aleppo on trade routes between Europe and Africa and Asia always made it a target of invaders. Around the year 1100, the city came under siege from the Crusaders on two occasions but they failed to capture it. The Mongol armies swept over it in the second half of the thirteenth century, destroying everything as effectively as any earthquake might do. Today the city is a large, modern, urban center of two to three million people, the second biggest city of Syria next to Damascus. It stands on the same site as it occupied for thousands of years; thus its rich history lies hidden beneath many buildings.

Aleppo is in a location that is extremely hot in summer but its elevation of more than a thousand feet above the surrounding plain, coupled with prevailing strong breezes, have always kept summer high temperatures below 110 degrees. Its modern name, Halab, is based on an ancient word for milk and traditions trace this name to the time of Abraham who, it is said, stopped here for a time on his journey to the Promised Land and grazed his cows in the area around the city. The traditional routes along the valleys of the Euphrates and Tigris and down the eastern Mediterranean coast make that a feasible story. Today, this ancient link with the Bible is reflected in a large Christian population in Aleppo, about 30 percent of the total, probably the largest concentration in any Middle East country, appropriately identified by the street called "Narrow." Another link with the Christian past is found in the Citadel mound. This place was a medieval castle, partially an imitation of the Crusader castles that were built all over the Middle East at that time. The crusaders brought with them the castle-building technology of Western Europe and in the years after they left the Middle East their technology is visible in the castles they abandoned. The castle in Aleppo is an excellent example of their work.

In addition to Christians, Aleppo had also from the very earliest times housed a big Jewish population. Their great synagogue held an ancient codex, now known as the Aleppo Codex, and it was dated in recent times as belonging to the ninth century. It somehow survived the catastrophes of the intervening centuries and is now housed in Jerusalem. There are other buildings too that define both its history and Aleppo's present place within Syria. A cathedral that was built in Roman times under the auspices of Saint Helena, mother of Constantine the Great is regarded as the burial place of John the Baptist's father. It was rebuilt in recent times. During the Crusades, when the invaders pillaged the surrounding countryside, the city's chief judge converted Saint Helena's cathedral into a mosque. Subsequently, it became a religious school. Aleppo's physical location defined its role through the centuries. It was a trading center. It maintained that role for a very long time, until Europeans began to use the Cape route to India and later the shorter route through the Suez Canal and Red Sea.

References for Further Study

Busquets, Joan. 2005. *Aleppo: Rehabilitation of the Old City*. Cambridge, MA: Harvard University Graduate School of Design.

Eldem, Edhem. 1999. *The Ottoman City between East and West: Aleppo, Izmir, and Istanbul*. New York: Cambridge University Press.

Meriwether, Margaret L. 1999. *The Kin Who Count: Family and Society in Medieval Aleppo*. Austin, TX: University of Texas Press.

Tabba, Yasser. 1997. *Constructions of Power and Piety in Medieval Aleppo*. University Park, PA: Pennsylvania State University Press.

10

Shaanxi, China, earthquake

1556 AD

In the Province of Shaanxi, China

The light loess soils of Northwest China are easily shaken by an earthquake. In 1556, a huge population lived there in underground homes and many were killed by this, the world's deadliest earthquake

The Shaanxi earthquake of 1556 was the deadliest ever experienced anywhere in the world. It happened in the northern interior of China not far from the city of Xi'an. It measured more than 8 on our scale of earthquake strength, damaged parts of ten neighboring provinces in addition to the Shaanxi one, and was so strong that half of China felt its impact. Aftershocks continued intermittently for six months. An area extending 250 miles outward from the epicenter was completely destroyed. Most of the population at that time lived in caves inside the loess cliffs. Loess is a relatively light type of soil and it disintegrated under the earthquake's pressure and shaking with the result that 830,000 people were killed.

In 1989, the Science Press of Beijing, with help from UNESCO, published a summary of the history of Chinese earthquakes. Its description of the 1556 one tells of mountains and rivers changing places and roads being completely destroyed. In several places earth movements pushed the surface up sufficiently to form new hills. At the same time, these same areas had sections that collapsed to form new valleys. Streams and gullies appeared in new locations. Overall, huts, official houses, temples, and city walls generally collapsed suddenly. Numerous valuable monuments were destroyed beyond repair. The important Small Goose Pagoda in Xi'an withstood the shaking but its height dropped by about six feet. The report from Beijing dealt with earthquakes of all kinds. It covered the long his-

Figure 7 Loess homes beneath terraced farms in China's oldest agricultural area; the site of the world's deadliest earthquake.

tory of China and demonstrated for the first time the constant threat that the nation always had to face. Ten earthquakes like the 1556 one were listed, each of magnitude 8 or more, and of these the largest cluster appeared in areas close to the city of Xi'an.

Provinces historically experiencing earthquakes of magnitude eight or more:

1303, Shaanxi
1556, Shaanxi
1604, Fujian
1654, Gansu
1668, Taucheng
1679, Hebei
1695, Shaanxi
1739, Yinchuan
1833, Yunnan
1879, Gansu
1976, Hebei

The Loess region is of great historic importance to the Chinese. It is the cradle of civilization for the country. In ancient times it was the meeting zone between the nomadic herders of the Mongolian and central Asian lands and the more settled farming communities of what would one day become China. It was on the margins of these loess areas that the great trading cities and capitals of empire first formed. Xi'an is one of the best known of these. Today it is a city of the same size as Chicago. In the 1930s and 1940s, fully aware of its historical significance to China, Mao Zedong and the Chinese Communist Party set up their headquarters here and made preparations for their conquest of China which happened in 1949. Today, some two hundred million people live in or near the loess lands with almost one quarter of them living in cave housing. The importance of this part of China is seen in the Great Wall of China, built to protect the high concentrations of people to the south of it from the marauding tribes to its north. The Mongol armies of eight hundred years ago were the strongest of these.

Loess is wind-born silt that has settled out over many thousands of years, frequently to a depth of three hundred feet in provinces in and around Shaanxi. Much of this loess accumulated in the aftermath of the last ice age as winds from the Mongolian Plateau picked up and transported tiny particles of rock from the barren land surfaces left by the ice. It has a yellowish to light brown color and has no structure of layering like sedimentary rocks. As a result, it breaks away easily whenever it is cut away by stream action, leaving high cliffs alongside the stream. These cliffs provide ready access for excavating cliff-side homes and people have taken advantage of this opportunity for thousands of years both in China and in parts of Central Europe. Caves provided warmth in winter and cool conditions in summer. The climate of Shaanxi is semi-arid with an annual rainfall of twenty inches. However, this amount of rain in some years may fall in a single day and in loess territory that can be catastrophic because the soil is easily eroded and washed away. Its lack of layering means it has no natural cohesion. Frequent landslides occur with heavy rain and they cause considerable loss of life.

The Hwanghe, or Yellow River as it is often named because of the load of yellow loess particles that it always carries, cut its channel over time through these mountains of loess. In its upper reaches, because of the interior location, occasional bursts of rain are experienced in the warmer months of summer and the river overflows the levees that hold the flow of water to its main channel. Farms get destroyed when this happens. The usual reaction in past times was to have thousands of workers rebuild the levees by painstaking hard manual work. It is very difficult to predict these overflows because of the large volume of yellow silt that the river carries. A buildup of this silt at a turning point in the river can quickly become cumulative as the silt slows down the flow of water, thus speeding up the rate at which silt is deposited.

Loess is an excellent parent material for the formation of rich dark soils so these soils coupled with plentiful supplies of water from the river gave rise to the earliest agricultural settlements in the country. Grains and cotton were grown there thousands of years ago and a variety of domestic animals were reared. These natural advantages gave rise to a high population density even in prehistoric times. Loess is a major factor in agriculture all over the world, not only in China. It is particularly well suited to the cultivation of grains. The wheat fields of the Ukraine, and those of Argentina and the U.S. are outstanding examples of the value of loess-based soils. Knowing how easily the Yellow River can erode loess, Chinese authorities have terraced steep slopes and planted trees on the flat areas thus created. The trees tend to hold the soil in place during heavy rain.

In order to gain greater control of the problems associated with loess, research was undertaken by the Chinese government in the last quarter of the twentieth century. Engineers from China and Europe studied bedrock geology, quaternary sediments, geomorphology, landslide distribution, land use, and geotechnical properties of loess soil. Their findings made possible a much higher density of population and industrial installations in provinces like Shaanxi. A new problem arose as increasing numbers of people came to live and work there. As modern life impacted the traditional ways of Shaanxi, many workers, especially younger people, insisted on leaving the underground caves and building new homes above ground. In the new economy in which they were involved, these people had the financial resources to make changes. There had always been problems of dampness and darkness in the loess caves, especially in the ones that had to be excavated vertically into flat areas in contrast to those that had been dug into cliff faces. Former generations had no choice but to accept these limitations and even today there are millions who still live in the cave dwellings.

The 1556 Shaanxi earthquake was not the worst disaster in Chinese history. Millions have died from time to time when flooding destroyed their farms and they starved because there was no emergency aid from government sources. The Yellow River has sometimes been called the pride of China and sometimes its sorrow. Over the thousands of years past, it changed its course completely five times and its levees collapsed as many as 1,500 times. The yellow loess is carried along by the river and wherever there is an obstacle in the streambed it builds up and builds up over time until it overtops the levee and floods the adjacent farms. One and a half billion tons of loess in the form of silt is deposited annually near its mouth by the Yellow River. Often people tried to prevent the flooding that occurs by building small dams on the river but this only accelerates the problem of buildup. The 1887 flood, which is described elsewhere, killed more than a million people. In 1938, as China was being invaded by Japanese troops, the government of that time broke the levees in order to stop the advance of the soldiers. In the flooding that followed, 700,000 died. Even in modern times authorities seem unable to cope with the buildup of silt behind dams.

In the 1950s, in order to prevent flooding and at the same time generate electricity, Chinese engineers built a gigantic concrete dam, assuming that the silt, being of a fine texture, would flow through the turbines rather than create a buildup behind the dam. They were wrong. The same old problem reappeared. The plan was to have a lake of almost 100 billion units of water. Within two years, 20 percent of this amount had been lost to silting and gradually over the following eight years the total amount of water in the dam shrunk to seven units. The plan was scrapped. Alongside these problems of silting and flooding there is uncertainty about rainfall as has already been mentioned. In 2006, for instance, Beijing and its surrounding area had a serious shortage of rainfall and, at the same time, experienced recurring sandstorms. Attempts were made to seed a few clouds by sending tiny sticks of iodide high into the sky. A small amount of rain was obtained by this method.

References for Further Study

Gongxu, Gu. (English edition.) 1989. *Catalogue of Chinese Earthquakes.* Beijing: Science Press.

McCoy, Floyd W., and Heiken, Grant, eds. 2000. *Volcanic Hazards and Disasters in Human Antiquity*. Boulder, CO: Geological Society of America.

Sinclair, Kevin. 2000. *The Yellow River*. Brook Vale, NSW, Australia: Child and Associates.

11

Arequipa, Peru, volcanic eruption

February 19, 1600
Southern Peru

A volcanic eruption of VEI strength 6 from a 13,000-foot-high mountain near Arequipa

On February 19, 1600, South America's biggest volcanic eruption in all of recorded human history occurred in a mountain close to Arequipa, a city in southern Peru. Its VEI was 6, the same as Krakatau's, and the type of eruption was also the same as Krakatau's, a Plinian one. By that term we mean that such an eruption sends ash, smoke, and fragments of volcanic rock with terrific force high into the atmosphere, frequently as high as twenty-five miles. Places within fifteen miles of the Arequipa volcano were devastated. The neighboring states of Chile and Bolivia received thick layers of ash, as did Lima, the capital and largest city of Peru. Later, ruins revealed the details of the communities that had been smothered by ash and rock fragments, just as Pompeii had been by a similar event in the year 79. The name Plinian was given to this type of eruption in honor of Pliny the Elder, the famous Roman who was killed when Mount Vesuvius erupted, killing him and most of the people of Pompeii.

Drainage, lakes, and transportation routes were all affected because of the huge amount of material that fell on them. In addition to the human losses, the loss of farmland, vineyards, crops, livestock, and water supplies completely disrupted the economy of the area. There were no international trading links, and no manufacturing or similar occupations to which people could turn in 1600 for their survival. They depended totally on what they could obtain from the ground. Fortunately, recovery was undertaken immediately. Arequipa was rebuilt and within a few years farming activities were close to pre-eruption standards, largely the result of life being very simple. In recent times, mainly through examining underground evidence of past climates, scientists have come to see that the impact of Arequipa was far greater than local records from 1600 would suggest. It affected countries all over the world. A few scientists said that it contributed to a worldwide cooling that occurred in the summer of the year 1601, the coldest summer within the past five hundred years.

The eruption was preceded by a series of earthquakes and explosions as magma made its way upward toward the surface. The volcanic mountain that was about to explode stood more than 13,000 feet high within the upper reaches of a broad valley. It had three vents high above the valley through which gas, smoke, and pumice was about to escape. Each one of the three was huge, about 300 feet deep and over 250 feet in diameter. The setting of the mountain was equally impressive, a valley that had been carved out of an ancient volcano's side and summit, a horseshoe-shaped amphitheater that looked like a glacial cirque. It is clear from the evidence that is being uncovered at the present time that the area around Arequipa experienced numerous volcanic eruptions over the past few millions of years. In the case of the 1600 eruption, tremors were felt long before February 19. By February 15, these movements increased in both number and intensity, and this condition was maintained right up to the night of February 18. On the fateful day of the eruption there was an explosion like the noise of a cannon, followed by a big fire that scared everyone. Within an hour of the explosion, the whole surrounding region became dark as large volumes of ash and other volcanic materials fell back to earth through the atmosphere. There was little change in this continuous flow of dark material until the eruption ended on the second of April. The following list summarizes the sequence of events.

February 15	Regular earthquakes begin
February 18	9 P.M.: Earthquakes increase in strength
	10 P.M.: People awakened by the strength of the earthquakes
February 19	Midday: two major quakes of intensity 11 (MM scale)
	5 P.M.: Eruption began, pumice and ash falls
	6 P.M.: Whole region dark with explosions every few seconds
February 20	Explosions and ash continue all day
	2 P.M.: All day was like midnight
	10 inches of sand and ash fall on Arequipa
	Eruption and earthquakes continue all day
February 28	A major earthquake
March 5	Ash fall finally stops
April 2	Atmosphere finally cleared

A flow of heavy, hot, pyroclastic material began to appear soon after the eruption. It formed new rivers as it traveled, disrupting the natural flow of water as well as the dams that had been built on the River Tambo. It was in the neighborhood of this river that most people lived. As volcanic material fell back from the sky and was added to the surface flow, the combined mass of material rolled down the steep slopes beneath the mountain and further disrupted everything on the surface. Fire and the weight of falling material did most of the damage. Today, geologists examining the scene of the 1600 eruption are finding plenty of evidence of the event. Thick layers of ash and pumice can be seen all over the area west of the River Tambo and the city of Arequipa. It is easy to see why most of the one thousand people of the region were killed. There is a record of the experiences of a hundred people who lived in one village. It tells of stones falling from the sky with many people and animals being killed, without giving them a chance to escape. Chaos and fear had gripped everybody; they hugged one another as hot ashes were falling and burning their homes.

The people were understandably terrified by the event, mainly because of ignorance and fears over the causes of volcanic eruptions. No one knew anything about tectonic plates in 1600. Records tell of Indians praying and casting magic spells because they felt that the church was unable to do anything about the eruption. Some local people prayed on their knees all day as one of their number played a doleful lament and asked for mercy. Fear drove people to walk around their community in a sort of dazed state. Churches kept their doors open all the time. Implicit in all of these reactions was the assumption that God was responsible for what happened and, since this particular event was troublesome and harmful, he must have done it as a punishment for bad behavior. To make matters worse, the local Spanish priest had warned his people at the time of the first small earthquakes that a hit from heaven was going to come to punish them for their sins. It was a similar story more than a hundred years later when Lisbon experienced a powerful earthquake on All Saints Day. Large numbers of people were in their churches when the earthquake struck. Lisbon was a very religious city and they were convinced that the earthquake was a punishment from God.

The warning from the priest was a particularly troubling factor for the social life of the community. The conquest of the area by the Spaniards, in the previous century, had brought to this village all that was best in the world. While it came by force of arms it nevertheless represented many things that were an improvement over their former lifestyle. Arequipa and its surrounding communities had been a traditional Indian village until the Incas captured it and made it the supply center for its capital of Cuzco nearby high in the mountains. Within a century of that development, the Spaniards arrived and took full control of the area. They immediately stopped the ancient practice of sacrificing humans and animals in order to appease the gods of the mountains but now, in 1600, the natives were in a helpless situation. The church could only threaten punishment. It could not stop the eruption. The mythology of the area told them that the devil was upset because they had abandoned sacrifices so he was going to punish them. Local wizards now persuaded them to find the nicest young girls, the best animals, and the prettiest flowers and sacrifice them. During the sacrifice the first burst came from the volcano and they were covered with ash.

There were reports from ships at sea experiencing ash falls, from as far as a thousand miles, just as there had been from Lima, in northern Peru, also a thousand miles away. However, most of the ash falls happened in Bolivia and Chile because the borders of all three countries are close to the site of the eruption. In the Pacific, offshore from Peru, sailors in a British pirate ship heard the explosions and thought they were about to be attacked by a Spanish warship. A merchant sailing south from Lima was caught in a storm of ash and pumice when his ship was off the coast two hundred miles west of Arequipa. The weight of ash dragged most of his boxes overboard. If we take the immediate communities in and around Arequipa for a distance of twelve miles outward from the city, it becomes clear that more than a thousand acres were covered with sufficient ash to make them unusable for many years. One factor that is rarely mentioned is the influence of rainfall on steep slopes when all the natural drainage channels have been dislocated. Rainfall is heavy on the west side of Peru's mountains and over the year or two following the eruption, without access to their natural channels, rainstorms washed away into the sea every movable thing on the sloping mountainside, including livestock, crops, and fish.

Volcanic eruptions along the west coast of Peru, as well as in other countries on that coast, are due to the accumulation of magma near the surface because of the subduction of the Nazca Plate beneath the continent of South America, disrupting both temperature and rock regimes deep below the surface. Peru experiences more earthquakes and volcanic eruptions than most of the countries on that coast. There are dozens of significant earthquakes every year, yet it seems that their familiarity with earthquakes and volcanic eruptions makes the people resilient, ready to start over when tragedy hits. It is an attitude similar to that found in Japan, another country well acquainted with earthquakes and volcanic eruptions. In 1784, Arequipa was hit with an earthquake that killed fifty people and destroyed almost all the buildings. Two others, in 1868 and 2001, did extensive damage. Despite the hazards, the city has grown rapidly through the years because it is located in a good agricultural area and it is strategically located for transportation. Arequipa's population has grown from about 20,000 at the end of the eighteenth century to 600,000 today, making it Peru's second biggest city.

The 1784 earthquake in Arequipa provided a better picture of the ways in which the Spanish overlords used local labor in the work of recovery. The records of the 1600 event do not tell us anything about relations be-

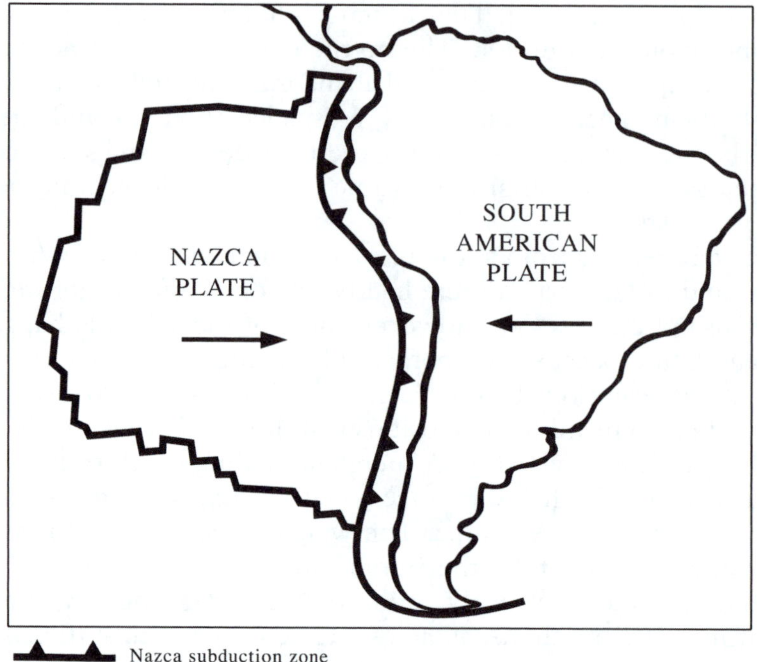

Figure 8 The eruption of Mt. Huaynaputina and many subsequent South American volcanic eruptions are linked to the subducting action of the Nazca Tectonic Plate.

tween the Spanish and the local people. In 1784 it is clear that forced labor was the method. Spanish royalty launched their conquest of South America in order to exploit its wealth, just as the British had done in America during the colonial period, and the Spanish would learn at a later time, just as the British did, that exploitation leads to revolution if the local people are not treated fairly. In 1784, the officer in charge arranged for a forced draft of six thousand Indians from neighboring areas to be brought to Arequipa to rebuild the city. There was little difficulty in arranging this as it was a common occurrence. An arrangement for ensuring adequate labor for the mines was a similar forced draft: every Indian community had to send one-seventh of their adult male population for a year to work in the mines. The low wages they were paid did not interfere seriously with the profits that had to be sent back to Spain, even after destructive earthquakes like this one in 1784 when the city was a much bigger place than in 1600.

Fortunately, recovery from the eruption in and around Arequipa did not take too long, perhaps because the area was not highly developed and the work of restoration consisted mainly of removing ash and other volcanic debris. During the eruption, ash had been falling so fast that the mayor of Arequipa gave orders to clear the roofs to protect them from collapsing. About three feet had fallen on the city by the time the eruption began to subside. For the cleanup the Spanish Commander commandeered six hundred natives and forty soldiers to clear the ground and rebuild the homes and public buildings. The work took a few years and Arequipa became known as the white city because of the volcanic stones used in construction; they were whitish in color and very hard, unlike pumice. It seems strange to use volcanic rock as the building material for a city destroyed by a volcanic eruption. Viticulture was a well-known traditional industry of the area and a particular tragedy was the loss of grape crops as a result of the ash fall. Seventeen years after the eruption, a visitor noted that very little development of agriculture had occurred since the eruption and no evidence anywhere of a revival of viticulture.

References for Further Study

Bullard, F. 1984. *Volcanoes of the Earth*. Austin, TX: University of Texas Press.

de Boer, Jelle Zeilinga, and Sanders, Donald T. 2002. *Volcanoes in Human History*. Princeton: Princeton University Press.

Francis, P. W., and de Silva, S. L. 1991. *Volcanoes of the Central Andes*. Heidelberg: Springer-Verlag.

Macdonald, G. 1972. *Volcanoes*. Englewood Cliffs, NJ: Prentice-Hall.

Simkin, T., and Siebert, L. 1994. *Volcanoes of the World*. Tucson, AZ: Geoscience Press.

12

London, England, Black Death plague

1665 AD

In the main built-up part of London, England

The Asian Bubonic Plague, known as the Black Death, hits London

No one knows why the bubonic plague, or Black Death as it came to be known in England, broke out in eastern Siberia in the 1300s and spread westward. There was very little knowledge, at that time, of the ways by which diseases are carried from place to place, so many of the efforts to get rid of them were ineffective. In later years it was discovered that infected fleas were the carriers. They passed on the disease to rats and when the rats died the fleas attacked humans. In 1347, a ship sailing from a Black Sea port to Messina in Italy, arrived at its destination with every person on board dead. It appears that the last to die were able to get the ship into port before they died. The port authorities in Italy, as soon as they saw what happened, had the ship carried out of the harbor, but their action was too late to stop the spread of the disease. Most of the people of Messina were already infected and, from this city, the disease spread quickly across Europe and across the English Channel, reaching London a year later, in 1348, where it killed close to half of the city's people. Within the following three centuries London suffered several different epidemics but these and even the experience of 1348 were relatively benign compared with the violence of the outbreak of Black Death that swept across London in 1665.

The name by which the bubonic plague came to be known was related to the formation of black boils in the armpits, neck, and groin of infected people, which were caused by dried blood accumulating under the skin after internal bleeding. People first experienced the bacterium of Black

Figure 9 The plague in 1665. The plague victims are being collected and loaded on a cart.

Death as chills, fever, vomiting, and diarrhea. Frequently, the disease spread to the lungs and almost always in these cases the victims died soon afterward. The name pneumonic plague was given to these cases. In all victims the disease spread easily from person to person through the air and, in the vast majority of instances, death ensued. London's population in 1665 was half a million; it was the biggest city in Europe. The first victim of the Black Death was diagnosed late in 1664 but it was in May of the following year that significant numbers of infections were being observed. By June, in the wake of a heat wave, more than seven thousand lives were being claimed by the Black Death every week. Those who could leave the city as the wave of death swept over it did so. The king and his retinue left. So did many of the clergy and nobility. The biggest surprise and the one that everyone condemned was the departure of the president of the Royal College of Physicians. All who were unable to leave the city, the vast majority, had to cope as best they could.

The usual practice of burying the dead in what was known as consecrated ground; that is to say, the cemetery on the grounds of the church, had to be abandoned as the number of dead mounted. Plague pits came into use to cope with the problem. As many as 100,000 lives were lost before winter killed the fleas and the epidemic began to taper off. The peak total of deaths came late in September, 1665, an interesting parallel with the time frame of the 1918 flu pandemic which lasted for a similar stretch of time. Presumably, those who are afflicted with such diseases develop antibodies after a time and fewer and fewer people then succumb. Doctors of the time could provide no explanation for the sickness, and most of them were afraid to offer treatment. In an attempt to keep from being infected, the few physicians who did risk exposure wore leather masks with glass eyes and a long beak filled with herbs and spices that were thought to ward off the illness. So terrified were the authorities that even if one person in a household showing plague-like symptoms a forty-day quarantine in the form of a red cross on the main door was imposed on the whole home. In many cases, it was a virtual death sentence for everyone living in the home because the black rat, the usual carrier of the disease, was an old inhabitant of London's homes. When these rats died from the disease the fleas used people as their hosts.

Daniel Defoe, who was a youngster in 1665, later wrote extensively of the effects of the Black Death. He described London as a city abandoned to despair, a place where every home and every street was a prison. One area near the center of the city that had no buildings on it became a mass grave where the dead were dumped unceremoniously and covered with loose soil. Every day, thousands of bodies were brought to this spot in what was described as dead carts. Farther out from the center of the city, as the disease spread, a burial pit was dug, forty by sixteen feet and twenty feet in depth, and this served as a mass grave. Defoe stressed the eerie silence everywhere. There was no traffic except for the dead carts. Anyone who risked going outside always walked in the middle of the street, at a distance from any building and as far away as possible from any other person. London's economic success, as evident in its huge population of half a million, led to overcrowding and neglect of hygiene, both conditions that encouraged the spread of diseases. Rat-infested slums that lacked running water added to the risk of infection. Paradoxically, the worst set of circumstances for those who showed initial symptoms was the five pest houses outside the city to which these people were sent. The unavoidable close contact with other patients made for easy transfer of the bacteria through breathing.

There have always been epidemics and outbreaks of sicknesses in London. This particular outbreak, the worst of all, had a predecessor in 1348, as has already been mentioned, which seemed to be the worst ever in its own time. A thousand years before the events of 1665 there was an earlier outburst of what must have been similar to the Black Death but was described differently at that time. Between the years 1550 and 1600 there were five severe attacks of Black Death, the last of which killed 30,000 Londoners. There were good reasons for these catastrophic experiences of diseases. Very little was known about public hygiene and open sewers were the norm. Homes were small and so tightly packed together that bacteria quickly moved around from person to person. Furthermore, London had for a long time been the center of national life and the place where there were opportunities in business and professional work. It had the biggest population of any English city. People kept arriving and living places became more and more crowded together in every part of the city.

There was a side effect from the frequency of diseases—the growth of what might be called healers. Charts were produced and circulated to show how the dates of saints or predictions about astrology related to the efficacy or otherwise for healing of different herbs. All kinds of superstitions were embraced, even the one about being cured if you touched the hand of a dead man. For centuries, the priests of the church were the doctors until the pope forbade them from drawing blood in any way. After that all kinds of lay doctors multiplied. Once a person managed to secure widespread publicity as a healer, large numbers of people accepted his cures without questioning them. The atmosphere of fear about new waves of disease was so great that the strangest type of cure was accepted. William Samson, a healer, practiced his art near the gates of Bartholomew's Hospital, a much-respected institution. Because of the location, his proposed remedies were readily accepted at the price he asked. Samson happened to be a bit of a psychiatrist and had evidence of people whom he claimed to have cured.

Before the Black Death had run its course an unexpected "cure" appeared in a rural setting in September of 1665. A tailor received a parcel of cloth from London that also contained some plague-infected fleas. Four days later the tailor was dead and, by the end of the month, five others died. Everyone had heard of the tragedy in London and panic set in after the deaths of the five. The whole community gathered together and arranged to have their village quarantined to prevent the disease spreading throughout the region. It seemed like suicide yet, a year later, when the first outsiders entered the village, they found that most of the residents were alive and healthy. How did so many live through the attack of a disease that had been consistently taking the lives of almost all those infected? It is here that two extraordinary stories from 1665 emerged, stories that affect life today. The first relates to Isaac Newton, the famous scientist who was studying at Cambridge when the Black Death began to reach that city. His mother took him home to northern England for two years and it was during that time of enforced isolation that he did most of the work on his Principia, meaning mathematical principles of natural philosophy, often regarded as one of the greatest scientific works of all time.

The second story relates to the survivors of Black Death. In London, as well as in the village where the tailor received the cloth with fleas, there were accounts of people who survived the Black Death in spite of close contact with family members who had been infected and died. Elizabeth Hancock was one of these. In 1665, she had buried her six children and her husband within a single week but never became ill. The village gravedigger who had close contact with hundreds of dead bodies also survived. Were these people somehow immune to the Black Death? In the last few years, as concern mounted over the possibility of a flu pandemic reaching North America, Dr. Stephen O'Brien of the National Institutes of Health in Washington, DC, decided to investigate the accounts of seventeenth century survival. He searched for descendants of the village where a number of infected people had clearly survived the disease. This was not easy as a dozen or so generations of families had successively spanned the long period of time. He finally succeeded and took their DNA record.

Dr. O'Brien had already been working with HIV patients and had discovered in 1996 that the modified form of a particular gene in these patients, one known as CCR5 and commonly described as Delta 32, prevents HIV from entering human cells and infecting the body. Based on this finding and convinced that the way in which Delta 32 protects the body from infection might apply to other diseases he took DNA samples from the surviving relatives of the lucky ones in 1665. As he examined them he made two startling discoveries based on both his work with HIV patients and the experiences of the surviving relatives. One copy of the mutation enables people to survive although they get very sick. Two copies, that is to say one gene from each of two parents, ensure that an individual will suffer no infection of any kind. Delta 32 has not been found in parts of Asia or Africa or other areas where bubonic plague or Black Death did not occur so this, for Dr. O'Brien, raised an interesting question: did some natural event create this mutation so that some would survive? It has been said that a destructive bacterium or virus does not want to destroy all of its hosts so that it can continue to infect others later. Was this what happened in the case of Delta 32?

References for Further Study

Bray, R. S. 2000. *Armies of Pestilence: The Impact of Disease on History.* New York: Barnes and Noble.

Cartwright, F. F. 1972. *Disease and History.* New York: Crowell.

Gottfried, R. S. 1983. *The Black Death: Natural and Human Disasters in Medieval Europe.* New York: Free Press.

Marks, G., and Beatty, W. K. 1976. *Epidemics.* New York: Scribner.

Shrewsbury, J. F. D. 1970. *A History of Bubonic Plague in the British Isles.* Cambridge, UK: Cambridge University Press.

13

London, England, fire

September 2, 1666
In the central area of London, England

London was well acquainted with fires but the Great Fire was by far the worst London ever experienced

About two o'clock on Sunday morning, the second of September, 1666, an assistant to the king's baker, who lived with the baker and his family above the bake house, awoke to find his tiny room full of smoke. He alerted the rest of the household, told them of the loud crackling of burning timber from below, and urged them to escape immediately. Within minutes flames began to consume the steps leading to the upstairs so there was no way of escape in that direction. They all climbed into the attic above, squeezed through the narrow window that opened on to the roof, and scrambled along to the next house from which they could reach the ground and escape. Many others were less fortunate as flames jumped from house to house across the city. Before the end of the day the fire was out of control and all efforts were focused on rescuing people and taking them to a safe place.

London was well acquainted with fires at this time and this familiarity tended to make people indifferent to reports of fires. People waited too long in 1666 and, as a result, many lives that could have been saved were lost. It is easy to understand Londoners' indifference to fire alarms; they have been experiencing fires from their earliest days during the time of Roman occupation of the city in the first century. In his classic publication, *London, the Biography*, Peter Ackroyd gives a list of dates for the known fires that swept over some or all of London in the years before 1666: 60, 125, 764, 798, 852, 893, 961, 982, 1077, 1087, 1093, 1132, 1136,

1203, 1212, 1220, and 1227. There were other fires in the more than four hundred years between 1227 and 1666 but records for these were not well kept. The slow reaction to the 1666 fire was almost universal, partly because people thought it was just one more fire that would soon go out but also because, for a short time after the first house went up in flames, there was a time delay before the second house caught fire.

Furthermore, there were underlying environmental factors that would make this fire more destructive than all the previous ones. The month of August, 1666, had been exceptionally hot with almost no rain so the thatch and timber of the crowded buildings were the kind of tinder that would quickly ignite. Additionally, as the fire grew from its beginnings in a house near London Bridge, it was aided by a wind from the southeast that pushed the flames westward and northwestward toward the vast majority of the houses and public buildings that were occupied by the city's half million, probably Europe's most populated city at that time. The narrow streets, all that were needed four hundred years ago for horse-drawn wagons, made it easy for fires to jump to the other side of a street. The houses on either side were even more accessible as they formed a continuous line of buildings so each home caught fire from its contact with the next. Public officials were not allowed to pull down parts of houses that had caught fire because they would be held responsible for all the damages if the building did not completely burn down. Therefore, they had to wait until the whole building was destroyed by fire before intervening.

The first line of flames followed the lower elevations running alongside the Thames River, but bursts of fire appeared nearby as embers were blown ahead in all directions by the following wind. As parish churches became engulfed in fire and smoke their clerks made desperate efforts to recover the parish records and get them out of the buildings. Their priorities were clear: if you can rescue only one thing, make it the records, not the money. It was a clear indication of the speed at which the fire advanced that almost all churches rescued only their parish registers. The most troublesome loss of all on this first day was the destruction of the water conduit, a large lead pipe that carried water uphill to the center of the city. The wooden wheels that pumped the water from the river burst into flames as the fire reached them and the lead melted under the heat. As we will see in later accounts of both fires and earthquakes, it was the loss of water rather than the actual flames that caused the greatest amount of damage. That was true for the San Francisco earthquake and the subsequent fire in 1906 and in the Tokyo earthquake of 1923. In the case of London, no one would get access to water in any quantity for more than a year, a particularly dangerous condition for a city that had so recently survived the scourge of the Black Death and was very much aware of the risks of endemic diseases.

As the fire reached the various quays along the river it found plenty of incendiary resources in sheltered areas and on the waterfront. Stacks of timber, hay, straw, and coal, all standard commodities of trade at that time, were piled up, ready to be transferred to the barges that would take them downstream to where the sea-going ships lay at anchor. There were also smaller quantities of other tinder-dry commodities—barrels of lamp oil, tar, pitch, and tallow. The heat that resulted from all of these products catching fire boiled the beer in the hundreds of barrels that had been stored in the various breweries on the waterfront. The barrels burst their staves and the beer flowed away into the river. Even at this stage, in the early hours of Sunday morning, no general alarm had been given. Samuel Pepys, the writer from whom we received much of our information about the fire and who lived in London at this time, told of his lack of interest in the fire when it was first reported to him. At first, in the middle of the night, when one of his servants awoke him, he looked out of his window and seeing the fire so far away decided to go back to bed. He was about to do the same four or five hours later but changed his mind when told that over three hundred houses had been burned down within the previous four hours. His home was close to the Tower Bridge so he dressed quickly and found his way to a high point on the bridge where he could see the extent of the fire. In his own words as he looked around there was "an infinite great fire burning in all directions."

Pepys took a boat and moved upstream under the bridge to observe more closely the rapid advance of the fire along the banks of the river. No one tried to fight the fire in any way and this surprised him. All efforts were directed at getting valuables out of homes before they went up in flames. Any barge or boat on the river became a target on to which people threw their clothes and other larger possessions. They then found their way, as best they could, on to these same boats or barges to watch the sad spectacle of their houses being destroyed, wondering all the time about their future prospects. Pepys watched with horror as one of the great landmarks of the city, the church of St. Laurence, which had a steeple that soared above all other buildings in the city, burst into flames while the main line of the fire was still some distance away. He concluded for the first time that this was no ordinary fire like those that had come before it. Others too came to the same conclusion. Up to this moment most of the city's population had gone about their normal activities, attending church and offering prayers for the unfortunate people along the river who had lost their homes. Now, as St. Laurence's steeple came crashing down before the eyes of most Londoners, a state of near panic set in.

By afternoon of the first day the fire had reached Whitehall and Westminster Abbey and every department of government was under threat yet, at the Palace of Charles the Second, little was known of the extent of the fire. Pepys arrived at the palace at this time where he told all the staff about the things he had seen. A general alarm soon spread as far as the king and Pepys was called in to repeat his report. He used the opportunity to urge the king and the Duke of York, who happened to be at the palace, to give command that houses be pulled down ahead of the fire. This move had been avoided up to this time because of the liability risks. Now it was apparent that no alternative could stop the fire so the king instructed Pepys to go to the lord mayor of London and command him to spare no houses in order to stop the spread of the fire. Pepys found it hard to get to the lord mayor's place in the eastern part of the city. Every spare wagon had been commandeered by a few who were escaping with their possessions and the streets were clogged with people. The lord mayor threw up his hands in desperation when told of the king's command. "What can I do?" was all he said. He went on to explain to Pepys that no one would obey him and whenever he and one or two others began to pull down houses the fire overtook them before they could complete their work. He had started the demolition of buildings in the night and was tired from six hours of continuous work.

Monday, the third of September and the second day of the fire, was another warm day with the strong wind from the southeast still blowing. It had become even stronger during the night, so strong that ships in the English Channel had to take shelter on the French side. The glare of light reflected from the smoke clouds overhead had been visible all night as the fire continued to sweep westward over the great houses in and around Westminster and farther west in and beyond Chelsea. The world outside London slowly became aware of the tragedy. Often half-burnt newspapers would be carried by the wind up river as far as Eton. One writer described London's yellow smoke as the output of a giant furnace ascending to heaven, a smoke so great that it darkened the sun at midday. No one person was yet fully aware of the scale of the fire. There were no methods of communication that could inform them. Thus, on this second day of the fire, people were still arriving at friends' houses with their belongings not knowing until they arrived that their friends were busy gathering what they could take away with them before the fire struck. September the fourth, the fire's third day, saw the wind abating and the advance of the fire firmly stopped by an order from the king to use gunpowder to blow up houses in the path of the fire and thus create an effective break.

As the smoke cleared and people could see the desolate mass of ruined homes, stumps of chimneys, and broken towers, many of them left the city for good with no hope or wish ever to return. Most of London had been destroyed. The work of reconstruction would be enormous. One sad aspect of the fire was the behavior of some who had carts and coaches for hire and decided to charge exorbitant prices for carrying personal possessions out of the city. Survivors had no choice; they had to pay the price or forfeit their possessions. Only one-fifth of the city was untouched by the fire. The reconstruction had to be seen as the creation of a new city and, to their credit, Londoners accepted the challenge and got to work. All the city homes were rebuilt or replaced within five years. The new streets were wider and brick became the common building material instead of wood. For the first time in the history of the city and after the many fires

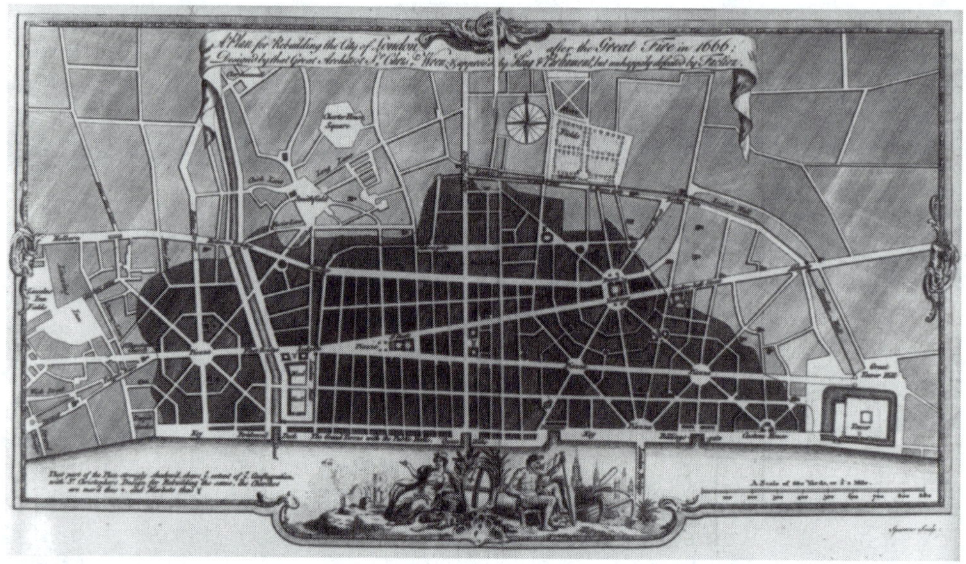

Figure 10 Christopher Wren's plan for rebuilding the city of London after the Great Fire in 1666.

that had assaulted it over that time, London now had a fire insurance plan in place. Never again would the possessions of hundreds of thousands of people be wiped out by a single fire.

References for Further Study

Ackroyd, Peter. 2001. *London the Biography*. London: Random House.

Bedford, John. 1966. *London' s Burning* London: Abelard-Schuman.

Fraser, Antonia. 1979. *Charles II: His Life and Times*. London: Weidenfeld and Nicholson.

Johns, Alessa. 1999. *Dreadful Visitations*. London: Routledge.

Kyl, Tanya Lloyd. 2004. *Fires: Ten Stories That Chronicle Some of the Most Destructive Fires in Human History*. Toronto: Annick Press.

14

Port Royal, Jamaica, earthquake

June 7, 1692
Harbor of Kingston, Jamaica

Port Royal was a city on a sand spit in the harbor of Jamaica, Kingston. It was hit with an earthquake and tsunami and the whole city sank into the ocean

On June 7, 1692, Port Royal, Jamaica, experienced a powerful earthquake and a tsunami. Larger houses collapsed almost immediately and smaller ones slid off the land into the harbor as a widespread state of liquefaction dislocated their sandy foundations. Before the end of the day most of the city had disappeared beneath the waters of Kingston Harbor. Most of those who were left standing in the midst of all the destruction were swept into the sea by the tsunami. Two thousand were killed immediately and an additional two thousand died later from injuries or disease. The city's graveyard was a victim of the earthquake so the survivors, as they sought to recover some of their possessions, had to cope with a frightening scene. There were coffins and bodies from the graveyard floating around along with those who had just been killed. As they continued their search they had to fight against a group of thieves who were taking advantage of the chaotic situation.

Few people seeing modern day Port Royal, Jamaica, a small isolated fishing village at the tip of a sand spit that extends into Kingston Harbor for about eighteen miles, would ever think that it once played a major role in the politics of the Caribbean and England. All the evidence now lies beneath the water of Kingston Harbor. Port Royal is the only sunken city in the western hemisphere. Founded soon after the conquest of the island of Jamaica from the Spanish by an English invasion force in 1655, Port Royal went through a spectacular rise in wealth and influence. Just before the

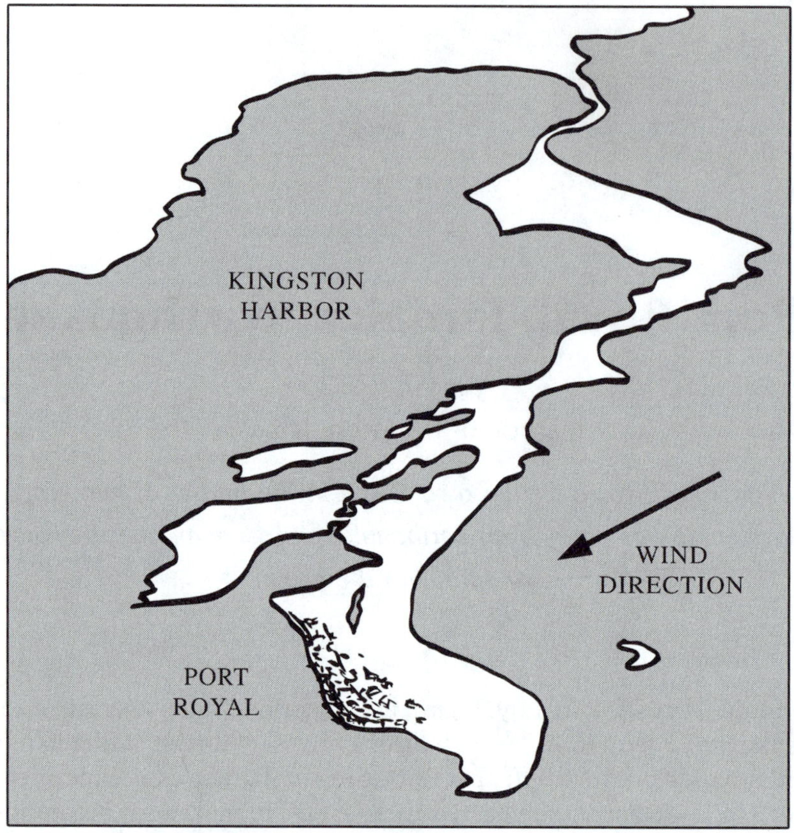

Figure 11 Port Royal, the city that sank beneath the sea in 1692.

earthquake it was the largest English town in the New World, and the most affluent. Every visitor was impressed with the multistoried brick buildings, quite a contrast to other English colonial towns in the New World. It had a population of more than seven thousand and rivaled Boston in size and economic power, the only other city of comparable importance at that time.

The English turned Port Royal into a strategic military and naval base. Its location in the middle of the Caribbean made it ideal for trade. Trade, as well as loot, dominated the economy in those times. The European powers extracted wealth from their colonies and brought it back to Europe in ships. If a country happened to have a powerful naval force it was considered fair game to raid the ships of other countries and empty their cargos of gold and other valuables. England was one country that engaged in that kind of enterprise. During its heyday, Port Royal was laid out with broad unpaved streets, named after familiar streets in London, each lined with buildings ranging in height from one to four stories. There were several sidewalks lined with bricks and rents ran as high as the highest found anywhere in London, maybe because London was still recovering from a devastating fire and an equally destructive plague. Port Royal in 1692 occupied a space of more than fifty acres at the western tip if the sand spit that extended out from Kingston Harbor, and after the earthquake only twenty of those acres were still above water. It was a little different on parts of the spit nearer to shore. Their underlying foundations of coral, below a hundred feet of unconsolidated sand, seemed to be more solid. Those who started running toward the shore at the first indication of an earthquake were saved.

The tsunamis that caused so much trouble came from submarine landslides. The various movements in the faults around the harbor of Kingston occurred horizontally, as strike-slip actions. There were no vertical displacements. The powerful earthquake created spaces for these landslides and the five-foot tsunami that ensued, mainly inside the harbor area between the peninsula and the main part of the island, swept more than twenty vessels off their moorings and sunk them into the harbor. At the same time, Port Royal was overwhelmed by the same tsunami and most of it sank into deep water to remain submerged for more than two centuries, providing scientists today with a well-preserved record of an early settlement. A brass watch that was recovered in later years appeared to have stopped at 11:43 and archeologists wondered if that represented the exact time of the earthquake. For earthquakes like the one of 1692, the return period lies between two hundred and five hundred years. Hence, a repeat of a similar earthquake and tsunamis could occur at any time.

The experiences of those who were still standing after the disaster, mainly by holding on to a branch or pole, provide a useful description of liquefaction. They told of streets rising and falling like waves of the sea. They saw people disappear in the sand and later reappear as stronger waves washed over the streets and carried quantities of sand out to sea. Others that sank into the sand never reappeared. Experiences of this type have often been documented in other earthquakes. Similar events happened in San Francisco in 1906, in Massachusetts in 1755, and more recently in New Orleans in 2005. The reasons for these recurrences are easy to understand. Unconsolidated stretches of sand, especially these near the sea in major cities, are valuable and suitable sites for building. Either because they did not know of the dangers of liquefaction, or because they did know but were able to persuade authorities to give them permission, construction companies have built large subdivisions on such places, hoping that the next earthquake would not arrive soon. In far too many places it was a false hope.

As so often occurs, in the midst of tragedy, there are instances of unexpected courage and generosity. The slave of one master of a ship decided to jump overboard to save his master after he had been swept off his ship into the sea. The slave reached his master and brought him safely back to the ship but then, too exhausted to stay afloat, lost his own life. Slaves were still slaves in 1692 and they were valuable property for those who owned them. In the chaotic situation that followed the earthquake slave owners were afraid that they would either start a revolt or escape—neither happened.

Reconstruction of Port Royal was ultimately a big problem. It had so little land left that everyone wondered how it could continue to carry its former responsibilities. Kingston was not an acceptable alternative for several reasons: it had a high death rate because it was so unhealthy and it was not easily defended if attacked by land and sea simultaneously. Furthermore, since sailing ships were the only kind available in the late seventeenth century, Kingston was not accessible in windy weather. England decided to let both ports, Kingston and Port Royal, share responsibilities for all shipping.

In 1907, a submarine landslide occurred in almost the same location as the one that occurred in 1692. This new submarine landslide generated a tsunami that overwhelmed the peninsula where Port Royal had stood. The earthquake that gave rise to the tsunami caused enormous damage to places all along the shores of Jamaica. At one location, the sea was observed to withdraw as far as three hundred feet within three minutes after the earthquake and to return as a destructive eight-foot wave. The fact that only three minutes elapsed between earthquake and tsunami makes it clear that the landslide happened very close to shore. A pilot and crew of a ship witnessed the return to shore of the tsunami. They saw both the peninsula and the town of Kingston disappear from view for some time. Shortly afterward, seiches as high as eight feet were observed in Kingston Harbor. One thousand people died in the town of Kingston, mainly from falling buildings, and another thousand were injured. Approximately 90,000 were left homeless.

Nothing like seventeenth-century Port Royal remains in that location today. Visitors now see a fishing community of less than 2,000 along with an abandoned British Naval Base, now used by the Jamaican Coast Guard. Jamaica is an independent nation now so the marks of former British activities lie, for the most part, under the sea. The ships and houses that sank in 1692 now form part of a magnificent museum and a unique center for archeological research. On land and sea above all these, in the years since 1692, Jamaica has experienced many more disasters. There was a fire in 1703, completely destroying all that was left or had been rebuilt of the old city of Port Royal. Hurricanes hit it in 1722 and again in 1744 and on both occasions everything came down and had to be rebuilt. Two earthquakes came later, one in 1770 and one in 1907. The former destroyed the hospital and the latter a large part of the dockyard. Another fire, in 1815, did extensive damage to all the buildings, and a third earthquake destroyed the old fortifications.

References for Further Study

Black, Clinton V. 1970. *Port Royal: A History and Guide*. Kingston, Jamaica: Bolivar Press.

Donachie, Madeleine J. 2003. *Household Ceramics at Port Royal, Jamaica, 1655– 1692* Oxford, UK: Archaeopress.
Pawson, Michael, and Buisseret, David. 1975. *Port Royal Jamaica*. Oxford, UK: Clarendon Press.
Smith, Horane. 2001. *Port Royal: A Novel*. Maple, Ontario: Boheme Press.

15

Cascadia earthquake

January 26, 1700
In and around Seattle

An earthquake, estimated at magnitude greater than 9, and accompanied with an equally powerful tsunami swept across the Pacific Northwest near Seattle

On the twenty-sixth of January 1700, a massive earthquake of magnitude greater than 9 shook the ocean floor west of Seattle. It occurred about one hundred miles off shore in the zone where the Juan de Fuca Tectonic Plate subducts beneath the North America Plate. A tsunami followed quickly because the distance from the epicenter to Seattle was small. A wall of water swept over the whole coastal area, destroying everything in its path. How do we know that these things happened? The only humans who lived in this area in 1700 were native people and they had no written records or indicators of time that could tell us. The answer lay in a series of events that began in the mid-1980s.

A nuclear power plant was being installed south of Seattle in the 1980s and the nuclear regulatory authorities wanted to know if there were any seismic concerns that ought to be taken into consideration. The initial response from geologists was that there was no record of big earthquakes in this area so a nuclear power plant would not be in danger, but the question that had been asked stimulated new questions that no one had previously asked. Geologists knew that, throughout historical time, there had not been any record of an earthquake of magnitude 8 or 9 at the Juan de Fuca site, yet all along the Pacific Coast of North and South America there were earthquakes of this magnitude in all the other regions. Is the Pacific Northwest unique? Do the gigantic Pacific and North American plates behave differently here than they do everywhere else? It was the remaining portion of an older Pacific spreading ridge, namely the Juan de Fuca Plate that caused the massive 1964 earthquake in Alaska, but that same plate is subducting beneath the Pacific Northwest. Why were there no big earthquakes there? These were the questions.

By the 1980s refinements in our knowledge of plate tectonics, particularly awareness of the much greater power in plates that are subducting when the distances from their spreading ridges are short as they were with the Juan de Fuca Ridge, persuaded scientists to search for evidence of past quakes in the Northwest. Perhaps, they speculated, there were powerful earthquakes in the past of which we know nothing because this part of the country has been settled for such a short time. Digging down beside a stream close to the coast, one geologist found layers of sand and mud below the surface. They extended downward for about six feet before coming to an abrupt stop at a junction with a layer of peat. As he dug down farther he found another layer of sand and mud below the peat. It was obvious

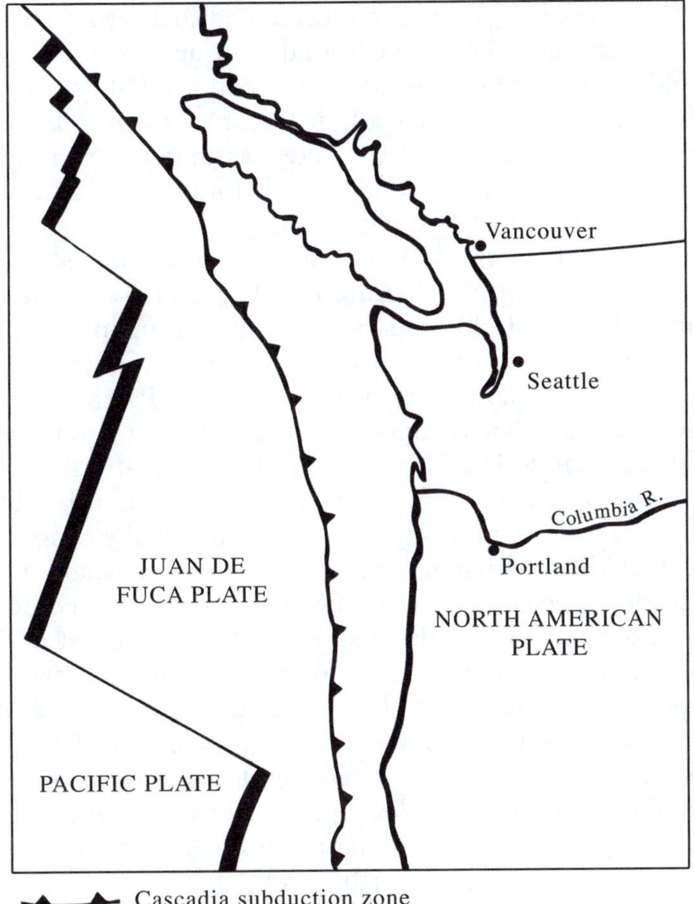

Figure 12 The massive Cascadia earthquake of 1700 was caused by the subducting action of the Juan de Fuca Tectonic Plate.

that this part of the coast had once been below high water, then above it, and then below it again before coming to its present state with topsoil in the uppermost eight inches. Furthermore, the sharp demarcation lines between peat and sand suggested that the changes from below to above water had been sudden, just the sort of thing known to be typical of subduction earthquakes.

If this was indeed the result of a former subduction earthquake there ought to be similar layers of mud and peat at the same depths all over the same place. Before long, evidence of such was found in abundance. In one place, a number of additional sets of layers were uncovered, suggesting that there might have been a succession of subduction quakes, separated by long periods of quiescence. As researchers moved farther and farther back from the coast, looking carefully at each location where layers of mud and peat were found, a very fine layer of sand on the peat seemed to become thinner and thinner the further you were from the coast. This is exactly what you would expect if a powerful tsunami had swept across the land following an earthquake. Samples of plant material and bits of wood from the top peat layer were collected and their age calculated using the carbon-14 technique. They were found to be approximately three hundred years old. At the same time, all sorts of additional data kept coming in, all confirming the original speculation that this region has always experienced massive subduction earthquakes, as many as thirteen over the past six thousand years, the last one being before there was any European settlement, about three hundred years ago.

It became clear that, in 1700, one of the world's largest earthquakes had hit the west coast of North America. The undersea Cascadia thrust fault ruptured along a six-hundred-mile length, from mid Vancouver Island to northern California in a great earthquake, producing tremendous shaking and a huge tsunami that swept across the Pacific. The Cascadia Fault is the boundary between two of the earth's tectonic plates: the smaller offshore Juan de Fuca Plate, formerly the Pacific Plate before the North American Plate had overtaken it, now the one that is sliding under the much larger North American Plate. This earthquake caused a shaking of the houses of the Cowichan people on Vancouver Island as we know from their stories. The shaking was so violent that people could not stand and so prolonged that it made them sick. On the west coast of Vancouver Island, the tsunami completely destroyed the winter village of the Pachena Bay people leaving no survivors. These events are recorded in the oral traditions of the First Nations people on Vancouver Island. The tsunami swept across the Pacific also causing destruction along the Pacific coast of Japan. It is the accurate descriptions of the tsunami and the accurate time keeping by the Japanese that allows us to confidently know the size and exact time of this great earthquake.

It was as geologists began to get firm data about the 1700 earthquake that they made contact with a Japanese seismologist who happened to be visiting North America and became interested in the Pacific Northwest.

This seismologist was well acquainted with subduction earthquakes and the tsunamis that so often accompanied them because they were common occurrences in his home country of Japan. He concluded that if one had occurred here about three hundred years ago it ought to be possible to prove that it had happened. Japan, being an older civilization, has records of earthquakes and tsunamis going back many hundreds of years. When he returned to his country he found that a powerful tsunami, of the kind that would be triggered by an earthquake of magnitude 9 or more, had struck Honshu, Japan's main island, exactly three hundred years ago and that it came from this part of North America. Knowing the speed of the tsunami he was able to say exactly when the earthquake took place. It was the twenty-sixth of January 1700.

A researcher from the Geological Survey of Japan, along with a team of scientists from the University of Tokyo, found Japanese records of tsunami occurrences along the country's eastern coastline between January 27 and 28, 1700. Careful analysis of these historic tsunami records indicated that several coastal villages were damaged. Accounts were recorded in different villages along Japan's coastline. Seawater was known to have covered land as if it had been high tide. Water went as far as the pine trees and returned to the ocean very fast. Reports indicated repeated waves of water coming in and going out as many as seven times before noon. Because the way the tide came in was so unusual, people were advised to move to higher ground. Some accounts tell of twenty houses being destroyed by waves ten feet high. Rice paddies were destroyed by these waves.

The long history of subduction activity is the key to the history of the Cascade Range of mountains that lie north and south of Seattle near the coast. These mountains are located approximately 170 miles from the coast. If we were to imagine a line descending directly downward into the earth from these mountains we would encounter the subducting ocean crust from the Juan de Fuca Plate at a depth of about seventy miles. Ocean crust from the Juan de Fuca ridges descends slowly so it has traveled some distance inland before it gets down to a depth of seventy miles. At that level the heat in the crust and in its associated water and other volatile material is high enough to create pockets of magma, which rise close to the surface. If a conduit permits any of this magma to break out on to the surface we have a volcanic eruption.

The Cascade Range is a series of stratovolcanoes; that is to say, volcanic mountains that are conical in shape because of the nature of the lava that built them over the past thousands of years. Other volcanoes, such as those in Hawaii, have a different shape because the lava that built them has a different chemical composition. The Cascades run from Mount Garibaldi north of the Canadian border all the way to Mount Lassen in northern California and each peak has its own unique history; some have a very violent past while others either took shape quietly or we do not know enough about their past. We will look briefly at some of these volcanic peaks, beginning at the south end at Mount Lassen. This mountain in northern California experienced a major eruption in 1915 with continuing action at different times over the following two years. The type of rock that erupted was mostly basalt, but in the explosive action accompanying the main event hot rocks were thrown on to its snow-covered sides, triggering major debris flows. In Lassen Volcanic National Park, which includes Mount Lassen and three smaller volcanic centers, the present-day geothermal system has a magma pool near enough to the surface to provide hot water. This system consists of a reservoir with a temperature of more than 400 degrees, underlain by a reservoir of hot water.

Crater Lake, farther to the north, in Oregon, is the remnant of a catastrophic eruption of what was once Mount Mazama, over 10,000 feet high. In that gigantic upheaval of 7,000 years ago, thousands of tons of matter were flung into the air in a pyroclastic flow that spread ash over large parts of eight states. It was an explosion that was probably ten times greater than the one that occurred later in Mount St. Helens. As often happens in an event of this magnitude, the summit of the mountain sank back into the now empty five-mile-wide inner magma chamber and went down below ground level. The empty caldera then filled with water to form the place we know as Crater Lake. Mount Baker has a summit rising to more than 9,000 feet. Apart from Mount St. Helens it is the most active volcano in Washington State. Steam and gas emissions from it were common during the 1970s. Glacier Peak is a volcanic mountain very similar to Mount Baker. Its height is more than 10,000 feet and, like Baker, its cone is less than one million years old. Mount Hood is the fourth highest peak. It has been active for more than twenty million years.

Mount Rainier is the highest mountain of the Cascades, towering more than 12,000 feet above sea level. It has the greatest concentration of glaciers of any mountain in the lower forty-eight. Like other peaks of the Cascades its growth occurred within the last million years but, within that period, all sorts of volcanic eruptions, landslides, and mudflows devastated the surrounding area. As recently as 1989 a gigantic rock avalanche crashed down on the north side of the mountain. Debris flows like this one give a great deal of concern to surrounding settlements. Glacial outburst floods originate when water stored at the base of glaciers is suddenly released, and floods of this kind have been launched from four of Mount Rainier's glaciers. The most prolific of the four is South Tahoma Glacier, which had fifteen of these outbursts between 1986 and 1992. These floods occur during periods of unusually hot weather in summer or early fall. Rainy weather can also be a trigger. I used the term debris flows in relation to these because the release of water triggers small landslides and picks up sediment on the way down. This flow of water, mud, and rocks at ground level then travels at about fourteen miles an hour, tearing up vegetation and damaging roads and facilities in Mount Rainier National Park.

Mount Rainier is receiving a lot of attention these days. Part of the concern relates to its rock structure, the presence of weak layers of rock high on the mountain, as well as its huge cap of snow and ice. These areas could collapse in even a small earthquake and disrupt life and industry in nearby Seattle. During the 1990s, Mount Rainier was selected by the United States Geological Service for intense study as one of three places that might cause major damage over the next decade or two. To emphasize the urgency of this study, it was pointed out that a fault line, known as the Seattle Fault, runs from a point near Mount Rainier to Seattle. Given the frequency of smaller earthquakes in and around Seattle, there is every justification for concentrated research efforts while, at the same time, keeping a close watch on the mountain's behavior.

We now know that a similar offshore event will happen sometime in the future and that it represents a considerable hazard to those who live in southwest British Columbia. However, because the fault is offshore, it is not the greatest earthquake hazard faced by major west coast cities. In the interval between great earthquakes, the tectonic plates become stuck together, yet continue to move toward each other. This causes tremendous strain and deformation of the earth's crust in the coastal region and causes ongoing earthquake activity. This is the situation that we are in now. Some onshore earthquakes can be quite large (there have been four magnitude 7+ earthquakes in the past 130 years in southwest British Columbia and northern Washington State). Because these inland earthquakes can be much closer to our urban areas and occur more frequently, they represent the greatest earthquake hazard. An inland magnitude 6.9 earthquake in 1995 in a similar geological setting beneath Kobe, Japan caused in excess of $200 billion damage.

At 9 P.M. on January 26, 1700 one of the world's largest earthquakes occurred along the west coast of North America. The undersea Cascadia thrust fault ruptured along a six-hundred-mile length, from mid-Vancouver Island to northern California in a great earthquake, producing tremendous shaking and a huge tsunami that swept across the Pacific. The Cascadia fault is the boundary between two of the earth's tectonic plates: the smaller offshore Juan de Fuca Plate that is sliding under the much larger North American Plate.

The shaking of the earthquake collapsed houses of the Cowichan people on Vancouver Island and caused numerous landslides. The earthquake also left unmistakable signatures in the geological record as the outer coastal regions subsided and drowned coastal marshlands and forests that were subsequently covered with younger sediments. The recognition of definitive signatures in the geological record tells us the January 26, 1700, event was not a unique event, but has repeated many times at irregular intervals of hundreds of years. Geological evidence indicates that thirteen great earthquakes have occurred in the last 6,000 years.

References for Further Study

Bolt, Bruce A. 1978. *Earthquakes: A Primer.* New York: W.H. Freeman.

Halacy, D. 1974. *Earthquakes: A Natural History.* Indianapolis: Bobbs-Merrill.

McKee, Bates. 1972. *The Geologic Evolution of the Pacific Northwest*. New York: McGraw-Hill.

Ritchie, D. 1981. *The Ring of Fire*. New York: Atheneum.

Yeats, Robert S. 2004. *Living with Earthquakes in the Pacific Northwest*. Eugene, OR: Oregon State University Press.

16

Lisbon, Portugal, earthquake and tsunami

November 1, 1755
The main city of Lisbon

An offshore earthquake of magnitude 9, followed by a tsunami destroyed Lisbon, Portugal. The combination of the earthquake and the tsunami, especially with little understanding of the nature of tsunamis, caused almost universal destruction in Lisbon

On November 1, 1755, an earthquake of magnitude 9 hit Lisbon. Houses and shops in the lower part of the city, which had been built on unconsolidated ground, were completely wiped out and most of the parish churches were also destroyed. The shock of the day on which this happened was as strong as the event itself. November 1 is All Saints Day, a sacred occasion in a Catholic country like Portugal. In such a religious place the middle of the eighteenth century there were deeply held convictions about all the earth being an orderly creation guided by its Creator for the benefit of humanity. How could such a tragedy occur on All Saints Day and how could it happen when most people were in churches and where so many of them lost their lives? There was a sense of bewilderment all around. Those who were able to get out of buildings before they collapsed ran down toward the open areas near the sea, tragically unaware that a powerful tsunami was about to overwhelm the very area they thought was safe.

The city of Lisbon is a short distance inland from the Atlantic coast on the northern bank of the River Tagus. As people moved toward the mouth of the river close to the coast they noticed that the water's edge had moved away from the land, leaving a broad stretch of beach covered with all kinds

Figure 13 Lisbon earthquake. An accompanying quote is from Voltaire's *Candide:* "The seas rose boiling in the harbour and broke up all the craft harboured there; the city burst into flames, and ashes covered the streets and squares; the houses came crashing down, roofs piling up on foundations, and even foundations were smashed to pieces. Thirty thousand inhabitants of both sexes and all ages were crushed to death under the ruins."

of sea life. What they were unaware of is that the withdrawal of water from beaches is frequently the first action of tsunamis as they reach shore. There is a pause as tsunamis encounter shallow water and friction is experienced by one part of the advancing wave. The wave stalls, then, like a suction pump, it withdraws all the water in front of it and recedes back out to sea, only to return later with much greater strength. There was no understanding of tsunamis 250 years ago so no one was prepared for the wall of water that subsequently crashed on to the shore destroying everything in its path. The wave was forty feet high at first and increased in height as it made its way up the valley of the River Tagus.

The epicenter of the earthquake was located at sea about seventy miles southwest of Lisbon in a location where two tectonic plates meet, the Azores Plate and the Gibraltar Plate. Historically, those have frequently given rise to tsunamis, particularly if the quake's magnitude is greater than 9. Thus, the result of the earthquake was first of all huge damage to

Lisbon, but then lesser destruction up and down the coast as far south as North Africa and northwards to Britain and even Scandinavia. Along the French coast lakes and sea inlets were flooded. There were several phases to the tsunami. It was not just one wave that came in but rather a sequence over a period of time, so places continued to be hit at a distance over time. Lisbon was a city of 275,000 people in 1755 and first reports told of 20,000 buildings having been destroyed but this was just the beginning of troubles. As has so often happened in earthquakes fires break out and quite soon they are out of control. This was the case in Lisbon and the same thing happened more recently in San Francisco's earthquake of 1906 and Tokyo's of 1923.

Fires always get out of control very quickly after earthquakes for similar reasons, because they originate in numerous places at the same time. In Lisbon, candles in churches were knocked over and open fires in kitchens were also tipped over. Wood, cloth, and paper, all highly flammable materials, were everywhere available to assist any flame. To make matters worse, strong northeasterly winds sprang up around the city. Fires blazed on for a week, destroying all that was left standing from the destruction cause by the earthquake. All kinds of valuable collections of silks, spices, and goods were destroyed by the fire, as were some outstanding buildings such as the Opera House, just built in the year of the earthquake, and the Patriarchal Church and Royal Palace. The major libraries of the city lost more than 70,000 volumes. Of special interest to those who disliked the authoritarian rule of the church was the news that one of the buildings destroyed was the headquarters of the Inquisition, the branch of the church that was responsible for the persecution and torture of all who opposed the beliefs of the church.

At least 30,000 people lost their lives in the city of Lisbon and a general state of chaos followed the tsunamis and the fires that followed. The sad situation that emerged was an opportunity for scavengers and thieves. They began to search all over the ruins of the city, among the living as well as the dead, to find what they could. Their behavior, added to all the destruction, gave rise to what can only be described as mass hysteria among survivors. The need for some form of authority coupled with effective control over crime became urgent. The government of Portugal had collapsed as a result of the widespread destruction and there was no obvious source that could exercise control. The king decided to appoint one man, on a temporary basis, to take complete charge of all the affairs of the city. He was given absolute authority. He had to launch quickly into three immediate tasks: establish order, fight the fires, and bury the dead. To make it clear to all who might try to steal or profit from the high demand for food, this man arranged to have several gallows erected in the city. The bodies of more than thirty looters were soon found on these gallows, left there for the public to see.

Securing the approval of the church to bury the dead quickly was a difficult task, despite his authority. Where you were buried was seen to be as important as how you had lived because it affected your fortunes in the afterlife. Burial in a consecrated plot beside the church was essential because that would mean your beliefs and behavior had been approved by the church. Without that approval you were certainly destined for hell. However, there were neither enough priests nor sufficient time to arrange for each burial and the man in charge wanted to conduct a mass burial at sea to prevent the spread of disease. Bodies had already been ignored for some days. The greater good prevailed and all bodies were buried at sea. The next task was to arrange temporary housing for the homeless along with public kitchens and food distribution centers. Both Portuguese and foreign ships that happened to be in the harbor were ordered to unload their provisions and sell them at reduced prices.

One foreigner visiting Lisbon who happened to be on the fringes of the city in a place that was largely untouched by the earthquake decided to record his observations of the event. It was probably all he could do because everywhere around him there was a situation of panic. He noted a slight tremor in the ground around 9:30 in the morning and thought it must be the result of a passing wagon. The tremor lasted for about two minutes and was followed, after a short pause, by a violent shaking that made nearby houses split and crack. This much stronger shaking went on for what he felt was about ten minutes and was accompanied by a steady build up of dust in the air, latterly so heavy and dark there was no daylight. Suddenly, he noted, the dust settled down and the sun appeared. There was a short period of nothing happening before he felt a third and far greater shaking. He could see at a distance building after building collapsing. Once again the sun was obscured and he began to hear the cries of pain from all directions. Soon afterward he saw fires springing up here and there and he could see people running away from them. A wind had sprung up and no one was trying to cope with the flames. Every person was trying to save his or her own life. Fortunately, this foreigner's written record was preserved and later added to the official documentation.

About an eighth of the 275,000 people of Lisbon had perished along with its buildings. The fires raged on for five days and Lisbon, one of the largest cities in Europe, famed for its architecture, was reduced to ashes. Architectural treasures from the days of Moorish occupation were lost. The city's opera house, built earlier in the same year as the earthquake, had gone. The cathedral and all the major churches were ruined and the Royal Palace was no longer habitable. The city's hospital was overtaken by fire and its destruction added significantly to the total loss of life. The total value of property losses was estimated to be $100 million. This earthquake was the first in all history to be subjected to very close scientific investigation. The same man who had been given absolute authority to bring order and provisions after the earthquake arranged for a questionnaire to be sent to every parish in all of Portugal asking them for all the information they could provide as to the time and duration of the shocks and aftershocks, how high the sea waves came, and how many people had been killed. This record was kept in Portugal's national archives and it has been a very valuable source of information for succeeding generations on the whole subject of earthquakes and their effects. Also included in this record were the notes from the foreign observer.

The work of restoration began quickly. Debris was cleared from the city within a year and by the end of that year the various branches of government were in place. Fortunately, the new prime minister decided to take account of the information that had been collected from all the areas affected by the earthquake and use it as a guide in the design of what would be a new city. There were many aspects of the old city that both contributed to earthquake destruction and hindered escape when tragedy struck. The new prime minister was determined to correct these weaknesses of design and, as a result of the work he did, he became known in history as the father of seismology. One improvement he introduced seems very simple to us today but was revolutionary in 1755. It was to make streets wider and remove curves. This one change would enable people to escape quickly from a collapsed building without having to cope with the debris that so often filled the older streets. In addition, fires could not jump easily from one side of a street to the other so they would not get out of control as quickly as they formerly had. Even in modern times, as was seen in Japan in the aftermath of the 1923 earthquake, a simple idea like this is not always implemented. Instead, in Japan, streets were left in the older narrow format.

To ensure against the collapse of buildings in an earthquake, the new prime minister did several things. First, he arranged to have models of buildings drawn to scale and then arranged for army units to parade backwards and forwards with their horses around the models to find out if their weights and activities affected the models in any way. As the design of new buildings progressed he finally settled on a new kind of structure consisting of a flexible wooden skeleton around which masonry walls would be built. The idea was that the flexible skeleton would be firmly anchored in order to hold the masonry walls in place during an earthquake. At the same time, the masonry would protect the wood from catching fire. This was perhaps the first occasion when a building design was carefully related to the effects of the earthquake. It may have been the first anti-earthquake building system ever designed. Such systems became fixed law for Portugal and guided Lisbon's new city plan. There were two other valuable initiatives that the prime minister added: he included the details about earthquake experience that had been collected and made them part of the overall plan for the city and added, in some detail, all that was known about the behavior of animals before and during earthquakes. Today we are well aware of the warning signals we get from all forms of life with regard to earthquakes but this was probably the first time they were given serious consideration.

References for Further Study

Braun, Theodore E. D., and Radner, John B., eds. 2005. *The Lisbon Earthquake of 1755: Representations and Reactions*. Oxford: Voltaire Foundation.

Brooks, Charles B. 1994. *Disaster at Lisbon: The Great Earthquake of 1755*. Long Beach, CA: Shangton Longley Press.

Fonseca, J. D. 2004. *The Lisbon Earthquake 1755*. Lisbon: Argumentum.

Kendrick, T. D. 1955. *The Lisbon Earthquake*. New York: J. B. Lippincott.

Satake, Kenji, ed. 2005. *Tsunamis*. Dordrecht: Springer.

Steinbrugge, Karl V. 1982. *Earthquakes, Volcanoes, and Tsunamis*. New York: Scandia American Group.

17

Massachusetts offshore earthquake

November 18, 1755

Two hundred miles off the coast of Massachusetts

An earthquake of magnitude 8 occurred offshore from Gloucester and damaged coastal areas; it was the largest earthquake experienced in Massachusetts up to that time

On November 18, 1755, a magnitude 8 earthquake, centered offshore two hundred miles east of Gloucester, severely damaged areas onshore. Heaviest damage occurred around Gloucester. It was the largest earthquake experienced in Massachusetts up to that time. Shaking was strongest all along the coastal areas southwards toward and around Boston. Within the city of Boston there was considerable damage. As many as 1,600 chimneys were knocked down and the brick walls and roofs of several buildings collapsed. Stone fences were thrown down throughout the countryside, particularly on a line extending from Boston to Montreal, reminiscent of an earlier earthquake around Montreal in the previous century which destroyed several stone chimneys in Boston.

Earth movements took place west and south of Boston; new springs formed, and old springs dried up. Cracks opened in the earth and water and fine sand issued from some of the ground cracks. The impact of the earthquake was felt in Halifax and Montreal in Canada, in Chesapeake Bay in Maryland, and on a ship that was at the epicenter. There, above the epicenter, the shock was felt so strongly that those on-board believed the ship had run aground. There were several aftershocks. An area of reclaimed land near the wharfs in Boston was damaged to a greater extent than anywhere else. It may have been one of the first examples of liquefaction, that is to say a ground surface changing to a mixture of water and mud during an earthquake, a problem that appeared later where buildings had been erected on unconsolidated sediments.

This earthquake may also be the first record of a tsunami in the U.S., now a familiar story in subsequent records of major earthquakes, especially the powerful 1964 earthquake in Alaska. In other countries, as we know from the devastating tsunami of 2004 in Sumatra, Indonesia, tsunamis have often been experienced. The Lisbon earthquake of the same year as the one in Massachusetts was one of the most powerful tsunamis ever known up to that time. This 1755 earthquake off Gloucester affected other vessels near the epicenter and left a few vessels aground in the Leeeward Islands, more than a thousand miles away to the south. In that area the typical tsunami effect of water being drawn back from the harbor was observed—fish were left on the banks along with anchored vessels and then, a short time afterward, a larger wave that was six feet higher than normal swept ashore.

The Gloucester earthquake, often referred to by the name "Cape Ann," was interpreted in the popular mind as a judgment from God for bad behavior. There were similar interpretations in other locations, at different times, including the United States today, despite our present understanding of the causes of earthquakes. In the case of the Gloucester quake there were additional reasons for attributing causation to the direct action of God. Widespread religious revivals had been taking place throughout New England under the leadership of Jonathan Edwards and they carried warnings of the imminent judgment of God against all who did not repent. Historians have identified a consistent theme in all the published sermons of that time, namely that the ground had shaken because of the moral imbalance in human behavior. In some southern states the influence of earthquakes on religious behavior was dramatically expressed in the increase of people attending Methodist churches. From 1811 to 1812, the dates of the Madrid quakes, their numbers jumped by 50 percent. For the prior decade this denomination's numbers had changed very little.

References for Further Study

Bolt, B., Horn, W., Macdonald, G., and Scott, R. 1975. *Geological Hazards*. Berlin: Springer-Verlag.

Bryant, Edward. 1991. *Natural Disasters*. New York: Cambridge University Press.

Ebel, J. E., and Kafka, A. L. 1991. *Earthquake activity in northeastern United States*. Boulder, CO: Geological Society of America.

Francis, P. 1994. *Volcanoes: A Planetary Perspective*. New York: Oxford University Press.

Steinberg, Ted. 2000. *The Unnatural History of Natural Disaster in America*. New York: Oxford University Press.

18

Bengal, India, famine

1770 AD

Northeast India, in the area now known as Bangladesh

British administration failed to prepare for times of inadequate rainfall so, when crops failed in 1770, no food supplies were available for the peasant farmers. Ultimately, the mass starvation of Indian peasants resulted from poor government administration

In the summer of 1770, the northeast of India, a region we now recognize as Assam Bihar and Bangladesh, experienced a famine that affected the entire area. By the end of that year ten million of the residents had died from starvation. The explanation given by the ruling authorities was that the tragedy was due to natural causes, but a closer examination of the circumstances associated with the sudden loss of rice, the principal food of the native people, revealed that the tragedy was due to two things: first, ignorance of rice agriculture on the part of the ruling authorities and, second, removal of the basic necessities of life by the same rulers in order to export or sell the rice and make a profit for the British government. At this time in its history Britain had no clear policy for its relations with colonial subjects other than to maximize its exploitation of local natural resources.

The East India Company was the ruling power in India at the time of the famine. Its work in that country dated from 1600 when the British government gave it the right to capture and control as much of India as they wished. Gradually they expanded their territory until they were the effective if not the official government of the whole country. Numerous trading posts were established along the east and west coasts and a large number of people came from Britain to look after these trading posts. The largest ones were in Calcutta, Bombay, and Madras. A successful military campaign in Bengal by the British leader Robert Clive in the year 1757, in which the local emperor was defeated, gave the East India Company complete control over the best and most extensive agricultural land in all of India. Plentiful supplies of water from the Brahmaputra and other rivers coupled with extensive tracts of flat, rich, alluvial soils enabled this part of India to sustain a high density of population. Summers were hot, ideally suited to rice cultivation. In addition, every summer brought the monsoon rains, high levels of rainfall that ensured adequate supplies of water for the paddy fields.

If the two causes of the tragedy are examined in more detail, the way that events unfolded become clear. The monsoon rains were always the key to successful cultivation of rice in Bengal. They arrived in onshore winds from the sea early in the hot summer months and they persisted into the fall when a reverse, cold, dry flow of air from the continental interior took their place. These gigantic movements of wind systems affected a much wider area than Bengal and it often happened that climatic changes in more distant places delayed the arrival of the summer rains, even causing an almost total absence of rain in some years. Two years before the famine, one of these monsoon anomalies began to appear. In 1768 there was a partial shortfall of rain. As a result, there was a reduction in the amount of rice harvested and in the following year there was even less rain and therefore a correspondingly smaller harvest. By September of 1769 there was a severe drought, and alarming reports were coming in of rural hunger. Early in 1770, reports of widespread starvation began to arrive at the East India Company Headquarters and they were followed by news of a rapid increase in the number of deaths.

In the midst of the developing tragedy, local authorities maintained a strict control over agricultural output. Their income depended on either the sale of the rice they demanded from the local small farmers or on the taxes they levied on the people producing the rice. The people, however, who decided who would benefit from the harvested rice were unfamiliar with rice farming. They knew almost nothing about the vicissitudes of the monsoon rains and they were equally ignorant of local customs, including the traditional ways of dealing with years of drought. It was normal practice among the people of this area to have some rice in reserve because they knew that on occasion they would experience the kind of situation that developed in 1768 and 1769. Thus, they had a reserve of rice to cope with bad years. The British rulers made no arrangements for some rice to be kept for emergencies. Worse still, they prevented the local residents from having such a traditional reserve. As conditions worsened in the early months of 1770 and the death toll mounted the only response from the local authorities was that a natural disaster had occurred and nothing could be done about it.

It is even more astonishing that the leaders of the East India Company, educated people who had come from England where humanitarian concerns for neighbors in distress was almost instinctive, could be so indifferent to the suffering that was taking place all around them. Instead of reducing demand on the harvest of 1769 and using all of it to provide emergency food supplies for the starving residents, they went in the opposite direction and increased the demand on available supplies of rice while continuing to increase the tax on the harvested rice. All the authorities cared about was the need to demonstrate to the British government that they made a profit year by year. If natural conditions reduced the harvest then, in their minds, the obvious thing to do was increase the tax on people so that the profits would remain at a high level. That is what happened. From the beginning of their control in Bengal, the Company had raised land taxes and trade tariffs up to half of the value of the agricultural produce. In 1770, with millions already dead from starvation, it raised these taxes and tariffs by 10 percent so that their profits would remain high.

Famine was everywhere in 1770. Peasants tried to sell their possessions, even the ploughs and bullocks that they would need for their survival in the future. The price of rice, their staple diet, kept going up, and soon nothing that they could sell would pay for enough food. Children were sold to anyone who would buy them and some of them ended up as slaves in European and Indian households. Conditions deteriorated to levels of desperation that give rise to cannibalism and, at the same time, to an increasing spread of disease. At first the starvation and rate of death was in the rural areas, where the population as a whole depended on the rice crop. Then, as out-migrations accelerated, most people headed for the capital of Calcutta in the hope of finding relief there. There was little for them there and soon the streets of that city were full of dead bodies. One or two members of the East India Company were so moved by the horror of the situation that they left the country and went back to England. Later they recounted the events that had made such an indelible mark on their memories. They had seen human corpses mangled by hungry dogs and by jackals and vultures. When the situation became too great a danger to public health the Company employed a hundred men to pick up the dead bodies and throw them into the River Ganges.

As a result of the famine, large rural areas were depopulated and allowed to revert to natural jungle. Many cultivated lands were completely abandoned. Bengal, formerly the richest part of the nation, became destitute and the East India Company was no longer able to maintain its formerly profitable status. The British Government appointed a governor-general to take charge and replace the Company. The famine had taken the lives of ten million peasants, about one-third of the total population of Bengal. The total may have been much higher; there had never been a census of the population and only the painstaking work of researchers in later years made it possible to confirm that the death toll was at least as high as ten million. The famine ended as quickly as it had begun. By the end of the year 1770 substantial rainfall ensured a plentiful harvest. The whole desperately tragic event needs to be placed in the context of previous and subsequent famines in India. Altogether there were about twenty-five substantial famines in different parts of the country during the period of British rule, some in the far south and several in areas west of Bengal. Estimates for the total loss of life in all of these exceeded thirty million. None of them was as catastrophic as the 1770 famine.

Famines were still present even in the final years before the country secured its independence from Britain in 1947. The last serious famine came in 1943, in the middle of World War II. Japanese forces had captured large areas of the south and the south east of Asia and they were advancing through Burma, at that time the largest exporter of rice in that part of the world. The British had encouraged the development of rice cultivation in Burma and, by 1940, was purchasing 15 percent of all India's needs of rice from that country. Bengal, because it was so close to Burma, depended to a greater extent on Burma's rice. About one person in every four of Bengal's population relied on imports of rice from Burma. If anything happened to that source there would be another famine. True to its former neglect of retaining resources to cope with possible emergencies, the British once again had nothing in reserve. What military authorities did do, and what proved to be more disastrous than anyone imagined, was to introduce emergency measures all across the Bengal area. Large areas of rice cultivation near the Burmese border were destroyed in order to slow down the advance of Japanese armies, depriving the area of all local food resources in the process. At the same time, almost all the rice available was transferred to other parts of India and other theatres of war. The residents of Bengal were told that they had to cope with less rice because so many of their agricultural areas had been destroyed.

In October of 1942, the whole east coast of Bengal was hit by a powerful tropical cyclone and areas of land as far as forty miles inland were flooded. The fall crops of rice were washed away and lost. Small quantities of what was already a reduced harvest, the part of the harvest that always had to be retained as seed for planting in the months of winter that followed, had to be consumed for food. As the hot weather of 1943 appeared and there was nothing to eat because nothing had been sown in the winter growing season, famine appeared and before the year was out four million had died. The military authorities had made no provision for food emergencies. Furthermore, all the military commanders in that region were concentrating on the war and gave little attention to domestic issues. The government of India tried to get help to the stricken areas but no one seemed to care in far away Britain at a time when World War II was at a peak of activity. Subsequent records of rice production for the year 1943 revealed that there was enough available to prevent starvation if only the military commanders had chosen to divert supplies of rice to the impoverished peasants.

In the late 1990s, Indian author Amartya Sen was awarded a Nobel Prize in economics for his studies of the Bengal and other famines in India. His conclusions were a damning indictment of British administration in India. He showed that rice production in India during the years 1941–1943 were pretty much normal and were sufficient to provide food for everyone. The totals, year by year, varied only slightly from the normal: 1940, eight million tons, 1941, seven million, 1942, nine million, and 1943, eight million tons. Sen was convinced that the 1943 famine was caused, not by a shortage of rice, but by the removal of supplies from the stricken areas to meet the needs of fighting troops. His thesis went on to show that, while malnutrition and hunger remained a common condition in India, no major famine occurred in fifty years following independence. Yet, in those years, 1951–2001, the total population grew from 360 million to more than a billion. By contrast, in one fifty-year period of British rule, 1891–1941, the population only grew from 287 million to 389 million. Sen selected the fifty years from 1951 because the immediate aftermath of independence led to considerable strife and disruption of agriculture.

References for Further Study

Baxter, C. 1997. *Bangladesh: From a Nation to a State*. Boulder, CO: Westview Press.

Duff, Romesh, Chunder. 2001. *The Economic History of India Under Early British Rule*. London: Routledge.

Kumkum, Chatterjee. 1996. *Merchants, Politics, and Society in Early Modern India*. Bihar: Brill.

Spear, Percival. 1963. *The Nabobs: A Study of the Social Life of the English in 18th Century India*. London: Oxford University Press.

Suleri, Sara. 1992. *The Rhetoric of English India*. Chicago: University of Chicago Press.

19

Connecticut earthquake

May 16, 1791

Along the lower reaches of the Connecticut River

The earthquake in 1791 was Connecticut's biggest earthquake up to that time. The earthquake hit east of New Haven and did extensive damage in the East Haddam Region of the Connecticut River

On May 16, 1791, along the lower reaches of the Connecticut River, east of New Haven, the state experienced its biggest earthquake up to that time. The felt intensity was 7 as based on the Modified Mercalli Scale, a measure that is similar to the Richter Scale but different in that it takes account of the effect of an earthquake rather than its power at source. In many older records of earthquakes all we have are accounts of the damage that was done. From these we can estimate its intensity on the Modified Mercalli Scale. The area affected by this earthquake is in and around East Haddam. It has a history of frequent earthquakes extending back to earliest settlement times.

The East Haddam region on the Connecticut River is known in Indian lore as a place of noises, presumably the noises of earthquakes. The first reported earthquake began on May 16 with two heavy shocks in quick succession. Stone walls were shaken down, tops of chimneys were knocked off, and latched doors were thrown open. A fissure several meters long formed in the ground. In a short time, thirty lighter shocks and more than one hundred other aftershocks continued during the night. Both the earthquake of May 16 and the many aftershocks were heard in Boston, Massachusetts, and in New York City.

References for Further Study

Bell, Michael. 1985. *The Face of Connecticut: People, Geology, and the Land.* Hartford: Connecticut Geological and Natural History Survey.

Jorgensen, Neil. 1977. *A Guide to New England' s Landscape* Chester, CT: Globe Pequot Press.

Merril, George P. 1924. *The First One Hundred Years of American Geology.* New Haven: Yale University Press.

Tedone, David, ed. 1982. *A History of Connecticut' s Coast* Hartford: Connecticut Department of Environmental Protection, Coastal Area Management Program.

Van Dusen, Albert E. 1961. *Connecticut.* New York: Random House.

20

New Madrid, Missouri, earthquakes

1811 and 1812

In and near New Madrid, a community close to where the states of Missouri, Arkansas, Kentucky, and Tennessee meet

The New Madrid earthquakes of 1811 and 1812 were the most powerful to hit contiguous United States in its history. The intraplate quakes of 1811 and 1812 were accompanied by numerous aftershocks and both the main shocks and those that followed were felt over most of the continental United States

The first of the 1811 and 1812 New Madrid earthquakes occurred on the sixteenth of December 1811. Its magnitude was 7.2. The second quake hit the same area on the fifth of February 1812. Its magnitude was 7.4. In between there were numerous aftershocks. Both earthquakes were centered on a part of the Mississippi embayment close to where the states of Missouri, Arkansas, Kentucky, and Tennessee meet. The ensuing destruction was similar and widespread for both events; buildings collapsed, trees toppled, and the Mississippi River changed course. What could be called minitsunamis appeared on the river as fissures opened and closed below the surface. The shock waves rang church bells in Washington, D.C., and they were felt from Indiana to Massachusetts. Fortunately, there were few people living in the area at the time so, in spite of the great intensity of the earthquakes, the loss of life was very small.

On the basis of the size of the area damaged and the extent to which awareness of the events was felt across the continent, the New Madrid earthquakes can be considered the most powerful to have hit the United

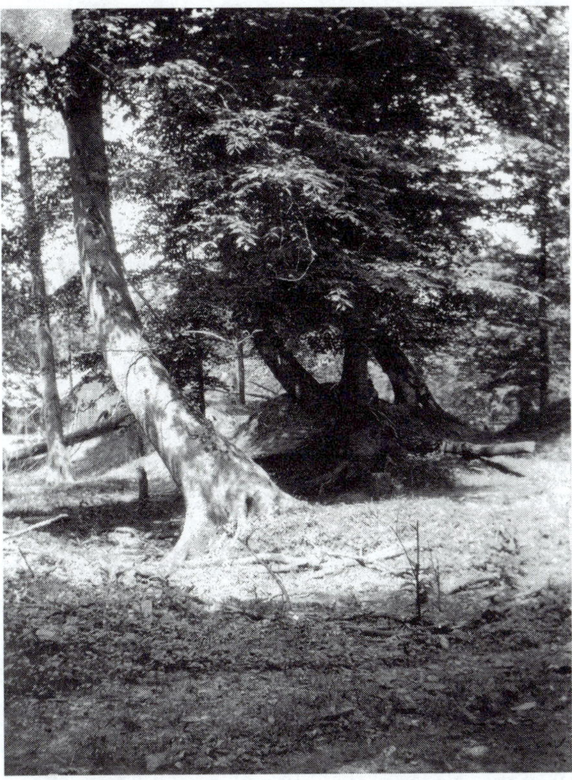

Figure 14 New Madrid earthquakes, 1811 and 1812. Trees tilted by the New Madrid earthquake at the Chickasaw Bluffs on the east side of Reelfoot Lake, Tennessee. Note the twist of trees into an upright position. 1904.

States since Europeans first settled here. An area of more than 200,000 square miles showed evidence of significant damage by these earthquakes and one million square miles experienced shaking that was strong enough to alarm the general population. This last-mentioned area can be compared with the effects of more recent events. It was more than twice the size of the area affected by the 1964 Alaska earthquake and ten times larger than that of the San Francisco earthquake of 1906. The complex physiographic changes that occurred on the Mississippi River within the earthquake areas were extensive. An uplift of land thirty miles long and fifteen miles wide raised the river's valley by as much as thirty feet.

The first effects of the earthquakes on those who lived in and around New Madrid were the sounds of timbers groaning, creaking, and cracking, of furniture being thrown around, and of chimneys crashing down. People got out of their homes as quickly as they could in order to avoid the falling debris. The log cabin was the most common type of building in the area, a structure that is well able to withstand earthquakes, yet one that did not stand up in this instance because of the extensive ground movements.

Earth waves similar to those experienced in water kept moving across the surface, bending trees and opening up deep cracks in the ground. Landslides, one after another, swept down from the steeper bluffs and hillsides and, simultaneously, large areas of land were uplifted. Water emerged from below through the cracks. On the river huge waves overwhelmed a number of boats. Others were thrown on to land high above the level of the water and the returning waves took back with them trees and other debris, rather like the actions of a tsunami. Whole islands in the river disappeared.

Aftershocks for both events were numerous and unusual when compared with those of other earthquakes. After the December event, these lesser shocks were almost continuous but with lesser intensities over time, then came two weeks of quiescence followed by several days in which the ground was in a state of constant tremor. Records of the aftershocks were kept locally and it seems that they continued in patterns similar to those of 1811 and early 1812 for about two years. In spite of the great intensity and widespread damage associated with these earthquakes, few lives were lost because the density of population at that time, in that area, was very low. One life was lost in New Madrid through falling buildings. Several drowned when they were thrown into the river as a result of landslides, and several boatmen drowned when their boats sank. A number of canoes had also been abandoned and it was concluded that their owners had drowned.

The most seriously affected areas were characterized by raised and sunken land with the former marked by fissures, sand blows, and landslides. These areas extended from Cairo in Illinois to Memphis in Tennessee, a distance of 150 miles, and southeastward from Crowleys Ridge, past Memphis for a distance of fifty miles. The extent to which the quakes were felt has already been identified in terms of area. It helps to put place names to that statistic: the shocks were felt from Canada all the way to New Orleans and from Montana to Boston. People in Washington, D.C., were frightened badly because the shock in that part of the Appalachians was more acute than in places closer to the coast. This difference was later related to a connection between the Appalachian system and the epicenter of the New Madrid earthquakes.

Precise locations of the epicenters of the New Madrid earthquakes of 1811 and 1812 are now known. The fault zone is one hundred twenty miles long and the epicenters show a northeast-southwest trend. Another series of events like those in the nineteenth century would be felt from Denver to New York City and damage buildings in eight states. Tennessee and the other three states bordering this earthquake zone would be devastated. Today there are more than fourteen million people living within the area that was devastated by the New Madrid earthquakes. Some comparisons can be made with the San Francisco quake of 1906, about which we know much more and the total population affected there was four million. Furthermore, because of the nature of the earth's crust in the central parts of the United States, the physical size of the area affected by any earthquake is much bigger. Geologists are always working on assessing the frequency rate of large earthquakes; that is to say, the average number of years between each big event. When they succeed preparations can be made to cope with the next occurrence.

The pressures that cause the massive tectonic plates to move will also cause them to rip apart because of the spherical shape of the earth's surface and therefore the differential rates of motion of the ocean crust as it moves away from the spreading ridges. The North American continent is therefore impacted on its east coast at different rates and so internal stresses are created. Studies of the New Madrid zone show that earthquakes like those in 1811 and 1812 did occur in the past. Exactly when and how consistently are the questions that researchers want to answer. Sand deposits and liquefaction are often useful in dating the past, for example, these two remnants of past earthquakes can be located quite easily today to show that powerful earthquakes hit New Madrid in 1811 and 1812. Charles Lyell, the British scientist who pioneered new developments in the field of geology and was Charles Darwin's mentor, visited New Madrid shortly after the nineteenth-century earthquakes and discovered that the native Indians had valuable information in their legends about past events.

Other geologists have followed up on the possibility of dating past events by examining the sites of ancient Indian settlements. It is known that native Indians used sandy areas for cooking, leaving on these places after they moved elsewhere fragments of their cooking utensils and charcoal residues. Archeologists can date items of pottery by their form and size; they can also date carbon or charcoal by the radiocarbon method. From evidence of this kind we now know that a major earthquake occurred in the New Madrid area sometime between 1180 and 1400. It was powerful enough to cause liquefaction. Evidence of much earlier earthquakes was also found, one of them being dated several thousand years ago. Large gaps of this kind between successive events are of little value for predicting future earthquakes so the search goes on. One alternative method employed by geologists involved examining earth fissures from the past, the same types of cracks in the surface that were seen in 1812, and looking for deposits of different material in them. By carbon dating these alien materials in the cracks they were able to locate one big earthquake somewhere between 780 and 1000 and another between 1260 and 1650. By interpolating from these it is now possible to come up with a rate of occurrence of 400–500 years.

If the 400–500 frequency rate were to be true for the future, Memphis, the nearest big city to New Madrid, need not expect a huge earthquake for another two hundred years. However, there are other considerations that illustrate the difficulty of being precise when it comes to predicting earthquakes. For one thing, the New Madrid area has been hit with more than twenty-four earthquakes since 1812, all of them events that did substantial damage. On national maps of the United States, New Madrid is shown as having a greater chance of being hit with an earthquake than any other place east of the Rocky Mountains. There is, additionally, one other variable affecting the time of the next earthquake. It has been found in several countries where the average rates of recurrence of earthquakes are known that sometimes the sequence is interrupted by a cluster of earthquakes. That was experienced in Australia when a series of five major earthquakes hit an interior area within a period of twenty years.

References for Further Study

Bagnall, Norma. 1996. *On Shaky Ground: The New Madrid Earthquakes of 1811– 1812* Columbia: University of Missouri Press.

Feldman, Jay. 2005. *When the Mississippi Ran Backwards: Empire, Intrigue, Murder, and the New Madrid Earthquakes*. New York: Free Press.

Fuller, Myron L. 1912. *New Madrid Earthquake*. Washington, DC: Government Printing Office.

Penick, James L. 1976. *New Madrid Earthquakes of 1811– 1812* Columbia: University of Missouri Press.

USGS Report on New Madrid Earthquakes of 1811– 1812 Available on Google and other Internet web sites.

21

West Ventura, California, earthquake

December 12, 1812

Epicenter of the quake was offshore, west of Santa Barbara

An earthquake of magnitude 7.1 struck western Ventura, including Santa Barbara. Extensive damage was done to the lightly-constructed Catholic missions in and around Santa Barbara

On December 21, 1812, one of the largest earthquakes in Californian history struck the western part of Ventura, including Santa Barbara. It had a magnitude of 7.1 and its epicenter was offshore, probable in the Santa Barbara Channel. Extensive destruction occurred in the lightly constructed buildings of the various Catholic missions. Three missions suffered the greatest damage—Santa Ynez, Santa Barbara, and Purisima. The experiences of Santa Ynez were typical of all three. One of the new homes next to the church was torn down and the upper interior walls along with the tiles on the roofs of all the adjacent houses were knocked down. Reports of a tsunami were persistent despite the rarity of such in the history of Californian earthquakes. Liquefaction was widespread along the coast. The effect of so much damage persuaded the Catholic authorities to remove most of their stations from the coastal areas to places farther inland.

The reports of sea waves were extensive, the only descriptions possible at that time for what we now call tsunamis, and it is highly likely that they occurred despite the absence of any reports of deaths from them. A Spanish ship at anchor thirty-eight miles offshore was substantially damaged at the time of the earthquake. People living at the Rancheria Mission where damage was minimal decided to move half a mile away from the coast because the waves threatened to flood them since they had already flooded two areas of Santa Barbara. At the Santa Barbara Presidio there were reports of the sea having changed its natural condition because the whole mission appeared to settle, presumably a reference to the land sinking because everyone ran away for fear of being engulfed by the sea. Another of the many scattered reports that were later recovered from the local archives told of an earthquake so violent that the sea receded and then rose up like a mountain. This account bears the marks of authenticity because it is exactly what would have happened, as we know from our present knowledge of plate tectonics, if indeed a tsunami had accompanied the earthquake.

An earthquake of magnitude 6.9 hit this same area thirteen days earlier but the epicenter was in a very different location, one hundred miles east of Santa Barbara, at Wrightwood, near the San Andreas Fault. This earthquake affected a wide area, reaching westward to damage some of the same places that were destroyed by the later one. It destroyed the church at Mission Santa Barbara, and caused major damage at Mission La Purisma Concepcion, near present-day Lompoc, causing that site to be abandoned, and a new Mission Purisma to be built several miles farther north. This earlier earthquake is often referred to as the San Juan Capistrano earthquake because it was responsible for the death of forty Native Americans who were attending mass at Mission San Juan Capistrano when the earthquake struck. The mortar in the church walls failed and the church collapsed. It had been poorly constructed. Damage was also reported at Mission San Gabriel and even as far away as San Diego and San Fernando.

Most of the overall damage was due to the December 21 quake but often, because both quakes sometimes hit the same place, we get explanations like the following of the additional damage done to a place that had already been hit by the December 8 quake. The damage at Mission La Purisima Concepcion on December 21 was extraordinary and horrifying. The earthquake completely ruined the church. It destroyed several statues and paintings, and ruined most of the art work. The ecclesiastical vestments were not damaged since they were in drawers. Some of the buildings were flattened to the ground while others may have been usable after repairs. The possessions and furnishings of the mission also suffered. Some were smashed, others broken, and all were damaged. The inclement weather with its copious rain did not allow people time to dig out or to repair roofs. The original mission was on the edge of a marsh and on sloping ground, which probably contributed to the extensive damage. Aftershocks caused considerable concern at Mission Santa Barbara. They were almost continuous at times. One person reported counting thirty on a given night and, in daytime, they arrived every fifteen minutes. All of this served to paralyze the community and delay restorative work. Priests were even afraid to conduct services because of the condition of the buildings.

References for Further Study

Briggs, P. 1972. *Will California Fall Into The Sea?* New York: McKay.

Coffman, Jerry L. 1982. *Earthquake History of The US*. Boulder, CO: United States Geological Survey.

Menard, H. 1964. *Marine Geology of The Pacific*. New York: McGraw-Hill.

Oakeshott, G. 1978. *California' s Changing Landscape* New York: McGraw-Hill.

Tazieff, H. 1964. *When the Earth Trembles*. New York: Harcourt, Brace, and World.

22

Tambora, Indonesia, volcanic eruption

April 5, 1815

On Mount Tambora in the eastern part of Indonesia

The earth's biggest eruption within historic times hit Indonesia in 1815. This eruption had a VEI of 7 and it not only devastated Indonesia but also changed climates all over the world for years

The area we now know as Indonesia experienced earth's two most powerful volcanic eruptions. The first, Toba, the biggest within the last two million years, had a VEI of 8 and was located in western Sumatra. It erupted 74,000 years ago. The second was Tambora, which had a VEI of 7 and was located east of Java. Tambora erupted in April of 1815 and was the biggest in all of recorded human history. It is likely that the tsunami of 2004, also in Indonesia, will go down in history as the most destructive tsunami ever experienced. Thus, Indonesia has come to be known as the locale of the world's most deadly earthquakes and eruptions. When Tambora erupted, two million tons of debris rose upwards to a height of twenty-eight miles. The heavier parts fell back to earth but the lighter particles stayed aloft, circling the earth and blocking out much of the sunlight. Temperatures dropped in every country of the world and many people subsequently referred to the year 1816 as the one without a summer.

Some sense of the immensity of this event can be gleaned from the dimensions of the mountain before and after the eruption. It was approximately thirteen thousand feet high before and nine thousand afterward and this loss of four thousand feet of height occurred in a mountain that was thirty-eight miles wide at its base. The total weight of the material that rose into the atmosphere was ten times greater than that of Krakatau in 1883 and one hundred times more than the amount ejected from Mount St. Helens in 1980. The sound of the explosion was heard in Western Sumatra, a thousand miles away. The heavier fragments of lava fell back into the ocean and the combination of heat and impact with the water created mini eruptions from which the finer quantities of dust were added to the already darkened atmosphere. The actual volume of ash produced by these secondary was ten times greater than the amount generated by the original eruption. For years, the average amount of sunshine reaching the earth was reduced. More than ninety thousand were killed by the eruption, most of them indirectly through the starvation and disease that followed as everything around them was obliterated. The mountain itself continued to burn for three months before finally coming to rest.

The local devastation in places within a hundred miles of the eruption is well illustrated in the experiences of the villagers of Bima, a small community at the eastern end of Sumbawa, the island on which Tambora previously stood. For several days following the eruption they were shaken day and night by the ongoing explosions that followed the main eruption. A dense ash cloud in the atmosphere above Bima completely shut out the sun for four days, similar to Vesuvius when the people there also experienced total darkness at midday. The weight of fallen ash was too much for most of the homes and they collapsed. At the same time, throughout the early hours following the eruption, tsunamis flooded the village just as they had done elsewhere on the Island of Sumbawa. Later, government officials found innumerable numbers of corpses of people and animals on the ground around Bima or floating nearby on the sea. In different places around the world the impact of Tambora was not as dramatic as it was in Bima but nonetheless enormously destructive.

Reports from northern Europe described the harvests for the year that followed as being so poor that starvation was common among poorer families. The industrial revolution was still young and most people were still totally dependent on what they could wrest from the soil. Many were reduced to eating rats. Grain prices rose four-fold in that part of the world and, when other countries tried to be capitalize on the shortage, the price of grain on the international market rose extremely high. France suffered more than other countries of Western Europe because it had been involved in Napoleonic wars right up to the year 1815 and the whole social life of the country had been severely strained from the stresses of warfare. In the year 1816, farmers were afraid to take their produce to market because of the dangers of being robbed by hungry people along the way. Government troops had to be called in frequently to protect these farmers. In the United States, farmers in New England had so many crop failures over such large areas that many of them migrated westward to Ohio and elsewhere.

All over Indonesia, in addition to the immediate destructive effects of the eruption, masses of ash, rock particles, and sulfur dioxide gas were deposited everywhere and they continued to give trouble year after year for some time. Sulfur dioxide is a poisonous gas used in the manufacture of sulfuric acid, a highly toxic substance. An invisible gas, the presence of sulfuric acid in the air created complications for the digestive system of both humans and animals and many died as a result. Lack of rain was another consequence of the disaster. Since all vegetation was destroyed, transpiration activity stopped. Normally new soil forms quickly in tropical areas that experience volcanic eruptions and the eruptions contribute to much of the tropical rainfall that comes frequently in latitudes such as those in Indonesia. Accordingly, population there is always dense and crops can be grown two or three times a year in such soil. However, it took several years before Indonesia was able to grow crops of the kind and quality needed to feed its huge population.

The collection of thousands of islands that we now call the nation of Indonesia always had a fascination for the people of Europe, largely the result of the value of spices in centuries past. Marco Polo was the first to acquaint the West with what was then called the Spice Islands. That was about eight hundred years ago but it was considerably later when the importance of spices appeared. By the middle of the nineteenth century and after considerable success in both farming and stock rearing, Europeans were faced with the problem of preserving meat in winter. Animals were slaughtered in the fall to reduce the cost of feeding them and the meat was then salted away in iceboxes to preserve it for six or more months. The taste of salted meat after all that time was, to say the least, not very attractive and Europeans discovered that one specific item from the Spice Islands, pepper, was the thing that would profoundly enhance its flavor. Trade in pepper between Indonesia and Europe became a top priority. So great was the value of this commodity that a single peppercorn was considered to be worth its weight in gold and this became evident in the rules governing stevedores at European ports. Whenever they had to handle peppercorn shipments from Indonesia their pockets were sewn up to minimize theft.

The island chain that is Indonesia extends in a curved form for more than 4,000 miles. Closely following the islands on their south side but deep below sea level stands the tectonic boundary between the Indo-Australian Tectonic Plate and the Eurasian one. The Indo-Australian Plate is moving northeastward beneath and at a slightly faster rate than the movement of the larger Eurasian Plate and this subduction is the main cause of the numerous volcanic eruptions and earthquakes we hear about from Indonesia. Within the overall picture of these two huge tectonic plates, there are smaller components of each that can at times be extraordinarily destructive. The gigantic earthquake of 2004 off the coast of Sumatra was caused by the Indian portion of the Indo-Australian Plate subducting under the Burma portion of the Eurasian Plate and creating one of the most powerful earthquakes of all time. The tsunami that accompanied this event and radiated outward from the entire 750 miles of plate that had been displaced is also likely to go down in history as the most destructive. It was literally an earth-shattering wave and it took several minutes for the displacement to be completed.

The island on which Tambora stood is more than two hundred miles north of the tectonic boundary. The magma that rises from below this boundary has to travel upward about one hundred miles from that boundary and from far below it to reach the summit of Tambora and cause the eruption. It is the work of geologists to trace as completely as they can both the source of the magma and its age. Only by doing this can information be found on the past history of volcanic activity as big as Tambora's and thereby be able to predict when another one might occur. The sea floor is the top of the outermost solid layer of the earth's surface, known as the crust, often several miles thick. Below the crust is where the magma exists and there have weaknesses or fault lines in that crust if the magma is going to rise to the surface. One such fault line stretches northwestward for 150 miles from the Island of Sumba across the tectonic boundary to the Island of Sumbawa, the site of Tambora.

It was through breaks in this fault line that magma built up over the centuries. Geologists did not know very much about either tectonic plates or subduction at the time of Tambora's eruption and it was about 150 years later that the secrets of earth's mosaic of tectonic plates became known. Ever since that time geologists have been busy making use of this new knowledge to trace the history of earthquakes and volcanic eruptions.

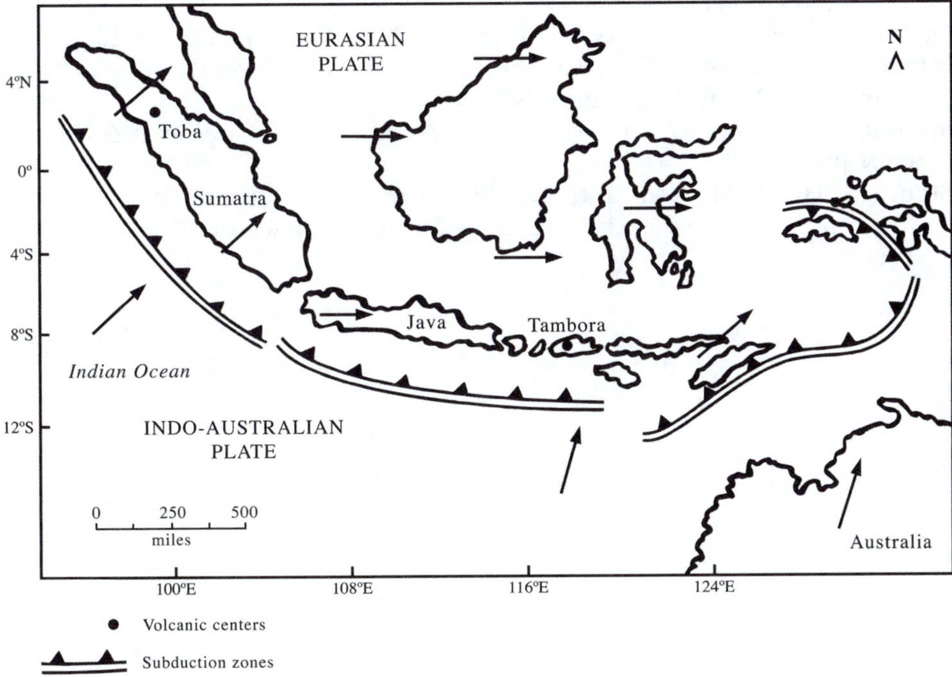

Figure 15 Locations for two of Indonesia's most powerful eruptions.

The age of the oldest lava on the site of Tambora is about 50,000 years and the youngest are the layers of ash and rock that were deposited on Indonesia in 1815. Beneath these deposits are some older rocks, about 5,000 years old. This discovery, while inconclusive, gave geologists at least one clue to the likelihood of another Tambora-type eruption arriving soon. If the time difference between the 1815 event and the one that came before it is 5,000 years, then one possibility is that there will not be another one before another 5,000 years.

More work needs to be done by geologists on the history of eruptions in this part of Indonesia in order to obtain the average time between these destructive events over the millions of years through which they have occurred. Only when armed with data of that kind can we estimate the future with some degree of accuracy. The final phase of the 1815 event seems to have begun three years earlier. Reports from local observers tell of noisy steam eruptions, sometimes followed by dark clouds of volcanic ash, happening from time to time between 1812 and 1815. These things were the result of hot magma encountering moisture as it rose within the mountain. Overall, in the course of the three years, there was a two-inch layer of ash on the sides of the volcano and on the ground.

References for Further Study

de Boer, Jelle Zeilinga, and Sanders, Donald T. 2002. *Volcanoes in Human History: The Far-Reaching Effects of Major Eruptions*. Princeton, NJ: Princeton University Press.

Decker, R., and Decker, B. 1989. *Volcanoes*. New York: W. H. Freeman.

Harrington, C. R. 1992. *The Year Without a Summer? World Climate in 1816*. Ottawa: Canadian Museum of Nature.

Simkin, T, and Siebert, L. 1994. *Volcanoes of the World*. Tucson, AZ: Geoscience Press.

Stommel, Henry M., and Stommel, Elizabeth. 1983. *Volcano Weather: The Story of 1816, The Year Without a Summer*. Newport, RI: Seven Seas Press.

23

Natchez, Mississippi, tornado

May 7, 1840

Natchez, a city on the lower Mississippi River

Natchez was almost totally destroyed by a mile-wide tornado and 317 lives were lost

Shortly after noon on May 7, 1840, a mile-wide tornado slammed into Natchez, Mississippi, a city on the Mississippi River, about 150 miles north of New Orleans. The storm was loaded with all kinds of debris it had picked up along its path. No one expected it and no one was warned of its approach even though the sounds of its destruction farther down the river could be heard in Natchez. Unlike the present time, there was no national weather service to alert people to an approaching storm and there were none of the things that individuals could have used to warn others, two-way radios, telephones, or cell phones. As the tornado struck Natchez, banks, homes, stores, steamboats, and other vessels were completely destroyed. Houses burst open. Three hundred and seventeen lost their lives. It was the second most deadly tornado in U.S. history.

About an hour before it struck Natchez, a thunderstorm with driving rain had formed in an area about twenty miles to the south and moments later a tornado began to form out of that same storm. The tornado gathered strength as it moved northward along the Mississippi valley. The United States gets about 1,000 significant tornadoes every year, more than the total number experienced by all other countries combined. Only one in every hundred is as powerful as Natchez. At the present time, in sharp contrast to 1840, few are killers. We now have the ability to identify the kind of weather that is likely to lead to a tornado and we can trace the paths of these twisters so that those in their paths can take shelter. Forecasting, detection, communications, and raised public awareness of the danger, all help to minimize the number of fatalities. The U.S. Weather Service in 1840 was only able to report on what was visible and measurable locally in terms of wind speed, temperature, and humidity. There was no system of communication that could relay these data quickly enough to provide a warning to those who were in the tornado's path.

As the tornado tracked northeast, heading for Natchez, people took advantage of the cooling rain to sit out in their porches, or to walk about even in the rain because the rain provided a cooler atmosphere than the usual hot dry conditions. Many were preparing to eat, fully aware of the dangers that any thunderstorm would present but unaware that this particular storm was much more than a thunderstorm. At the very moment that the tornado struck, the dinner bells in large hotels had rung and most citizens were sitting at their tables. It is difficult for us today to appreciate the scene in Natchez in the year 1840. This was pre-Civil War America and there were two social classes of humanity living and working in the plantations and in the home—ordinary Americans and slaves. There is no reference to the deaths of slaves in the various newspapers apart from one sentence in one paper, saying that hundreds of slaves died. They died in their homes or at work in the plantations. It is quite clear from the details of life on the river, and the large number of deaths that occurred there, that the vast majority of the 317 deaths occurred among the merchants who were transporting goods on their flatboats. The hundreds of slaves who died were considered property losses.

The approaching tornado raced up the river from a point seven miles south of Natchez. As it traveled it stripped the forest from both sides of the river. Those on the river were the first to hear what must have been a thunderous roar from the river as it churned with massive waves and whitecaps. Up and down the river on either side of Natchez scores of vessels, steamboats, flatboats, and skiffs, were crowded together in great numbers, including many itinerant boatmen who traded everything from furs to liquor. Flatboats and people were tossed into the air like toys and, as they came down, they were drowned. The volume of debris as well as the tumultuous state of the water made it impossible for anyone to be rescued. One or two survived because they were thrown on to the land. As the tornado swept northwards, the central and northern parts of the town were demolished. Survivors described the air as being black, filled with spinning pieces of walls, roofs, and chimneys and with large timbers flying through the air as if shot by a catapult. Beneath the ruins lay the crushed bodies of many strangers. There were many escapes and many heartrending scenes. A woman named Mrs. Alexander was rescued from the ruins of the Steam Boat Hotel. She was seriously injured and was holding on to two dead children.

The destruction of the flat boats was an immense blow to the economy of the area. At least sixty of them were lost. It was impossible to calculate the total value of the boats and their contents. The steamboat *Hinds*, with most of her crew, went to the bottom, and the *Prairie* from St. Louis was so much wrecked as to be unfit for use. The steamer *St. Lawrence*, at the upper cotton press, was a total wreck. It was difficult to tell how widespread the ruin had been. Reports of major damage came in from plantations twenty miles away in the state of Louisiana. Looking back from today's vantage point, these losses were all the more unfortunate because there were none of the aids with which we are now familiar: Red Cross, National Guard, presidential disaster decree, and mobilization of doctors and emergency personnel from other places. The townsfolk did the best they could and, as always in these earlier days, the unexpected was attributed to the deliberate action of God. One newspaper described the whole scene as the voice of the Almighty and hence prudence should dictate reverence rather than execration. Total costs of the disaster were estimated at 1.3 million dollars at the 1840 value of money.

References for Further Study

Hemingway, Lorian. 2002. *A World Turned Over: A Killer Tornado and the Lives it Changed Forever*. New York: Simon and Schuster.

Nova, Craig. 1989. *Tornado Alley*. New York: Delacorte Press.

Taylor, James B., Zurcher, Louis A., and Key, William H. 1970. *Tornado: A Community Responds to Disaster*. Seattle: University of Washington Press.

24

Fort Tejon, California, earthquake

January 9, 1857
Fort Tejon, about thirty miles south of Bakersfield

California's most powerful earthquake ever struck Fort Tejon, a place near the San Andreas Fault. The quake's epicenter was some distance north of Fort Tejon and the scar it left alongside the San Andreas Fault was two hundred miles long

On January 9, 1857, California's greatest ever earthquake struck the central part of the state near the San Andreas Fault. It left a surface scar of more than two hundred miles along the line of the fault and caused a horizontal displacement as large as thirty feet. Its magnitude was 7.9. The Owens Valley Earthquake and the great San Francisco event of 1906 make up, with Fort Tejon, California's three biggest historical earthquakes. The 1906 San Francisco guake was 7.8 and that in Owens Valley was 7.4. The epicenter of the 1857 event was not at Fort Tejon but rather about sixty miles farther north but, because Fort Tejon was a well-known place in a thinly populated area, the earthquake was named after it. The earthquake itself caused one fatality, evidence of the low density of population. If we compare San Francisco in 1906 with Fort Tejon in 1857, the break in the San Andreas Fault was longer in the former but the maximum and average displacements were larger in the latter.

The effects of the quake were quite dramatic, even frightening. Were the Fort Tejon shock to happen today in the context of present population, the damage would run into billions of dollars, and the loss of life would be substantial. In 1857, the population density was extremely low and native people were the principal residents. When the earthquake actual hit strong shaking ensued, which lasted from one to three minutes. Property loss was heavy at Fort Tejon as five buildings were severely damaged and several others sustained moderate damage. Trees were uprooted and fish were thrown out of Tulare Lake. Ground fissures appeared in the beds of several rivers and evidence of liquefaction was found between Stockton and Sacramento. Additionally, there were two significant aftershocks within a week of the main event. Ground openings and fissures were reported from Sacramento to the delta of the Colorado River and changes in the flows of rivers occurred in several locations. In Los Angeles, a city of 4,000 people at that time, minor damage was done to homes.

The San Andreas Fault extends for more than eight hundred miles from the northern Californian coast to the Gulf of California. It is at the heart of almost all California's earthquakes. Interaction between the North American and Pacific plates along this fault takes place within an elongate zone, broadening from sixty miles at its north end to three times that width in southern California. The fault is close to the east side of this zone in the south and it gradually migrates across the zone, lying on the west edge at its northern end. The constant interaction between the Pacific and the North American tectonic plates takes place in opposite directions along this fault, with the Pacific Plate moving northwards and the North American Plate moving southwards, but these movements are not always smooth. Many factors interfere with their movements, including the presence of subsidiary faults, different types of rock, and the differential rates of plate movements because they are moving on the globe, a curved, not a flat surface. Much of the energy expended is, therefore, unable to do its work of moving the tectonic plate forward. It gets stored elastically, that is to say under pressure, in the upper crust of California's bedrock, close to the fault. From time to time the fault slips, the stored energy is released, and an earthquake occurs.

California in 1857 was thinly populated with Europeans, except for the two dominant settlements, San Francisco and Sacramento. The first big gold rush of the many that would happen later in the nineteenth century—in the Klondike, Australia and South Africa—had created a feverish scramble among people everywhere to get to California and be the first finder of the mother lode, the place with the biggest gold nuggets. There were no roads or trains across the United States and the gold seekers had to find their way either across land near Panama or by sea around Cape Horn. In this year of 1857, the gold rush was in its ninth year of diggings and things were beginning to slow down. There was less and less gold to be found but, in the few years of frantic efforts to strike it rich, San Francisco had become a big city, the only big city west of the Rockies. Its population was 53,000 and the only other city, Sacramento, the state capital, had a population of 12,000. It was fortunate for us today, as we seek to understand better the huge earthquake of 1857, that there were newspaper descriptions and other reports of the event published in these two cities at the time and we can examine these accounts today. San Francisco had six newspapers at the time and Sacraments had five.

Most of these records deal with human reactions and damage to buildings, all of which were either of adobe or brick construction. In either case, in a frontier location like this, the masonry used would be weak so that minor shocks could be very destructive. From Marysville, fifty miles north of Sacramento, all the way to the southern border of the state and eastward as far as Las Vegas some level of shock was experienced. The main area affected, however, while still large, is limited to a hundred-mile stretch of territory from 34 degrees north to 36.5 degrees north. Shocks of strength 7 on the Modified Mercalli Scale were experienced everywhere within this area. Typical newspaper accounts of the shocks experienced were as follows: we all ran outside as our building cracked because we saw that others had collapsed. It was difficult to remain in a standing position. We saw men being physically thrown down by the force of the earthquake. Reports by those who were close to the epicenter of the quake described homes collapsing and trees being knocked down. Everywhere, people were afraid. They did not have our present knowledge of earthquakes so, understandably, they had no idea what might happen next.

The intensity experienced in Los Angeles, at that time a pueblo in the location we know today as downtown, was described as moderate. People were frightened but the only damage to buildings was the cracking of walls. It was a similar level of shock in San Bernardino and Santa Barbara. From data such as these it is reasonable to conclude that a repeat of the 1857 earthquake today would not cause serious damage to low-rise buildings in Los Angeles. There were many mild aftershocks to this momentous earthquake of 1857 but among them two seemed to have been sufficiently strong to attract the attention of several newspapers. One occurred on the evening of the day of the main shock. The second one arrived a week later. Both were described as severe but there was no record of damage. The duration of each of these two strong aftershocks was short, much less than the timing of the main shock, and they continued for three minutes in San Bernardino and two minutes in Fort Tejon.

The close link between the 1857 and 1906 earthquakes, coupled with the growing body of research findings on previous powerful quakes along the San Andreas Fault, has given rise to calculations and possible predictions about the future. When might another magnitude 8 earthquake occur here? That question has occupied the minds of many geologists. One of the first pointers to an answer came with investigations of past quakes. One geologist used evidences of past displacements on the fault, deformations of the crust, and distances between the two tectonic plates that move on opposite sides of the fault to propose a timetable for the future. His calculations were based on a time period of twenty million years so many of his colleagues treated his estimates as very-long-predictions; that is to say, estimates that might prove to be statistically good but incapable of giving much guidance for the immediate future. His prediction was that another large earthquake would occur at intervals of from fifty to two hundred years. Another researcher, Kerry E. Sieh of the California Institute of Technology, focused his investigations in one place, the same area affected by the 1857 quake, and examined the earth's crust vertically rather than horizontally as was done by the geologist who considered the past twenty million years.

Sieh discovered evidence of at least nine earthquakes over the past 1,400 years. Later, as he continued his investigations, he expanded the number to twelve. Based on these findings that cover a relatively short time, geologically speaking, he concluded that the average recurrence interval would be between 140 and 150 years. His work was carried out in the mid 1970s and many scientists commented on his findings in later years. In 1985, for example, two geologists wrote a major article on predicting future San Andreas earthquakes in the journal *Scientific American*. They noted that the time interval from the 1857 earthquake was 128 years at the time of their writing and added that this figure was alarmingly close to Sieh's estimate for a recurrence. More than twenty years after the publication of their article, the San Andreas Fault still awaits its next magnitude 8 event. These two attempts, one looking back twenty million years and the other 1,400 years, are a useful reminder of the great difficulties in predicting earthquakes. Nevertheless, the attempts continue and, as mentioned in the introduction, they have expanded in China and Japan to observations of the behavior of wildlife just prior to earthquakes.

Sieh's findings were incorporated into the prediction that the Geological Survey was asked to provide to the National Security Council. Preparations have to be made in anticipation of future earthquakes even if there is no certainty about specific dates. These preparations take account of all kinds of data in the hope that they will, one day, be able to anticipate a catastrophic earthquake. Experts know, just to add another item of information to what they already have, that strain accumulates on the San Andreas Fault at a rate of a little more than an inch a year. Thus, if one were to calculate the strain since 1857, it would amount to twelve and a half feet by the year 2007. Deductions from such data as well as from the earlier ones are not reliable. Even when the recurrence rate of a major event in the San Andreas Fault is known, activities in other domains may disrupt our calculations. Slight changes in the earth's rotation or in its normal distance from the sun can change the behavior of the tectonic plates that are a vital causal factor in California's earthquakes. The massive Indonesian earthquake of December, 2004, was sufficiently powerful to do what had never before been observed in human history. It slowed down for a fraction of a second the earth's rate of rotation.

The value of knowing when the next earthquake may strike becomes more and more important with the passage of time. There are so many elements of our total environment that human society can now control, and so much technology with which we can do what is needed, that the quest for answers to earthquake prediction must be pursued. In 1857, the total population of California was not much more than 10,000, perhaps not even as great as that. In the early years of the present century its population is thirty-five million and growing at a rate that is above the national average. It added fifteen million since 1970. Today, a single county may be the custodian of most of the nation's wealth. Santa Clara County suffered heavy damage in the 1906 earthquake; today it is the principal home to the nation's supplies of semi-conductors. Urbanization has added its own urgency to the demand for earthquake prediction. Most of the state's people live in cities and San Francisco is now a huge urban agglomeration, not just a single city as it was in 1906. There are estimates of casualties if a magnitude 8 quake should hit the San Andreas Fault within the next decade. They vary according to the time of day that such an event occurred. At two in the morning it would be over 13,000 and proportionately less at various other times of day.

References for Further Study

Bolt, Bruce A. 1978. *Earthquakes: A Primer*. New York: W. H. Freeman.

Coffman, Jerry L. 1982. *Earthquake History of The US*. Boulder, CO: United States Geological Society.

de Boer, Jelle Zeilinga, and Sanders, Donald T. 2005. *Earthquakes in Human History*. Princeton: Princeton University Press.

Iacopi, R. 1973. *Earthquake Country*. Menlo Park, CA: Lane.

Rikitaki, T. 1976. *Earthquake Prediction*. Amsterdam: Elsevier.

25

Calcutta, India, cyclone

October 5, 1864
Calcutta, India

Cyclones from the Bay of Bengal in the northeast of India frequently cause extensive damage. This cyclone took 60,000 lives and flooded the entire city of Calcutta

On October 5, 1864 most of the city of Calcutta, India, was flooded and destroyed by a cyclone. Sixty thousand people were killed at once and many thousands of others died later from the sicknesses and diseases that followed. The cyclone crossed the east coast of India south of the Hooghly River, one of the streams that constitute the delta of the River Ganges, shortly after 10 A.M. As the cyclone entered the narrowing waterway the water level rose until it became a towering forty-foot-high wall. Its height had been raised to a maximum by the arrival of high tide before noon on the same day. Everything was washed away in its path as the water swept inland. In the months that followed, the city, the surrounding area, and the harbor had to be rebuilt.

Different parts of the world have different names and different definitions for the storms they experience. In Asia, a storm with speeds less than 39 mph is called a tropical depression. If the circulating speed is above 39 mph it is named a storm and, if above 73 mph, it is classified as a cyclone. The meteorological conditions in India are very different from the Caribbean. Winds are stronger, rainfall is heavier, and preparations for weather extremes were almost non-existent in the nineteenth century. Hence, there are records of huge losses of life and widespread damage to buildings from that period of history. Even today, as was seen when the Indonesian tsunami of 2004 struck India, many lives can be lost if preparations for coping with disasters are inadequate. A comparison of the Caribbean and

Southeast United States storm environment with that of India helps to explain why India's storms are enormously destructive.

The first thing to note is the temperature difference. India lies south of the Tropic of Cancer while the Southeast United States is north of this line so water temperatures are generally higher in the waters around India. The winds, therefore, are able to carry greater volumes of water vapor at any given time and bring high levels of rain if they are moved over land. In the areas around Calcutta, especially in the mountainous regions north of it, the highest rainfall records in the world are found. Cherrapunji is a community 300 miles northeast of Calcutta and 4,000 feet in elevation, in the country of Bangladesh. It holds the world record for being the wettest place anywhere. Its average annual rainfall is 450 inches but many years have totals far beyond that figure. Calcutta's rainfall is much less than Cherrapunji, even though it experiences the same winds, because its elevation is close to sea level. The second thing to note is the huge expanse of the Indian Ocean compared with the Caribbean and the equally massive extent of the landmass north of India. The air masses that build up over these areas are larger and denser than we find over either the Caribbean or the United States and, hence, their winds are stronger when storms or cyclones form.

In October of 1737, the coastal area of the Bay of Bengal north and south of Calcutta was hit by a cyclone. Numerous ships in the waterways of the Ganges delta were destroyed and many thousands of Indians lost their lives. It was a similar story twenty-five years after the 1864 cyclone, and with similar devastating outcomes. This part of India will always be at risk as the huge air masses that move over it create storms and cyclones. At the same time, the benefits of the monsoon rains they bring are felt and welcomed all over India as they have sustained a human population of a billion. These seasonal winds, blowing toward the land of India from May to October, and blowing in the opposite direction for the rest of the year, bring large volumes of rain. Indian farmers depend on them for their livelihood and if they are delayed for any reason, and sometimes this happens due to unusual behavior of air masses, the result can be disastrous. Many of the accounts of famines in India are related to a major delay in the arrival of the monsoon rains. For various reasons, often because forests were cut down, the ground does not preserve much of the water that comes in the wet season. Even in Cherrapunji there is an inadequate amount of water in the dry season and the people have had to travel great distances, on foot, to find clean drinkable water.

In addition to their unfamiliarity with India's physical environment, British colonial officers had to cope with the limited knowledge of meteorology when they had to cope with cyclones. Temperature and pressure measurements and reports from ships at sea constituted almost all of their available data and the ships at sea in 1864 were often sailing ships. Powerful cyclones could completely destroy both ships and their cargoes so captains were always eager to detect approaching storms and report their findings to shore by wireless telegraph. One vessel, the *Proserpine*, was caught in the1864 Calcutta storm as it made its way out of port and found itself in the spiral winds of the cyclone almost two hundred miles from its center. Within an hour of entering the storm area, the captain of the *Proserpine* discovered that the winds were too strong for his ship, even though it was a steamboat, so he just let it be carried along under the force of the winds. Three hours later he noted that the winds had greatly increased in strength, perhaps because his ship had been drawn further into the storm area. The ship began to roll violently and the engine-room started filling with water.

Over the following six hours every member of the ship's crew was busy pumping out water. At the same time, everything that could possibly be spared was thrown overboard in order to make the ship as light as possible and so minimize its resistance to the waves that swept over it. In the hold there was a quantity of wooden beams, part of the cargo, and they too would have been thrown overboard if they had been lighter. As the ship lurched backwards and forwards the cargo of beams also moved and the captain was afraid that they would make a hole in the ship's hull. Twenty-four hours after their first encounter with the storm, the *Proserpine* entered calmer water beyond the storm. It had barely managed to stay afloat. Everyone was exhausted after all the hours of pumping out water and they could imagine conditions in and around Calcutta when such a powerful cyclone would reach land. That scene of devastation has already been described.

References for Further Study

Bunbury, B. 1994. *Cyclone Tracy: Picking Up the Pieces Twenty Years after Cyclone Tracy*. South Freemantle: Freemantle Arts Centre Press.

Eliot, John. 1890. *Cyclonic Storms in the Bay of Bengal*. Calcutta: Government Printing Office.

Grazulis, T. P. 2001. *The Tornado: Nature' s Ultimate Windstorm* Norman: University of Oklahoma Press.

Nalivkin, D. V. 1983. *Hurricanes, Storms, and Tornadoes*. Rotterdam: Balkema.

26

Kau, Hawaii, earthquake

April 3, 1868

The epicenter was on the south coast of Hawaii, known as the Big Island

An earthquake of magnitude 7.9, the biggest ever, hit the island of Hawaii. The earthquake caused enormous damage in Hawaii Island and was felt three hundred miles away

Every year thousands of earthquakes hit the state of Hawaii, the vast majority of them occurring on the biggest and youngest of all the islands that form the state, The island of Hawaii, known as the Big Island. On the third of April 1868, this island experienced Hawaii's biggest earthquake ever, magnitude 7.9, which caused damage all across the hundred-mile-long island. Its epicenter was in the district of Kau on the south coast, on the southeast flank of Mauna Loa, a volcano that rises more than 27,000 feet into the air, higher than Mount Everest if you count its height from the ocean floor where it begins. The earthquake, which could be heard more than three hundred miles away on the Island of Kauai, caused a mudflow, a rare aspect of Hawaii's many earthquakes, an occurrence that killed thirty-one villagers. It also caused coastal subsidence west of the epicenter and created a tsunami that flooded several villages in Kau and drowned forty-six people.

All along the south coast of Hawaii the earthquake knocked wooden homes off their foundations and, in the villages where straw was the main building material, it tore homes to shreds. Even the more substantial structures of stone were demolished. In the community of Hilo, some distance away on the east coast of the island, every building was damaged. Farther north, almost a hundred miles from the epicenter, in the Kohala Mountains, there were ground waves rising as high as two feet that made it almost impossible for people to stand. Ground fissures of varying depths extended from Pahala to the Kilauea Crater, a total distance of twenty-five miles. Landslides were common all over the island and there was subsidence on the southwest coast to depths of six feet. Much of the destruction was a direct result of the tsunami in which water at times rose as high as forty-five feet. Its impact was also felt beyond the Big Island, on Maui, Lanai, Oahu, and Kauai.

The state of Hawaii is a chain of volcanic islands near the center of the Pacific Ocean. Every part of the state has a volcanic origin. The following is a list of the eight main islands, in descending order of size: Hawaii, Maui, Oahu, Kauai, Molokai, Lanai, Niihau, and Kahoolawe. These eight constitute 90 percent of all the land area of the state but there are numerous smaller islands. There are also many very large islands but they are farther west and are below sea level. The name of the island of Hawaii is a bit of a problem because references to it in books and news reports are often confused with the whole state. It is not only the biggest island; it is more than twice the size of all the other islands combined and it contains the biggest volcano in the state in terms of total mass, Mauna Loa. Because of its location at the eastern end of the state, Hawaii is the youngest volcanic island and therefore the one where most volcanic activity is taking place. The reason for the greatest volcanic activity being at the eastern end of the state is because the hot spot, that is to say the opening down below in the crust of the earth, is directly below the Big Island.

Big Island has five volcanic mountains, approximately twenty miles apart, separated from one another by saddles formed from past lava flows. As the newest island it has none of the coral reefs that are common on the far western, much older islands, and little of its coast has yet been affected by erosion. Maui, Molokai, Lanai, and Kahoolawe, which were once probably a single volcanic peak, are all now separated by distances averaging eight miles and by shallow waters usually three thousand feet deep. Oahu, third in size, is the location of the state capital, Pearl Harbor, The East-West Center, and the well-known tourist attractions of Diamond Head and Waikiki Beach. Kauai and Niihau stand apart from other islands. They are at considerable distances from their nearest neighbors and the water in between is quite deep compared with most of the other islands.

The whole of the state of Hawaii is part of a large volcanic mountain range, most of which is beneath the sea, the islands forming the state being the youngest and, therefore, the highest and most visible parts. The whole mountain chain was formed by what some call a hot spot beneath Big Island in the earth's mantle. This hot spot does not move relative to motions on the surface of the earth and for the past few million years it has been underneath the Big Island. Hence, the frequencies of earthquakes and volcanic eruptions are more frequent here than anywhere else. The Pacific Tectonic Plate on which all the islands stand does move very slowly from east to west. As it moves it takes all the islands with it so the ones we see today as the farthest west are the coldest and least active because they are farthest away from the hot spot. The Pacific Plate moves northwards and then northwestwards, first at a rate of about three inches a year, then four inches, and this has gone on for the past seventy million years. Mama, magma from areas seventy miles below sea level erupted continually at the location of the hot spot, creating, over time, the volcanic mountains that constitute the state.

The history of the Pacific Plate's movements is told in the evolution of the Hawaiian-Emperor Chain, a dogleg series of volcanic mountains stretching thousands of miles across the North Pacific from Hawaii to the Kurile Trench, a subduction zone close to the Kamchatka Peninsula. It also provides a concrete illustration of sea floor spreading. The dogleg section, the change of direction when the Pacific Plate switched from moving northward and took a northwesterly course, was caused by collisions between the Indian subcontinent and the Eurasian land mass forty million years ago. Volcanic mountains in the chain that would now be counted as are older than seventy million years were carried down into the Kurile subduction zone. This series of volcanic peaks consists of more than one hundred individual volcanoes, most of them are below the sea. Their ages are progressively older and their heights lower as they move away from the hot spot. The history of any one of these volcanoes can now be better understood because a new one, Loihi, presently under active study, is developing under the sea twenty miles to the east of the Big Island. Its peak is still less than a mile below sea level.

The heights of some of these volcanoes can readily be overlooked because so much of them is below sea level. Take the two highest, for example, Mauna Kea and Mauna Loa, and note that they stand, like all the others, on an undersea platform that rises far above the general level of the seafloor. A single contour line representing one and a half miles of depth can be drawn to encompass all of Kauai, Oahu, Maui, and Big Island. Even this measurement does not reach far enough. The average depth of the ocean floor in this part of the Pacific is approximately three miles. The identification of a hot spot anywhere on the surface of the globe provides one location that is fixed with respect to the earth's mantle. This is very valuable because all else is relative. All the plates are moving and have no fixed reference to the interior of the earth. It's the same with mid-ocean ridges, oceans, and continents. These hot spots are found in a number of places all round the world but their behavior over time is difficult to track if they occur on land. It is a much easier task when the spot is in the ocean so the Hawaiian-Emperor Chain is an ideal model for studying the historical process.

Over the long seventy million years that we can trace this chain before the oldest of the volcanoes disappears beneath the Asian continent at Kamchatka, we can see a clear pattern developing for each individual volcano. First, as the Pacific Plate moves westward and volcanic eruptions decrease, the rock that formed the mountain gets cooler and cooler and therefore heavier. This increasingly heavy mass then presses down on the seafloor and pushes it downward. At the same time, erosive forces go to work on the top of the peak, first rain and wind, then ocean waves, until it is almost flat. The end result is a series of underwater volcanic mountains, each the same height above the seafloor, but with the flat top of each progressively deeper and deeper below sea level. The ocean floor had sunk but each mountain ended up as a similar landform.

Because of their universal and multi-faceted influence over conditions in the state of Hawaii, we need to be aware of the evolution of a typical Hawaiian volcano before examining its effects in daily life. Although the final appearance and size of a volcano will be unique, each one in the chain evolved and is evolving through the same sequence of stages. First comes the eruption of small quantities of lava deep in the ocean over the hot spot, gradually increasing in quantity until it reaches a peak about half a million years later, after which the amounts decline. Several million years may pass before eruptive activity finally ends and the volcano becomes extinct.

The volcano's life begins deep down below the ocean surface as submarine eruptions build a steep-sided, small mountain with a shallow caldera. As the young volcano grows, small landslides cut into its steep slopes, scarring them. This first phase lasts about 200,000 years but produces only a small part of the final mass. An increase in the frequency and volume of eruptions marks the second phase along with changes in the composition of the basaltic lava. This is Loihi's present stage of development and, before it is completed, Loihi will be close to the surface of the ocean and explosive, ash-generating eruptions will become common as lava mixes with water.

The third phase is when the volcano has grown to more than two thousand feet above sea level and explosive eruptions begin to taper off. Lava flows are now low in volume and continue intermittently for several hundred thousand years. The type of lava emitted is shaped by the slope of the ground and the physical properties of the erupted basalt, and is most commonly basalt. Lava that flows into the ocean shatters into sand and gravel-size fragments and these blanket the submarine slopes. During all three phases, the summit caldera repeatedly collapses, fills up, then collapses again. By the end of half a million years, more than 90 percent of the volcano's mass has been accumulated and it looks like a warrior's shield, hence it has come to be known as a shield volcano.

Weathering and erosion now take their toll of the high, steep-side mountain. The side of the mountain that is closest to the sea and therefore not supported as well as the landward side slips readily toward the ocean, creating large faults and causing major earthquakes. Occasionally there are catastrophic landslides. Recently, vast fields of debris, some of it in large blocks, have been discovered all around the major islands. These submarine deposits suggest that major landslides must have occurred every 150,000 years on the average. Over time, deep canyons cut into the flanks, often along faults previously created by landslides.

At the same time, the volcano's enormous weight pushes the underlying lithosphere downward. Mauna Loa, for example, the world's biggest volcano, has a volume of more than one and a half million cubic feet. Under these conditions the volcano begins to sink and as this happens fringing coral reefs grow at the shoreline with sediments from the reefs accumulating in lagoons. In some Hawaiian islands, remnants of these ancient reefs can be seen. During times of global cooling when polar ice caps grew and sea levels dropped the volcanic shorelines remained at the same level for long periods of time, allowing numerous large reefs to grow.

Beneath Mauna Loa, because of its enormous weight, the ocean crust is depressed approximately 1,500 feet, forming a hollow known as the Hawaiian Deep. In the adjacent waters the seafloor rises by about the same amount to form the Hawaiian Arch. Kilauea is 250,000 years ahead of Loihi in its evolution. It rose above the surface of the ocean 200,000 years ago and within the following 100,000 years had grown to a height of 2,000 feet above sea level. One of the interesting comparisons between Loihi and Kilauea is that both have three main areas of volcanic activity: the summit and two flanking rift zones. Though widely separated in time it seems that their patterns of growth take similar paths.

References for Further Study

Cox, D. C., et al. 1977. *Local Tsunamis and Possible Local Tsunamis in Hawaii.* Honolulu: Hawaiian Institute of Geophysics.

Heliker, C. 1933. *Volcanic and Seismic Hazards on the Island of Hawaii.* Honolulu: Bishop Museum Press.

Macdonald, G. A., et al. 1970. *Volcanoes in the Sea.* Honolulu: University of Hawaii Press.

Stearns, H. T., et al. 1935. *Geology and Groundwater Resources of the Island of Oahu.* Honolulu: Hawaiian Division of Hydrography.

U.S. Geological Survey. 1976. *Natural Hazards on the Island of Hawaii.* Washington: U.S. Government Printing Office.

27

Chicago, Illinois, fire

October 8, 1871

In the barn of a farmer in the city center

A bigger fire, compared with all the previous ones, broke out in the center of the city of Chicago. Inability of firemen to get to the fire quickly gave the flames a quick start from which, aided by a brisk wind, they were able to push the fire beyond the control of the fire department

This fire began in the barn of a farmer near the center of the city in the evening of October 8, 1871. There was considerable delay in responding to the fire. The alarm was not sounded for more than an hour and then the firemen were sent at first to the wrong place. These factors allowed the fire to make a quick start. Additionally, weekends seem to be favorite times for tragedies of this kind. It was on a weekend, early Sunday morning, that the great fire of London of 1666 broke out and it was also on a weekend that the tragic Coconut Grove Club fire in Boston occurred, killing five hundred of the people who had packed into that club for the evening of November 28, 1942. There was an additional troubling factor affecting the Chicago fire: weeks of extremely dry weather had caused a rash of fires. Daily the city's fire bell kept ringing every three or four hours. Firemen were completely exhausted by the time the big fire broke out on October 8.

Chicago, the windy city, unfortunately lived up to its reputation on this occasion. Soon after the start of the fire a strong wind began to blow from the southwest. This was the trigger that accelerated the conflagration, pushing it beyond control within a couple of hours. The wind rose to 60 mph, flaming bits of debris were blown from one building to another, and soon large numbers of people were running toward Lake Michigan's

Figure 16 A view from the west side of the great fire at Chicago October 9, 1871.

beaches for safety. The reality that firemen had to face was that Chicago was a city almost entirely constructed with wood and all of this wood had become as dry as tinder in three months of drought since early July. Less than three inches of rain had fallen in those months. Wood was the universal raw material for homes and streets at that time and writers often referred to Chicago as being all wood. The arrival of blacktop was still a long way ahead in time. Walkways, paths, and even streets, were made of wood planks. There were hundreds of miles of wood in Chicago and every home and almost every building was a wooden structure.

The city in 1871 had become the national center for the meat packing industry and so the entire ground area in the newly opened stockyards were paved with wooden blocks to prevent damage to the feet of cattle, sheep, and hogs. The ships in the Chicago River were made of wood and so were the bridges that spanned it. There were wooden fences and wooden barns and outbuildings, wooden stables behind the wealthier homes and even among the large buildings of the city most of them were built of wood. The poorer residential homes stood next to lumber and coal yards, paint sheds, furniture factories, and other buildings of an industrial kind that were filled with flammable goods, so they constituted a fire trap in the given situation. That situation included widespread neglect of such fire and safety regulations that were in place. The considerations with which we are familiar today were absent in these early days of burgeoning western cities. Nowadays, the cost of a fire in a major city is so great that strict controls and high penalties for neglect are installed in all vulnerable sites.

By the time the fire eased, which would be eighteen hours later, there was a huge population of homeless people. Late on Monday evening, that is almost a day and a half after its inception, the fire burned itself out. Flames had swept over more than 2,000 acres of land and destroyed an estimated $200 million worth of property. The worst feature of all was that the areas that had been destroyed were the ones that the city could least afford to lose. The center of the city's commercial, cultural, and civic life was destroyed. As so often happened in situations of this kind, it was hard to control looters. The authorities did what they could and the military units that were drawn in to control the situation were given orders to shoot at sight anybody who was looting. However, that did not seem to inhibit the amount of looting. There was a national and international outpouring of charitable contributions and a remarkable amount of work was accomplished in a short period of time for the many who were homeless. Reconstructing the city was a big task. Eighteen thousand buildings had been destroyed, three hundred had died, and there were a hundred thousand people without homes.

References for Further Study

Andreas, A. T. 1884. *History of Chicago*. Chicago: A.T. Andreas Publishing Company.

Bales, Richard F. 2002. *The Great Chicago Fire and the Myth of Mrs. O' Leary' s Cow*. Jefferson, NC: McFarland & Company.

Chicago Historical Society. 1971. *The Great Chicago Fire*. Chicago: Rand McNally.

Cromie, Robert. 1994. *The Great Chicago Fire*. Nashville, TN: Rutledge Hill.

Goodspeed, Edgar. 1871. *Great Fires in Chicago and the West*. Chicago: Goodspeed.

28

Owens Valley, California, earthquake

March 26, 1872

Lone Pine was a small community two hundred miles north of Los Angeles and close to the Nevada border

The town of Lone Pine, California, was hit with an earthquake of magnitude 7.4. This earthquake destroyed a seventy-mile fault line and killed twenty-seven. Although one of the largest quakes in California's history the death toll was small because there were few people living here in 1872

The town of Lone Pine, California, two hundred miles north of Los Angeles and fifty miles west of the Nevada border, was virtually leveled when the entire seventy-mile length of the Owens Valley fault ruptured on March 26, 1872. It was one of the largest earthquakes in United States history with a magnitude of 7.4. There were fewer than three hundred people in Lone Pine. Twenty-seven of them were killed and fifty-six others suffered cuts and bruises. All the adobe homes were destroyed. The event was felt throughout most of California and Nevada, and as far as Salt Lake City, Utah. Adobe and brick buildings sustained the brunt of the damage. Minor damage also occurred two hundred and fifty miles away in the San Joaquin and Sacramento Valleys on the western side of the Sierra Nevada. In Yosemite Valley one hundred and fifty miles to the north the earthquake triggered a landslide.

As severe as the ground shaking must have been, it was noted that no one would have been killed or hurt if the houses had been made of wood. The characteristic log homes of early settlement always provided good protection against earthquakes. Numerous depressions and uplifts occurred in and around Lone Pine as would be expected from an event that displaced the Owens Valley fault horizontally by as much as twenty feet. In one location, an area two hundred and fifty feet long sank twenty-five feet while a neighboring stretch of land of comparable size rose by twenty feet. Many comparisons have been drawn between the Owens Valley earthquake and the great San Andrea earthquakes of 1857, the Fort Tejon earthquake, and 1906, the Great San Francisco event. The extent of the land area shaken by each of these three events is comparable, as are the maximum fault displacements. All of them can be classified as great on the basis of the lengths of the ruptures that occurred in the faults but their seismic magnitudes are all much smaller than, for instance, the Alaska earthquake of 1964.

References for Further Study

Bolt, Bruce A. 1993. *Earthquakes*. New York: W. H. Freeman.
McPhee, J. 1980. *Basin and Range*. New York: Farrar, Straus, Giroux.
Sieh, Kerry, et al. 1998. *The Earth in Turmoil*. New York: W. H. Freeman.
Yeats, R, et al. 1993. *The Geology of Earthquakes*. New York: W. H. Freeman.

29

Bangladesh cyclone

October 31, 1876

Southern coastal area of what is now Bangladesh

A cyclone in the area we now know as Bangladesh destroyed the city of Chittagong. At least 200,000 people in Chittagong and its surrounding area died as a result of the cyclone

On October 31, 1876, the community of Chittagong, in a part of India that is now in the nation of Bangladesh, experienced a powerful cyclone that swept inland up the River Meghna, part of the Ganges River's delta. As the surge of water moved upstream into the shallower and narrower stretches of the river it rose in height until it became a monstrous wall of ocean water, thirty to forty feet high. Bangladesh, on the eastern part of the Bay of Bengal, experiences cyclones twice a year, in October and in May. These two months represent the turning points of the monsoon winds. In May they begin to move on shore and in October they move southward from the cold air mass in the north to dominate the atmosphere of India for almost six months. It seems that these turning points, because they represent for a time a mixing of the two contrasting wind systems, trigger the cyclones. The impact of this cyclone in 1876 was devastating in every way. A hundred thousand persons drowned and another hundred thousand perished from diseases or famine.

There is, initially, an accumulation of water in the various small sea inlets along the coast as the cyclone pushes water toward the land. This is a slow process because the Bay of Bengal is quite shallow for a distance of several miles outward from the land. Other factors too, in addition to the depth of the ocean, determine the rate at which water accumulates. A spring tide, a higher than normal level of tidal water, if it were to coincide with the arrival of a cyclone, would greatly increase the breadth of destruction because tidal waters influence the entire shore. This coincidence occurred several times in the recent past, in 1970, 1981, and 1991, fortunately with less loss of life, presumably because disaster preparedness was greater than in 1876. The wind strength of the cyclone and the angle of impact with the shore are two other factors influencing the amount of destruction.

Bangladesh seems to have received more of the types of cyclones that result in high death rates than has any other country in South or Southeast Asia. One statement that gives support to this claim is based on a list of deaths from cyclones that occurred only in those countries and in those cyclones in which there were more than 5,000 deaths. The data reveals that Bangladesh featured in more than half of the countries listed. One physical factor in the environment of Bangladesh may be a contributing cause. The country's overall low elevation makes it easy for relatively small storms to transform its coastal area into a vast sea. With regard to the future, scientists have debated the implications of global warming with respect to the nature of cyclones in the Bay of Bengal. The only tentative conclusions arrived at to date are that sea temperatures will increase and these cyclones, as a result, will likely be more intense and therefore more destructive.

References for Further Study

Eliot, John. 1890. *Cyclonic Storms in the Bay of Bengal*. Calcutta: Government Printing Office.

Holthouse, H. 1986. *A Century of Cyclonic Destruction*. Sydney: Angus and Robertson.

Lamb, H. H. 1982. *Climate, History, and the Modern World*. London: Methuen.

30

Marshfield, Missouri, tornado

April 18, 1880
Marshfield, Missouri

A fast-moving category 4 tornado swept through downtown Marshfield, Missouri. Most of its buildings were destroyed

A massive category 4 tornado left little standing after it had swept through downtown Marshfield, Missouri, on April 18, 1880. It arrived from northeast of Springfield. Seven people were killed in that city as it passed through and ninety-two lost their lives in Marshfield. This was one of the worst natural disasters to strike a small town anywhere in the country, at least up to 1880. All but fifteen buildings in Marshfield, a community of 1,100 people, were destroyed. Memories remain strong when a small community suffers such a large degree of destruction and some of these memories were recalled many years later. They provide a vivid picture of the nature of a tornado and the suddenness in both forming into a vortex and traveling at high speed across the ground.

One man recalled that the day of the tornado was warm and without any wind, an ideal day for young people to be out of doors playing. This is what he remembers doing. It was a Sunday and nothing changed in the appearance of the sky from three in the afternoon to five. From 5 P.M. to 6 P.M. everything seemed to happen. First came the darkening of the sky by a series of black clouds that looked like smoke coming from one of the old coal-fired steam engines. Then almost immediately one could see a mass of these same clouds coming in their direction. This man remembered the reaction of his father at this stage. He had recognized the signs of a tornado and without a moment's delay began to run toward the one place that was known to be a safe refuge in a tornado, the courthouse. As he ran he pushed or dragged every member of the family with him. Family members remember the fear that was evident as they ran.

In the short space of time between identifying an approaching tornado and running the hundred yards to the courthouse, the air and ground all around had filled up with all kinds of debris. Anyone who was still outside could only hold on to anything that seemed firm and hope for the best. The wind was a howling, greater than 100 mph force, sweeping away anything and anyone in its path. Those who remembered noted how quickly it was all over. So quickly, in fact, that no one wanted to leave the courthouse for some time. When they did leave it was to witness their demolished homes, and cope with the horror of dead and injured neighbors.

References for Further Study

Eagleman, J. R. 1983. *Severe and Unusual Weather*. New York: Van Nostrand Reinhold.

Simpson, R., ed. 2003. *Hurricane: Coping with disaster*. Washington, D.C.: American Geophysical Union.

Whipple, A. B. C. 1980. *Storms*. Amsterdam: Time-Life Books.

31

Georgia/South Carolina hurricane

August 1881

The hurricane made landfall at Ossabaw Island

A category 2 hurricane struck the coastal and interior areas of Georgia and South Carolina. Damage was greatest in Georgia where the majority of those killed had lived

In August of 1881, a category 2 hurricane struck the coastal and interior areas of South Carolina and Georgia, in and around Savannah. The hurricane made landfall on Ossabaw Island so it has been named Georgia/South Carolina rather than South Carolina/Georgia to indicate the dominance of damage in Georgia where most of the seven hundred people who were killed by the hurricane had lived. This particular storm was somewhat overlooked in records of the time, probably because it was limited in its lateral coverage. However, very low pressures were recorded in Savannah at the hurricane's peak and one instrument for measuring wind speed was blown away at 80 mph. Based on modern storm surge predictions, a category 2 storm that made landfall at the time of high tide would have inundated large portions of Isle of Hope. The Georgia/South Carolina storm was an example of the worst possible outcome from a category 2 event. After landfall it turned sharply toward the west and died out over northwestern Mississippi on August 29.

Hurricanes that strike Georgia and the Carolinas usually originate in the Atlantic Ocean east of the Bahamas. Many hurricanes that track north of the Greater Antilles eventually threaten this portion of the southeastern United States. Periodically, storms in the eastern Gulf of Mexico pass over the Florida peninsula and move up the Atlantic coast toward the Carolinas. Cold fronts that sit over the subtropical waters off the southeast coast have, on occasion, formed into hurricanes. Many of the largest and most intense tropical cyclones that strike the southeastern United States have long tracks covering thousands of miles. Numerous powerful hurricanes reached the Carolinas in the decades after 1881. Georgia, however, despite its earlier experience of several powerful hurricanes prior to 1881, has been largely free of major hurricanes for most of the twentieth century.

References for Further Study

Barnes, Jay. 1998. *North Carolina' s Hurricane History* Chapel Hill: University of North Caroline Press.

Barnes, Jay. 1998. *Florida' s Hurricane History* Chapel Hill: University of North Carolina Press.

Nalivkin, D. V. 1983. *Hurricanes, Storms, and Tornadoes.* Rotterdam: Balkema.

Tannehill, Ivan Ray. 1956. *Hurricanes: Their Nature and History.* Princeton: Princeton University Press.

32

Haiphong, Vietnam, typhoon

September 15, 1881
Haiphong, Vietnam

A monstrous typhoon struck Haiphong, Vietnam, killing 300,000. Haiphong, poorly prepared in 1881 for typhoons, was devastated

Haiphong, Vietnam, in the Gulf of Tonkin, lies directly in one of the most frequently used paths for those Pacific typhoons that originate in and around the Philippines and reach the Asian mainland through the Gulf of Tonkin. The typhoon that arrived on September 15, 1881, was very powerful and it devastated Haiphong and the surrounding coastal area. Three hundred thousand died. Little is known of the social and environmental conditions there at that time. It seems that no protective barriers were in place to protect people against a typhoon. Even today it is often difficult to protect people and buildings. Admiral William Halsey, commanding the U.S. Fleet during World War II, discovered something of the power of these storms when he found his ships caught in one. Seven hundred and eighty men were killed, three destroyers sunk, and more than a hundred aircraft lost. The storm had been more destructive than many of his encounters with enemy fleets.

Long before the typhoon of 1881, the Japanese, like Admiral Halsey, discovered the power of typhoons. In 1281, a Mongol fleet attempted to invade Japan but the ships were destroyed by a typhoon. The event was immortalized in the Japanese word "kamikaze," meaning divine wind, and later in the suicides of the kamikaze pilots of World War II. Haiphong, Vietnam, is located in the delta of the Red River, approximately sixty miles from Hanoi, the Vietnamese capital. Haiphong is the main seaport for the northern region of the country and has, for centuries, been one of Vietnam's principal trading centers. Earlier in the nineteenth century, when Vietnam became a colony of France, the city was France's main naval base in Indochina. After

World War II, when Vietnam attempted to regain its independence, Haiphong was the site of the first military action undertaken by the French. Later, during the Vietnam War of the mid-twentieth century, Haiphong was subjected to heavy bombing by the United States due to its status as country's major port. After the war, the city was built up as a major industrial center and years later, early in the morning of September 27, 2005, Haiphong was struck once again by a strong Pacific typhoon.

Aware that the 2005 typhoon was approaching, preparations were made on the previous day to provide shelter from the storm by moving 2,000 people to areas away from the coast and giving them supplies of food and water that would suffice for several days. Dikes near the coast, built some years earlier to minimize the effects of storm surges of water, were already in place. The typhoon began as a tropical storm in the Philippine Sea east of the Philippines on the twentieth of September, 2005 but, as it passed over Luzon and moved into the warm waters of the South China Sea, it became a typhoon. The typhoon crossed over Hainan Island on the twenty-fifth of September and reached the coast of Vietnam early on the twenty-seventh with sustained winds of 100 mph. Chinese and Vietnamese authorities had been watching the approach of this typhoon with much concern and it turned out to be the worst typhoon they had experienced in several decades as its winds caused widespread flooding and destruction along the coast. Ultimately, the 2005 typhoon caused more than 150 deaths, almost half of them in Haiphong, before it moved on westward into China.

Vietnam's deputy prime minister, accompanied by representatives of various government departments, spent most of September 27 on tours of the city assessing the damage. They discovered that the Maritime Search and Rescue Center was rendered helpless as a major dike protecting it had collapsed under the typhoon. The Center's inability to rescue the people overwhelmed by storm surge may account for the high death toll. Elsewhere on the coast and throughout the city the deputy prime minister and his representatives encountered a scene of almost complete destruction. Within a few days, the government of Vietnam issued a worldwide appeal for help, asking for the equivalent of US$1 million in cash, goods, or on-site help. The appeal said that five thousand families, involving 25,000 people, needed both immediate and long-term care, the latter for at least twelve months. The government added that it had already contributed from its disaster emergency fund one quarter of the amount requested in order to begin the restoration work.

References for Further Study

Bunbury, B. 1994. *Cyclone Tracy: Picking Up the Pieces Twenty Years after Cyclone Tracy*. South Freemantle: Freemantle Arts Centre Press.

Holthouse, H. 1986. *A Century of Cyclonic Destruction*. Sydney: Angus and Robertson.

McGuire, Bill. 1999. *Apocalypse*. London, UK: Cassell.

Unesco. 1955. *Symposium on Typhoons*. Tokyo: Unesco.

33

Krakatau, Indonesia, volcanic eruption

August 27, 1883

Krakatau was seen before the eruption as a small group of islands with the main part towering high above the others in the ocean between the islands of Java and Sumatra

The main part of Krakatau stood 6,000 feet above sea level before the eruption; afterward it was below sea level

In the course of the nineteenth century, Indonesia was struck by two of the most powerful volcanic eruptions it had experienced in the past 10,000 years—Tambora in 1815, in the eastern part of the country, and Krakatau in 1883, farther west between Java and Sumatra. Krakatau had one tenth of Tambora's power but, nevertheless. was sufficiently destructive to profoundly affect places all over the world. Following tremors and minor explosions during the previous night there was one massive outburst of pyroclastic material that rose more than six miles into the upper atmosphere on the morning of the twenty-seventh and at the same time swept across Indonesia, darkening the sky for as far as one could see. The explosion was followed by several tsunamis ranging in height from 40 to 120 feet. Most of the 36,000 who died were victims of the tsunami.

The Krakatau Islands in the Sunda Strait were the above sea level portions of a single volcano that had erupted more than once over the previous million years. Just before its last phase of activity, many centuries before 1883, Krakatau was a mountain that stood 6,000 feet above sea level. When it erupted in 1883 the entire top of the mountain and much of the portion below sea level disappeared and in their place was a huge four mile-wide crater, known as a caldera. The caldera was mostly below sea level and all that remained visible of Krakatau after the event in 1883 were the four Krakatau Islands, composed of the higher parts of the caldera. At the time of the 1883 eruption, because the eruption originated below sea level and was so massive, the noises of pyroclastic material mixing with water were the most powerful and long lasting experiences of all who witnessed the event. For thousands of miles from Sunda Strait, in places as far away as Australia, the sounds of explosions were heard, and in countries all over the world the atmospheric shock caused by the eruption were registered in their barometers.

Some estimate of the power of the explosion on August 27 can be seen in reports from the time. The place we now know as Indonesia was a European colonial territory in 1883, mainly a Dutch possession and to a lesser extent a British one. A Dutch warship was close to the site at the time of the eruption. As a result, the ship was carried inland for more than a mile and was left there at an elevation of thirty feet above sea level. Extensive damage was done both on land and in the sea. Towns on both sides of the Sunda Strait were completely destroyed; blocks of coral, some as heavy as 600 tons, were torn away from their locations and left on shore; and more than 5,000 boats were sunk. In Australia, four hours after the eruption, a thousand-foot-high tsunami reached almost one mile inland. On the eastern coast of India, in Calcutta, three hundred riverboats were sunk by the tsunami and, still further away at the southern tip of

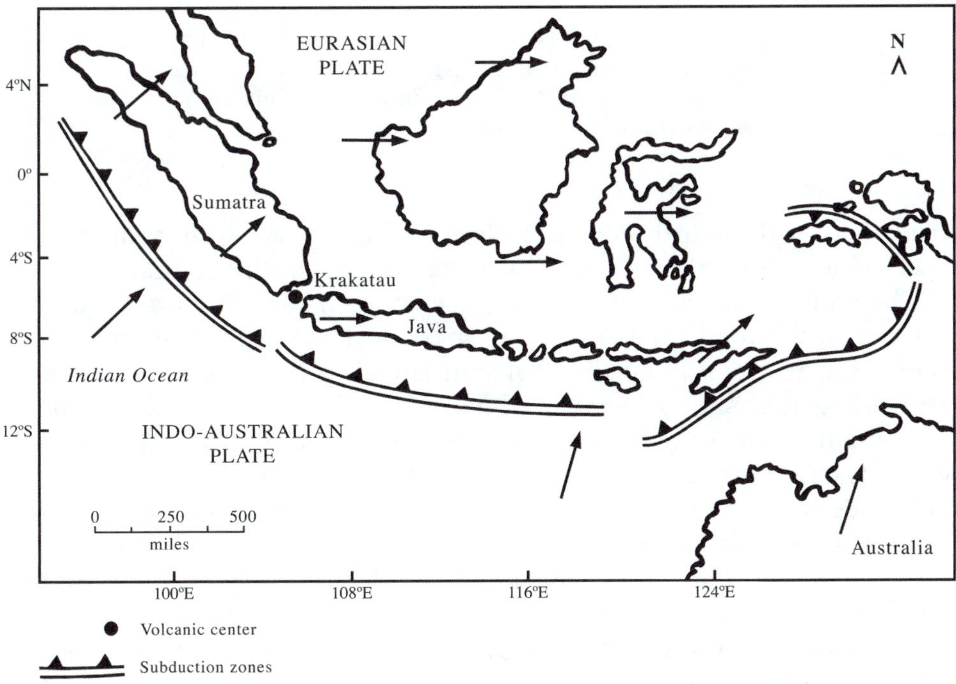

Figure 17 The site of the Krakatau eruption.

Figure 18 Krakatau is located in the Sunda Strait, between Sumatra and Java. It is famous for its devastating 1883 eruption, one of the largest in history. This drawing shows the ash cloud from the 1883 eruption.

Africa and in the North Island of New Zealand, there were some minor repercussions from this powerful wave of water from Indonesia.

The volume of material that was ejected from Krakatau on August 27 was not understood for many years, not until extensive measurements were taken in and around the Krakatau Islands about one hundred years later. Altogether six cubic miles of materials of different kinds had been thrown out by the eruption and most of that material came back to earth or sea in areas quite close to their source. So heavy was the deposit on the north side that two new islands were formed just below sea level. Coastlines were extended on both sides of Sunda Strait and the ocean around Krakatau was shallower as a result of the deposits. All of these events together gave rise to the two events that were vividly remembered by the people who lived there at the time: the explosive noises of magma and rocks at temperatures of more than 700 degrees entering water, and the tsunamis that were created by the huge displacement of water. The caldera that remained had a diameter of four miles and it was more than two hundred feet below sea level.

Fortunately for us today, detailed records of the events of 1883 were sent back to Europe soon after the eruption by the Dutch and British colonial authorities in Indonesia. Alexander Cameron, the British Consul in Batavia, now the city of Jakarta, wrote a letter to the British Prime Minister, William Gladstone, five days after the volcanic eruption. In the letter, Cameron identified what had happened as one of the greatest calamities of the century. Uppermost in his report were two things: the loud noises that were identical to artillery shells exploding, and the darkness that covered the area around him. He described the latter as a thick cloud of grey ashes that gradually reduced light from twilight conditions to total darkness by midday as the cloud moved eastward. Cameron's report went on to describe the tsunamis that followed the eruption and affected the neighboring shores of Java and Sumatra, stressing their height and speed. Details of the damage caused and the numbers of lives lost were still unknown as his report was being written because all forms of communication had been interrupted.

Others also recorded their observations. A representative of Lloyd's of London Insurance Company who was based in Batavia reported to his head office in London that all methods of communication, including roads, had been destroyed, and that the principal peak in the Krakatau Islands—which was almost 3,000 feet high—was no longer there. Other observations came from a harbor pilot whose home was in Anjer on the shore of Java and whose work was to guide ships through the Sunda Strait. The pilot was walking on the beach near his home on the afternoon of August 27 because hot volcanic fragments had been dropping from the sky all day and he was afraid that they would set his home on fire if the thatch on the roof were to be ignited. As he stood on the beach he saw a dark, black object moving toward the shore, something he had never seen before in his many years on the ocean. As the object approached he could see that it was a high wall of water. This was the first of several tsunamis that would, over the following twelve hours, cause the deaths of almost all of the 36,000 who lost their lives.

The deadly tsunamis made the Krakatau eruption different from other events of this kind elsewhere in the world. Approximately 10 percent of the world's peoples live close to volcanic sites that are either active now or potentially active in the lifetime of those living nearby. Volcanic eruptions occur somewhere in the world every year yet, over the past two centuries during which there are records of close to a hundred tsunamis that were created by volcanic eruptions, not one of them was responsible for as many deaths as were caused by Krakatau's tsunamis. The more than 150 villages in Java and Sumatra in which people were killed were not the only places destroyed by these tsunamis. Numerous small boats were sunk near shore and those in them drowned as telegraph cables were severed, and all kinds of docking and other shore installations were swept out to sea. A number of larger ships that were some distance from Sunda Strait when the eruption occurred were not affected in any way as they were still in deep water.

As soon as the scale of the disaster became known, corrective steps were taken to minimize additional damage. Warships were stationed on both north and south entrances to the Sunda Strait to stop all approaching ships. This was normally a very busy shipping area so, until the nature and extent of the changes that occurred below sea level were known, the Strait had become an unsafe waterway. On land, the damage affected both human and animal life. Agriculture, the main livelihood of almost all of the people, was suddenly and completely stopped because of the deep layer of ash everywhere. Fodder for animals was unavailable so emergency food supplies had to be found for them. Fruit and palm trees constituted a major source of wealth for the native people and they depended for food on other crops that had been destroyed. The loss of coffee and tea plantations created additional concerns among the colonial officers. These plantations were the sources of profits for the European nations concerned and the main reason for their presence in that area.

References for Further Study

Furneaux, R. 1964. *Krakatau*. Englwood Cliffs, NJ: Prentice-Hall.

Simkin, T., and Fiske, R. S. 1983. *Krakatau 1883: The Volcanic Eruption and Its Effects*. Washington, DC: Smithsonian Institution Press.

Symons, G. J., ed. 1888. *The Eruption of Krakatau and Subsequent Phenomena: Report of the Krakatau Committee of the Royal Society*. London: Trubner and Company.

Verbeek, R. D. M. 1885. *Krakatau*. Batavia, Indonesia: Government Press.

Winchester, Simon. 2003. *Krakatau*. New York: HarperCollins.

34

Charleston, South Carolina, earthquake

August 31, 1886

The epicenter located sixteen miles north of Charleston

Charleston, South Carolina, experienced the most powerful earthquake ever to strike the east coast of the United States. Because of the epicenter's closeness to the city, damage was extensive in and around Charleston and the quake was felt in places all the way from Canada to the Gulf of Mexico

Charleston was the scene of a 7.3 strength earthquake on August 31, 1886, the greatest quake to hit the east coast of the United States in historical times. More than a hundred buildings and many thousands of chimneys in the city were destroyed. About sixty people were killed. The reason for the enormous amount of damage to chimneys and the lesser destruction of buildings generally stems from an edict dating back more than forty years following a disastrous city fire. During that fire, older wooden buildings had been burned to the ground so it was mandated that, for all future construction, brick was required. Unfortunately, an inferior type of mortar was used in the construction of many of the newer buildings and, accordingly, these were the buildings that toppled in the August 31 event. This earthquake was felt all the way from Canada to the Gulf of Mexico.

Any earthquake in this part of the nation in and surrounding Charleston, South Carolina, causes damage over an area larger than that influenced by comparable quakes in the West both because of lower bedrock density and because of its location within the continental plate rather than at the area of interaction between two plates. This Charleston event was similar to three events in the eastern and central parts of the United States: the offshore earthquake in Massachusetts in 1755 and the Madrid earthquakes of 1811 and 1812. Overall, the pressures at work were similar for all three of these. The ocean crust moved westward from the Mid-Atlantic Ridge, pushing North America slowly toward Asia and, in doing so, created tensions in the continental lithosphere that caused these major earthquakes as well as numerous minor ones. Pressure from the Juan de FICA Plate as it moves crust in the opposite direction heightened these tensions, slowing the process slightly but not stopping it.

There were numerous aftershocks after the 1886 earthquake and earthquakes will occur again in or near Charleston. Of the over 400 earthquakes reported to have occurred in this area since 1774, most were aftershocks from the 1886 event. Furthermore, recent research revealed evidence of large quakes near Charleston approximately 600 and 1,300 years ago, suggesting that the frequency of these monster quakes may be of the order of every 500 years. After the 1886 quake, people reinforced their buildings with wall anchors that tied walls and roofs to the floor in order to prevent them being blown out in another earthquake. The effectiveness of these measures has yet to be tested and may not be tested in the lifetimes of

Figure 19 Derailed locomotive on Ten Mile Hill after the August 31, 1886, earthquake in Charleston, South Carolina.

Figure 20 The worst earthquake wreck in Charleston, South Carolina.

the next several generations. For the present, there needs to be a change of attitude toward the danger of earthquakes in the eastern part of the continent. The western portion of the continent tends to receive the majority of the attention when it comes to earthquakes because of the frequency and size of the events that occur in that area. Since the 1960s and the deployment of the Global Seismograph Network (GSN) which records small quakes as well as larger ones we now know that a small earthquake strikes somewhere within the regions of Appalachia and the Coastal Plains every day.

In the aftermath of the 1886 earthquake, railroad tracks buckled in a number of locations and telegraph wires were cut, leaving Charleston with no communication links to the rest of the world for a couple of days. Even then, there was no serious lack of food but the means for preparing the food that was available were inadequate since few houses escaped damage and many were totally destroyed. Much of Charleston was built on what was known as "made" land; that is, land formed by filling in existing creeks or extending shorelines with deposits of sand and rock. Older houses stood up better than newer ones because they had employed handmade bricks with a rough surface that were able to maintain a strong bond with mortar. One family that lived in an older house slept through the earthquake without knowing it had occurred. Well-built wooden homes with parts carefully pinned together withstood the shaking as well. These homes had an elastic quality enabling them to stretch under pressure and then return to their original shape.

There were two epicenters for this earthquake, one sixteen miles north of the city and the other thirteen miles to the west. The close proximity of these epicenters to Charleston accounted for so much widespread damage. Summerville, a town of about 2,000 people near the north epicenter, experienced sounds like major explosions on October 27 and 28. When the earthquake struck people in the town were tossed from side to side and frequently thrown to the ground. Houses appeared to be receiving heavy blows from below; chimneys fell down, sometimes carrying fireplaces with them as they collapsed into a heap of rubble. All indications pointed to strong vertical motion. Aftershocks gave a powerful boom sound. Ground fissures were everywhere and from some of them water was extruding, sometimes in the form of jets, at other times mixed with sand. The severity of the earthquake was felt over a much bigger area than the environs of Charleston, albeit in terms of lesser amounts of damage. For an area within eight hundred miles of the city severe shaking was experienced.

References for Further Study

Fuchs, Sir Vivian. 1977. *Forces of Nature*. London: Thames and Hudson.

Moores, E. M., ed. 1990. *Shaping the Earth: Tectonics of Continents and Oceans*. New York: W. H. Freeman.

Morrison, H. R., et al. 1981. *America' s Atlantic Isles* Washington: National Geographic Society.

Pilkey, Orrin H., et al. 1998. *North Carolina and Its Barrier Islands: Restless Ribbons of Sand*. Durham: Duke University Press.

35

Yellow River, China, flood

1887 AD

The flood occurred in Henan Province

High rain fall caused the Yellow River to overtop its banks leading to a widespread flood and the deaths of 900,000

Throughout China's history, on both of its major rivers, flooding has always been a common experience. This has been especially true on the Yellow River, locally known as the Huanghe, because of the large volume of loess silt that it carries. This kind of light silt can easily be dislodged from the side of the river and carried along by the stream. At the lower reaches of the river, where the land is relatively flat the speed of the river decreases, much of the silt is deposited. The dykes on both sides of the river were originally built to prevent river overflows that would destroy the farmlands, the only source of livelihood for the peasants who own and work the farms. From time to time, however, sudden heavy rainfall can make the river overtop these dykes and flood the neighboring farms. That is what happened in 1887 when the worst flood in Chinese history occurred. The Yellow River overtopped its dikes in Henan Province in the lower reaches of the river. Five thousand square miles were inundated. Eleven large towns and hundreds of villages were destroyed. Nine hundred thousand people died, and two million were left homeless. "River of Sorrow" is another name that has been given to the Hwanghe and it is easy to understand why.

The process by which a catastrophic flood occurs is tied to both the amount of silt and the height of the dykes. Throughout most of its history, the Huanghe was not dredged so there was always a slow buildup in the level of the river compared with the surrounding land. Earthen dykes supported by stones were built on the sides of the river and periodically raised to higher levels as the river rose so that river water was always below overtop level. Thus, in the thousands of years over which farming was carried on beside the river, the overall picture was of a river flowing along at a high level above the adjacent land. When the river overtopped its banks the damage caused was enormous because of the advantage of height. The kinetic energy in the water leaving the river enabled it to wash away large segments of the dykes. The overflow of water then continued until it reached the lowest point in the broken dykes. It took some time for the water to drop to this level and then the hard manual work of rebuilding the dykes had to be undertaken.

As a precaution against flooding, people had to watch the weather and the level of water in the river. As soon as the water level became too high, an army of people was supposed to rush to the scene and raise the level of the dykes. It was not always possible to identify the right moment to do this or to get people in place in time to do this corrective work. In the year 1887, heavy rains poured right through the latter part of summer and into September. On the twenty-eighth of that month, a major collapse of dykes took place unexpectedly and water began to spill all over the land on both sides. The province of Henan where this happened has an average elevation above sea level of six hundred feet or less, very different from the mountainous regions from which the Yellow River had come. Henan is close to the sea and close to the mouth of the Yellow River. It is often referred to as the North China Plain. Immediately after the break in the dykes the alarm was sounded and a large number of people rushed quickly to the river in the hope of repairing the breaches. Before they could reach the river, the breaks had expanded to more than 2,000 feet in length. There was little that could be done. Many of the people tried to run or walk upstream in order to reach a level above that of the flooded area, but they were caught in the fast-moving huge volume of water and drowned.

The breaches in the dykes took place near the city of Zhengzhou and, within an hour, a lake as big as Lake Ontario had formed on the adjacent plain. People from the city attempted to reach as many victims as they could by rowing around in small boats. Some of the peasants were able to reach terraces that were slightly higher than the water level and there they waited for someone to reach them. Others desperately tried to stay alive by clinging to straw barrows. The overall temperature is quite low by the end of September and on the day of the tragedy there was a strong wind that made everyone feel colder than it was. It was slow work for the small boats as they tried to go from terrace to terrace and take people to safety. Often there would be as many as a hundred families on one terrace. Some homes were still erect though under water and survivors stood on these as long as they could before either hunger or cold took over and they lost their lives. Here and there an old tall tree was standing and people of all ages were seen clinging to branches in the hope that help would arrive. One family, knowing that it had no chance of surviving, placed a baby on top of a chest along with some food and a piece of paper with its name, and this chest stayed afloat long enough for the child to be rescued.

There was very little organization or resources for the rescue work. Foreign missionary societies shared their meager food supplies with survivors but their food supplies did little for the starving thousands. One report described the situation as thousands of people all around, stunned and hungry, crying out for food. Efforts by individuals and government agencies continued unabated all through the winter months. It took a lot of time because there was so little organization in China at that time for dealing with emergencies. When the water finally stopped residents saw a plain on which there lay a heap of loess mud about eight feet deep. As it dried out, the whole region looked like the Sahara Desert rather than the green fertile plain that was there a few days before. People unfamiliar with life around the Yellow River often wonder why peasants insist on living and working in such dangerous areas. The same people also wonder why peasants live and work very close to volcanoes. The answer in both instances is the same: it is near volcanoes that the best soils for farming are found.

The cleanup of the farm fields and the rebuilding of the dykes had to be undertaken immediately despite the approaching cold weather of winter. Farm work in this part of China is a year round activity. Furthermore, the danger of a new flood would increase once the warmer weather of the following year came around. Every person was familiar with the routine for dyke repair. Thousands of tons of earth had to be moved in wheelbarrows and, in the process of both removing the mud from their farms and rebuilding the dykes, almost all of it had to be passed from place to place by hand buckets. The stones needed for the work had to be carried in ox carts from places as far away as a hundred miles.

Thousands of feet of damaged dyke were subject to constant crumbling and when wet the silt facing was slippery. From the top of the dyke the river may be forty feet below, so it is easy to imagine the amount of work that had to be done to build up the dyke to prevent any further breaches. It was a common experience for workers to see their fellow laborers lose their footing and fall to their death in the river. It was not until the early part of 1889 that the dykes were finally closed. By that time the spread of disease had added its troubles to all that had been experienced from the flood and the famine.

In ancient times, dykes would often be deliberately broken in order to flood the fields of an attacking enemy but no one was prepared for the use of that same technique in the twentieth century. In the 1930s, years before World War II began, China was invaded by Japanese soldiers in flagrant violation of international agreements and by 1938 had captured and destroyed large areas of the country. In June of that year, a large part of the Japanese army was about to march westward across the North China Plain, a few miles south of the Yellow River, in order to capture a major railway juncture. The Chinese government of that time decided that its only hope of survival was to use the age-old method of breaking the dykes. This they did and it certainly stopped the Japanese advance, but there were terrible unexpected consequences from its action. The Yellow River flooded an area of about nine thousand square miles and drowned half a million Chinese peasants. Millions of others were left homeless. The plain remained flooded until the end of World War II and the surrender of Japan, seven years later. In 1947, with help from the United Nations, China returned the Yellow River to its former channel and two million acres of farmland was once again in productive use.

References for Further Study

Czaya. E. 1983. *Rivers of the World*. Cambridge: Cambridge University Press.
Sinclair, Kevin. 2000. *The Yellow River*. Brook Vale, NSW: Child and Associates.
Tungsheng, Liu. 1985. *Loess in China*. Beijing: China Ocean Press.

36

Johnstown, Pennsylvania, flood

May 31, 1889

A dam above and north of Johnstown

The town of Johnstown, Pennsylvania, was devastated by the nation's worst flood. Poor maintenance had allowed a dam built high above Johnstown to give way and flood the town

On May 31, 1889, the town of Johnstown, Pennsylvania, population 30,000, was devastated by the worst flood in the nation's history. Over 2,200 died and many others were homeless. A small lake, about four hundred feet higher than the elevation of Johnstown, once used to supply the old Pennsylvania canals, had been purchased by a private group, The Hunting and Fishing Club, and they had enlarged it, raising its dam to a height of one hundred feet. This club failed to give attention to the old sluiceways at the bottom of the dam so that, as heavy rain raised the water level in the lake, the only escape route for water was over the top and the dam had never been designed to restrain the weight of water at that level. On May 31, 1889, heavy rains raised the lake level to the top of the dam. Leaks began to appear in several places and within a short time the whole dam collapsed. The waters of the entire three-square-mile lake thundered down the valley to Johnstown.

Johnstown was a steel-company town in 1899, a growing and industrious community known for the quality of its steel. Founded in 1794, Johnstown prospered with the building of the Pennsylvania Mainline Canal in 1834 and still more with the arrival of the Pennsylvania Railroad and the chartering of the Cambria Iron Company in the 1850s. There was one drawback to living in the city—Johnstown had been built on a flood plain at the fork of the Conemaugh and Stony Creek rivers. Because the growing city had narrowed the river to gain building space, heavy rainfall quickly raised the river's water level, frequently flooding parts of the town. Fourteen miles up the Conemaugh River, Lake Conemaugh, at an elevation of four hundred feet above Johnstown, with a poorly maintained dam, was a constant source of concern to the people farther down the valley. Every spring, as heavier rain arrived, there was talk that it might not hold back the water, especially if its level rose very high.

At 4:00 P.M. on the wet afternoon of May 31, 1889, the inhabitants heard a low rumble that grew to a roar like thunder. Some knew immediately what had happened. After a night of heavy rain, the South Fork Dam had finally broken, sending sixteen million tons of water crashing down the narrow valley. Boiling with huge chunks of debris, the wall of floodwater grew at times to sixty feet high, tearing downhill at 40 mph, leveling everything in its path. Thousands of people desperately tried to escape the wave. Those caught by it were swept up in a torrent of oily, muddy water, surrounded by tons of grinding debris, which crushed some while providing rafts for others. Many became helplessly entangled in miles of barbed wire. There were no telephones or anything similar beyond the telegraph stations at different locations to warn the people of Johnstown of the approaching deluge.

A young civil engineer who was the first to see the impending break in the South Fork Dam rode his horse as fast as he could down the valley shouting, "The dam is breaking, run for your lives." At South Fork Station he stopped to send a telegraph message to Johnstown, ten miles down the valley. Some paid attention to his cry, most ignored him. He lost his life

Figure 21 Wreck of the Iron Bridge at Williamsport, Pennsylvania, after the Johnstown flood.

as he crossed a railway bridge below Johnstown and was caught in a wall of water and debris as the bridge collapsed. It was all over in ten minutes, but for some the worst was still yet to come. As darkness fell, thousands were huddled in attics, others were floating on the debris, and many more had been swept downstream to the old Stone Bridge at the junction of the rivers. Piled up against the arches, much of the debris caught fire, entrapping forever eighty people who had survived the initial flood wave.

Floods are familiar events in most parts of the world and they most frequently occur when humans compete for the use of flood plains. The natural function of a flood plain is to carry away excess water when there is a flood. Our failure to recognize this fundamental fact has led to extensive development on flood plains, without adequate attention being paid to the behavior of water, and hence an increase in floods. Because these places are ideal locations for agriculture, there are good reasons for living and farming there. In this book and in the second volume, there are examples of human use of flood plains and also the disastrous consequences of inadequate planning in time of flood. One of these examples is China's terrible experience of a flood on the Yellow River in 1887. In that event, heavy rains raised the water level in the river so high that the levees were overtopped and then partly destroyed so the flood plain became a deep lake. Close to a million people lost their lives. While this example involved huge numbers of people and a large amount of land, the cause of the tragedy was exactly the same as the Johnstown one. There had not been sufficient strength in the methods used to hold back the water neither in the levees in China nor in the dam above Johnstown.

The outstanding example of flood plain problems is the Mississippi River basin. It is the largest in the world and it occupies almost half of the total surface area of coterminous United Sates. Floods have been a constant feature of this river from the beginning of historical records. For most of this time period, Mississippi's floods were considered to be local responsibilities. When the flood of 1927 occurred, killing 246 people, flooding 137,000 buildings, and leaving 700,000 people homeless, it became clear to all that national action was essential if the ravages of flood damage were to be effectively minimized. At the mouth of the Mississippi, human activity of various kinds is destroying the wetlands that would normally develop if the river were free to deposit its silt naturally. Sixty square miles of wetlands are lost annually in this area, a higher percentage that occurs on any other U.S. coastal area. Yet we know now, in the aftermath of Hurricane Katrina, that these wetlands provide the first line of defense against deadly hurricanes, by both limiting the storms' access to the warm ocean water that drives them and by creating a physical barrier to the floodwaters that they generate.

Johnstown is not the only example of flooding in the U.S. caused by a dam failure. There are numerous other examples, large and small, of similar failures. Two of them are described in one of these two volumes, Buffalo Creek and Teton, each quite different from the other. The dam failure

Figure 22 The Johnstown flood and "A slightly damaged house."

in Buffalo Creek was very similar to that in Johnstown—it was the failure of a dam in a community that, like Johnstown, was dominated by a single company, a coal-mining company in Buffalo Creek. As so often happens when a single owner has complete control of the economic life of a community, there is a temptation to minimize safety precautions and maximize profits. In the case of Johnstown various officials provided ample warning that the dam posed a great risk to the whole community and external, objective advice was needed to assess that risk. In spite of these recommendations the Cambria Iron Company decided to assess the risk, concluding that the dam was safe. No one seemed to be able to insist on a second opinion. The Teton Dam was quite a different story. It was a public corporation set up to access the water supplies of a region to provide both flood control and, at the same time, supply water for irrigation. The disaster that occurred was caused by technical errors on the part of the geological engineers who designed the dam.

Once the dam collapsed and the wall of water and debris started moving down the valley toward Johnstown there was little that anyone could do to save lives. The only communications possible were shouts of warning. Within twenty minutes of the dam's collapse it was all over. Men, women, and children had been carried along to their deaths in a tornado of water and debris, frantically shrieking for help. The speed of the flow of water and materials made it impossible to rescue anyone and the aftermath was painful in every way. Recriminations soon appeared. Why was the water level in the dam allowed to rise so high? Even as late as May 30, action could have been taken to release large quantities of water from the dam. The most urgent task was the burial of bodies, large numbers of them unknown by name or association. A mass funeral and mass burial was arranged but there were no pallbearers. Ox teams and carts, each cart carrying six burial boxes, brought the bodies to a mass grave. There were memories of the final day recounted many times, stories of heroes and of villains as is always the case in such situations.

In the offices of the Cambria Iron Company, south of Johnstown, an assistant cashier noticed that the water had reached as far as the second floor where he was and where the money for the workers was kept in a safe. The dam had not yet collapsed but the numerous leaks had already turned the river into a torrent that was steadily rising higher and higher. The cashier took the money from the safe—it was in packages of bills, altogether amounting to 12,000 dollars—and climbed to the next floor and within a short time went on to the roof, the only place that was still above water. Moments later the entire office building disintegrated and he jumped on to a house that was floating past. This temporary spot carried him downstream and, fortunately, the house got stuck for a time against a bank. He managed to clamber his way on to land and then found his way into the woods where he hid for the night in order to safeguard the money. There were other memories too from the days immediately following the tragedy. Memories that people would like to forget but cannot. Some young men came from Pittsburgh, fifty miles away, to observe the scene, found some barrels of whisky and in a state of intoxication began to rifle the dead bodies. Rings, clothing, jewelery, and anything else that might have value were stolen.

The telegraph line was the only form of communication with other places at this time, so the telegraph operator was always a vital part of efforts at saving people. Some telegraph lines had been swept away by the flood and later partly reconnected by volunteers who strung wires across trees wherever they could. As had happened elsewhere in similar situations, the importance of the telegraph connection was so important that operators often stood there until it was too late to escape. That was the story of the lady who had been telegraph operator for the Western Union Telegraph Office. She sent messages to every place that might be affected but waited too long to save her own life. In the days and weeks that followed, aid money and help of all kinds poured in from governments, businesses, and people in all walks of life. President Benjamin Harrison, who had been sworn in as president in the same year as the flood, convened a meeting of eminent citizens to plan relief. He also sent a gift of money as a personal contribution to the community.

References for Further Study

Johnson, Willis, Fletcher. 1889. *History of the Johnstown Flood*. Edgewood: Edgewood Publishing Company.

Mayer, L., and Nash, D. 1987. *Catastrophic Flooding*. London: Allen and Unwin.

McCulloch, David Willis. 1987. *The Johnstown Flood*. Riverside, NJ: Simon and Schuster.

37

Louisville, Kentucky, tornado

March 27, 1890

The downtown area of Louisville, Kentucky

A tornado of strength 4 struck Louisville, Kentucky, killing seventy-six. The tornado's path was wider than Louisville had ever experienced. Most of the city was devastated

A tornado of strength 4 swept through the downtown section of Louisville, Kentucky, on the evening of March 27, 1890. Its path was wider than the city had ever previously experienced and because of the violence of the damage inflicted there was some doubt about categorizing it as a strength 4 storm. In all likelihood it was the main part of series of storms that arrived almost simultaneously. It gained the name of the Louisville Cyclone. All through the day air pressure kept falling but news that the tornado was imminent did not reach the city in enough time for people to take shelter. The impact on Louisville lasted only five minutes but in that time most of the city was devastated. Seventy-six people lost their lives.

Dozens of residences, businesses, large stone warehouses, the railroad station, and several churches were among the places destroyed in these five minutes. One of the most tragic sites of the storm's violence was the Falls City Hall, on West Market Street, where a local chapter of the Knights and Ladies of Honor were meeting when the storm hit. Located in the same building on the lower floor were fifty-five children and their mothers who were taking dancing lessons. The building collapsed, burying about two hundred people, forty-four of whom died. This was one of America's greatest loses to a tornado in one building. The first sign of danger was the rocking of the building. Shortly after, a window was blown from its casings and plaster began to drop from the ceiling. The floors gave way and all fell to the basement level with parts of walls and debris on top of them.

The Union depot railroad station on Seventh Street completely col-

Figure 23 Stereoscopic image of the destruction of the 1890 Louisville, Kentucky tornado.

lapsed. Some heard the large building crack. The wind struck from the south and lifted the roof from the structure, throwing it several feet away. It was estimated that some fifty people were in the station when the cyclone struck. Many were trapped and seriously injured, but fortunately no one died. A special concern was the destruction of the Waterworks stand tower, which could have resulted in cutting off the water supply to the whole city. The standpipe through which all water was forced into the reservoir was demolished; there was only enough water available to last six days. There was fear of a water famine. Special notices appeared in the newspapers for water consumers to limit their use of water to cooking and drinking.

The newspapers were full of notices for relief efforts and aid for the cyclone victims. It became a national, as well as, an international interest. Telegrams came from all over the world offering to help with whatever aid was needed. At the same time, familiar problems common to disasters worldwide surfaced; namely the activities of thieves seeking to take advantage of the disorder. The mayor and chief of police ordered the Louisville Legion to patrol the affected streets, to control the crowds and to warn looters that they would be shot on site, not arrested. The path that the tornado had taken from the south, at times on the Indiana side of the Ohio River where it caused three deaths and $150,000 worth of damage, at other times and finally on the southwest part of Louisville, was almost identical to the route taken by another tornado that hit the city in 1852.

References for Further Study

Bluestein, Howard B. 1999. *Monster storms of the Great Plains*. New York: Oxford University Press.

Church, Christopher R. 1993. *The Tornado: Its Structure, Dynamics, Prediction, and Hazards.* Washington, DC: American Geophysical Union.

Grazulis, T. P. 1993. *Significant tornadoes, 1680– 1991.* St. Johnsbury, VT: Environmental Films.

38

Japan earthquake

October 28, 1891

The epicenter was in Nobi, the provincial capital of that region

The Nobi Region north of Nagoya, Japan, was hit with an earthquake of magnitude 8. The earthquake was felt all over the island of Honshu as many buildings came down and 7,000 lost their lives

On October 28, 1891, The Nobi region of Japan, a rich agricultural area north of Nagoya, experienced an earthquake of magnitude 8. It rocked the main island of Honshu all the way from Tokyo to Osaka. Iron bridges and brick walls of buildings came tumbling down, about 7,000 people lost their lives, tens of thousands were injured, and 100,000 became homeless. Most of the destruction was in the smaller towns and agricultural hamlets. Gifu, the provincial capital of Nobi, and Ogaki, both large towns, were completely destroyed. They were very close to the epicenter. Extensive fires broke out in the city of Nagoya because pipelines and communications had been broken.

Earthquakes are familiar to the people of Japan. School drills in preparation for the next one are a regular feature of life as are also the positive, creative responses of people in all walks of life to an earthquake. Nevertheless, there are times when one arrives at critical moments in the nation's history. Old-standing attitudes appear at such times and the earthquake is explained in terms of political events or the choices made by leaders. In 1891, Japan, like the rest of the world, knew little about how earthquakes happen. It was prior to the 1991 event that Japan had come through two revolutionary changes: the Meiji Restoration, the restoring of imperial rule and moving the capital from Kyoto to Tokyo and, secondly, the establishment of new strong ties with the Western World. There was a determination to make use of the expertise of countries like the United States and Britain in order to create a modern economy and society. Students were sent to Europe and the United States to study modern science and technology, while foreign experts were hired to help in the design of factories and educational institutions. Many Japanese suggested that the quake was punishment for bad choices like these.

These thoughts about the cause of the 1891 event became evident as the details of damages were publicized. For example, news of what happened in Osaka, Nagoya, and Kobe was known before anyone was aware of the damage to rural areas. In these big cities many buildings were constructed of brick. Two large textile mills, built of brick, had collapsed in Nagoya and Osaka and the supports of a western-style steel railway bridge had given way. One newspaper focused on these details, adding that although Osaka had been severely shaken almost all of its Japanese-style houses survived. The editor concluded that it was because of their wood construction that the Japanese houses had survived. Conversely, other buildings had collapsed because they were made of brick. The newspaper went on to affirm that all the foreign-built factories were more or less destroyed. When the reports from the rural areas came in it was clear that tens of thousands of Japanese wooden homes had collapsed and burned. However, by that time, a picture had emerged of a failed, foreign, type of building, a view that persisted as Japan sought to come to terms with its new relationships with foreigners.

References for Further Study

Adams, W. ed. 1970. *Tsunamis in the Pacific Ocean*. Honolulu: East-West Center Press.

Ikeye, Motoji. 2004. *Earthquakes and Animals*. Singapore: World Scientific Publishing Company.

Milne, John. 1913. *Earthquakes*. London: Kegan Paul.

Panel on Earthquake Prediction. 1976. Washington, DC: National Academy of Sciences.

39

Imperial Valley, California, earthquake

February 23, 1892

Uncertainty persisted over the exact location of the epicenter as this area had few residents in 1892

An area close to the California–Mexico border experienced an earthquake of magnitude 7.8. Damage was caused in San Diego County and as far south as San Quentin in Baya, California

On February 23, 1892 an earthquake of magnitude 7.8 struck an area close to the California–Mexico border. The destructive power of this earthquake demolished all adobe buildings in San Diego County and did comparable damage 250 miles east of San Diego, in Arizona. South of the California border, along the Pacific Coast, major damage was reported as far south as San Quentin, Baja California, 180 miles south of the border. Aftershocks were felt all along the coast northwards to Santa Barbara and there was one report of aftershocks in Visalia, five hundred miles north of the Imperial Valley. In Ensenada, fifty miles south of the border, in Baja California, local residents declared that they had never in living memory experienced an earthquake of this strength. There were numerous aftershocks with one weather station having recorded 155 of shocks within a twenty-four hour period. Large parts of the total area affected was unoccupied by people who might have provided detailed information about the earthquake, as a result we do not have a clear indication of the epicenter's location.

References for Further Study

Bolt, Bruce A. 1982. *Inside the Earth*. San Francisco: W. H. Freeman.

Bonson, William. 1959. *The Earth Shook, The Sky Burned*. Garden City, NY: Doubleday.

Brazee, Rutlage, J, and Cloud, William K. 1957. *United States Earthquakes*. Washington, DC: U.S. Department of Commerce.

Hallam, A. 1983. *Great Geological Controversies*. Oxford: Oxford University Press.

40

Georgia/South Carolina hurricane

August 1893
The hurricane made landfall at Savannah, Georgia

A hurricane of strength 3 struck South Carolina and Georgia in 1893 killing 1,500, making it the deadliest U.S. storm prior to 1900

A category 3 hurricane, known as the "Sea Islands Hurricane," made landfall in South Carolina in August of 1893 killing 1,500 people in Georgia and South Carolina, making it the deadliest U.S. storm prior to 1900. This hurricane was born as a tropical storm in the Cape Verde Islands and became a hurricane a week later. After a second week of travel, the hurricane reached South Carolina late in August. It gained its name because of the extensive damage it caused in the Sea Islands. Many of the people on these islands decided to leave before the storm actually hit, so the death toll there was minimal. The storm gradually turned toward the north, running parallel with the coast for about one hundred miles. Landfall occurred north of Savannah, Georgia, and from there it moved up the U.S. coast until it dissipated in the colder waters of the North Atlantic.

A heavy storm surge, at times as high as sixteen feet, accompanied the hurricane during its passage along the coast and at landfall. Destruction was widespread, homes everywhere having been destroyed. About 30,000 residents were homeless as a result. The tragedy was worsened by a delay in the arrival of the American Red Cross. The Red Cross had been fully occupied with the destruction caused by an earlier hurricane and was unable to reach Savannah until early in October. Even after its arrival, further delays occurred as some staff were called away to assist with damage from yet another storm. On the Atlantic Coast, in terms of number of hurricanes, the decade of the 1990s was one of the busiest ever. Not until the 1950s was there a comparable rate of hurricanes.

Hurricanes in the Southeast United States have always come in cycles rather than in trends toward more frequent or stronger storms. The period of the 1850s to the mid 1860s was quiet, the late 1860s through the 1890s were busy, and the first decade of the 1900s was quiet. There were five hurricane seasons with at least ten hurricanes per year in the active period of the late 1860s–1890s and none in the quiet periods. Earlier work had linked these cycles of busy and quiet hurricane periods in the twentieth century to natural changes in Atlantic Ocean temperatures. Advocates of the dangers of global warming continue to support this point of view; they feel that the devastation of New Orleans in 2005 supports their position. It is not a view that is held by all experts at the U.S. Hurricane Center and some from that center point out that the tragedy of New Orleans was due to faulty levees not temperature.

References for Further Study

Barnes, Jay. 1998. *North Carolina' s Hurricane History* Chapel Hill: University of North Caroline Press.

Barnes, Jay. 1998. *Florida' s Hurricane History* Chapel Hill: University of North Carolina Press.

Nalivkin, D. V. 1983. *Hurricanes, Storms, and Tornadoes*. Rotterdam: Balkema.

Tannehill, Ivan Ray. 1956. *Hurricanes: Their Nature and History*. Princeton: Princeton University Press.

41

Louisiana hurricane

October 2, 1893
Beginning with areas southeast of New Orleans
this storm moved to the northeast over Alabama

A hurricane of strength 4 struck the area southeast of present-day New Orleans. This hurricane left behind a trail of enormous destruction, including the death of at least 2,000

On the morning of October 2, 1893, Hurricane Chenier Caminanda, with winds peaking at a speed of 135 mph, struck the area southeast of present-day New Orleans. The hurricane then curved eastward across southeast Louisiana and turned northward over Alabama. Leaving behind a trail of destruction and caused the death of 2,000. This became the second deadliest hurricane in U.S. history prior to Hurricane Katrina in 2005. Indeed, the 1893 hurricane began in the Caribbean five days before hitting land and followed a route that became familiar at the time of Katrina, first moving to the northwest and striking the Yucatan Peninsula before moving into the warmer waters of the Gulf where it gathered enough strength to become a category 4 hurricane as it reached New Orleans.

It is difficult to be precise about the causes of death during the 1893 hurricane. Throughout almost the entire nineteenth century, New Orleans suffered from yellow fever with occasional outbursts of epidemics that killed large numbers of people. The question arises whether Chenier Caminanda's destruction caused additional deaths besides those that would already have occurred from yellow fever. Overall, more than 41,000 people died in the city from yellow fever between 1817 and 1905. The number of fatalities ranged from zero, in the few years in which the plague caused no casualties, to more than a thousand in nine of the eighty-eight years during which the fever was active. The cause of the yellow fever outbreaks was quite readily identified as inadequate disposal of human waste. A city that is about at the same elevation as the sea needs a special system to dispose of the contents of home privies and, for most of the century, no plan proved to be effective. Only during the Civil War, in order to protect the soldiers, and then only for a period of three years, was waste disposal efficiently handled.

Following a serious epidemic in 1853, a city ordinance was enacted by which every home had to empty its privy when its contents reached a level of one foot below the land surface. The homeowner was required to deposit the contents into the river or the sea and, if he failed, public authorities were required to ensure that it was done. For various reasons the plan never worked. An observation by the local medical officer describes the failure in simple but tragic language. He stated that the people have a huge privy in common and the inhabitants of New Orleans live upon a dung heap. A yellow fever epidemic struck the city in 1878, much worse than that which struck in 1853. The disease started in New Orleans in July and took nearly four months to run its course through the Mississippi Valley. When it was over, the nation reported more than 100,000 cases of fever and a toll of 20,000 deaths. Particularly hard hit was New Orleans where 5,000 lost their lives.

References for Further Study

Barnes, Jay. 1998. *Florida' s Hurricane History* Chapel Hill: University of North Carolina Press.

Fitzpatrick, P. J. 1999. *Natural Disasters, Hurricanes.* Santa Barbara: ABC–CLIO.

Lee, Sally. 1993. *Hurricanes.* New York: Franklin Watts Publishing.

Simpson, R., ed. 2003. *Hurricane: Coping with Disaster.* Washington, DC: American Geophysical Union.

42

St. Louis, Missouri, tornado

May 27, 1896
In and near St. Louis

A series of tornadoes struck St. Louis and east St. Louis. Two of the tornadoes, both F4 in strength, impacted St. Louis and East St. Louis

At 6:30 P.M., May 27, 1896, two F4 tornadoes touched down near and on St. Louis, Missouri, almost simultaneously. One passed over the city and moved in a southeasterly direction, leveling entire farms in such communities as Richview and Irvington sixty miles east of St. Louis. The other, a much more powerful tornado, was the third deadliest tornado in U.S. history, responsible for the deaths of 255 people on both sides of the river before it finally petered out in East St. Louis, Illinois. People died in homes, factories, saloons, hospitals, mills, railroad yards, and churches, as the half-mile-wide swath of this killer tornado cut its way across the center of St. Louis. At least 137 people died and 300 were seriously injured. People living on shanty boats may have perished in the Mississippi River, but were not counted because their bodies were washed downstream. In east St. Louis, the swath of the tornado narrowed and, as so often happens in such circumstances, the funnel's speed and power increased. Devastation was complete and 118 people died. Two million dollars worth of damage had been done in east St. Louis.

The tornadoes did not carry away the majority of roofs and trees in most areas. Instead, tress and roofs were thrown to the ground while homes were swept away in other areas. Lafayette Park became a wasteland of stripped trees and stumps. One record of barometric pressure was retained.

Photo by Strauss.
ANCHOR HALL, JEFFERSON AND PARK AVENUES—From what remains standing of the front, it will be seen that this was a well constructed 4-story heavy structure. One side was comptetely blown in, killing several people; the roof was removed, and the number of stories reduced to two.

Figure 24 Anchor Hall, Jefferson and Park Avenues. In: "Photographic Views of the Great Cyclone at St. Louis, May 27, 1896."

It stood at 26.74 inches, a rare level of low pressure and a clear definition of the power of the tornado. A bridge across the Mississippi that had been built as tornado proof in the aftermath of earlier tornadoes was covered with iron plate, with a thickness of five-sixteenth of an inch. The tornado pierced the bridge with a two by ten inch white pine plank. The plank did not weaken the strength of the bridge but it illustrated the ability of a powerful tornado to generate missiles. On every side lay the bodies of dead horses, overturned heavy freight cars that had been lifted from their tracks in their entirety and hurled yards away, frequently plunging down embankments and landing upside down.

By the water's edge are the battered steamboats, thrown high and dry upon the shore. Many steamboats went to the bottom of the river. One agency estimated the property loss at $50,000,000. This loss is as complete and thorough as though its equivalent in money had been thrown into the ocean, for there was so little tornado insurance carried in the city that its total barely covered a small fraction of the losses. A fund of $15,000 for the immediate relief of the homeless was quickly raised on the floor of the Merchant's Exchange and this sum could have been increased to $100,000 if necessary. Congressman Joy introduced a resolution in Congress, arranging for the use of army tents for those who were homeless.

Photo by Strauss.
BROADWAY AND SOULARD STREETS.—This was a case of utter annihilation. Buildings were literally brought to the ground, and those within hem had no possibility of escape. At the corner itself, nothing but wreckage remained and the adjoining houses were badly dismantled.

Figure 25 Broadway and Soulard Streets. In: "Photographic Views of the Great Cyclone at St. Louis, May 27, 1896."

President Cleveland promised to sign the resolution. Conditions in east St. Louis were worse than in St. Louis because of the greater power of the tornado as it reached that place.

References for Further Study

Bradford, Marlene. 2001. *Scanning the Skies: A History of Tornado Forecasting*. Norman: University of Oklahoma Press.

Grazulis, T. P. 1993. *Significant Tornadoes, 1680– 1991.* St. Johnsbury,VT: Environmental Films.

Lamb, H. H. 1982. *Climate, History, and the Modern World*. London: Methuen.

43

Sanriku, Japan, earthquake and tsunami

June 15, 1896

The earthquake occurred offshore from the northeast coast of Honshu Island, in the prefecture of Iwate. The epicenter was ninety miles from shore

This disaster included a powerful earthquake of magnitude 8.5, followed by a massive tsunami. It struck the northeast coast of Japan. There was little awareness of the earthquake because of its distance from shore and because of its character, but the tsunami that ensued was massive and did overwhelming damage on shore and killed 26,000 people

On June 15, 1896, an earthquake of magnitude 8.5 struck the Sanriku coast on the northeast of Honshu, Japan, in the Iwate Prefecture. Its epicenter was ninety miles offshore, near an area of very deep water known as the Japan Trench. The impact on shore was much weaker than would normally be expected from such a powerful earthquake so there was little expectation of a tsunami, even though this part of the Japanese coast experiences earthquakes frequently. Thirty-five minutes after the earthquake, the most devastating tsunami in Japan's history reached the shore at the same time as high tide. The first wave receded back out to sea and returned in a second wave five minutes later. At times the tsunami's wave reached a height of 125 feet. Everything in its path was totally devastated. Twenty-six thousand people were killed and nine thousand homes destroyed. Its epicenter on a reverse fault near the Japan Trench was the reason for the mild impact felt on shore. The earthquake lasted for five minutes and was accompanied by a slow shaking.

Many villagers were at the beach celebrating two events when the earthquake occurred: the return of soldiers from a successful war with China, the first Sino-Japanese War of 1894, and the annual Boys' Festival. Villagers observed minor shocks in the earlier part of the day, many hours before the earthquake. There were also reports of unusual phenomenon on that same day—low water levels in wells and large numbers of tunas every day. The violence of the tsunami was yet another unusual feature of the day. Usually victims in tsunami disasters die by drowning but, in the Sanriku tsunami, there was extensive damage to the bodies of victims; fractured skulls, bodies heavily scarred, and legs and arms broken. The impact of this tsunami carried across the Pacific. In Hawaii, wharves were demolished and several houses swept away. In California a 9.5 foot-high wave arrived. Unfortunately, in spite of the long history of tsunamis on this coast, very little beyond immediate humanitarian assistance was done by public authorities.

On June 16, the day following the tsunami disaster, a telegram reporting the disaster reached the Interior Ministry. After reporting to the Meiji emperor, the minister of the Interior Ministry contacted all ministries to deliver relief and rescue for the tsunami victims. The emperor delegated one person to visit the disaster site and cheer up the survivors with encouraging words. The governmental agencies dispatched inspectors and the army sent medical specialists. The military authorities also sent soldiers to secure public order, military engineers to recover bodies from the rubble, and the navy to search the water for bodies of the victims. The Japanese Red Cross Society and the Nurse Association sent doctors and nurses to treat the injured. However, it took a further thirty years before action was taken on detailed preventive measures.

In 1937, another very strong tsunami hit the coast of Sanriku. This time the local authorities were better prepared for it. They had installed tidal embankments, trees, and escape roads. They also prepared a booklet on precautions for preventing a disaster. This booklet included a warning about weak earthquake shocks, the kind of event that was so much misunderstood in 1896. At the same time it pointed out that a loud noise like thunder might indicate an approaching tsunami. Other things listed in the booklet included avoiding the recession of the tsunami's first wave and being prepared to evacuate the coast quickly and move to higher ground.

References for Further Study

Adams, W., ed. 1970. *Tsunamis in the Pacific Ocean*. Honolulu: East-West Center Press.

Eiby, G. 1980. *Earthquakes*. Auckland, New Zealand: Heineman.

Satake, Kenji, ed. 2005. *Tsunamis*. Dordrecht, Netherlands: Springer.

Smith, F. 1973. *The Seas in Motion*. New York: Crowell.

Yeats, R., et al. 1993. *The Geology of Earthquakes*. New York: W. H. Freeman.

44

Assam, India, earthquake

June 12, 1897

The area we now know as Bangladesh experienced the main force of the quake

A violent earthquake of magnitude 8.7 struck northeast India in 1897. Destruction was massive all over northeast India and 6,000 people lost their lives

The Assam earthquake of June 12, 1897 was a violent 8.7 in magnitude and reduced to rubble all buildings within an area equal in size to several New England states. Reports from north, south, and west of India all told of the earthquake having been felt in these places. Dacca, south of Assam, and now the capital of Bangladesh, experienced the largest number of deaths. In all, 6,000 people lost their lives and fifty miles of railway track were completely destroyed. In Darjeeling in the far northwest of Assam, the tea industry was destroyed, including both buildings and crops. The eastern Bengal railway line was closed down due to several bridges having collapsed. The weather added additional hardship. Temperatures were 120 degrees in the shade and rain was heavy as the monsoon was just beginning. Cherrapunji, the world's wettest place, is in Assam. It has an average of 450 inches of rain every year and in some years it is much more.

A lady living in a tea garden in Assam wrote to her friends in Britain a day after the disaster. The letter arrived several weeks later and gives a good picture of the devastation caused by the quake and also of the limited resources available at that time for coping with disasters. This lady was sitting in bed when the earthquake struck. She had been ill and was quite unable to get out of her house. The thunderous noise of the quake from below coupled with a general shaking of everything made her crawl toward the door where her native servant met her to take her free of falling objects. In her letter she told of the impossibility of standing. Her servant somehow managed to get her away from the building before it, along with everything else around, collapsed. The earthquake was described as the worst she had ever experienced or even heard about. It was raining hard as the monsoon rains had just arrived and those buildings that were still standing were swaying backwards and forwards like a ship in a bad storm. The ground too was moving in waves like those of the sea. All communications with other places had been severed; that is, there was no telegraphic link, the only direct method of communication available in 1897, so this person had no knowledge of conditions in other places. Her concluding observations included masses of debris everywhere, deep holes in roads, and an ongoing series of earth tremors, aftershocks, which lasted for the rest of the day.

Assam is a plateau, often referred to as the Shillong Plateau, Shillong being the capital city for the region. It is set in the midst of a mountainous area where elevations range from sea level to that of Mount Everest, but the Shillong Plateau is less than five hundred feet above sea level. It is well watered by the monsoon rains and its soils are rich, the gift of the Brahmaputra River, India's biggest in the eastern part of the country. The plateau rises in the Himalayas and flows through Assam at a point where it is still a thousand miles from the sea. Assam, or the Shillong Plateau, lies between several countries—China on its north, Nepal on its west, Myanmar on its east, and Bangladesh on its south. It is no surprise that Britain, as the colonial ruler of the time, was particularly interested in this part of India. Its low elevation, warm climate, and good soils made it an ideal agricultural region, able to produce large quantities of rice, the staple food of the native people and the product whose surplus could be sold to secure a profit for Britain. Tea plantations were developed there to meet the British demand for this drink and Darjeeling, in the northwest of Assam, became for a time the tea capital of the world.

The British colonial authorities were totally unprepared for a major disaster. This was evident over a hundred years earlier at the time of the Bengal famine. Furthermore, colonial powers were mainly and sometimes only concerned with how to make a profit for the home country not the welfare of their colonial subjects. It seems that by 1897 they had learned a few lessons about the importance of native rights because their behavior was in sharp contrast to their former actions. There were no public medical services, no disaster preparations, and no established social services such as food banks and emergency shelters for coping with emergencies. Anything that might help the native people who had lost their homes and were sleeping outside in the midst of the rainy season had to come from the generosity of the colonial governor. He decided to open all the government buildings that remained standing and allow the homeless to take shelter in them. At the same time he decided to donate the money planned for the Queen's celebrations to help those in need of food. A celebration in honor of the Queen's diamond jubilee had been planned for some time. This particular jubilee year, 1897, was the sixtieth anniversary of Queen Victoria's accession to the throne so it was an important occasion to recognize. Queen Victoria must have heard of these decisions because she sent a message of sympathy regarding the earthquake and congratulations on the action taken to help the natives.

It took many years of research and consultation to establish the cause of the 1897 earthquake. Nothing on this scale had ever been experienced anywhere in India. It was more than a century later that researchers from the universities of Colorado and Oxford finally arrived at certainty over the nature of the forces at work. They concluded that for the past five million years the Indian Tectonic Plate was restricted in its advance within Assam as it pushed against the Himalayas. As a result, there was a build up of pressure against the Shillong Plateau and it was the release of this pressure that caused the earthquake. Two adjacent faults, both of them about seventy miles long and located ten miles underground, slipped and triggered the earthquake. The slope of these faults was downward toward the south away from the Himalayas and they moved by as much as forty-five feet, one of the largest slips ever calculated for any earthquake anywhere. The extreme violence of the quake forced the overlying Shillong Plateau to shoot upwards by as much as fifty feet in a matter of a few seconds. Boulders, tombstones, and anything else on the surface, even people, were thrown into the air. Fortunately, an earthquake as powerful as this one only occurs once in 3,000 years.

References for Further Study

Bolt, Bruce A. 1982. *Inside the Earth*. San Francisco: W. H. Freeman.

Bolt, Bruce A. 1993. *Earthquakes and Geological Discovery*. New York: Scientific American Library.

Hallam, A. 1983. *Great Geological Controversies*. Oxford: Oxford University Press.

Motz, Lloyd, ed. 1979. *Rediscovery of the Earth*. New York: Van Nostrand Reinhold Company.

Sullivan, Walter. 1974. *Continents in Motion*. New York: McGraw-Hill.

45

Eureka, California, earthquake

April 16, 1899

Coastal area around Eureka, California.

This earthquake had a magnitude of 7 and, while extensive damage was done, there was no loss of life because few people lived here in 1899

On April 16, 1899, a magnitude 7 earthquake struck a coastal area north and south of Eureka, California. It was one of the severest ever experienced in this part of the country. In spite of the unusually long duration of the main shock–fifteen seconds–only a lumber mill in Eureka suffered damage. The reason for the low mortality was simply that few people, other than the native population, were living here at the time. Shocks were experienced along a two hundred mile coastal stretch from Crescent City, near the Oregon border, to Albion in the south.

References for Further Study

Ayre, Robert S. 1975. *Earthquake and Tsunami Hazards in the United States.* Boulder, CO: Institute of Behavioral Science.

Brazee, Rutlage J., and Cloud, William K. 1957. *United States Earthquakes.* Washington, DC: United States Department of Commerce.

Hansen, R. J., ed. 1970. *Seismic Design for Nuclear Power Plants.* Cambridge: MIT Press.

Iacopi, Robert. 1964. *Earthquake Country.* Menlo Park, CA: Lane Book Company.

46

New Richmond, Wisconsin, tornado

June 12, 1899
New Richmond, Wisconsin

An F5 tornado struck New Richmond, Wisconsin. As the tornado traveled toward New Richmond it destroyed many farms, killing in all 117 and injuring 200 others

On June 12, 1899, the New Richmond tornado of F5 level strength originated as a waterspout on Lake St. Croix, about twenty-five miles northeast of New Richmond, Wisconsin. As it became a tornado and moved southwest toward New Richmond it leveled farms on its way and killed three people in them. The tornado entered New Richmond about 4:30 P.M., shortly after a crowd of 1,000 had dispersed. The crowd had come in from surrounding areas to watch a circus that was there for the day. New Richmond had virtually all of its buildings either totally destroyed or seriously damaged as the tornado passed through the center of the community. A total of 117 people lost their lives and more than 200 were injured. The damage was estimated at $300,000. The death toll might well have been much higher had visibility been poor, as it was, the funnel cloud could be seen at a considerable distance and many were able to get to safe shelters.

The massive amount of flying debris resulted in multiple deaths in twenty-six families. Each of six families lost four of their members. The main reason for these unexpected multiple deaths was the presence of the Gollmar Brothers Circus and the large numbers of whole families that had come into New Richmond for the occasion. Schools had closed down at the end of the previous week so children were free to join the rest of their

Figure 26 A cropped view of a panoramic photograph taken after the New Richmond, Wisconsin, cyclone of June 12, 1899.

family. A 3,000 pound safe was picked up and carried for a distance equal to the length of one block. Trees and timber were thrown high into the air. The community's electrical plant and water facilities were destroyed, so fires were out of control. Many bodies found in the aftermath were burnt beyond recognition. It was impossible to tell if they had died from the tornado or from being trapped and burned alive. The damage wrought by the tornado was so complete that the town had to be rebuilt.

References for Further Study

Bluestein, Howard B. 1999. *Monster Storms of the Great Plains*. New York: Oxford University Press.

Grazulis, T. P. 2001. *The Tornado: Nature' s Ultimate Windstorm* Norman: University of Oklahoma Press.

Weems, John Edward. 1991. *The Tornado*. College Station: Texas A&M University Press.

47

Yakutat, Alaska, earthquake

September 10, 1899
Yakut region of Alaska

A series of earthquakes, all of them of magnitude 7 or more, struck the Yakut region of Alaska. The main quake had a magnitude of 8 and struck on September 10, 1899. The whole coastal area of Alaska north and south of Yakutat Bay was shaken for a distance of six hundred miles

During the month of September 1899 the region of Yakutat Bay was shaken by a series of very severe earthquakes, all of them of magnitude 7 or more. Fortunately, the number of people living in this region was very small and no one was killed. All of these events profoundly changed the topography of the area, raising the elevation of the land in places by as much as forty-seven feet, the greatest amount of displacement by an earthquake ever known in historic times. The most powerful earthquake of the series was the magnitude 8 quake that struck on the tenth of September. This earthquake was experienced as a strong shaking from Fairbanks all the way to Sitka, a distance of more than six hundred miles. The geologists who visited the area five years later found dead barnacles and other shellfish everywhere. They saw several uplifted beaches and areas of subsidence as deep as six feet. The tenth of September earthquake lasted ninety minutes and was followed by many aftershocks.

The whole southern coast of Alaska, including the Aleutian chain of islands that stretch westward as far as the International Date Line, is a 1,500-mile-long chain of volcanic activity constituting the volcanic capital of America. There are more active volcanoes or earthquakes here than in all the other United States combined, an average of one event occurs every year. The Aleutian Islands, many of them standing high above sea level, together with the mountains of the main part of Alaska, are all outcomes of millions of years of volcanic eruptions and earthquakes. The Pacific Tectonic Plate is constantly pressing against and sliding beneath the North American Plate. The contact area between these two massive plates is curved and this condition gave rise to subsidiary movements around faults, or cracks in the seabed, that force the main plates to slide past each other rather than collide. Often the sliding past type of action can be more destructive than a head-on collision. Two of these subsidiary faults, the Queen Charlotte and the Transition, especially the Transition, are the ones most involved in the earthquake of the tenth of September 1899. Their actions in causing earthquakes are not yet fully understood but it is clear from what happened that they are very important.

Yakutat Bay is a deep indentation in an otherwise unbroken concave stretch of coastline between Cross Sound and Controller Bay. Eastward of this coastline are the St. Elias and Fairweather ranges—St. Elias with heights of 18,000 and 19,500 feet respectively in Mount St. Elias and Mount Logan. These mountains do not rise directly from the sea, but are faced by a low foreland, or coastal plain, made up of glacial debris. The northwest side of Yakutat Bay is still occupied by the ice plateau of the Malaspina Glacier. On its west side, the bay is bordered by a foreland of glacial gravels which are still being deposited by streams issuing from the Malaspina and other glaciers. The changes that the earthquake effected in the glaciers included a rapid retreat of Muir Glacier, 150 miles to the southeast, and a general advance of several other glaciers near Yakutat Bay. Muir Glacier, which hundreds of travelers had visited annually up to 1899, became inaccessible to tourist vessels in that year and remained so until 1907. By 1903 the glacier had retreated by as much as three miles and, by 1907, almost eight miles. Before examining further the details of the earthquake of September 10, 1899, a short account of Alaska's earthquake history will help to set the stage.

Early reports of earthquakes in Alaska were fragmentary. The first event in this incomplete record occurred in July 1788 when a tsunami inundated the islands of Sanak and Unga and a part of the Alaska Peninsula. Overall, the record of earthquakes identifies two areas as having experienced most of the state's seismic activity—one area is the Aleutian Island Chain and the other is the coastal and inland region north and south of Yakutat Bay. From 1899 to 1969, eight earthquakes of magnitude 8 or more on the Richter Scale occurred in Alaska. Four of these caused extensive property damage and topographic changes; the other four were centered in areas with no nearby towns, and, except for being recorded by seismographs, went relatively unnoticed. The Alaskan earthquake that is outstanding in the memory of most is the Anchorage quake of 1964. It had a magnitude of more than 9 and it will be described in detail later in this book. In October of 1900 a magnitude 7.9 earthquake was felt from Yakutat Bay to Kodiak, and probably even farther westward. On Kodiak

Island chimneys were downed, and a man was thrown from his bed. The shock was probably centered in southeastern Alaska. Property damage was very moderate for such a great shock because of the low population densities in the affected areas

Andreanof Island sustained an earthquake of magnitude 8.8 in 1957 which caused very severe damage on Adak and Unimak Islands. This earthquake initiated a tsunami and its forty-foot wall of water smashed the coastline of Unimak Island. On Adak Island two bridges were destroyed and considerable damage was done to roads and docks. The tsunami caused millions of dollars of damage in Japan and Hawaii, both parts of the world that have suffered damage from Alaskan tsunamis from time to time. During the period 1899 to 1969, eight great earthquakes of magnitudes 7–7.9 occurred in Alaska. Thirteen earthquakes occurred in or near populated regions and caused minor to severe damage. On July 22, 1937, a magnitude 7.3 earthquake occurred in central Alaska, about twenty-five miles southeast of Fairbanks. It was felt over most of Alaska's interior, over an area of 300,000 square miles. About ten years later, on October 15, 1947, a magnitude 7.3 shock occurred in the same region. It was preceded by a swarm of shocks, some very minute, others violent. On April 7, 1958, a magnitude 7.3 earthquake hit central Alaska. Within a 40–50 miles radius of Huslia, cracks in lake and river ice, and many ground cracks and mudflows, were observed. The strongest shock since those of September 1899 at Yakutat hit southeastern Alaska on July 9, 1958. It was rated magnitude 7.9 on the Richter Scale.

The U.S. team of geologists who visited Yakutat Bay in 1905 came upon clear evidence of recent uplift in barnacles attached to ledges high above the reach of the present tide. They conducted detailed observations along the affected shoreline until practically every foot of its 150 miles had been examined, and evidences documented of uplift, depression, faulting, avalanches, earthquake waves, and changes in the locations of glaciers. Local native fishermen and prospectors provided detailed accounts of what had happened when the earthquake struck. For example, eight men were in the fiord portion of the Yakutat Bay inlet on the tenth of September. They had camped on the east side of the moraine-covered margin of Hubbard Glacier. They were prospectors, washing the gravels they had collected in hope of finding gold. Alaska and Yukon Territory in Canada had been the center of gold rushes a few years earlier and the findings from that time were still inspiring new seekers of gold. These men lost everything they possessed when the earthquake struck and they almost lost their lives too. For the team of geologists they provided good descriptions, as much as they could remember in the context of a terrifying experience.

As nearly as can be made out from the prospectors' descriptions, their camps were on the moraines and alluvial fans. Three men were on one side of a glacial stream and the others were on the opposite side. As is common in major earthquakes or volcanic eruptions, there are minor tremors that precede the main event. The men decided to rig up a simple device that would indicate the strengths of these tremors. In 1899 very little was known about the forces that cause earthquakes and there were no instruments suitable for measuring their strengths. All the men could do was improvise. They hung up two hunting knives in such a way that their points were touching. Any earth tremor would cause a jingle between the knives and the strength of the sound would give them some idea of the power of the tremor. These men were well acquainted with earthquakes from their experiences in Alaska and they hoped to be able to detect danger moments among the tremors and so get away to a safe place before the main quake struck. They counted fifty-two tremors in all before the big quake struck but it was difficult to identify increasing strengths in them. Their plan was a clever one; unfortunately, it failed to give them the kind of advance warning they needed.

One man was about six miles from the spot where the shore was lifted up forty-seven feet and two miles away from another spot where the shore had been uplifted seven feet. It was impossible for anyone to stand unaided as everything around was moving. Even the ground cover of alder bushes kept shaking and bending over as if they were under the influence of a strong wind. All of the enormous uplifts of shore areas began to take place early, around nine, and this was followed by a succession of further shocks that ended with the biggest shock of the day around two in the afternoon. At that time the men were sitting in their tent. As they tried to get out one of them was physically thrown over the camp stove and across the length of the tent. The other men took hold of the tent pole and held on to it for the duration of the quake. The ground below was moving like waves in the sea for the minutes it took for the earthquake to subside. Immediately, a pause occurred in the total amount of movement all around, the men then ran outside, leaving everything. They never recovered any of their possessions. As they watched they saw the Hubbard Glacier, one that measured five miles in diameter, slide out half a mile into Yakutat Bay. At the same time a lake of two acres in size and thirty feet in depth that had stood above the men broke away from its site and crashed down on the place where their camp had stood. The men were already away from the area by this time.

They had started running away from their camp as soon as there was a slight pause in the violent ground shaking. They felt that the safest place was the lowest elevation and so they had made for the shore. The collapse of the lake brought water, rocks, and debris down the mountainside but, within a short time, a tidal wave, triggered by the uplift of land, brought a wall of water twenty feet high on to the high ground, sweeping the debris from the lake back up on to the moraines. The men heard the sound of this ocean wave but by that time they had found a place of safety and they stayed there. Notching the fiord walls at various levels was a series of sea cliffs, which the waves had cut in the headlands and which, with their associated rock benches, were hoisted above sea level during the faulting.

The benches are broadest and the cliffs highest where the weaker rocks outcrop on exposed points and they are narrowest and the cliffs lowest where the more resistant strata occur. These elevated benches are not remnants of glacial marginal channels, as is proved by the barnacles and other sea forms still attached to their ledges. All in all, they form one of the most striking, obvious, and spectacular of the physiographic evidences of uplift. The amount of land created from the sea during these changes of level far exceeded the amount submerged by the sea in places where there were depressions.

In summary, these earthquakes were most severe on two dates, September 3 and 10, especially on the tenth, when there were more than fifty small shocks and two violent ones, the second of which was extremely violent and probably caused the greater part of the changes observed in and around Yakutat Bay. There were many additional shocks. The view of the geologists who visited the area within five years of the events concluded that they had no record of any other region on earth that experienced such shaking as had occurred here. The great earthquake in the afternoon of the tenth of September was concentrated in Yakutat Bay. The shock of it, though locally sharp and of world-shaking caliber, seems to have been more restricted and was observed at fewer localities in Alaska than the earlier earthquake on the same day. The volume affected by the earth movement must be great in order to shake such a wide area. During all these seismic disturbances there was no recorded loss of life and little damage to property, simply because of the sparseness of population in the shaken area and the fact that few buildings were there. Most of the buildings were low, one-story rustic cabins built loosely of heavy logs or boards. Past experience has shown that homes of this kind are well able to withstand earthquakes as they are difficult to tear apart by shaking.

References for Further Study

Ayre, Robert S. 1975. *Earthquake and Tsunami Hazards in the United States*. Boulder, CO: Institute of Behavioral Science.

Chapin, F. S., III, et al. 1991. *Arctic Ecosystems in a Changing Climate: An Ecophysiological Perspective*. San Diego: Academic Press.

Smith, Peter J. 1986. *The Earth*. New York: Macmillan.

Steinbrugge, Karl V. 1982. *Earthquakes, Volcanoes, and Tsunamis*. New York: Scandia American Group.

Verhoogen, J., et al. 1970. *The Earth*. New York: Holt, Rinehart, and Winston.

48

Galveston, Texas, hurricane

September 8, 1900
The island on which Galveston stood

The worst natural disaster before Hurricane Katrina struck Galveston in 1900. This hurricane flooded the island where Galveston was located, destroyed buildings, and caused the loss of 8,000 lives

Galveston, Texas, was the site of the worst natural disaster ever to strike the United States up to that time. On the eighth of September 1900 a hurricane with wind speeds of more than 140 mph created a twenty-foot storm surge that covered the entire island on which Galveston stood. At least 8,000 people died, more than lost their lives in any one of the Chicago Fire, the Johnstown Flood, or the San Francisco Earthquake of 1906. Thousands of buildings were destroyed. U.S. Weather Bureau forecasters believed the storm would travel northeast and affect the mid-Atlantic coast. This was based on an assumption that when storms begin to curve in a particular direction they continue on that course. Weather forecasting in 1900 was largely amateurish. Few of today's technological tools were available. Cuban forecasters disagreed with their U.S. counterparts. They were convinced that the hurricane would continue to move to the west. Unfortunately there was little cooperation between the U.S. and Cuban forecasters and the U.S. view prevailed.

Early on the Saturday morning of the eighth, the level of the ocean continued to rise despite only partly cloudy skies. Largely because of this weather condition as well as the weakness of the warnings that came in, few residents paid much attention to the threatening storm. Forecasters at the U.S. Weather Service had seen their earlier prediction fail. The storm had not reached Florida and the East Coast, and reports were coming in from stations along the Gulf Coast showing clearly that a storm was moving westward in the Gulf. The warnings that came in from the Weather Service never used the word hurricane. There was a reason for not using this term. The Director of the U.S. Weather Service in Galveston had long been convinced that Galveston would never be seriously damaged by a tropical storm. Thus, by Saturday afternoon few people had left the city across Galveston's bridges to the mainland. By the time people became fully aware of the impending disaster it was too late to attempt an escape. Throughout the afternoon and into the early evening, as the sea level rose and wind speed increased, people sought shelter in homes and large buildings.

Galveston in 1900 was a major port, about fifty miles southeast of Houston, on the northeast end of the thirty-two-mile-long Galveston Island. Highways and ferries linked the city to other places. With a population of 42,000 and an annual growth rate of 3 percent it was the most important city of Texas, just as New Orleans was for Louisiana, and it competed with Houston to gain recognition as the state's premier port. One newspaper called it the New York of the Gulf. However, it was a city on an island where the average elevation of the land was five feet above sea level, only slightly higher than New Orleans. Furthermore, the coastal area offshore to the south of Galveston is shallow for a great distance and the water is therefore warmer than in deep water. As the hurricane neared landfall it was greatly strengthened by this warm water. Of even greater importance to the citizens of Galveston on this Saturday in the year 1900 was the fact that a storm had hit the island about sixty years earlier, totally submerging it to such a degree that ships were able to sail across it.

The twenty-foot storm surge of water that swept over the island in the evening of the eighth of September, fifteen feet above the elevation of the land, leveled everything in its path with wind, waves, and the debris it collected. Houses on the waterfront were the first to go and, as they disintegrated, their timbers became flying missiles that were lethal for anyone in their path and weapons of destruction against any structures farther inland that were still standing. Very few buildings survived this onslaught. No one thought that the hurricane would be so violent because no one had given the city any indication of its strength. All telegraph communication between the island and the mainland had been cut off by mid-afternoon. A ship at sea close to Galveston was battered by the storm and almost unable to stay afloat. It recorded a very low level of air pressure, only slightly higher than 28.47 inches, the one registered at Galveston during the storm. This ship had no means of transmitting this valuable information to shore, always an accurate indication of a storm's strength, because the techniques of wireless that had been invented in the late 1990s were not yet installed in ships.

Isaac Cline was the U.S. Weather Bureau's director in Galveston, the person who had said, nine years earlier, that it was absurd to imagine that his city would ever be seriously damaged by a storm. As the city was being destroyed he gathered his family and forty-five others around him within his house. Shortly afterward the house collapsed. Cline, his brother, and three others were among the eighteen of the fifty who survived by clinging to pieces of debris. Most of those who died had drowned or been crushed as the waves pounded the debris that had been their homes hours earlier. Many survived the storm itself, but died after being trapped for several days under the wreckage of the city. Rescuers were unable to reach them. On the mainland on the other side of Galveston Bay no news of the disaster reached the rest of the country for two days until one of the few ships that survived the storm sailed into Galveston Bay. Messages were sent to the State Governor Joseph Sayers and the U.S. President William McKinley.

The bodies were so numerous that arrangements for individual burials

Figure 27 Lucas Terrace under which fifty-one people were buried during the Galveston, Texas, hurricane of 1900.

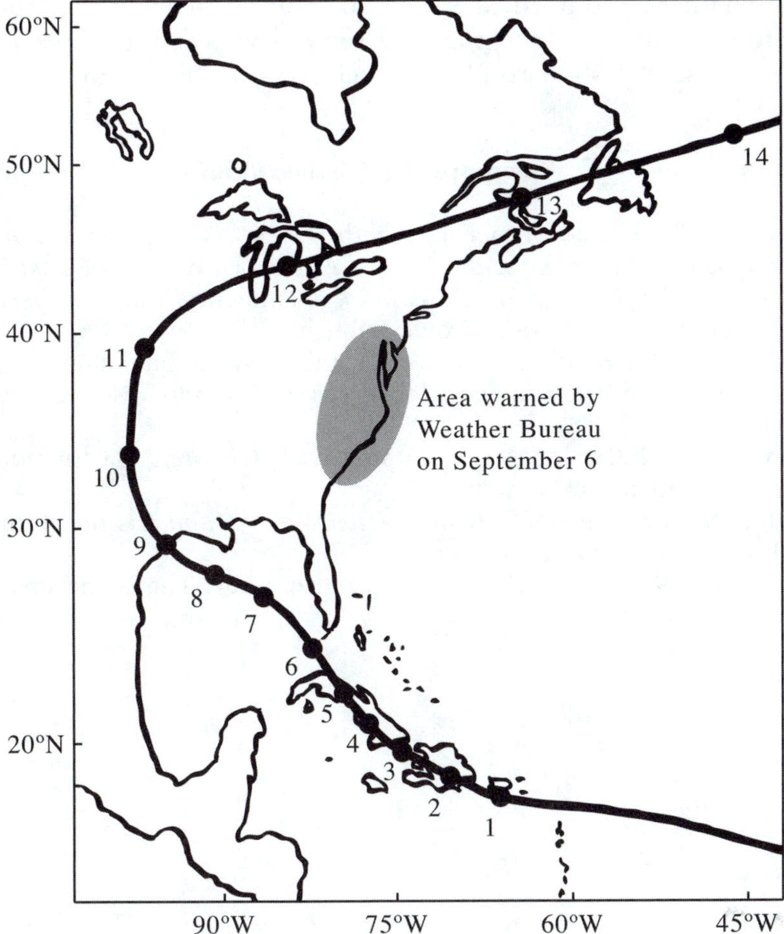

Figure 28 The path taken by the Galveston hurricane of 1900.

were impossible. Funeral pyres were set up wherever the dead were found. These pyres burned for weeks. Survivors set up temporary shelters in surplus U.S. Army tents along the shore. Others constructed lumber homes from the debris. Within four days, basic water service was restored and Western Union began providing minimal telegraph service. Within three weeks, cotton was again being shipped out of the port. Reconstruction work began almost immediately. A massive seventeen-foot seawall was built along the entire Gulf side of the city, extending along the coast for eight miles. The most extraordinary effort of reconstruction was the raising of the level of the city. Dredged sand was used to accomplish this feat, bringing the whole city to a height of seventeen feet above sea level. Many buildings, including St. Patrick's Church, were restored to their places in the city, now at the new elevation. In the year 2001, the American Society of Civil Engineers honored the reconstruction work by naming it a National Historical Civil Engineering Landmark. In 1915, a hurricane of the same strength as the hurricane of 1900 struck Galveston. It brought a twelve-foot storm surge and the new seawall was able to repel it. Two hundred and seventy-five people lost their lives in this storm.

References for Further Study

Bixel, Patricia Bellis, and Turner, Elizabeth Hayes. 2000. *Galveston and The 1900 Storm: Catastrophe and Catalyst*. Austin: University of Texas Press.

Larson, Erik. 1999. *Isaac' s Storm: A Man, a Time, and the Deadliest Hurricane in History*. New York: Crown Publishers.

Lee, Sally. 1993. *Hurricanes*. New York: Franklin Watts Publishing.

Nalivkin, D. V. 1983. *Hurricanes, Storms, and Tornadoes*. Rotterdam: Balkema.

Simpson, R., ed. 2003. *Hurricane: Coping with Disaster*. Washington, DC: American Geophysical Union.

Tannehill, Ivan Ray. 1956. *Hurricanes: Their Nature and History*. Princeton: Princeton University Press.

Tucker, Terry. 1995. *Beware the Hurricane*. Bermuda: The Island Press Limited.

49

Cook Inlet, Alaska, earthquake

December 31, 1901
Cokk Inlet reaches inland 180 miles from the Gulf of Alaska to Anchorage

Earthquakes are frequent in Alaska but less frequent in magnitudes over 7. This 1901, magnitude 7.1, earthquake was related to a volcano nearby that erupted frequently. The earthquake caused widespread destruction and triggered a tsunami but, because there were so few people living in the area in 1901, there was no record of casualties

On the morning of December 31, 1901, a 7.1 magnitude earthquake shook Cook Inlet in Alaska. The quake was accompanied or followed soon after by several tsunamis, all of them created by the Augustine stratovolcano on the Island of Augustine in Cook Inlet. It, like other stratovolcanoes, has a symmetrical, cone-shaped appearance and over the past two centuries it has erupted more frequently than any other of the many volcanoes in this southern part of Alaska where most of the state's people live. It was active in 1812, 1883, 1902, 1935, 1963, 1971, 1976, and 1986. As recently as 2006, the volcano was very active again, sending plumes of smoke and ash 30,000 feet into the air. It is hard to separate the earthquakes of Cook Inlet from the volcanic eruptions on Augustine Island. Both are so frequent that it is likely that they are interrelated. Between 1899 and 1903, the period within which the 1901 occurred, there were five earthquakes in and around Cook Inlet, each one of magnitude greater than 7, a rare thing even for Alaska.

The tsunamis that Augustine produced in 1883, a well documented event, rose as high as sixty feet in inlets like the one at Port Graham, fifty miles from Augustine on the east side of Cook Inlet. Elsewhere on the inlet, at Homer and Anchor Point seventy-five miles northeast of Augustine, deposits from earlier tsunamis were later identified at elevations of twenty-four feet above sea level. A description of the 1883 event indicated that the summit was destroyed, leaving a jagged crater at the top of the mountain. The tsunamis that accompanied the eruption completely destroyed the boats that were moored at English Bay and Port Graham and they also deluged the homes that were close to the ocean. Smoke and ash flows covered the whole area. These features were repeated again and again in the eruptions of subsequent years. Cook Inlet had become famous a hundred years earlier as the site where Captain Cook attempted to claim this part of the world for Britain. In 1778 Captain Cook sent a boat ashore on what is now Turnagain Arm with one of his lieutenants who was instructed to bury an earthen bottle with a parchment inside it on which he wrote a formal ownership claim for England of all the land drained by the waters of Cook Inlet. The bottle has never been found and this may explain why Alaska became the property of Russia until it was purchased by the United States in 1866.

During this age of exploration, the latter part of the eighteenth century, it was common for captains to make a formal act of possession when they found lands that no other country had already claimed. When Cook left England in 1776 he knew the Spanish were planning another voyage to the Northwest Coast, so he made his first claim north of where he thought the Spanish might have reached. He succeeded in getting closer to places such as Cook Inlet and Prince William Sound than any other explorer of that time. The Russians had only reached the western coastal areas of Alaska. Cook met with Russian explorers and they shared charts. Quite apart from discovering new lands there was another purpose behind Britain's desire to explore the northernmost part of the Pacific Ocean. Different European nations wanted to find an ocean passage to Asia via northern Canada. Both before Cook's time and after it different explorers had tried to find such a sea passage but none of them were any more successful than Cook. We know today that theirs was an impossible task, even in summertime, with the kinds of ships they had in the eighteenth century. Now, in the light of global warming and the increasing volume of ice that is seen to be disappearing from the Arctic Ocean, it might be a very different story if people on wooden sailing ships were to try again.

Apart from the competition among Europeans to be the first to find new lands to claim, there was very little about southern Alaska in 1901 that interested either the U.S. or Europe. The contrast between 1901 and today is as great as one could find anywhere in the world. Air travel and oil have transformed life for everyone in Alaska. A brief summary of Augustine's eruption in 1976, an event that was carefully monitored simply because, by that time, major commercial and industrial enterprises were active in southern Alaska and they needed to know the extent to which they might be harmed by Augustine's eruptions. Advance warnings of impending action came in the form of swarms of earthquakes deep down within the mountain. This was followed by six major explosive eruptions. Ash was repeatedly blasted skyward to heights of 40,000 feet, then fell back to cover an area of more than 100,000 square miles. In between the explosive episodes, ash and gas avalanches swept down gullies in the mountain's sides, often at speeds of 100 mph, to end up in Cook Inlet. The internal temperatures in these flows reached 1,000 degrees Fahrenheit. The destructive effects of the ash were felt in many places. It stripped the wax from skis, irritated eyes, especially those with contact lens, and endangered turbines, forcing industries to stop and clean their machines.

In the late 1980s before Alaska's Volcano Observatory was installed, Anchorage was being used as a refueling stop for flights between the U.S. or Europe and Asian cities. The great circle route, the shortest path between two points, happens to pass through Anchorage so more and more airlines used this city as a convenient stopover. On December 15, 1989, a Boeing 747 en route from Amsterdam, carrying 231 passengers and a crew of thirteen, began its descent into Anchorage. Another 747 had followed the same descent path only twenty minutes earlier and had landed safely. The plane from Amsterdam however ran into a cloud of ash 150 miles downwind while still at an altitude of 22,000 feet. The volcano had erupted about ninety minutes earlier. As the pilot attempted to climb out of the ash, some particles that were melted by the heat of the engines began to solidify, forming a glassy coating on the turbine blades, thus restricting air intake. All four engines shut down. For the next eight minutes the plane glided steeply, losing 12,000 feet of altitude before the pilot was able to restart the engines. He managed to get the plane back to Anchorage and land it safely. All four engines and the electrical circuits had to be replaced and all the fine ash removed. Total cost of these repairs was $80 million. Shortly after this incident new efforts were launched by the installation and constant monitoring of the Alaska Volcano Observatory to make sure, as far as was humanly possible, that an event of this kind would not happen again. There are monitoring stations now all along the volcanic arc, with special additional sites close to the main airport.

When volcanoes erupt explosively, high-speed flows of pyroclastic ash and landslides can devastate areas ten or more miles away, and huge mudflows of volcanic ash and debris can inundate valleys more than fifty miles downstream. Around island volcanoes, like Augustine in Cook Inlet, pyroclastic flows and landslides can generate tsunamis that threaten nearby coastal communities. Explosive eruptions can also produce large earthquakes. In 1912, at Katmai, fourteen quakes of magnitude 6 to 7 rocked the region, and countless smaller shocks occurred. However, the greatest hazard posed by eruptions of most Alaskan volcanoes is ash. Minor amounts can create health problems, close roads and airports, disrupt utilities, and contaminate water supplies for hundreds of miles downwind. Since it is now possible, through observation of the frequency and strength of earthquakes immediately prior to an eruption, to predict to within a few hours when the eruption will occur, people will not again be taken by surprise. To cope with the difficulty of seeing the Augustine Volcano during an eruption, seismometers were installed. These instruments can sense earthquakes caused by magma and other fluids moving beneath and within the volcano. The challenge of safe air travel is one, and perhaps the easier of the two revolutionary developments that have changed the face of Alaska in the second half of the twentieth century. The other challenge is oil. The cold northern shores of Alaska do not look like a place that once was a warm tropical environment, full of rich vegetation, but that is exactly what it once was, hundreds of millions of years ago. Oil and gas are being extracted from this area and moved by pipeline to the south coast of Alaska for onward transportation by ship.

The permafrost terrain through which the oil has to be taken is a constant challenge to the engineering skills of those involved. Equally challenging is the problem of remediation when accidents occur. The Arctic environment is fragile and the low temperatures of water ensure that pollutants remain in place for long periods of time. The oil and gas reserves for the whole petroleum province, with a concentration in and around Prudhoe Bay amounting to seventy billion barrels of oil and forty trillion cubic feet of gas, is one of the largest in the United States and represents about one-fourth of the nation's production of oil. There is a continuous flow of oil tankers, day and night, transporting oil to southern places and they have to approach land through narrow channels. As they move in and out they have to contend with unexpected masses of ice released from eruptions on volcanoes like Augustine and scattered over the neighboring ocean. In 1989, the oil tanker *Exxon Valdez* ran aground on Bligh Island in Prince William Sound, spilling ten million gallons of oil. More than 5,000 kilometers of Alaska's coastline was contaminated and all kinds of marine life were decimated. While mistakes were made in the course of navigating the ship though the Sound, the initial source of the problem was the rerouting of the ship to avoid a sudden mass of ice that had covered the normal route.

In 1912, Alaska was very sparsely populated, and there were few airplanes. Now, nearly three-quarters of a million people live in the state, and aircraft carrying more than 15,000 passengers and millions of dollars in cargo pass near Alaska's more than forty historically active volcanoes each day. The heavy ash fall produced by another eruption like the one that happened at Katmai in 1912 would bring the state's economy to a standstill and kill or injure hundreds. Clinics would be overwhelmed by people with eye, throat, and lung damage. Building ventilation systems would have to be closed to outside air. Ash entering computers, bankcard machines, and other electronic equipment would cause them to break down. Automobile, snowmobile, and boat engines would also be damaged. Airports, including Anchorage, which handles the largest amount of air cargo of any airport in the United States and is a refueling stop for many trans-Pacific flights, would be closed until runways could be cleared of ash. To avoid the ash cloud, aircraft would have to be diverted around most of Alaska, Canada, and the Northern United States, seriously disrupting national and international commerce.

References for Further Study

Cas, R. A. F., et al. 1987. *Volcanic Successions Modern and Ancient*. London: Allen and Unwin.

Chapin, F. S., III, et al. 1991. *Arctic Ecosystems in a Changing Climate: An Ecophysiological Perspective*. San Diego: Academic Press.

Fisher, R. V., et al. 1984. *Pyroclastic Rocks*. Berlin: Springer-Verlag.

Sieh, Kerry, et al. 1998. *The Earth in Turmoil*. New York: W. H. Freeman.

50

Mount Pelee volcanic eruption

May 8, 1902

Island of Martinique in the Lesser Antilles

The eruption burst out of the side of the volcano rather than from the top. As a result the cloud of pyroclastic material swept rapidly across the ground, overwhelming the city of Saint-Pierre

On May 8, 1902, Mount Pelee, a volcano on the Island of Martinique in the Lesser Antilles, Caribbean, erupted and destroyed Saint-Pierre, a city of 30,000 people that was located about four miles from the volcano. Every person in the city, with a few exceptions, was killed. A pyroclastic flow of superheated gases and fragments of volcanic material had swept rapidly along the surface of the ground instead of moving upward into the atmosphere as often happens with volcanic eruptions. In this case it seems that a mass of magma had solidified near the top of the volcano, preventing the escape of material vertically when internal pressures reached the point of eruption, thus forcing a horizontal outburst of hot lava and gases. The people of Saint-Pierre as well as those on ships in the harbor were overwhelmed by a mass of red-hot volcanic material racing toward the city at 100 mph.

Martinique, in 1902, was a colony of France with a total population of less than 50,000. Its first European occupant was Christopher Columbus in 1502 but European permanent settlement did not occur for another 133 years. In 1535, one French company took possession of the island and set up plantation for the production of cotton, tobacco, and sugar. Slavery was introduced early in the eighteenth century in order to provide sufficient labor for these plantations. Slavery was finally abolished in 1848 and today it is a self-governing overseas department of France with a population of half a million. Martinique forms part of a chain of islands in the eastern

Figure 29 Mount Pelee erupting, 1902.

Caribbean south of the Tropic of Cancer. Mount Pelee is still there, inactive, towering 4,000 feet high over Saint-Pierre, now just a village. In 1902 it was the principal city on the island, often referred to as the Paris of the West Indies, a popular tourist destination. There were plenty of warnings in 1902 of the approaching eruption. For more than a week before May 8 there had been a continuous sequence of minor explosions at the summit and numerous tremors and showers of ash that reached Saint-Pierre making breathing difficult. In addition, large numbers of red ants, centipedes, and snakes moved away from the mountain and invaded the city. Fifty people died as a result of snakebites during this time. A group of colonial officials visited the mountain four days before the eruption and declared that there was no need for an evacuation.

When the volcano actually erupted and the pyroclastic flow reached the city, thousands of barrels of rum stored in the city's warehouses exploded, sending rivers of the flaming liquid through the streets and into the sea. The flow continued to advance over the harbor to destroy twenty ships anchored offshore. The hurricane force of the blast capsized the steamship *Grappler*, and its scorching heat set ablaze the American sailing ship *Roraima*, killing most of her passengers and crew. The *Roraima* had the misfortune of arriving only a few hours before the eruption. Those on board could only watch in horror as the cloud descended on them after annihilating the city of Saint-Pierre. Two sailors managed to get overboard into the protection of water. The surface water was too hot but by staying at a deeper level as long as they could and only coming to the surface briefly for air they were able to survive until temperatures dropped to a level that would not destroy their lungs. They saw the city covered with a dark, dense cloud, from beneath which emerged a constant roar, like the noise of cannons, as homes and storage units caught fire. When the black cloud lifted for a few minutes they saw that there was another layer of cloud beneath, a yellow one, presumably sulfur gases. Later, as the temperature became bearable, they swam to shore. They found a scene of total desolation with no sign of life of any kind and no ships anywhere.

The only ship that managed to escape from the harbor on May 8 was the *Roddam*, a steam-powered vessel from England. One or two sailors were able to slip the anchor chain and allow the ship to crawl away. The captain was seriously injured and in great pain but was able to navigate his ship to port in Saint Lucia, an island fifty miles south of Martinique.

Figure 30 Reflections of ruin in the streets of Rum, St. Pierre, Martinique, French West Indies.

Those from there who came aboard the *Roddam* described its condition. A fine bluish mass of dust covered everything. It looked like cement and was five feet deep in places. It was evident that the dust had fallen all over the ship in a red-hot state, setting fire to everything that was flammable. It fell on people, burning off limbs and large pieces of flesh. Much of the latter was uncovered after debris was removed from the deck. Eighteen dead bodies lay on the deck. All the rigging, tarpaulins, and awnings had been either charred or burned. Stanchions and spars had gone overboard, skylights were smashed, and the cabins below them were filled with volcanic dust. Some of the more substantial stone buildings in Saint-Pierre, though seriously damaged by the eruption, were still erect next day, but an aftershock from Mount Pelee hit the area less than two weeks after the first one and reduced to rubble whatever remained standing. Saint-Pierre became a dead city. Fort-de-France is now the main urban center for the island.

One lucky person happened to be a prisoner when the eruption occurred. He had been sentenced to solitary confinement for a week in the prison's dungeon. On May 8, he was alone in his dungeon with only a small grated opening cut into the wall above the door. In the morning of May 8 his cell became dark and he was overcome by intense gusts of hot air mixed with ash that had entered through the grated opening. He held his breath as much as he could in spite of the intense pain of having to inhale red-hot air. Gradually the heat subsided. He was severely burned but fortunately the amount of hot air that came into his prison was far less than the amounts experienced by everyone else in Saint-Pierre. He remained in his prison for four days, managing to survive in a half-conscious state, suffering great pain and having difficulty breathing, until people found him. After he recovered, he received a pardon and eventually joined the Barnum & Bailey Circus, where he toured the world billed as the "Lone Survivor of Saint-Pierre." The saddest aspect of the whole terrible catastrophe that had struck Saint-Pierre was the appearance of looters. They came looking for money, jewels, and other valuables in the ruins. The French colonial authorities were ruthless with situations of this type. Their marines put an immediate stop to it, often shooting looters on sight when necessary.

Mount Pelee's geological setting explains the frequency of its eruptions. The Caribbean Tectonic Plate of which Martinique forms a part is being pushed upward as the North American Plate slides beneath it. This plate includes an area of the Atlantic beyond the land areas of the continent. At a rate of about an inch a year North American Plate slides westward beneath the Caribbean Plate. The magma that moves upward into Mount Pelee originated in an area between the North American Tectonia Plate and the crust near the surface of Mount Pelee. Mount Pelee first erupted about 200,000 years ago and, over the years, geologists have found eruptions emanating from it at intervals of 50–150 years. Over historic times this mountain was active in the following years: 1792, 1851, 1902, and right up to the present time. The remains of three craters are visible at the higher elevations of Pelee. The largest and oldest of these was the focus of eruptions from earliest times right up to 40,000 years ago but over the years since that time the topography of the mountain has changed considerably until by 1902 only the two smaller craters were visible. By 1898 the first signs of new activity became clear. Tragically, politics—concentrating on an upcoming election—and lack of knowledge of volcanic eruptions, contributed to the indifference that was shown by the people of Martinique to the warning signs that came before May 8.

One day before the eruption of Mount Pelee, an almost identical type of event occurred on the island of Saint Vincent, a hundred miles south of Martinique in the same chain of islands that form the Lesser Antilles. The volcanic mountain that erupted on Saint Vincent was La Soufriere. The day before the eruption there was an earthquake in the same location and many concluded that this earthquake was the trigger than initiated the eruption. Fortunately, unlike Martinique, the people of Saint Vincent had taken precautions as they saw menacing signs coming from the mountain so the death toll was much less than it would otherwise have been. As La Soufriere erupted, a red-hot ash cloud, mixed with steam and gas, swept down on the citizens in the towns below. People perished quickly from ash asphyxiation or from burns. Some escaped by going into cellars and others were able to get into the ocean before the deadly blast of volcanic material reached them. Two thousand people lost their lives. One newspaper report from that time described Saint Vincent as being covered with ashes to an average depth of eighteen inches, so that all crops were ruined and many homes had collapsed under the weight of falling ash. Five thousand destitute citizens were in need of assistance from their government.

Saint Vincent had to cope with the problem of burying those who died, a task that never arose in Martinique since the devastation was total and very little was left of the bodies of the dead. This part of the world has a very hot climate, so bodies decompose quickly. Gangs of men were organized to pick up the dead and arrange to have them buried in mass graves. It was not always possible to do this as many had taken shelter in huts and they died there. It was difficult to get each body out of these huts and there was little time available for the task before decomposition raised the danger of disease. Decisions had to be made quickly because this was a Catholic society, used to burying people in the ground, and the situation demanded incineration. Quite apart from the urgency of burying the dead there were large numbers of injured people who needed attention. The Ambulance Corps attempted to help these victims. They were in great pain, wanting a drink of water but unable to consume it because of the damage done to their faces. Almost all of them died within a short time.

Many eminent researchers visited Mount Pelee and Soufriere after the eruptions because they were interested in the exceptionally high death toll and the unusual feature of Mount Pelee's eruption emerging as a horizontal blast of volcanic substances. A new aspect of the study of volcanology began to take shape. Among the scientists there was one, Thomas Jaggar, an assistant professor of geology at MIT, who was overcome by the high death rate and the extensive level of destruction. He decided, then and there, to devote his career to studying eruptions in order to save lives and began to search for a place that would be suitable for such a research center. The quest took him to the state of Hawaii and to the Kilauea Volcano. He managed to raise funds for the establishment of a research center at the site of that volcano. He searched the world for a volcano suitable for continuous study and chose Kilauea. The entrepreneurial Jaggar raised the funds, took a leave of absence from MIT, and established the new Hawaiian Volcanic Observatory (HVO) in 1912. HVO would be dedicated to the development of monitoring tools, strategies, and knowledge. All focused on his motto for HVO, "no more shall the cities be destroyed."

References for Future Study

Fisher, R. V., et al. 1997. *Volcanoes: Crucibles of Change.* Princeton: Princeton University Press.

Francis, P. 1976. *Volcanoes.* Harmondsworth: Penguin.

Simkin, T., et al. 1981. *Volcanoes of the World.* Stroudsburg: Hutchinson Ross.

Tazieff, H., et al. 1983. *Forecasting Volcanic Events.* Amsterdam: Elsevier.

Williams, H., et al. 1979. *Volcanology.* San Francisco: Freeman, Cooper and Company.

51

Goliad, Texas, tornado

May 18, 1902

Goliad, Texas, south of San Antonio

This tornado claimed 114 lives, injured 230 others, and caused damage equal to $50,000 in 1902 dollars

The Goliad Tornado struck the town of Goliad, Texas, on May 18, 1902, touching down on the south side of the San Antonio River at 3:35 P.M. It claimed 114 lives, injured 230 people, and caused damage equal in value to $50,000 in 1902 dollars. It is considered to be one of the two most destructive tornadoes in the history of Texas, the other being the Waco strike of 1953. Of the 114 deaths, fifty were members of an African-American Methodist church who died when their church was destroyed. This tornado sounded like a heavily loaded freight train. The northwest section of the town saw an area one mile long and half a mile wide, totally wiped out and one hundred homes lost. The dead were buried in one long trench, for there was no time to dig separate graves or conduct individual funerals. Following the disaster, the Goliad County Courthouse served as a temporary hospital and morgue.

The town of Goliad is built around its courthouse a building designed by Texas architect Alfred Giles and erected in 1894. Limestone was used in the construction, hauled from Austin by oxcart. The courtyard was enlarged and restored in 1964. Along with the nineteenth and early twentieth century structures surrounding it the courthouse was entered on the National Register of Historic Places in 1976. Goliad today is primarily based on oil, agriculture, and cattle, but tourism is also a vital component. The moderate climate provides habitat for a variety of wildlife and rich grasslands for ranching. Landscape is an important historical resource, from the plants and animals that thrive there to modern day roadways that follow centuries-old trade routes. Giant oak trees dominate the land cover, traditionally used for grazing herds of cattle and horses. The San Antonio River flows through the town. On the north lawn of the courthouse there is a tree called "The Hanging Tree." At various times between 1846 and 1870, this tree served as the site of court sessions. Death sentences pronounced by the court were carried out immediately with a rope and a strong limb. During the 1857 Cart War, in which Texan freighters perpetrated a series of vicious attacks against Mexican cart drivers along the Indianola-Goliad-San Antonio Road, this site witnessed a number of unauthorized executions before the conflict was brought to an end by Texas rangers.

By the early eighteenth century, when Spanish missionaries and soldiers arrived in the mid-coastal area of Texas, they found the native peoples as long time residents of the area. The Mission Espiritu Santo was founded in 1722 to serve these native people. The site was abandoned in 1724 and the mission moved twice to places within the Indian community. Later it moved back to the original site near Goliad. Mission Espiritu Santo became the first large cattle ranch in Texas, with jurisdiction over all land between the Guadalupe and San Antonio Rivers as far north as Capote Hills near Gonzales. On this land, the mission's 40,000 or more cattle grazed. The mission continued as a mission for more than a hundred years, longer than any other Spanish colonial mission in Texas. In 1848, the Goliad City Council rebuilt its principal structures for use as public school facilities. Later it became Aranama College, the first institution in Texas established for education of Spanish-speaking Texans. The college for men lasted until the outbreak of the Civil War when the student body marched off to join the Confederate Army.

Designated a National Historic Landmark in 1967 and considered the world's finest example of a Spanish frontier fort, Presidio La Bahia had first been founded on the banks of Garcitas Creek, near Lavaca Bay. Previously owned by the Catholic Church and currently operated by the Catholic Church, the Presidio dates from its present site next to Goliad in 1749. It is the oldest fort in the western United States, and the only Texas Revolution site with its original 1836 appearance. As a permanent settlement by Spain in the early days it had been given the name La Bahia meaning "The Bay." The Spaniards used the fort as protection. Nine flags of different nations have flown over the Presidio in the course of its long history. It is the place where the first Declaration of Texas Independence was signed on December 20, 1835. The saddest page of Texas history, the Goliad Massacre, the largest single loss of life in the cause of Texas Independence, occurred here. Nine miles east of Goliad on Highway 59 is the site of the Battle of Coleto Creek. In March 1836, during the Texas Revolution, Texas troops under Colonel James Fannin surrendered here to superior Mexican forces after a day and a half of fighting. Colonel Fannin was one of the wounded individuals from the battle of Coleto Creek. He was helped out of the chapel where the prisoners and wounded had been held for a week. On Palm Sunday, March 2, 1836, the men were led out in three directions from La Bahia and massacred; the wounded were shot in the compound of the fort. The bodies were stripped and left unburied. When the shooting ended, 302 men were dead and about twenty-eight escaped. Fannin and thirty-nine other men who were wounded at the battle of Coleto Creek the week before the massacre were killed inside the Presidio, bringing the total killed to 342. A monument marks the grave of Colonel Fannin and 342 men who had surrendered to Mexican forces during the Texan Revolution and massacred at the orders of General Santa Anna.

References for Further Study

Church, Christopher R. 1993. *The Tornado: Its Structure, Dynamics, Prediction, and Hazards*. Washington, DC: American Geophysical Union.

Grazulis, T. P. 2001. *The Tornado: Nature' s Ultimate Windstorm* Norman: University of Oklahoma Press.

Weems, John Edward. 1991. *The Tornado*. College Station: Texas A&M University Press.

52

Santa Maria, Guatemala, volcanic eruption

October 24, 1902
Santa Maria, near the city of Quezaltenango in northwestern Guatemala

Santa Maria's first eruption in five hundred years exploded into action with a VEI of 6, the same size as that of Krakatau. The eruption devastated 120,000 square miles of surrounding territory and killed 5,000 people

The first eruption of Santa Maria in recorded history occurred on October 24, 1902. Before 1902 it had been dormant for at least five hundred years. The eruption, with a VEI of 6, equivalent in magnitude to both Krakatau in Indonesia in 1883 and Katmai in Alaska in 1912, was the second biggest of the twentieth century. The eruption formed a large crater on the mountain's southwest flank and blasted volcanic ash twenty miles into the atmosphere. The ash that subsequently fell devastated most of the 120,000 square miles of surrounding territory. Volcanic ash was detected as far away as San Francisco—a distance of 2,500 miles. The crater on the southwest flank was half a mile in width and a thousand feet deep. It stretched from just below the summit down to the 7,000-foot level. Because of the lack of previous activity at Santa Maria, local people failed to recognize the warning signs that arrived in the days before October 24. At least 5,000 people were killed by the eruption. Many more died from a subsequent outbreak of malaria.

The city of Quezaltenango sits below the 11,000-foot-high Santa Maria. It is the second most populous city of Guatemala and has a present population of 300,000. It is located in the Sierra Madre range of volcanoes that extend along the western part of Guatemala, separated from the Pacific Ocean by a broad plain. These volcanoes are formed by the subduction of the Cocos Plate under the Caribbean Plate. Eruptions at Santa Maria are estimated to have begun about 30,000 years ago and continued intermittingly for many thousands of years right up to the quiescent period that preceded the event of 1902. This enormous blast of ash and pyroclastic material was followed by twenty years of dormancy. Then, in 1922, a new volcanic vent formed within the existing crater, forming a new volcano. It was named Santiaguito and it has been erupting ever since and now forms a cone a thousand feet tall, reaching a height of 7,000 feet. Thus, today it is possible to climb to the top of Santa Maria and look down on the ongoing eruptions at Santiaguito, 4,000 feet below.

Dome growth at Santiaguito has alternated between growth caused by the emission of lava flows, and inflation caused by the injection of magma into the middle of the dome. Activity has been concentrated at several different vents, and Santiaguito now has the appearance of several overlapping domes.

Although most of Santiaguito's eruptive activity has been gentle, occasional larger explosions have occurred. In 1929, part of the dome collapsed, generating pyroclastic flows and killing several hundred people. Occasional rockfalls have generated smaller pyroclastic flows, and vertical eruptions of ash to heights of 2,000 feet above the dome are common. The areas to the south of Santa Maria are substantially affected by volcanic activity at Santiaguito. The most common damage comes from mudflows in the rainy season due to heavy rainfall on loose volcanic deposits. The town of El Palmar was twice destroyed by these mudflows and infrastructure such as roads and bridges have been repeatedly hit. One hazard, potentially devastating, is the possibility of the collapse of Santa Maria. The 1902 crater has left the southern flank of the mountain above Santiaguito very steep. A large earthquake or an eruption from Santiaguito could trigger a huge landslide.

In light of the threat it poses to nearby populations, Santa Maria has been designated a Decade Volcano, identifying it as a target for detailed study. Since volcanic eruptions can have additional local effects such as the disruption of air traffic by ash clouds, the unique perspective provided by views from a space shuttle or from the International Space Station (ISS) enable scientists to see not only the horizontal influence of the eruption within the atmosphere, but also the vertical effects. The ISS can plan passes over any give target two or more times daily, so that astronauts can photograph happenings many times and can coordinate with ground observers as well. Volcanic eruptions, another Dynamic Events target of Crew Earth Observations, produce aerosols that are distributed globally and influence atmospheric temperatures, cloud formation, and rainfall.

References for Further Study

Fisher, R. V., et al. 1984. *Pyroclastic Rocks*. Berlin: Springer-Verlag.

Sheets, P. D., et al. 1979. *Volcanic Activity and Human Ecology*. London: Academic Press.

Simkin, T., et al. 1981. *Volcanoes of the World*. Stroudsburg: Hutchinson Ross.

Tazieff, H., et al. 1983. *Forecasting Volcanic Events*. Amsterdam: Elsevier.

53

Turtle Mountain, Alberta, Canada, landslide

April 29, 1903

Turtle Mountain is near Coleman, Alberta, Canada

Excessive amounts of coal were removed from the mountain without adequate protection from overlying layers of rock. As a result seventy people in the small town of Frank were killed

Early in the morning of April 29, 1903, a gigantic slab of limestone rock broke away from Turtle Mountain at the 3,000-foot level. It weighed about seventy-five million tons, was half a mile wide, and as it crashed down the side of the mountain it broke apart into huge boulders. With the momentum acquired in descent this mass of rocks cut across the valley of the Old Man River at the foot of the mountain, continued up the slopes on the other side of the valley, and destroyed most of the town of Frank. Seventy of the town's residents were killed. Debris from the landslide can still be seen today.

Turtle Mountain was built up in the ancient past with sedimentary rock, mainly limestone. Geological structures of this kind are a common setting for coal deposits. Layers of coal seams are found alternating with layers of rock. In this location mining the coal was especially easy as the seams slanted downward toward the face where the mine entrance was. Gravity did most of the work, and very little blasting was needed. One thousand tons of coal was being extracted daily within the first year of operation but, despite some telltale signs, little thought was given to the effects of the work on the stability of the mountain. On any given shift seventeen miners extracted coal somewhere along a ten-foot-wide seam that, after a year, stretched back for 5,000 feet into the mountain. Early in 1903 miners

Figure 31 Results of the rock slide of 1903 at Frank, Alberta, Canada. In less than two minutes, forty million cubic yards of rock from Turtle Mountain slid along a plane of structural weakness to cover the town of Frank.

noticed, as they came to work, that some of the supporting pillars were badly splintered, pillars that had been in good shape at the end of the previous day's shift. With today's understanding of geology it is easy to explain what was happening, but that was not obvious in 1903.

The sedimentary formations of rock that constituted Turtle Mountain form a series of horizontal strata. Some of these may be coal, some limestone. Any weakening in one of these layers can trigger a slide, allowing upper layers of rock to cascade downwards along the general slope. In Turtle Mountain this slope was quite steep so any movement would be accelerated by gravity. When the landslide occurred, the mine entrance was blocked, leaving seventeen men trapped inside. Three other men who had just left the work area to take loads of coal to the entrance escaped the trap that caught the seventeen men but they were overtaken by the cascading material of the landslide and were never seen again, buried forever under tons of rock. As the reality of the event became obvious to the seventeen men inside, they ran to the mine entrance, only to find that it was now a heap of shattered timbers and fallen rock. They were now cut off from the outside world at a point three hundred feet inside the mountain. Before their lamps faded they examined their options. First they made their way to a lower level, hoping that the exit there was still open, only to find that the river had flooded that entrance and was rapidly backing up into the mine.

They realized that closures of entrances together with widespread flooding might have already cut off their supplies of fresh air. They had to act fast before their small amounts of fresh air would soon be used up. Hoping that they were sufficiently close to the surface they decided to try to cut a tunnel upwards and outwards. To remove the mass of material at the entrance was impossible. Over a period of twelve hours they worked steadily in shifts and finally came out on the face of the mountain to stare at the destruction below. The scene before their eyes was terrifying. Where their homes had been there was now a mass of white limestone rock. All but a part of the town's center was gone. The falling rock had swept across a mile of intervening ground before landing on the town of Frank. A mile-long section of double-track railway line, the main highway, and the coal-mining plant had been destroyed. Old Man River began to back up and form a lake behind the mass of rock. A freight train entering Frank at the moment of the slide was lucky enough to escape. It arrived as the landslide began to move down the mountain and it was able to speed past the town before everything crashed around it.

The rock mass that constituted the landslide was shattered by impacts against the side of the mountain as it came down. Long before it reached the valley below it had been transformed into several large boulders plus a myriad of fragments of all sizes so, in one sense, it was no longer a landslide. It began as one but ended up as something else. The different pieces of rock traveled for one or two miles from the base of the mountain over uneven ground by a series of skips and jumps until it reached the 400-foot level on the other side of the Valley of the Old Man River. There was no way of escape for the residents of Frank before the rocks reached it. The total amount of time involved was less than a minute. The history of the landslide can be read today in the indentations made on rocky surfaces by bouncing boulders as they made their way across the valley. As the mountain was examined after the event it became clear that the dislodged slab of rock had broken away along lines that were ancient fissures formed by successive faulting throughout the long history of the buildup of the mountain to its size in 1903.

One man who kept a boarding house in Frank woke up when he heard the sound of the slide and rushed to the entrance of his house. He was just in time to see the masses of rock fragments sweep past him at a distance of a few feet. Another workman who lived in one of the cottages that was destroyed woke up and, before he could do anything, was aware that his cottage was rocking backwards and forwards. The only thing he remembered after that was that he was forty feet from the house with his bed lying twenty feet farther away. His leg was broken and he had been wounded in several places by small rocks. The story was similar with many of the others who survived. In one home when a couple and their children were asleep there was no time to escape before their home was shattered and they somehow survived, albeit with numerous injuries.

The first action of both the Mining Company and the government of

Canada inspectors was the assessment of the cause of the disaster. Some accusations had already been made such as that the mining company had not provided adequate support of the higher strata, thus reducing pressure on them and so endangering their stability. The Mining Company insisted that the mine was in first class condition before the landslide and that the few instances of movements in the coal walls were normal for any mine. A senior miner pointed out that new movements of walls were observed from time to time in the six months before the landslide, each one occurring between one and three in the morning, presumably when temperatures were at their lowest. This miner described the experience of these movements as being like a ship's violent shaking when struck with a large wave and he added that they alarmed many of the workers. Some left the mine because of the shaking. Weather records were examined and it was established that the day before the landslide was warm and wet and the night that followed recorded temperatures far below anything experienced throughout the previous six months.

The weather factor, it was agreed, was one causal factor. Water expands and contracts wherever there are places that allow water in. These are all normal processes of nature that will be at work everywhere whether or not there is human intervention. Mining inevitably creates new spaces into which water can enter. In addition, even with the maximum number of supporting pillars, the removal of a thousand tons of coal daily changes the density or weight of one part of the mountain and, as was the case in the early weeks of April 1903, if there is a sudden increase in the amount of coal being removed every day, this change in the distribution of weight on he mountain accelerates the strain on its stability. The fact that the mountain was composed of a series of horizontal layers of rock and coal makes it particularly sensitive to any movement that would interfere with its stability. Since the coal seams sloped parallel to the mountain's layers there was a constant challenge facing the Mining Company to ensure that the supporting pillars were always doing their work.

The government inspectors concluded that the landslide could not be explained by a single cause. A combination of factors, acting together, led to the disaster. Nevertheless, it is difficult to get away from the conviction that the coal mining operations were the main cause, especially when it was noted, after the event, that the location of the edges of the break where the mass of rock came away from the mountain coincided exactly with the upper limit of operations of the coal workings. The coal was being removed from within huge spaces measuring more than three hundred feet in height. Loosened coal offers very little resistance to the enormous pressure from above, that is to say the pressure from the rest of the mountain, so inevitably there must have been some movement from time to time along the roof of the coal seams. The Mining Company was well aware of the reports brought back by the miners regarding the splintering of the wood pillars that supported the overhanging rock and this should have persuaded the company to install more and stronger timbers.

When coal mining resumed at Frank years later, safety features that should have been there in 1903 were firmly in place. After 1903, some people began to move away from the mountain, fearing another slide. The town did expand over the years, but there was nowhere for it to grow eastward, so the town of New Frank took root just northwest of the original town. In 1911, a Royal Commission study found the North Peak of Turtle Mountain to be structurally unstable. In reaction to this study, the government ordered everyone out of that section of Frank. People moved to other areas and many settled in New Frank, the present location of Frank. Today, the remains of the old town of Frank and the rocks that came down the mountain in 1903 form a tourist attraction. Limestone rocks in depths ranging from 5 to 100 feet litter the entire area. There is an information booth beside the highway and a number of displays that re-enact the events of more than a century earlier.

References for Further Study

Benedict, Michael, ed. 2000. *In the Face of Disaster*. Toronto: Viking.

Bird, Michael J. 1962. *The Town that Died*. Toronto: Ryerson Press.

Looker, Janet. 2000. *Disaster Canada*. Toronto: Lynx Images.

McConnell, R. G., and Brock, R. W. 2003. *Report on the Great Landslide at Frank, Alberta*.

54

Chicago, Illinois, fire

December 30, 1903
Iroquois Theater, Chicago

The theater that was claimed to be fireproof went up in flames shortly after its first opening. Of the 1,900 people in attendance six hundred lost their lives

Chicago's deadliest fire of the twentieth century occurred shortly after the opening of the new, fireproof, Iroquois Theater. On December 30, 1903, when the Iroquois Theater was packed for a holiday matinee of the popular musical "Mr. Blue Beard, Jr.," a fire suddenly broke out. The management was quite unprepared for the panic that ensued. Out of the 1,900 people in attendance, mostly women and children, six hundred lost their lives. The United States had a long history of fires, and this was not the only twentieth century urban fire, but it was a particularly tragic event. The new fire precautions had been well established and were well known. Several theaters had already implemented them. Sadly, at the Iroquois, there was indifference to two extremely important safety procedures: ways of getting people out of the building quickly and stationing firemen close to the stage with fire extinguishers and hoses ready for use. Neither of these procedures was in place on December 30.

There were firemen on duty in the theater at the time of the fire but the only firefighting equipment they had was a quantity of powder to sprinkle on a fire. The powder proved to be quite useless. When a velvet curtain ignited at the stage, an asbestos backup curtain, standard equipment in all theaters of that time, failed to drop down and contain the fire. Someone had raised the curtain higher than its usual position in order to provide a better view of the stage for those on the balcony. It got stuck in the higher position. Additionally, there were no ushers at the exits to guide people out and avoid panic. Iron gates had been installed over exit doors and some of these were locked. Those that were unlocked were difficult to open because of a lever that was unfamiliar to most patrons. The result was a combination of panic and pileup at the exits. A large number of casualties, perhaps the majority of the six hundred, were people and children who had been trampled to death at the doors or were killed when they jumped down from the balcony. The speed with which everything happened added to the rush and confusion. Canvas backdrops on stage, painted with highly inflammable oil paints and mounted in the air, had caught fire instantly and created a firestorm. It was all over in fifteen minutes.

The Cook County Coroner's Inquest documented the tragic sequence of events and came down hard on the theater's management. It listed 571 deaths and hundreds of people injured. Thirty of these latter died in the weeks that followed. The fact that the casualties were mostly women and children, and that it happened so near to Christmas, made it all the more poignant and blameworthy. It was Chicago's worst tragedy since the fire of 1871. Out of the tragedy came new, stronger regulations for theaters. New laws about fire safety were passed. Among them was the requirement that all exits had to be clearly marked and their doors so arranged that they could be pushed open from the inside. The largely undamaged Iro-

Figure 32 The stage of the Iroquois Theater, looking down from the balcony.

quois building reopened less than a year after the fire and ran on for a further twenty years. Both before this fire and after it there were other urban fires across America. Wood was still the dominant building material in use for homes, for piers, and even for walkways in some of the newer communities. The New Jersey shore of the Hudson River was a busy shipping center at the start of the twentieth century. There were many wooden piers at which ships tied up while awaiting the loading of their cargoes.

On Saturday afternoon, in June 1900, stacks of baled cotton and about a hundred barrels of whiskey were stacked on one New Jersey pier when a fire broke out in one of the cotton bales. Cargoes of flammable materials lay around waiting to be put on board. Fire immediately erupted. Dozens of kegs of whiskey were ignited and these exploded and added fuel to the fire. The cause of the fire was not known; it could have been smoldering for some days before bursting into flame. In spite of efforts to limit the spread of the fire things got out of hand within an hour. Several ships and numerous smaller vessels caught fire as most of the crews from ships were ashore and large numbers of visitors were visiting the ships. There were also many canal boats and barges loaded with oil, coal, cotton, and gasoline, all highly inflammable materials which were being transferred to the ships. These added fuel to the already raging fires, helping to spread the flames to neighboring piers. All the ingredients for a devastating fire were at hand. The piers were old, already saturated with oil from previous ship-

Figure 33 Investigators standing inside the Iroquois Theater after the fire.

ments. Cargoes of flammable materials lay around waiting to be put on board.

Tied up at a pier, on the New Jersey side of New York harbor, were four ships of 5,000–10,000 tons in size. A 14,000-ton liner, the *Kaiser Wilhelm der Grosse*, held the Blue Riband, the much-coveted Atlantic-crossing record. This ship was the pride of the German marine fleet. It was built in 1897, carried a crew of five hundred men, and had an average speed of 20 mph. It was the first ship built with four stacks and the first to be fitted with remote-controlled watertight doors. It was also the first ship to carry a radio. In 1900 it carried a radio that had a range of twenty-five miles. The *Kaiser Wilhelm* plied the Atlantic sea lanes for years after the Hoboken fire then, at the outbreak of World War I, it was converted into an armed merchant vessel but was sunk within a month of the war's outbreak. A red and yellow plume shot skyward as flames spread from place to place and longshoremen soon realized that the wooden piers under them were catching fire They shouted a warning to others and ran for their lives. Forty men who did not move fast enough were incinerated. Trapped on the ships, some on deck and others below the level of the deck, were hundreds of visitors. Many of the casualties were people who were unable to get away in time.

The nearest horse-drawn fire-fighting carriage arrived within six minutes and the men on it fought the fire all evening and through the night until they finally got it out by the morning. The *Kaiser Wilhelm* had hundreds of sightseers on deck and many of them panicked when flames engulfed her bow. Tugs rushed to the rescue from both sides of the harbor and pushed the big ship into mid-stream. The stern also caught fire but the crew was well organized and fought every outbreak persistently, even using their uniforms to smother the smaller fires. No lives were lost. It was a very different story on the other ships. All of them were completely on fire and the tugs attempting to pull them away from the pier caught fire too and had to give up. The damage to the three ships was extensive and they had to stay in port for some time for repairs. Since the piers in this area of Hoboken were under the care of the North German Lloyd Steamship Company, owners of the *Kaiser Wilhelm* and the other three ships, the company had to make arrangements for the burial of those who died. For most of them it was almost impossible to establish any identity. The tools that are at our disposal today were not available at that time. A mass burial was arranged at the Flower Hills Cemetery nearby and the shipping company, to its credit, looked after the maintenance and repair of this burial site for the whole of the twentieth century.

Lack of attention to fire regulations and inexperience in dealing with new hazards were also evident in ships at sea. One of the favorite trips of the 1930s was a pleasure cruise from New York to Havana. Cuba was a very different place at that time than it is today. Costs were low compared with their equivalents in the United States and large numbers of New Yorkers made the short two-way trip to the capital, Havana. The *Morrow*

Castle was one of the ships that plied regularly between these two places and, in September of 1934, it was returning to New York when a small fire broke out in the writing room in the middle of the night. Instead of notifying the captain, three sailors decided to put out the fire on their own. When they found that the fire was spreading and they were unable to control it they sent an urgent message to the captain who should have been on the bridge because the ship was quite close to New York at this the time. What they did not know was that the captain had had a heart attack and died a few hours earlier. His chief officer, in accordance with standing regulations, had immediately taken command but he was quite inexperienced and did not know what to do about the fire. A second message went to the bridge but again there was no response. Within an hour the fire was out of control and the new captain sent out an SOS message. Chaos followed. A few managed to get away in lifeboats. Out of the total of 550 on board, one hundred thirty-five either drowned or were incinerated.

All of these fires occurred in places of entertainment and commerce. It was a very different story in a fire that broke out in New York in 1911, in a place where new immigrants to America had just secured their first jobs, where pay was at a minimum level, and where working conditions were poor. These new immigrants fitted the traditional description, "tired and poor," and probably spent their last nickel to get to America. The garment industry in Lower Manhattan gave many of them their first job in the new world, a job that required little prior experience and hence paid little. They had to work long hours each day to make enough money. The history of New York's clothing industry is full of examples of poor working conditions and inadequate safety precautions. It was common practice for management to lock the emergency doors during working hours, as was done in one tragic instance. This was to prevent workers stealing things and leaving the building via fire exits instead of the main doors. Shirtwaist, or ladies' blouse, was a popular item in the early 1900s, worth a significant amount of money, the sort of thing that workers might be tempted to steal.

The Triangle Shirtwaist Factory was one of the thousands of clothing factories in lower Manhattan. They employed the immigrants, mostly Jewish and Italian, who streamed into New York and factory managers were able to take advantage of these new arrivals. Even after fifteen hours of work a day many of them had to take clothing home to be finished there in order to make enough money. No health or insurance benefits were provided, no extra money for working overtime, and frequently children were employed. "Sweatshops" and "fire and death traps," were the terms often used to describe these places of work. It was in these factories that some of the strongest trade unions took shape to fight for better working conditions. They had to work hard for the right to present workers' grievances to managers. In many cases the managers refused to recognize their existence and even threatened workers who supported them. In 1909, facing persistent refusal from management to listen to their complaints,

20,000 shirtwaist workers, mainly women, went on strike. There were no laws guaranteeing them this right so business leaders persuaded the police to arrest them for lawless behavior. There were also acts of brutality by the police to intimidate them. In spite of the conflict the strike secured some concessions and there was a general pay raise and the workweek was fixed at a maximum of fifty-two hours.

The Asch Building at the south of Manhattan Island, New York, was a modern structure and had a reputation for being fireproof. It had ten floors and the top three floors belonged to the Triangle Shirtwaist factory. Five hundred women worked in these three floors. Shortly before five o'clock in the afternoon of a day in March of 1911, as workers were about to leave, a fire broke out on the eighth floor. Like the two other floors above it, this floor was filled with sewing machines crammed so close together that little aisle space was left for moving about. Scraps of cloth and paper patterns lay around and they soon increased the spread of flames and smoke. The fire had started quickly and flared out just as rapidly. A number of workers from the eighth floor rushed to the stairway in time to see the whole floor erupt in a mass of flames. Many of them managed to escape with their clothes on fire. It was a different story on the ninth floor. The elevator quit and never reached that floor. The emergency door leading to the fire escape had been locked previously and by the time someone broke it down the fire escape had collapsed under the heat of the fire. A few who reached the fire escape were killed as it collapsed. Others, desperate and with nowhere to turn, chose to jump to their death rather than be incinerated.

Firemen had difficulty bringing a ladder into position because of the bodies strewed over the pavement, not all of them yet dead. Furthermore, their ladder, when it was erected, could only reach as far as the eighth floor. Life nets were brought in to try and catch those falling down but the women fell with such force that they went right through the nets. In less than two hours 147 bodies lay dead on the sidewalk below. The events of March 1911 were exceptional because of the large number of workers killed but other aspects were typical of the times. The fire and its effects were all over in two hours and firemen were left with the task of removing the bodies of those who had died on one of the upper floors. By the standards of the time the Triangle Shirtwaist Company was not held responsible for the fire and loss of life even though it was quite obvious that it had failed to ensure safety for its workers. Action was taken immediately by city authorities to institute factory inspections, fireproofing, and installation of sprinkler systems. The union representing the garment workers was not satisfied with these moves. They felt they could no longer trust anyone but themselves for their safety and took action within a few days of the tragedy.

Parents and friends of the victims of the fire met with the Ladies' Waist and Dress Makers' Union a few days after the tragedy to give them support. They were completely in favor of the union's demand that the company owners be brought to trial. They were also concerned, as was the union, about the disposal of the $100,000 that had been collected for the families of the victims. These two issues galvanized the union. They were convinced that appeals to authorities for corrective action were simply not working and they resolved to be more militant in the future. This is what their president said at the time: "Just because a safety committee was appointed and newspapers devoted pages to the problems in the factories, we cannot assume that the 30,000 shops in the city will suddenly become perfect. As long as the enforcement of labor laws is in the hands of political people, factories will remain unsafe and unhealthy. We must depend entirely upon ourselves for improvements." In later years other trade unions referred back to them as pioneers of the trade union movement.

References for Further Study

Cornell, James. 1976. *The Great International Disaster Book*. New York: Charles Scribner's Sons.

Everett, Marshall. 1904. *The Great Chicago Theater Disaster*. Chicago: Publishers Union of America.

Nash, Robert J. 1977. *Darkest Hours*. New York: Pocket Books.

Sherrow, Victoria. 1995. *The Triangle Factory Fire*. Brookfield, CT: The Millbrook Press.

55

St. Petersburg, Russia, revolution

January 22, 1905
St. Petersburg at the Winter Palace

A thousand of the workers were killed and thousands more were injured when the Czar's soldiers opened fire on the protesters. The Czar of Russia had absolute power at this time and his cruel actions contributed to the bigger revolution that followed twelve years later

Russia's emperor in 1905 was Czar Nicholas II. As czar, Nicholas had absolute power. In other words the country's form of government was an autocratic monarchy. Any protest that the czar disliked was met with force and as the country became industrialized the confrontations between impoverished workers and the state became more and more violent. Many were killed in the course of these protests and the number of strikes increased year by year. On January 22 1905, one hundred thousand workers, led by a priest, marched peacefully to the czar's Winter Palace in the Russian capital of St. Petersburg. They were demanding better working conditions. Instead of a friendly reception the workers met a volley of bullets. A thousand were killed and thousands more wounded. It was a turning point in Russian history.

The peaceful protests of January 22 at the Winter Palace in the nation's capital of St. Petersburg were intended to resolve growing tensions without confrontation. The opposite was the outcome as extreme violence erupted. In the months that followed, Czar Nicholas II knew that he could no longer stop protests with bullets. That era of Russian dictatorship belonged to the past and he recognized the necessity of making some concessions. The wide publicity that had been given to the march made it different from others. If the czar's representative had acted differently when the protesters arrived at the Palace, the more bloody events of 1911, the Communist Revolution, might never have taken place. As it happened, they were only delayed for six years. The amount of concessions that the czar granted in the course of the year that followed were inadequate and they only ensured some delay before the bigger confrontation of 1911 became inevitable.

On the Saturday evening prior to the protest, Father George Gapon, who organized the event, sent a letter to the emperor assuring him that everyone would behave peacefully. Gapon was well-known as a follower of Tolstoy's creed of non-violence so there was every reason to treat his assurances as credible. Gapon knew that the czar had arranged for extensive military protection all around the Winter Palace so in his letter he urged him not to use force against innocent civilians. He said this because he was afraid the czar's ministers might have given him false information about the protest. He then made a special personal appeal to the emperor, asking him to receive his address of devotion which he was going to bring along with a statement of the people's needs. His final words declared that he and all the workers with him would guarantee what he called "The inviolability of your person."

The origin of the march was unrelated to the various political groups that formed in the preceding years. Rather it was a reaction to the way management had victimized a group of workers for participating in a strike. Gabon felt that every worker had the right to strike and so he was convinced that a personal appeal to the czar would support his position. Gabon was a priest and for a time had been a prison chaplain but his main interest was the ongoing fight for workers' rights. He knew that the planned protest march to the Winter Palace was illegal. The police knew this as well but they did nothing to warn him. Even when Gabon sent the details of the march to the city authorities ahead of time nothing happened. The czar would not be in the palace on the day of the march so all decisions would be left to the Grand Duke Vladimir, the military commander of St. Petersburg.

The marchers set out in five columns all moving toward the great square in front of the Winter Palace. The authorities knew their route because they had been given the details a day before. No one among the thousands felt concerned about the outcome. They felt that their peaceful purpose would be enough to prevent violence. As they marched through the city the police made way for them, holding up traffic where necessary to let them pass. Banners were held aloft, while holy icons and portraits of the czar were also prominent. Onlookers gave them respectful attention as they passed by. It was only as they came near their goal, the great square, that they encountered firm opposition and were told to stop. They continued to move forward but within a few minutes they were physically confronted and pushed back by a cavalry troop. Clearly the soldiers had been given orders to stop the march.

Gabon requested a hearing for the petition they carried but the response by the soldiers remained the same. No one and no petition would be allowed past the entrance to the palace. Meanwhile the crowd of 200,000 waited. Gapon, dressed in his golden vestments and holding aloft a crucifix, requested that the petition be forwarded to the emperor. The officer in charge refused. For a few moments, the mass of marchers stopped, then, after a few moments of discussion among themselves, they decided to oppose the order to stop and moved forward. A volley of shots rang out from the soldiers on guard, fortunately all blanks, but it was followed a moment later with live bullets. Within a minute there was a third volley of live bullets. Men, women, and children fell in heaps and those who could escape scattered in all directions. Father Gapon, who was not hit, stood still, aghast. A thousand, maybe five thousand as was reported elsewhere, had been killed and thousands more wounded.

Reports in U.S. newspapers on the following day contained accounts of the extraordinary strength of the protesters. Even after a violent attack on them by cavalry with horsemen wielding swords, they persisted in moving forward toward the palace, calling for the emperor and shouting abuse at the troops, yet avoiding any appearance of acting violently. Their form of passive resistance made little difference to the soldiers' actions. Within half an hour of the previous violent assault on helpless citizens a second attack occurred on those who remained. They were told to disperse but before they could get away volleys of shots rang out. Most were shot in their backs as they attempted to escape. Bodies were scattered over the sidewalk. A witness to the tragedy identified women, children, as well as men, among the dead. Splashes and streams of blood stained the snow. Only a very few survived because the volleys were fired from twenty feet away. Ambulances had little to do. Policemen found a large number of sleighs to carry off the dead. Cries of anguish and despair were mingled with shouts of "murderers, murderers!"

Early in the morning of January 23 it could have been obvious to anyone that the military commander at the palace anticipated a major revolt, despite his recognition of Gabon's opposition to any form of violence. What the commander was opposed to, obviously, was any form of protest, however harmless. Every street and every bridge crossing the River Neva had been ringed with triple rows of defenses, as if an invading army was at the city gates. Because different things were happening in different places it was difficult to get an overall picture. Some days later it was discovered that large numbers of protesters in suburban areas had been shot before their procession began to move. On January 24, the military commander declared martial law and went on to station troop detachments at all strategic points around St. Petersburg. The *New York Times*, because of the time delay, was able to carry the previous day's news on its January 23 issue. The front page was headlines with phrases like "Day of Terror in Russia," and "Czar's subjects arm for revolt."

Bloody Sunday, as the January 22 event was known, led to further unrest as people became radicalized by the treatment they received. In the weeks that followed disturbances broke out throughout the country. In factory after factory close to half a million workers went on strike. Uprisings also took place in territories that bordered Russia and were part of its empire such as Russian Poland, the Baltic countries, and Finland. Sailors on one battleship mutinied. Maxim Gorky, the Russian novelist, took the side of the strikers. On Monday morning he spoke of the previous day as inaugurating revolution in Russia. He said that the emperor's prestige had been irrevocably shattered by the behavior of the military units. Gorky was arrested in Riga, Latvia, two days later and held in prison for a month, after which he was released on bail.

Gorky pointed out that Father Gapon persuaded the workers to believe that a direct approach to the one he called "Little Father" would be successful. Now he and all with him have been deceived. Gorky went on to say that peaceful means of change will not work and therefore force must be employed. He insisted in speeches to large crowds that the country now has no emperor because too much blood lies between him and the people. Because of the great respect accorded him, Gorky's words carried a lot of weight, especially when he urged his listeners to begin the people's struggle for freedom. Some began an appeal for arms. Others proposed a letter condemning the soldiers at the Winter Palace while commending those in Moscow who had refused to fire on protesters.

The czar knew for the first time that he could no longer solve peaceful protests with bullets; he had to make some concessions. He faced what Vladimir Lenin would later call a revolutionary situation. His style of addressing the situation sounds strange to us but it underlines the reality of the absolute power he held. Even the smallest concession on his part would represent a major change for all of Russia. Eight months after Bloody Sunday he issued a proclamation to the country. In it he describes himself as "We, Nicholas the II, Emperor and Autocrat of All the Russias, Czar of Poland, Grand Duke of Finland," which is a strange way for a single individual to talk. He then went on to say how the people's sorrow was also his and, therefore, that we, using that same word again, must do everything possible to bring an end to unrest. Maybe he was including his wife and children along with himself when he made the plural reference to the czar.

There were three parts to the proclamation. First, everyone was assured civic freedom based on the integrity of the individual. This included freedoms of speech, conscience, assembly, and association. Second, all those who were at that time deprived of their franchise would be given access to the country's parliament, the Duma, and have an opportunity to vote in it. Third, the Duma would have full power to pass or reject whatever laws were proposed. Implied in these new freedoms was the right of work-

9 января 1905 года
С картины художника И. Владимирова
Годы 1901—1904 ознаменовались подъемом революционного рабочего движения в России. Назревала первая буржуазно-демократическая революция. Ее началом были события 9 января 1905 года — расстрел безоружных рабочих у Зимнего дворца в Петербурге

Figure 34 Reproduction of a Russian propaganda painting of czarist soldiers in front of the palace firing on protesting workers, St. Petersburg, Russia, January 1905.

ers to form trade unions and peasants to create their own individual small farms. Up to that time all lands were held in common with no individual owning land. All of these changes, while modest as we might see them, changed Russia forever. Russia could never go back to being a dictatorship. The people's revolution had succeeded in getting a constitution that gave them new and permanent rights.

At the same time, power remained in the hands of those who held the large tracts of land because this was still a rural society and whoever had most land got most votes in the Duma. Society became divided in a new way. No longer was it the people against the czar. Now two social classes appeared, the have-nots and the haves. In later years as the communist revolution of 1917 broke out and transformed Russia back into another dictatorship for seventy years, the revolution of 1905 was seen as its dress rehearsal. The many workers' movements that emerged in the interim twelve years created opportunities for Lenin who was able to unite the most powerful among them. He then used these groups to set up the new communist dictatorship by force.

References for Further Study

Ascher, Abraham. 1992. *The Revolution of 1905: 2 Vols*. Stanford, CA: Stanford University Press.

Sablinsky, Walter. 1976. *The Road to Bloody Sunday: Father Gapon and the St. Petersburg Massacre of 1905*. Princeton: Princeton University Press.

Schwarz, Solomon M. 1989. *The Russian Revolution of 1905: The Workers' Movement and the Formation of Bolshevism and Menshevism*. Chicago: University of Chicago Press.

56

Mongolia earthquake

July 9, 1905

An area of Mongolia, close to the Chinese border

A vast area of two million square miles was damaged by this earthquake and the shaking was felt over a distance of 1,500 miles

On July 9, 1905, an earthquake of magnitude 8.4 occurred in the Gobi–Altai region of southwestern Mongolia, close to the Chinese border. At that time very little was known or documented about geological changes in that part of the world. This catastrophic event in 1905 was an exception. It was one of the very few for which detailed data was available. An aftershock of almost the same magnitude occurred in the same location two weeks later. A land area in parts of Mongolia, China, and Russia, covering as much as two million square miles, was affected by these events and people experienced the shaking from east to west over a distance of 1,500 miles. A large number of rocks rolled down from the 12,000 feet high surrounding mountains, trees were uprooted, and two lakes, each of eight acres in size, disappeared.

Deep fissures, one stretching for seventy-five miles and another for two hundred miles, formed in the wake of the July earthquakes and from within these fissures water was forced out on to the surface. Subsequent research, mainly in modern times after World War II, identified a series of earthquakes subsequent to the 1905 quake. One occurred in 1931, one in 1957, and one in 1967, each one of magnitude 8 or greater, a rare record in the history of earthquakes anywhere in the world. Additionally, each one of these events gave rise to fault movements as big as twenty feet and rupture lengths of several hundred miles. How could so many catastrophic earthquakes occur within a single century and within two hundred miles of one another? Geologists have concluded that, in this poorly understood region, events like these appeared in cycles over geological time with recurrence rates of several thousands of years. All of the information we now have about the 1905 event came from one Russian seismologist who traveled to the area of the earthquake at his own expense, in 1905, and by primitive means of transportation. His notes and maps lay in the archives of the Russian Geographic Society until they were discovered in 1957.

With the data from 1905 available to them in 1957, and encouraged by the new interest in eastern Siberia by political leaders, geologists began to study the Gobi–Altai region in greater detail than had ever been previously attempted. U.S. geologists in particular saw similarities between the layout of fault lines in this part of Mongolia and the fault lines associated with the Venture and the San Andreas faults. In particular they saw that what had happened in the Gobi–Altai earthquake, namely the simultaneous rupturing of two major faults, were to happen in California, it would be worse than anything that had yet hit that state. The new interest in the Gobi–Altai Region enabled the geological societies of Russia, China, and Mongolia to work together in the investigation of the 1957 earthquake when it struck. A year later the Academy of Sciences of the USSR, the name of the country at that time, appointed a group of geologists to investigate the Gobi–Altai area, to map it in detail and to carry out seismological investigations over a large area.

References for Further Study

Izdatelstvo, Akademii Nauk SSSR. 1965. *The Gobi-Alti Earthquake: Translation*. Jerusalem: University of Jerusalem.

Moores, E. M. ed. 1990. *Shaping the Earth: Tectonics of Continents and Oceans*. New York: W. H. Freeman.

Press, F., and Siever, R. 1986. *Earth*. New York: Freeman.

57

San Francisco, California, earthquake

April 18, 1906
In and around the city of San Francisco

This was the first devastating Californian earthquake to destroy a major city. Three thousand lost their lives because of it

Early in the morning of April 18, 1906, while most people were still in their beds, a 7.8 strength earthquake hit San Francisco. The shock lasted for less than a minute but that seemed like a year to those who were rudely awakened and had to rush out into the streets with whatever clothing they could lay hands on. Aftershocks soon followed and the destruction they could see in every direction convinced most people to stay away from their crumbling homes. The worst horror came later in the morning with fires all over the city, sixty in all. A firestorm erupted to add to the terror. The fires raged for three days with a total destructive power twenty times that of the earthquake, one of the most devastating in the history of California. There were three thousand deaths.

It took this event, the first major assault on a big city by an earthquake, to set in motion a serious quest for the cause of the earthquake. About five hundred city blocks had been devastated. Masonry buildings collapsed but wood frame homes and skyscrapers withstood the shock. One exception was the landfill areas in Marina District near the water. Wood frame homes there simply disintegrated. There is a special reason for the damage in this area. This district, south of Market Street, was a filled area; that is, it had been constructed by pouring unconsolidated materials, sand and rocks, on stream beds and other places that were too close to the water line to allow for construction. Buildings were then erected on this artificial foundation, and when the shaking from an earthquake occurred, liquefaction took place. Water seeped from below and changed land that formerly seemed quite solid into a watery mess, quite incapable of supporting buildings. Because this was the industrial part of the city people felt they could risk the possibility of a disaster from an earthquake. The cost of building on filled land was much lower than anywhere else in the city and industrialists felt that this lower cost would offset the price of reconstruction after a quake.

Unfortunately, as so often happens in human-induced disasters like this one, the lessons learned are not remembered when there is a different kind of event involving filled land. Over the years, people forgot the dangers of filled land and the area that had been an industrial site was rebuilt again, this time as a fashionable residential subdivision. When the Loma Prieta earthquake struck in 1989, this area was totally demolished and many lives were lost. San Francisco was not the only city to forget the past. Tokyo did the same thing, or rather allowed the same thing to happen. Many years before the 1923 earthquake, one area of the city had been built up on filled land and the authorities in the city knew that this was the case. They also knew about the San Francisco earthquake because Japan experiences more earthquakes than almost any other place on earth and there are always ongoing studies of earthquakes in other parts of the world. Nevertheless, nothing was done about the filled land and new homes were built on it after 1906. When the 1923 event hit Tokyo the buildings on filled land collapsed immediately and many people died. One part of the San Francisco filled land that did not collapse was the Palace Hotel, although it did catch fire.

Most of the buildings in the city were built of wood and, as such, they would normally withstand earthquakes because of the ability of wood to expand and contract under shaking. Most of them were lost because of fire and even those that survived had trouble because their chimneys toppled, ripping plaster off ceilings and walls and breaking floors as they fell. Some places at considerable distances from the city suffered severe damage, far more than other locations at equivalent distances from San Francisco, simply because they happened to be on one of the many faults that stretch out from or run parallel to the main fault. Santa Rosa was one of those places. It is nineteen miles away from the source of the earthquake and it experienced extreme damage. Fifty people were killed there. It was a similar story in several places west of the San Joaquin Valley even though they were thirty miles south of the earthquake's epicenter. Because of their proximity to water courses these areas experienced liquefaction, rift fissures, avalanches, and earth slumps.

Electrical power lines, water mains, and all the other normal services were cut off. When the first fire broke out nothing could be done about it because there was no water. Then a firestorm erupted. These fires raged for three days and the whole city was incinerated. All attempts to create firebreaks failed. There were probably three or more thousand killed, 1 percent of the total population. When the fires finally subsided people searched for their homes or what might be left of them. It was a difficult task. All the familiar landmarks had vanished. The quake was felt over an area close to 200,000 square miles, all the way from Oregon to south of Los Angeles and eastward to Nevada. Cities closer in proximity suffered varying amounts of damage. Stanford University was one of the worst affected. Several buildings were completely destroyed there. One person's observation on the morning of the earthquake sums up the experience of most: the street was undulating as if it were the ocean with waves sweeping toward me. I was terrified.

Earth waves rolled across the state with clear depressions between the swells. When they finally broke open there were parallel fissures with lengths of six hundred feet or more. Another type of fissure took the form of a rectangular-shaped block that dropped, leaving a trench with vertical sides. Landslides occurred wherever the banks of rivers were steep and where there were steep bluffs. Frequently forests were carried down or were overthrown by the slides. Several sections of land were raised as much as twenty feet above the highest flood level for the area concerned. Other places dropped by as much as fifteen feet although the majority of these were of the order of seven feet. The forests of different areas, that altogether added up to 150,000 acres, were completely destroyed. About forty miles to the south of San Francisco, near the limit of the earth-

Figure 35 San Francisco, California, earthquake, April 18, 1906. Downtown San Francisco showing residents watching fire after the 1906 earthquake.

Figure 36 San Francisco, California, earthquake, April 18, 1906. Stanford University. Looking towards Chemistry Building after the Statue of L. Agassiz fell from a height of thirty feet and pierced the concrete sidewalk.

quake's destructive power, the Spanish mission of San Juan Bautista, built a hundred years earlier, was severely damaged.

San Francisco was a flourishing city in 1906. It had sprung into fame as the premier city of the West Coast during the gold rushes of fifty-five years earlier and at the time of the earthquake it had a population of 400,000. San Francisco's prosperity was due to new mining developments in western Nevada, to truck farming from surrounding agricultural areas and, most of all, as a seaport for Asian trade. Fires destroyed large parts of the city six times in the course of its short history and their frequency persuaded builders to switch from wood to brick and stone. They also inspired the leaders of the city to create a brand new fire department. It earned the name of being the best in the world. Sadly, the one consideration that ought to have been uppermost in the minds of the city officials was missing—the provision of emergency supplies of water in the event of the city's mains being severed by an earthquake. As had happened with filled land, so here too, San Francisco's lack of emergency water supplies was a mistake that was repeated in subsequent urban earthquakes, as in Tokyo in 1923. A plan to pump emergency water supplies from San Francisco Bay had been laid out but never implemented.

Figure 37 San Francisco, California, earthquake, April 18, 1906. View showing damage the San Francisco City Hall resulting from the San Francisco earthquake and fire of 1906.

The fear of earthquakes was never evident in San Francisco in spite of the fact that the city had experienced the tremors of three quakes, those of 1836, 1838, and 1868. Memories seemed to be short. In the immediate aftermath of the quake and fires, with all the awareness of their neglect of adequate preparation for emergencies, and with a quarter of a million of the city's population, more than a half of the total, homeless, everyone took responsibility for the task of reconstruction. Money contributions, practical help, and the provision of military units from the federal government all helped to speed up the recovery. Every individual could, and did, participate in the clean up and in the practical work of either building homes or carrying supplies to building sites. Within three years San Francisco was back to a near normal level of operation and was growing at a fast rate.

San Francisco has the highest density of underground faults of any urban area in the United States. Furthermore, the break in the San Andreas Fault that caused the disaster was six miles below ground and the amount of lateral displacement was as much as twenty feet in places. Costs in 1906 dollars were close to $500 million. That would be about $7 billion

Figure 38 San Francisco, California, earthquake, April 18, 1906. View south from 4th and Market streets, showing results of fire. April 20, 1906. San Francsico County, California. April 1906.

today, a figure close to the cost of the 1989 Loma Prieta earthquake. Earthquakes had struck California before. In 1812, an area south of Los Angeles was hit and more than thirty people were killed by it. In 1857, another quake caused considerable damage over an area northeast of Los Angeles. Some decades later a geologist from the University of California who had observed a fault line south of San Francisco, decided to trace its extension north and south. He and his students found, to their surprise, that this was no ordinary fault. It was the San Andreas Fault and it ran almost the full length of the state, close to the coast for the most part but veering inland in the south.

This discovery was made in the 1890s, long before there was any understanding of plate tectonics, so little was done with the new information. Now, with hindsight and present knowledge of tectonic plates, the story of the San Andreas Fault is the key to understanding most of California's earthquakes. First attempts to understand its behavior began within a year of the 1906 disaster, first by a geologist who had lived through the quake. He recognized that the cause of the earthquake was slippage on part of the San Andreas Fault, later identified as a segment that stretched for 250 miles from Monterey Bay northwards. Pipelines and roads that crossed the fault line had been broken and displaced by an average of twelve feet with the western side always moving northwards with respect to the eastern side. It was evidently a strike-slip fault but until the era of plate tectonics everyone regarded it as an anomaly, a one of a kind event unique to California. With the increasing public concern today about the potential for destructive earthquakes in California since the great Alaska earthquake of 1964, and the general acceptance of the concept of plate tectonics and seafloor spreading in the late 1960's, the San Andreas Fault has received new attention. It is closely related to such recent earthquakes as the Loma Prieta of 1989 as well as the much earlier quake in Fort Tejon in 1857.

At the northwest end of the fault system, the Mendocino triple junction represents an intriguing structural knot where the North American, Pacific, and Gorda plates join. A fourth block at depth, made up of material below the North American Plate but east of the San Andreas Fault and south of the Gorda Plate, is juxtaposed with these three named plates. The San Andreas Fault is the one that dominates in the interaction between the huge Pacific and the North American plates and some of its effects are felt far inland across the western part of the country. It is a rare situation to find these two plates, the Pacific and the North American, meeting on land as they do here. As a strike-slip one it moves as much as two inches a year and it has been doing this for more than fifty million years with a total displacement of hundreds of miles. Massive earthquakes are associated with it. Both the Pacific and North American plates are moving relative to the deeper parts of the earth, so the San Andreas Fault boundary is also moving, changing its shape in the process as the adjacent plates deform. In southern California, the sector of the fault from north of Los Angeles to east of San Bernardino has been rotating slowly counterclockwise. We tend to think of the margins between these plates as narrow lines because this is the way they are depicted on maps and we also tend to imagine the rest of the Cordillera as being static. The reality is quite different. The plates are moving on a sphere, not on a flat surface. In some places the plate margin may be hundreds of miles wide and the whole of California may be in motion at different rates in different places.

References for Further Study

Jordan, D. S., ed. 1907. *The California Earthquake of 1906*. San Francisco: A. M. Robertson.

Kurzman, Dan. 2001. *Disaster!: The Great San Francisco Earthquake and Fire of 1906*. New York: William Morrow.

Lawson, A. 1908. *The California Earthquake of April 18, 1906: The Report of the State Earthquake Investigation Commission*. Washington, DC: Carnegie Institution.

Morris, Charles. 1906. *The San Francisco Calamity by Earthquake and Fire*. Philadelphia: World Bible House.

Richards, Rand. 2001. *Historic San Francisco: A Concise History and Guide*. San Francisco: Heritage House.

Winchester, Simon. 2005. *A Crack in the Edge of the World: America and the Great California Earthquake of 1906*. New York: HarperCollins.

58

Socorro I, New Mexico, earthquake

July 16, 1906
Socorro, 150 miles north of the Mexican border

Considerable damage was done to homes but little loss of life, as far as is known, because of the low population density in 1906

On July 16 of 1906 Socorro, a town in New Mexico in the Valley of the Rio Grande, 150 miles north of the Mexican border, experienced an earthquake with a magnitude of at least 7. Numerous tremors preceded the event of July 16. They began on July 2 and there were equally numerous aftershocks that followed. Albuquerque, a hundred miles north of Socorro and even San Antonio in Texas, more than five hundred miles away, were shaken by this earthquake. Within the town of Socorro the walls of adobe houses were cracked and brick chimneys thrown down. Many people left their homes and lived in tents for a time to avoid the risk of their homes collapsing on them. The Socorro Hotel, a brick building in the eastern part of the town, had to be abandoned because of the severe damage it sustained.

The ground movements experienced during this earthquake were unusual. Boulders rolled on to railway tracks, breaking the tracks in some places and destroying ties elsewhere. Fissures formed in the ground near the center of the town and the land surface moved in waves as if it had been a lake. The entire business block in the center of town was very heavily damaged. Newspapers, in one or two cases, provided sensational accounts of what happened. One reported that the temperature of nearby hot springs had increased and another that the entire town of Socorro was in ruins with all its inhabitants fleeing. These were subsequently recognized as being false. In addition, as had happened prior to the earthquake, aftershocks in the form of recurring smaller tremors continued throughout the following months right up to the major event of November 15 of the same year.

References for Further Study

Ayre, Robert S. 1975. *Earthquake and Tsunami Hazards in the United States.* Boulder, CO: Institute of Behavioral Science.

Iacopi, R. 1964. *Earthquake Country.* San Francisco: Lane Book Company.

McPhee, J. 1980. *Basin and Range.* New York: Farrar, Straus, Giroux.

59

Socorro 2, New Mexico, earthquake

November 15, 1906

Socorro, 150 miles north of the Mexican border

Considerable damage was done to homes but little loss of life, as far as is known. Damage was much more extensive than in the July 16 earthquake because some development had occurred in the intervening months

An earthquake with a magnitude of at least 7 hit the town of Socorro on November 15, 1906. It was more powerful than the one that had occurred on July 16 of the same year. In the months between July and November there had been a succession of lesser tremors. Any place within 180 miles of Socorro felt the impact of this earthquake. It greatly increased the damage done by the July 16 quake and, in total, represented the most severe shock of the year 1906. Chimneys on the County Courthouse that had been rebuilt after previous damage were thrown down, plaster shaken from walls, upper floors of some two-storey buildings collapsed, and bricks were dislodged from a few houses. Many people in Texas and Arizona remembered the earthquake.

Isoseismals, lines joining places with equal earthquake intensity, are difficult to draw for this earthquake or for its predecessor in July of the same year, because of the limited amount of data available. Nevertheless, it was well known that strong shaking was experienced by people all over New Mexico and in parts of Arizona and Texas. Smaller shocks were observed to be single vibrations backwards and forwards while stronger ones vibrated in different directions. This pattern is usual in strong earthquakes like that experienced in November. There were also different sounds accompanying the vibrations. The search for the epicenter of this earthquake leads to an examination of the geological history, especially the existence of fault lines. The formation of new fault lines or volcanic eruptions or both of these are the two known causes of earthquakes. The lack of volcanic eruptions and the general character of the shocks suggest that no new fault lines appeared. It seemed likely that the cause of the earthquake was a slip action on an existing fault and its location was on the west side of Socorro.

The evidence for the location of the epicenter is found in the different things that happened. The overthrown chimneys and gables fell to the east. Both the directions taken by falling objects, and the directions in which earth movements occurred were measured in 1906 by hanging pendulums and marking the extent and direction of movement on the floor beneath. These pendulums had to be watched as they moved in response to the earthquake and the length of support as well as the end weight had to be consistent in order to make comparisons over time. The fact that both the July and the November earthquakes were preceded and followed by smaller tremors is consistent with the geological history of this region. Earthquakes have frequently occurred here in clusters over the past few thousand years. One series of earthquakes hit the area between 1898 and 1900. The November 1906 shock was the strongest recorded since 1869.

References for Further Study

Ayre, Robert S. 1975. *Earthquake and Tsunami Hazards in the United States.* Boulder, CO: Institute of Behavioral Science.

Iacopi, R. 1964. *Earthquake Country.* San Francisco: Lane Book Company.

McPhee, J. 1980. *Basin and Range.* New York: Farrar, Straus, Giroux.

60

Ecuador offshore earthquake

December 31, 1906
Offshore off Colombia, Ecuador, and Peru

An earthquake of this extraordinary size is capable of great damage. It created a huge tsunami that killed a thousand people along the coasts of the three countries and destroyed a large number of homes

Three very large earthquakes shook North and South America in 1906, the first on April 18 in San Francisco, California, the second on August 17 in Valparaiso, Chile, and the third on December 31 in the Colombia-Ecuador region. In all three cases, the earthquakes caused massive destruction of cities and a large number of casualties. Since early in the twentieth century seismic source investigations have revealed considerable information about earthquakes, though scientists are still unable to predict when they will occur, and these three dramatic events have give us fresh understandings of the enormous amount of activity occurring between tectonic plates all along the eastern coasts of the Pacific Ocean. In the case of the San Francisco earthquake it was a slip-slide movement of the plates on either side of the San Andreas Fault rather than subduction, and in South America it was the subduction of the Nazca Plate beneath the South American Plate.

With all the earthquakes that we hear about in Indonesia and Alaska, most of them of the subduction type, just like the ones of 1906, we get the impression that these two areas of the world have the biggest earthquakes of this type. This is not the case. A 1960 earthquake off the coast of Chile accounted for almost half of all the seismic action released worldwide in that year. The 1906 quake in Ecuador, beneath the margin of the South

American Plate, carried a rupture than was three hundred miles in length and was of magnitude 8.8, a rare event in geological history, only matched by such extraordinary events as the Alaska earthquake in 1964 and the Indonesia quake in 2004. Furthermore, the speed of subduction by the Nazca Plate is much greater every year when compared with Indonesia or Alaska. Subduction earthquakes occur when tectonic plates, as they gradually and continually move beneath other plates, encounter some resistance that slows them down. As tension builds up over time under mounting pressure from below there comes a moment when resistance snaps and one of the plates, usually the upper one, moves and causes an earthquake.

When one plate, usually the lighter continental crust, rides up over the top of the other it's called a subduction zone, because one plate margin is being subducted under the other. The lighter continental South American Plate is riding up over the heavier oceanic Nazca Plate. Deep down where the leading edge of the Nazca Plate is diving down under the South American Plate it makes contact with the molten magma of the earth's mantle. This melts the Nazca Plate margin sending magma chambers rising to the surface where they sometimes break through in volcanic eruptions. The chain of volcanic mountains known as the Andes is a result of the rumpling of the South American Plate where the Nazca Plate crashes into it. In view of the huge impact on land by these subduction earthquakes, why are there not more reports of damage to people? One reason is that the earthquakes are frequently offshore and another is that they equally frequently occur in places of low population density. The western part of Indonesia and the coastal areas of Peru and Chile are exceptions to these patterns and hence it is common to have large loss of life with South American events.

Whenever an earthquake as strong as the 1906 earthquake in Ecuador occurs, tsunamis can follow. In this particular case, about a thousand people on the coasts of Peru and Colombia were killed by the tsunami and many homes were destroyed. Other places also experienced tsunamis from this source. It was felt all along the coasts of Central America and in California. In the harbor at San Diego, boats at anchor were shaken and swung around by the force of the tsunami wave that reached this part of the United States. Similar effects were felt in San Francisco where tidal charts showed a rise in water level above normal. The Valparaiso earthquake of August 1906 triggered a tsunami that had similar effects in these Californian cities. Across the Pacific the Ecuador tsunami reached the Big Island of Hawaii about twelve hours after the earthquake and did a lot of damage around the port of Hilo. It must have traveled across the Pacific at more than 400 mph. Tsunamis can travel much faster than that depending on the obstructions they encounter. Japan too was hit by this same tsunami.

The story was the same when another earthquake, this time one in the interior of the continent, shook the interior of Chile. It was an intra-plate quake, on the border between northern Chile and Argentina, in the southern part of the province of Atacama. It struck on November 11, 1922, and it had a magnitude of 8. A tidal wave swept over Coquimbo, a coastal city about 250 miles to the south of the epicenter taking the lives of several hundred people and caused enormous property damage, subsequently estimated as ranging from $5 to $25 million. As happened with so many other earthquakes in South America the tsunami from this eathquake also hit Hawaii, reaching Hilo on the Big Island, the nearest point to Chile, in 14.5 hours with a wave height of seven feet. Many boats were washed away, and some damage was done. The tsunami reached the next part of Hawaii, Honolulu, half an hour later. On the west coasts of California the same tsunami wave was recorded at both San Diego and San Francisco with wave heights of less than a foot.

The Valparaiso quake of August 17 was more deadly than the one in Ecuador. The city of Valparaiso was destroyed and twenty thousand people lost their lives. The following description is taken from reports of people who lived through the tragedy. The earthquake seemed to go on for about fifteen minutes and the whole experience felt like standing on a wagon racing across uneven ground. Everything was thrown down, chairs, tables and desks inside, and buildings everywhere outside. The cries and the behavior of animals shocked us. Their squealing and lowing, coupled with the cries of people everywhere made the whole scene all the more terrifying. Rail lines and bridges were all out of action and the telegraph communications cut. A locomotive on a siding was thrown to one side and ended upside down beside the track. Huge openings in the ground appeared here and there, one of them big enough to swallow a large trunk. In addition, shallow fissures appeared in the ground, some over six feet wide and two hundred yards long. Large rocks rolled down from neighboring mountainsides and blocked roads.

References for Further Study

Ayre, Robert S. 1975. *Earthquake and Tsunami Hazards in the United States*. Boulder, CO: Institute of Behavioral Science.

Bascom, Willard. 1980. *Waves and Beaches: The Dynamics of the Ocean Surface*. Garden City, NY: Anchor Press.

Dudley, Walter C., and Lee, Min. 1998. *Tsunami*. Honolulu: University of Hawaii Press.

Yeats, R., et al. 1993. *The Geology of Earthquakes*. New York: W. H. Freeman.

61

Monongah, Pennsylvania, explosion

December 6, 1907
Monongah, Pennsylvania

Monongah was an exceptional example of the great risks that have always faced miners. While some reduction in risks has occurred as technological improvements are brought into use, the risks still remain at an unacceptably high level

Pennsylvania and West Virginia were major producers of coal in the early years of the twentieth century. In Monongah, West Virginia, on December 6, 1907, the full horror of mining's dangers was brought home to everyone when 363 miners went down below to work and only one returned. Work began early on that morning soon after five o'clock. Coal dust, a potentially lethal material unless it is thoroughly dampened, lay all over the floor of the pits and was used by the men to pack the holes they had drilled and loaded with black powder explosives to loosen the coal. It was always a risky business as they used carbide lamps with open flames as their only source of light. Five hours after work began a huge explosion shattered the two connected pits. The explosion rocked the buildings above ground and was heard eight miles away. The devastation below was total and it was amazing that even one man escaped. He happened to be at the site of an open-air vent that reached the surface. For all the others death was instantaneous.

Dozens of bodies were so badly dismembered by the explosion that they could not be identified. The night before the explosion, instructions had been given to have the coal dust watered down but the person responsible

Figure 39 The day after the massive explosion at Monongah Mines in Marion County, West Virginia, that killed 361 coal miners in 1907.

for that work was moved to another mine shortly before he was due to do this work. The whole tragedy was the worst coal disaster in the nation's history and it marked the beginning of, for that time, new safety regulations. Connecting of underground mines in order to make them a single operation was made illegal immediately in West Virginia. Three years later the United States Bureau of Mines was established and it stopped nationally both the use of black powder as an explosive and the tamping of drill holes with coal dust. Accidents continued to occur across the United States for one of three reasons—explosions, fires, or roofs collapsing—and, in the years from 1900 to 1910, human error led to many tragedies. Knowledge of the dangers and ability to cope with them were both poor.

Throughout Europe, North America, and Australia, coal was the early twentieth century's primary source of energy for industry and transportation. It was mined intensively and often with inadequate attention to safety. The accelerating demands of industry led to shortcuts that increased output but endangered the lives of miners. Coal still remains a major source of energy, particularly for generating electricity, and there are enormous quantities available across the United States. At present rates of consumption supplies could last a thousand years. The room and pillar method of mining, in which in which masses of coal seams were left standing to support the overlying rock while the coal around them was taken out, was in widespread use. In this environment miners had to encounter and get used to new areas of work all the time. Death rates were very high. Even today they are higher than in most other industries.

In 1946, immediately after World War II, these rates in U.S. mines were still high, over seven hundred annually. Thirty years later, the death rate every year had dropped to one-third of the 1946 figure. Sometimes a whole underground region was endangered when a mine was not carefully closed down. In one place in Pennsylvania a mine was abandoned after a fire but some smoldering embers were ignored. Twenty years later the underground fire was still slowly burning.

Prior to the devastation at Monongah, similar disasters were occurring in different locations across the United States. Coal resources were widely available and the demand for coal continued to grow. Local initiatives could be launched to meet the needs of the market. In the period before 1910 there was little federal regulation of operations, and there was also limited state supervision. Mines were planned and worked by their owners and supervised by owner-appointed inspectors. On May 1, 1900, at the Pleasant Valley Company's Schofield Mine in Utah, two hundred lives were lost when a series of explosions occurred in two shafts. The cause of the tragedy was either ignorance or indifference. Thirty containers of black powder had been stored in one of the pits. None of the miners at work on an adjacent pit, using explosives, were told of the bomb next door. The story was often similar in other countries. Australia, like Britain and the United States, was heavily dependent on coal in the first part of the twentieth century. On July 31, 1902, a gas explosion occurred at a mine on the coast, fifty miles south of Sydney, killing ninety-six and injuring 152 others.

At this particular Australian mine, operations date back to 1883 where an eight-foot seam of coal was being worked. It was located some distance below ground and access was gained via a horizontal shaft below the coal seam. By the very nature of the site it was clear from the beginning that an explosion and fire would trap every miner and make escape or rescue almost impossible. An explosion would release quantities of coal, adding fuel to the fire and blocking off exits. For this reason responsibility lay heavily on the mine manager to ensure that no one went underground if there was the slightest indication of gas, especially since, at the time of the explosion in1902, open-flame lamps were still in use. As the explosion occurred roofs collapsed and coal cars were thrown about like toys. Blasts of hot gas swept through the work areas. Subsequent inquiries revealed that the mine manager was aware of small pockets of gas in the mine, despite his assurance to the miners, on the day of the explosion, that there was none. The explosion and subsequent tragedy was caused by contact between a miner's lamp and one of the gas pockets.

For the most part, in the early years of the twentieth century, most mine disasters were the result of either not dampening coal dust or not checking carefully for the presence of gas. With open flame lamps as the normal type of lighting it is easy to see now that these two things should have been given top priority. On July 10, 1902, at the Johnstown Mine in Pennsylvania, 112 men lost their lives in an explosion because no one checked for the presence of gas even though the mine was known to have gas. At the Hanna Mine, Wyoming, on June 30, 1903, the same neglect occurred and 169 miners were killed in the explosion and fire that ensued. Conditions were even worse then elsewhere in this case. Work was stopped for a time because of the accident but later resumed on a different level without attending to the problem that had led to the work stoppage. There was a second explosion and fifty-nine miners died. Local outrage forced the permanent closure of the mine.

In Alabama the men who worked the mines were often black chain-gang inmates who were serving time in hard labor. There was little recourse open to these men if something went wrong and this may explain why managers often took greater risks there than they should. Short fuses were sometimes used to save costs but that meant that workers had less time to get away from a blast site. On March 23, 1905, too much dynamite was used in one blast, triggering a general explosion that killed 112 men. Two years later, at another mine, an explosion took the lives of thirty-seven convicts because the management had not dampened the heavy layers of coal dust on the pit floor. Four years later, on April 8, 1911, at Alabama's Banner Mine, the same neglect of failing to check for gas and not dampening the coal dust caused an explosion that killed 128 men. The story of inadequate safety can be traced to other states where attention to the presence of gas and dry coal dust was neglected. In Colorado on April 27, 1917, managers of a mine with a history of tragedies allowed 120 men to go below without first checking for gas. All 120 were killed in the explosion that followed. It was the same outcome and again due to the same neglect of the mine's lethal elements that caused the death of 170 miners in Utah on March 8, 1924. The similar tragedy of 1900 in Utah seemed to have been forgotten.

Other factors than gas and coal dust can sometimes lead to catastrophic mining events. The Cherry Mine in Illinois had an excellent record for safety. On November 13, 1909, however, because there was a temporary problem with the electrical power circuit, electric lamps could not be used so open-flame gas lamps were introduced for the day. Mules were being used at this time to haul the mine carts and fodder for them, bales of hay, were stacked at the mine's entrance. A miner's lamp touched one of the bales but no one took any notice of it for some time. The hay smoked a little but there was no fire. Quite suddenly a flame shot up into the air and workers scrambled to get the hay away from the mine entrance, unaware that the big ventilation fans had already boosted the fire. It was too late to stop it and the heat forced everyone to step back.

Flames soon spread to the mine's wooden support pillars and almost simultaneously triggered gas explosions within the mine. The mules panicked and ran back into the shaft to get away from the smoke and heat. So did the miners who knew the lethal power of gas and smoke in the small spaces where they worked. The small handful of men who were outside the mine when the fire broke out decided to go down in the cage and rescue those trapped below. They were overcome by gas fumes and were all dead when the cage was pulled back up. In an equally futile and ill-informed move, the mine superintendent sealed off the entrance thinking that this would smother the fire. Underground damage was widespread and nothing could be done until the morning of November 14 when it was safe for rescuers to go down below. Rescuers found 170 men still alive. They had been able to get into small crevices away from the smoke. Another 259 men had died. It was the worst mine disaster in the history of Illinois.

In all of the above instances the tragedies were due to one of two things, carelessness or lack of experience on the part of miners, or failure by mine managers to take adequate safety precautions. The idea of a safe mine is now a top priority throughout the industry. The growing environment movement is expressing concerns about pollution and health risks. Companies are determined to show that, whatever environmental damage they may cause, at least they are deeply concerned for the safety of the miners. There is greater understanding of the geology of mine structures, better and safer equipment for all aspects of mining, and emergency resource kits. All these make it easier to safeguard the lives of those who work below ground.

References for Further Study

Brown, Malcolm Johnson. 1941. *Seven Stranded Coal Towns: A Study of an American Depressed Area*. Washington, DC: Government Printing Office.

Freese, Barbara. 2002. *Coal: a Human Story*. New York: Perseus Books Group.

Harvey, Curtis E. 1977. *The Economics of Kentucky Coal*. Lexington: University of Kentucky Press.

Peng, Syd S. 1978. *Coal Mine Ground Control*. New York: Wiley Publishers.

62

Amite, Louisiana, tornado

April 24, 1908
Amite, Louisiana, north of New Orleans

A series of tornadoes was triggered by thunderstorms. Amite was the strongest of these and it was responsible for the deaths of 143 people out of a total death toll of three hundred

In the first half of 1908 a series of severe thunderstorms triggered eighteen tornadoes across the central part of the Gulf states, killing more than three hundred people. The strongest of these was Amite, so named because it was in Amite that it did the greatest amount of damage. This F4 strength tornado arrived on April 24, 1908, and swept bare a path two miles wide as it raced along through Louisiana into Mississippi. Most of the town of Purvis, Mississippi, a town of 2,000, was leveled by it, leaving only seven of its 150 houses standing and causing half a million dollars worth of damage. By day's end Amite was responsible for the deaths of 143 and the injuring of 770 others, making it one of the country's deadliest.

Amite began as a two-mile-wide tornado and, as it passed on into Mississippi, its path narrowed to a width of half a mile and then to two hundred yards. As always happens when a tornado's path is narrowed, its destructive power increases, and so Mississippi experienced a more devastating storm than was seen in Louisiana. A railroad crew at work hid from the approaching storm inside boxcars but their refuge was far from being safe. The boxcars were thrown a distance of 150 feet and torn apart in the process. Seven people lost their lives in them. Thousands of tall pine trees were uprooted, broken and scattered.

References for Further Study

Bradford, Marlene. 2001. *Scanning the Skies: A History of Tornado Forecasting*. Norman: University of Oklahoma Press.

Grazulis, T. P. 2001. *The Tornado: Nature' s Ultimate Windstorm* Norman: University of Oklahoma Press.

McGuire, Bill. 1999. *Apocalypse*. London, UK: Cassell.

63

Louisiana hurricane

September 20, 1909

Grand Isle, south of and close to the city of New Orleans

Six million dollars of damage was caused in New Orleans and 350 people were killed

The Louisiana hurricane of September 20, 1909, is often referred to as The Grand Isle Hurricane because it was in Grand Isle that it first touched down and where it completely devastated everything around it. It came ashore on September 20, 1909, as a category 4 hurricane and moved across New Orleans causing huge amounts of additional damage, later estimated at six million dollars. It also was responsible for the deaths of 350 people largely as a result of the fifteen-foot storm surge brought by the hurricane. Extensive flooding occurred in its wake in the northern undeveloped swamp area north of New Orleans. Extensive flooding of this kind in New Orleans is exactly what happened in Katrina but, because low lying areas within the city limits at that time had little residential build up, the consequences of the flooding were much less severe than those of Katrina. The storm dissipated over Southern Missouri by September 22, leaving a memory of being one of the deadliest ever to hit the United States.

Hurricanes are part of a family of weather systems known as tropical cyclones. The word hurricane comes from a West Indian word that means big wind and it normally begins its life as a storm system over warm, tropical waters in the Atlantic. When a storm becomes more organized, it is classified as a tropical depression and given a number by the National Hurricane Center. If the winds increase to 40 mph, it is re- classified and given a name. Later, when the winds reach 75 mph it is upgraded to a hurricane. The winds of a hurricane are structured around a central eye, which is an area free of clouds and relatively calm. Around this eye, clouds wrap in a counter-clockwise direction. This wall of clouds, wind, and rain, is the most destructive part of the storm. In fact, it is the wall that creates the eye, since the rapid spinning clouds in the wall reduce the pressure in the eye and suck out any clouds that may be there. Hurricanes are usually compact storms, with maximum wind velocities extending out from 7 to 80 mph from the eye. Of course, one can still experience gale-force winds as far way as three hundred miles from the eye.

An overview of a season sometimes helps to understand a particular event within a season. The 1909 Atlantic hurricane season for example began officially on June 1, 1909, and lasted until November 30, 1909. These are the dates that conventionally define the period of each year when most tropical cyclones form in the Atlantic basin. The 1909 season was an average but destructive season; eleven storms formed, of which six became hurricanes. Four of those hurricanes became major hurricanes with winds of greater than 111 mph. The season started early, with two tropical storms and a hurricane. The first storm hit Nicaragua in mid-June and the second hit Texas as a category 2 hurricane near Brownsville. The third hit southeast Florida in late June. Activity continued through July, when a fourth, a tropical depression, formed over the southern Lesser Antilles in Mid-July. The storm attained tropical storm strength south of Jamaica, and reached hurricane strength near the western tip of Cuba. It ultimately hit near Freeport, Texas, on July 21 as a category 3 hurricane; with a ten-foot storm surge, this was the first test of Galveston's seawall, built after the destructive 1900 hurricane. Damage came to $2 million and forty-one people died.

The fifth tropical storm of the season formed on August 6 and hit Mexico twice, first on the Yucatán Peninsula and then near the border between Veracruz and Tamaulipas. The sixth storm formed east of the Lesser Antilles on August 20. The storm went westward, hitting the Dominican Republic and Southeast Cuba. The storm strengthend to a category 3 hurricane and hit the Northeast corner of the Yucatán Peninsula; a transmission on the hurricane from a vessel near the Peninsula became the first "ship report" to be used in a forecast. After weakening, it regained strength and hit Tamaulipas as a major hurricane on August 27. The death toll from this storm was staggering. Floods and landslides killed an estimated 1,500 people. The seventh storm formed over the Bahamas on August 28, hit near Miami as a tropical storm, and went out to sea. The eighth storm formed south of Hispaniola on September 13. It reached hurricane strength south of Cuba, and eventually hit southern Louisiana as a category 3 or 4 hurricane, making landfall at Grand Isle with a fifteen-foot storm surge. Warnings came to New Orleans before 1909 and even more after that date, reminding the city of its vulnerability to hurricanes long before the days of Katrina in 2005. A major hurricane hit the city in September of 1722, leveling many of the buildings in the young city. The year 1794 was perhaps as dreadful a year as the city of New Orleans ever experienced, as it was hit by two hurricanes in addition to a major fire.

References for Further Study

Barnes, Jay. 1998. *North Carolina' s Hurricane History* Chapel Hill: University of North Caroline Press.

Barnes, Jay. 1998. *Florida' s Hurricane History* Chapel Hill: University of North Carolina Press.

Tannehill, Ivan Ray. 1956. *Hurricanes: Their Nature and History*. Princeton: Princeton University Press.

64

Oregon earthquake

August 5, 1910

Offshore from Oregon's coast

The strongest earthquake in Oregon's history hit the State from an offshore epicenter. Damage from this particular earthquake was minimal

Two of the largest earthquakes in Oregon occurred in 1910 and 1993. The 1910 earthquake was the largest historical shock within the state's boundaries at a magnitude of 6.8, but it occurred too far offshore to cause damage, whereas the damaging 1993 earthquake was the largest historical earthquake beneath the land area of Oregon, with a magnitude of 5.9. There have been no big earthquakes in Oregon's brief history, and there is no question that damaging earthquakes have been far less frequent in Oregon than in California or Washington. However, geologic research tells scientists that Oregon will some day experience big earthquakes, and both the Scotts Mills earthquake of March 25, 1993, and the Klamath Falls earthquake of September 20, 1993, confirm such research. Because the Oregon is poorly prepared, the damage could be great.

Geologic research has shown that Oregon and Washington have probably been shaken by numerous subduction zone earthquakes during the last several thousand years. Subduction zone earthquakes occur when two great crystal plates slide past each other beneath the coast of Oregon and Washington. These earthquakes occur, on average, every 300–600 years, and the most recent was about three hundred years ago. The subduction zone earthquakes were probably centered just off the coast of Oregon and Washington and may have been as large as magnitude 8 to magnitude 9. Such earthquakes would cause significant shaking and damage in much of western Oregon. Scientists cannot predict whether the next such event might occur in two years or two hundred years.

Local earthquakes are most common in the Portland metropolitan area, northern Willamette Valley, and Klamath Falls area and may threaten the coast from Coos Bay south to Brookings. There is little knowledge at the present time as to the risk of local earthquakes in most other parts of western Oregon. All of Oregon west of the Cascades, as has been pointed out above, is at risk from the subduction earthquakes that will come some day as the Juan de Fuca Plate continues to move beneath the North American Plate. The amount of earthquake damage at any place will depend on its distance from the epicenter, local soil conditions, and types of construction. To date, no fault in western Oregon has been proven to be likely to move in an earthquake. Although many faults have been identified, it cannot be said yet whether being near a fault is any more hazardous than being far from one.

References for Further Study

Ayre, Robert S. 1975. *Earthquake and Tsunami Hazards in the United States.* Boulder, CO: Institute of Behavioral Science.

Bolt, Bruce A. 1982. *Inside the Earth.* San Francisco: W. H. Freeman.

Fried, J. 1973. *Life Along the San Andreas Fault.* New York: Saturday Review Press.

65

Titanic iceburg tragedy

April 15, 1912

The North Atlantic, four hundred miles south of St. John's, Newfoundland, and eight hundred miles east of New York

The unsinkable Titanic *was suddenly sunk as it collided with an iceberg. Through a variety of failures the* Titanic *was sunk by an iceberg and, due to an equally tragic series of failures in terms of sufficient lifeboats, 1,490 lost their lives*

Their regulations had been written in 1894 and they stipulated that every ship over 10,000 tons must carry sixteen lifeboats. The ship's designers knew that the *Titanic* could stay afloat if four of its sixteen watertight compartments were flooded, but it could not survive if five were flooded. No one ever suspected that as many as four would be flooded at one time and this fact may have given rise to the idea that the ship was unsinkable. On April 10, 1912, the *Titanic* left Southampton on its maiden voyage to New York. Next day the ship received radio messages telling of large icebergs that were much farther south than usual. Captain Smith accordingly altered course toward the south, maintained speed at twenty-two knots and gave instructions to lookouts to be especially vigilant.

Titanic, on its first transatlantic voyage from Southampton to New York, was eight hundred miles east of Halifax, Canada, on April 15, 1912, when it hit an iceberg. Within a minute or two, a 300-foot gash was cut in the ship's steel side and about an hour later the *Titanic* was listing seriously. The captain ordered everyone to take to the lifeboats and two hours later the ship sank. Of the 2,227 passengers aboard 1,490 lost their lives.

In the years before World War I there was heavy sea traffic between Europe and North America. Immigration from Europe to the United States was at a peak and the growing industrialization of the United States was a magnet for European businessmen. Ships competed for both economy and luxury travel. Speed of travel was also in demand and some ship owners concentrated on that. In 1907, the British White Star Line decided to build ships that would focus on luxury, size, comfort, and safety, rather than speed. On May 31, 1911, four years later, the first of these ships, the *Titanic*, was launched. From its moment of launch it was known as a "safe" ship compared with all other vessels of that time.

The *Titanic* weighed more than 46,000 tons, stood eleven stories high and four city blocks long, was divided into sixteen watertight compartments for safety, and carried twenty lifeboats. This was four more lifeboats than the Board of Trade regulations required. The *Titanic*'s reputation of being unsinkable created an atmosphere of complacency, almost arrogant indifference, from the captain all the way down to the least deck hand. So widespread was this outlook that when the call to abandon ship was made a large number of passengers refused to believe what they were told. There was a casual approach to safety in the minds of the ship's officers as evidenced by the things that were not done. No formal boat drill was arranged for passengers, a normal procedure to ensure orderly behavior in an emergency. There were lifeboats for only one-third of the passengers, legally correct but hardly responsible, and there was little concern over the danger of icebergs.

Radio was a fairly new thing in 1912 and large numbers of passengers used it to send messages to friends in Europe and the United States, describing life aboard the *Titanic*. The ship's radio operator was so heavily engaged in sending these private communications that he paid little atten-

Figure 40 The *Titanic*.

tion to the warning signals about icebergs from other ships. Some urgent messages about icebergs that arrived at noon did not reach the navigation officer until 7:00 P.M. Even a drop in the outside air temperature around the ship, a clear indication of proximity to an iceberg, from forty-three degrees to freezing in the course of one day was ignored by those in command. Sunday, April 14, 1912, was cold but visibility was good. Messages kept arriving from other ships warning of the presence of icebergs in the main shipping lanes. The *Titanic*'s Captain Smith still seemed indifferent to these warnings.

It was well known that most of an iceberg's bulk floats below the surface so it was always important to keep a safe distance from the part one could see above water. Captain Smith may have been more concerned with the hope of gaining a new crossing record because, instead of slowing down to make sure that the ship kept well clear of icebergs, he maintained a speed of twenty-two knots, about 25 mph, a high speed for ships at that time. Shortly before ten o'clock in the evening the seventh ice warning of the day arrived, telling of a huge mass of ice less than eighty miles directly ahead. An hour later an urgent message was sent to all ships in the area from a ship, the *Californian*, twenty miles away, which had stopped its engines because of an eighty-mile stretch of ice directly ahead. At the same time, the *Californian' s*radio operator tried to call the *Titanic* but, finding that he was met with a blunt "Keep out" response, decided to retire for the night.

Close to midnight, as the *Titanic* pushed ahead, lookouts in the crow's nest, high up on the foremost mast, spotted an iceberg off the right side of the ship, almost directly ahead and towering sixty feet above the water. The warning signal was triggered. The engine room was ordered to stop the ship and then go full speed astern, but the warning came too late. Even as it began to swing away toward its left side, the ship hit the iceberg below the surface. The crew felt a bump and heard a scraping sound. They concluded that nothing serious had happened but the first officer as a precaution decided to close all the watertight doors below the waterline. The elapsed time from the moment of sighting until the watertight doors were closed was about half a minute.

The ice had gashed a series of openings in the steel side of the ship and water was pouring in. Within ten minutes, fourteen feet of water filled the forward part of the ship. All five compartments were flooded and, after another ten minutes, water rose to twenty-four feet above the keel. Captain Smith and the managing-director of the shipyard that built the ship, Thomas Andrews, were by now on the bridge assessing the damage. Andrews knew that the ship could only stay afloat for a little more than one hour if five compartments were flooded and he told Smith so. Distress signals were immediately sent out and preparations made for abandoning ship. The bow area was already sinking. Twenty-five minutes after the first sighting of the iceberg, Captain Smith gave orders that the lifeboats be made ready.

The captain knew that the lifeboats could only carry 1,178 out of the 2,227 on board even if every boat was filled to capacity, and he was anxious to avoid panic. Rockets were fired aloft and the *Californian*, which was still nearby, saw the rockets but the ship's operator had retired for the night soon after getting the earlier rejection from the *Titanic*. He had been at his station for sixteen hours. The *Californian* tried to make contact using light signals but, when that failed, it made no further attempts. Several other ships received the radio signals but they were all some distance away.

About an hour after hitting the iceberg the first lifeboat was launched, but inadequate planning together with passenger apathy saw it leave with twenty-eight people instead of its capacity load of sixty-five. Even as this boat was being lowered into the water many passengers felt it was safer to stay on the ship. They refused to believe that the *Titanic* would sink despite the abandon ship order. Other lifeboats too left with partial loads, one with forty-two, a second with thirty-two, and a third with thirty-nine. Much later, when the tally of survivors was examined, there were questions. Why did one boat leave with seven, two members of the crew and five who were mostly from first-class cabins? Was it impossible for passengers from down below to reach the boats in time because of the barriers that separated third from first class sections of the ship?

Approximately two hours after it had hit the iceberg the *Titanic* was

Figure 41 *Titanic* lifeboats on their way to the *Carpathia*.

listing heavily to port, its bow close to the water. People found it hard to keep their balance and panic was setting in. As one of the last boats was being launched and was already almost full, a group of passengers tried to jump in. An officer in the boat had to fire two warning shots to hold them back. As another boat was being loaded the crew linked arms and formed a chain around the boat, allowing only women and children to get on board. Captain Smith walked around, thanking various ones for the work done then headed for the bridge to go down with his ship, a long-standing maritime tradition. In the final moments many jumped off the ship. By hanging on to pieces of wreckage or, in a few cases, by being taken on board a lifeboat, some of these survived.

The *Carpathia*, a ship that was sixty miles away, received the distress messages and headed for the location of the *Titanic*, arriving shortly after 4:00 A.M. long after the *Titanic* had completely disappeared. For several hours the *Carpathia* took on board those in lifeboats as well as survivors from the sea, thus succeeding in rescuing 711 who were taken to New York. One thousand four hundred and ninety lives were lost, the worst ever tragedy at sea. Many were lost because they were unable to cope with the near zero temperatures. Ships from Halifax, Canada, were dispatched to pick up bodies. One hundred and ninety were recovered and these were interred in Halifax. Many years later, in 2001, some of these remains were exhumed in attempts at identification, using DNA techniques.

A British public inquiry was conducted as soon as the survivors were able to attend. They were delayed for some time in order to answer questions from the U.S. Senate. The inquiry was held in London and it centered on possible navigational negligence on the night of the disaster. Was the ship traveling too fast? Were officers attentive to the various warnings of ice? Why was it that the total number of survivors was far less than the total capacity of all the lifeboats? Were the third class passengers held back and locked below decks in order to allow those in second and first class to escape? The inquiry exonerated the captain and crew in words like the following: while the collision with an iceberg could have been avoided it was not a direct result of negligence on the part of either Captain Smith or any member of his crew.

Captain Rostron, *Carpathia'* sskipper, was commended by members of both U.S. and British authorities for his courageous efforts to reach the *Titanic* in time to save her passengers. In pushing his ship to its limits and dashing through treacherous waters he was seen as a true hero. The captain of the liner *Californian*, on the other hand, was regarded as almost a villain because he did not do all he could to save lives. Almost immediately after the public inquiries were completed dramatic changes were made in the rules regarding icebergs and lifeboats. The International Ice Patrol was instituted, ensuring constant watch on errant icebergs, and winter shipping lanes were moved farther south. Twenty-four-hour radio watch was required for all ships and sufficient lifeboats to accommodate everyone became mandatory.

These outcomes from the U.S. and British formal inquiries concentrated on the shipping errors and loss of life, but beneath all of these and only lightly touched on by the investigators lay some serious social issues. Not least of these was a tradition of class distinction when filling lifeboats. While the owners of the *Titanic* denied that any such practice existed, it was well known among other ships of that time. When the liner *Republic* went down, four years earlier, the captain told the passengers as they approached the lifeboats, remember women and children first, then first class passengers followed by all the rest. Whatever might have been the unspoken rules on the *Titanic*, the reality was blatant discrimination.

Out of the first class women passengers, 3 percent lost their lives, while 16 percent of second class women drowned, and in steerage, the lowest class, 45 percent of the women died. The barriers set up to keep the different classes of passengers from mixing became death traps. Steerage passengers were seen climbing out on whatever protrusions they could access on the sides of the ship in order to reach a deck above the water. When the last lifeboat was launched and the ship's officers were convinced that all women had been accounted for, dozens suddenly appeared from steerage sections. Such was the pathetic lack of organization for coping with an emergency. Two women from steerage were stopped as they walked toward one of the boats on the first class deck and ordered to go down to their own deck to board there, something that was quite impossible at that stage.

This traditional class distinction appeared again in New York as the *Carpathia* brought survivors ashore. Survivors' stories became headlines in newspapers but they were almost all from first class passengers. The horror of more children from steerage being drowned than men from first class was hardly noted. Investigators from both members of Congress and the British authorities ignored the steerage passengers. It was a similar story among the media representatives, at least for a time. Then questions began to surface about how some important men survived while a hundred women were lost. By exposing so many of these habits of class distinctions, the *Titanic* put an end to many of them. It destroyed much of an era of privilege that looked inappropriate, even indecent, in the light of the unfair treatment accorded people on that night of April 15, 1912.

Seventy-three years later, Robert Ballard and his team from Woods Hole Oceanographic Institution, Boston, discovered and photographed the wreck of the *Titanic* as it lay on the seabed at a depth of two miles, three hundred miles south of Newfoundland. Ballard's wish was that all who followed him would respect the site and not interfere with it. He felt it was a gravesite that ought to be left undisturbed. Interest in the wreck, however, was too strong for others to accept that recommendation. Two years after Ballard's discovery, a French expedition, backed by money from the United States, went to the site and recovered artifacts. The French submersible *Nautile*, used by the expedition, dived more than thirty times and spent about two hundred hours on the ocean floor.

Approximately nine hundred artifacts were discovered, many of them objects that no one knew had been aboard the ship. New light was cast on the *Titanic* and the condition of the wreck. There was a cache of Spode china with blue and gold patterns that caught historians of the *Titanic* by surprise. A bag stuffed with jewelry, U.S. banknotes and gold coins was also recovered. Some of the important navigational and communication instruments were also salvaged, such as the ship's telegraph, operated by a system of wires and pulleys. There were many other interesting objects including sterling silver knives, forks, and spoons, cut-glass carafes, white ceramic egg dishes, a bottle of champagne, a teapot, and a jar of skin cream.

References for Further Study

Ballard, Robert D. 1989. *The Discovery of the Titanic*. Toronto: Madison Press Books.

Butler, Daniel Allen. 1998. *Unsinkable: The Full Story of RMS Titanic*. London: Stackpole Books.

Lord, Walter. 1997. *A Night to Remember*. New York: Bantam.

Lynch, Donald, and Marschall, Ken. 1995. *Titanic: An Illustrated History*. New York: Hyperion.

Wade, Wyn Craig. 1986. *The Titanic: End of a Dream*. London: Penguin Books.

66

Katmai, Alaska, volcanic eruption

June 6, 1912

Mount Katmai, west of Kodiak Island

Volcanic ash in volume greater than the sum of all other volcanic eruptions in Alaska was ejected and devastated every place within miles of the eruption

The largest twentieth century eruption anywhere on Earth occurred in Alaska, on June 6, 1912, creating the Katmai Caldera and the Valley of Ten Thousand Smokes. Volcanic ash, in quantities more than from all other historical eruptions in Alaska combined, devastated areas hundreds of miles away. An ominous cloud rose into the sky above Mount Katmai, reached an altitude of twenty miles, and within four hours ash from this huge volcanic eruption began to fall on the village of Kodiak, one hundred miles to the southeast. By the end of the eruption, the ash cloud, measuring thousands of miles across, shrouded southern Alaska and western Canada, and sulfurous ash was falling on Vancouver, British Columbia, and Seattle, Washington. On June 7, the cloud passed over Virginia and by June 17, it had reached Algeria in Africa.

During the three days of the eruption, darkness and suffocating conditions caused by falling ash and sulfur dioxide gas immobilized the population of Kodiak. Sore eyes and respiratory distress were rampant, and water became undrinkable. Radio communications were totally disrupted and, with visibility near zero, ships were unable to dock. Roofs in Kodiak collapsed under the weight of more than a foot of ash, buildings were overwhelmed with ash, and many structures were burned. Novarupta, mean-

Figure 42 W. A. Hesse taking moving pictures of Katmai Volcano in 1912.

ing "new eruption," is a volcano that sits below Mount Katmai and that shared in the eruption, an event that was ten times more powerful than the 1980 eruption of Mount St. Helens. More than three cubic miles of volcanic material was ejected over two and a half days. The 1815 eruption of Tambora, by comparison, displaced about seven times as much material. The 1883 eruption of Indonesia's Krakatoa displaced twice as much. Magma from underneath Mount Katmai area was drained away, leaving a collapsed caldera that measured four square miles in surface area.

Several villages were abandoned forever and much animal and plant life had been decimated by ash and acid rain. Bears and other large animals were blinded by ash and starved when large numbers of the plants and small animals they lived on were wiped out. Millions of dead birds that had been blinded and coated by volcanic ash littered the ground. Aquatic organisms, such as mussels, insect larvae, and kelp, as well as the fish that fed upon them, perished in ash-choked shallow water. Alaska's salmon-fishing industry was devastated, especially from 1915 to 1919, because of the failure of many adult fish to spawn. Augustine is a good example of the frequency of volcanic eruptions in and around Cook Inlet, but Mount Katmai, a 6,000 foot peak, is an example of quite a different kind: as the world's largest twentieth century eruption it is certainly Alaska's worst ever within historic times. Mount Katmai and its sister mountain, Novarupta, are about ninety-five miles southwest of Augustine and three hundred miles southwest of Anchorage, within what is now known as Katmai National Park and Preserve. When the eruption happened, after centuries of silence from both of these mountains, more than three cubic miles of ash and small particles were blown into the sky, giving rise to a new name for the area—"Valley of Ten Thousand Smokes." Villagers from Katmai and other nearby communities moved away to a safer location.

The Katmai area was permanently changed by the eruption. Enormous quantities of hot, glowing pumice and ash flowed over the terrain, destroying all life in its path. Trees up slope were snapped off and carbonized by the blasts of hot wind and gas. For several days after the explosion ash, pumice, and gas created a haze that darkened the sky over most of the Northern Hemisphere. When it was over, more than forty square miles of lush green land lay buried beneath volcanic deposits as deep as seven hundred feet deep. For two full days, people in nearby Kodiak could not see a lantern held at arm's length. Acid rain caused clothes to disintegrate on clotheslines as far away as Vancouver, Canada. In the valleys of Knife Creek and the Ukak River, innumerable small holes and cracks developed in the ash deposits, permitting gas and steam from the heated groundwater to escape. A ship moored in Kodiak harbor at the time of the eruption gave this account of events. Five inches of ash fell everywhere, choking all wells and streams on shore. Visibility dropped to fifty feet and after about two more hours, at a time when the sun would have been shining brightly, pitch darkness set in and continued into the morning of the next day. Decks, masts, and lifeboats were all covered with a fine, yellowish-colored dust.

Avalanches of ashes could be heard sliding down the neighboring hills and sending out clouds of suffocating dust. The crew on ships kept working continually with shovels and hoses to try to get rid of the ash. The amount on the ground of Kodiak averaged one foot in height. Like other gigantic events of this kind, where ash and other materials are flung high into the upper atmosphere, the effects of Katmai's eruptions were felt far and near. There were over 40,000 square miles of the surrounding area covered with ash to an average depth of two inches. Smaller amounts of ash fell on Juneau, more than seven hundred miles to the southeast and still less on Seattle, about 1,500 miles to the south. Some ash particles reached far enough into the atmosphere that they were caught in global circulation patterns and provided spectacular red sunsets for months. In terms of the original volume of molten rock released, comparisons can be made with other major events. On this basis, there were three cubic miles of magma ejected from Katmai, thirty times greater than the volume of magma released in the 1980 eruption of Mount St. Helens. Even the 1991 eruption of Mount Pinatubo, the second largest of the twentieth century, was less than half the size of Katmai's.

In 1916, a National Geographic Society expedition led by Robert Griggs visited Mount Katmai and found a two-mile-wide crater where its summit had been before 1912. Nearby, the expedition discovered a newly formed lava dome they called "Novarupta" and huge flows of volcanic ash filling what they named the "Valley of Ten Thousand Smokes" for the numerous plumes of steam rising from the still-hot ground. Griggs' descriptions of these spectacular features helped persuade President Woodrow Wilson to create Katmai National Monument (now Katmai National Park) in 1918. In the 1950's, volcanologists discovered that the great Alaskan eruption of 1912 was not really from Mount Katmai, as previously thought, but from a new vent at Novarupta. The eruption removed so much molten rock (magma) from beneath Mount Katmai, however, that a cubic mile of Katmai's summit collapsed to form a two-mile-wide volcanic depression, a caldera, now a lake eight hundred feet deep. Despite the fact that the eruption was so close to the Continental United States and comparable in magnitude to that of Krakatau of 1883, it was hardly known at the time because the area was so remote from the world's main population centers.

Almost a hundred years after it happened, researchers are paying attention to Katmai because it is near the Arctic Circle and its impact on climate appears to be quite different from that of volcanoes in lower latitudes. When a volcano erupts anywhere, it does more than spew clouds of ash locally and shadow a region from sunlight so that it cools for a few days; it also blows sulfur dioxide, a gas irritating to the lungs and smelling like rotten eggs. If the eruption is strongly vertical, it shoots that sulfur dioxide high into the stratosphere as far as ten miles above the Earth. In the stratosphere, sulfur dioxide reacts with water vapor to form sulfate aerosols. Because these aerosols float above the altitude of rain, they don't get washed out, they linger, reflecting sunlight and cooling Earth's surface. A condition of this kind can create a kind of nuclear winter for a year or more after an eruption. In April 1815, for instance, the Tambora volcano in Indonesia erupted. The following year, 1816, was called "the year without a summer," with snow falling across the United States in July. Even the smaller, June 1991, eruption of Pinatubo in the Philippines cooled the average temperature of the northern hemisphere summer of 1992 to well below average. However, both of these eruptions, as well as Krakatau, were tropical events. Katmai and Novarupta are just south of the Arctic Circle.

Using a NASA computer model at the Goddard Institute for Space Studies (GISS), Professor Alan Robock of Rutgers University and colleagues found that Katmai's effects on the world's climate would have been different. The stratosphere's average circulation is from the equator to the poles, so aerosols from tropical volcanoes tend to spread across all latitudes both north and south of the Equator, quickly circulating to all parts of the globe. Aerosols from an arctic eruption tend to stay north of 30°N; that is, no further south than the Continental United States or Europe. These aerosols would mix with the rest of Earth's atmosphere only very slowly. This bottling up of arctic aerosols in the north would make itself felt, according to the findings of GISS, in India. According to the computer model, the Katmai blast would have weakened India's summer monsoon, producing an abnormally warm and dry summer over northern India. Why India? Cooling of the northern hemisphere by Katmai would set in motion a chain of events involving land and sea surface temperatures, the flow of air over the Himalayan mountains and, finally, clouds and rain over India. This is an unusual and rather complicated conclusion from Robock's research and it only became clear when the supercomputers were employed in the calculations.

To check the results of his study, Robock and colleagues are examining weather and river flow data from Asia, India, and Africa in 1913, the year after Katmai. They are also investigating the consequences of other high-latitude eruptions in the last few centuries. The fact that the stratosphere in high latitudes is shallower than at the tropics means that even small eruptions near the North Pole may deposit more aerosols than bigger events in the tropics. Furthermore, they would remain in circulation longer as happened with Katmai. Indians will need to keep an eye on Arctic eruptions. There is yet another consideration: even years after an eruption, volcanic ash deposited within two hundred miles of the eruption site would be remobilized by windstorms and blown high into the atmosphere, renewing the hazards for people and machinery. Fish and wildlife would be devastated as they were after the 1912 eruption, wreaking prolonged havoc on Alaska's now large and economically important fishing and tourism industries.

The chance of another Katmai-scale eruption occurring in any given year is small, but such cataclysmic volcanic events are certain to happen again in Alaska. Within five hundred miles of Anchorage, volcanologists have identified at least seven deposits of volcanic ash younger than 4,000 years that approach or exceed the volume of ash ejected by Katmai in 1912, including a thick layer of ash erupted from Hayes Volcano, only ninety miles northwest of Anchorage. Of the numerous volcanoes scattered across southern Alaska, at least ten are capable of exploding in a 1912-scale eruption.

References for Further Study

Cas, R. A. F., et al. 1987. *Volcanic Successions Modern and Ancient*. London: Allen and Unwin.

Chapin, F. S., III, et al. 1991. *Arctic Ecosystems in a Changing Climate: An Ecophysiological Perspective*. San Diego: Academic Press.

Fisher, R. V., et al. 1984. *Pyroclastic Rocks*. Berlin: Springer-Verlag.

Francis, P. 1976. *Volcanoes*. Harmondsworth: Penguin.

Peters, R. L., and Lovejoy, T. E., eds. 1990. *Global Warming and Biological Diversity*. New Haven, CT: Yale University Press.

Sheets, P. D., et al. 1979. *Volcanic Activity and Human Ecology*. London: Academic Press.

67

Omaha, Nebraska, tornado

March 23, 1913

A mile-wide twister in the city of Omaha

This tornado took the lives of ninety-six people, destroyed six hundred homes, and damaged more than 1,100 others

On the evening of Easter Sunday, March 23, 1913, a tornado storm of multiple parts passed through Nebraska and hit Omaha. It was close to a half mile wide and it stretched back as far as forty miles. This storm marked the darkest day in Nebraska's history as far as weather extremes are concerned. It started in Sarpy County, ripping its way northeast through Ralston, where seven people were killed. The twister then cut across Omaha and killed ninety-six people, destroyed six hundred homes, and damaged more than 1,100 others. The tornado followed the path of Little Papillion Creek as it entered the city before moving through the west side of town alongside the Missouri Pacific Railroad, destroying the small workers cottages in that area. This storm was so strong that steel train cars were pierced by pieces of shattered lumber from the demolished homes.

Easter Sunday began under cloudy skies in Omaha in1913. Rain threatened but never fell on the city, and by noon the skies had brightened to the point where the sun began to peek through. In the afternoon the skies darkened again as a massive storm system moved into the area from western Nebraska. At 5:45 P.M. the tornado touched down near Kramer, and then raced northeast to reach the outskirts of Omaha by 6 P.M. By the time the funnel cloud reached Dewey Avenue it was five blocks wide. When it reached Farnham Hill it followed a shallow valley through this upscale neighborhood. Even the large mansions of Farnham were unable to cope with the winds and many houses were torn to pieces. Others were later found chopped in half, pipes and supports dangling in space. At 24th and

Figure 43 Omaha, Nebraska, at 24th and Lake Streets, after the tornado in 1913.

Lake Streets a large crowd was enjoying a show at the Diamond Moving Picture Theater. The tornado flattened the building. Other brick structures in this small commercial district took similar hits, and this became the place where most of the casualties occurred. A streetcar running down 24th Street encountered the tornado near this area. Thanks to the quick actions of the streetcar's operator, every passenger survived. Later, people who saw the wrecked streetcar called it the streetcar of death because they were sure that no one had survived, given the immense amount of damage it had sustained.

References for Further Study

Bluestein, Howard B. 1999. *Monster Storms of the Great Plains*. New York: Oxford University Press.

McGuire, Bill. 1999. *Apocalypse*. London: Cassell.

Murname, Richard J., and Liu, Kam-biu. 2004. *Hurricanes and Typhoons: Past, Present, and Future*. New York: Columbia University Press.

68

Texas hurricane

August 4, 1915
Galveston on Galveston Island

A storm surge of twelve feet inundated the business district of the city to a depth of six feet and killed 275 people

A monstrous hurricane formed near the Cape Verde Islands on August 4, 1915, and moved just south of the Greater Antilles, reaching the Texas coast near Galveston on August 16. In Galveston many people, with memories of the 1900 hurricane still fresh in their minds, left town as soon as it was clear that the storm would hit Galveston. Storm surges of twelve feet were seen at Galveston, inundating the business district to a depth of five or six feet. Many houses were demolished and all beach houses were washed away. Overall this hurricane, one that was a category 4 hurricane as it touched down, caused a great deal of destruction in its path, leaving 275 people dead and causing $50 million dollars worth of damage.

In Galveston, with strong winds, tides nine feet above normal, and a storm surge of sixteen feet, the ten-foot-high seawall built after the 1900 hurricane was unable to withstand the volume of water. It was partly damaged and this led to severe flooding in different parts of the city and the removal of twenty-five feet of the beach close to he seawall. Close to three hundred homes outside the seawall were destroyed. Despite the damage done to it, the seawall did achieve widespread protection for the city as a whole as evidenced by the low death toll compared with 1900. The devastation occasioned by the powerful hurricane of that year, the deadliest of its kind anywhere in the United States in modern times, led to the massive reconstruction of the whole city. Recovering from the 1900 storm involved building a seawall and raising the island's elevation significantly above sea level. In effect, the plan involved changing the entire natural environment of the city. The people of New Orleans must have often wondered why the same thing was never contemplated for their city. They have the same problem as Galveston, living on territory that in places is barely above sea level.

The challenge of raising an entire city began with a decision to raise its elevation by seventeen feet and surround the whole uplifted area with a ten-foot seawall. On the ocean side of this wall the land would slope down to the water on a slope of one foot for every 1,500 feet. To get the required quantities of sand, sixteen million cubic yards, enough to fill more than a million dump trucks, Galveston's ship channel was dredged and the sand was piped into the city in a slurry form. Quarter-mile sections of the city were marked off and protective walls erected around them. The theory was that, as the water drained away, the sand would remain as a hard surface. Before any work could be initiated, every building had to be raised and all service lines, sewer, water, and gas lines, had also to be raised. Even some gravestones had to be raised. The wall went up in stages year by year and the 1915 hurricane, with the same strength as the hurricane of 1900, was the first real test of the wall and the elevated interior. After leaving Galveston, the weakening 1915 storm took a turn to the northeast and passed Houston as a category 1 hurricane before dropping to tropical storm status later that day. In Galveston a series of fires broke out after the storm's passage and relief aid was slow because the causeway that connected Galveston to mainland Texas had been badly damaged by the hurricane.

References for Further Study

Tannehill, Ivan Ray. 1956. *Hurricanes: Their Nature and History*. Princeton: Princeton University Press.

Tucker, Terry. 1995. *Beware the Hurricane*. Bermuda: The Island Press Limited.

Williams, J. M., and Duedall, I. W. 1997. *Florida Hurricanes and Tropical Storms*. Gainesville: University of Florida Press.

69

Pleasant Valley, Nevada, earthquake

October 3, 1915
Pleasant Valley, south of Winnemucca

Pleasant Valley was thinly populated and the main impact of the quake was geological, creating a twenty-mile scarp at the base of the Sonoma Mountains

The largest earthquake in Nevada's history up to 1915 occurred on October 3, 1915, and was centered in Pleasant Valley, south of Winnemucca. This earthquake had a magnitude of 7.1 and it was followed by several aftershocks that disturbed a large part of northern Nevada. It destroyed or seriously damaged many adobe houses in Pleasant Valley. Most of the damage was confined to the towns of Kennedy, Lovelock, and Winnemucca. The earthquake was felt over a very wide area, from Baker, Oregon, to San Diego, California, and from the Pacific coast to beyond Salt Lake City, Utah. A scarp four to fourteen feet high and more than twenty miles long was formed parallel to the base of the Sonoma Mountains. It broke the surface in four different places for a distance of thirty-seven miles. The largest offset of the ground was nineteen feet of vertical movement.

This earthquake occurred along a fault on the eastern side of Pleasant Valley, about forty miles southeast of Winnemucca, in the north-central part of Nevada. This location of the epicenter was almost uninhabited and, therefore, property damage was less than might have been expected. Damage was confined mainly to an area within forty-five miles of the Pleasant Valley Fault. The combined length of the scarps was thirty-five miles, the average vertical displacement six feet, and the maximum dis-

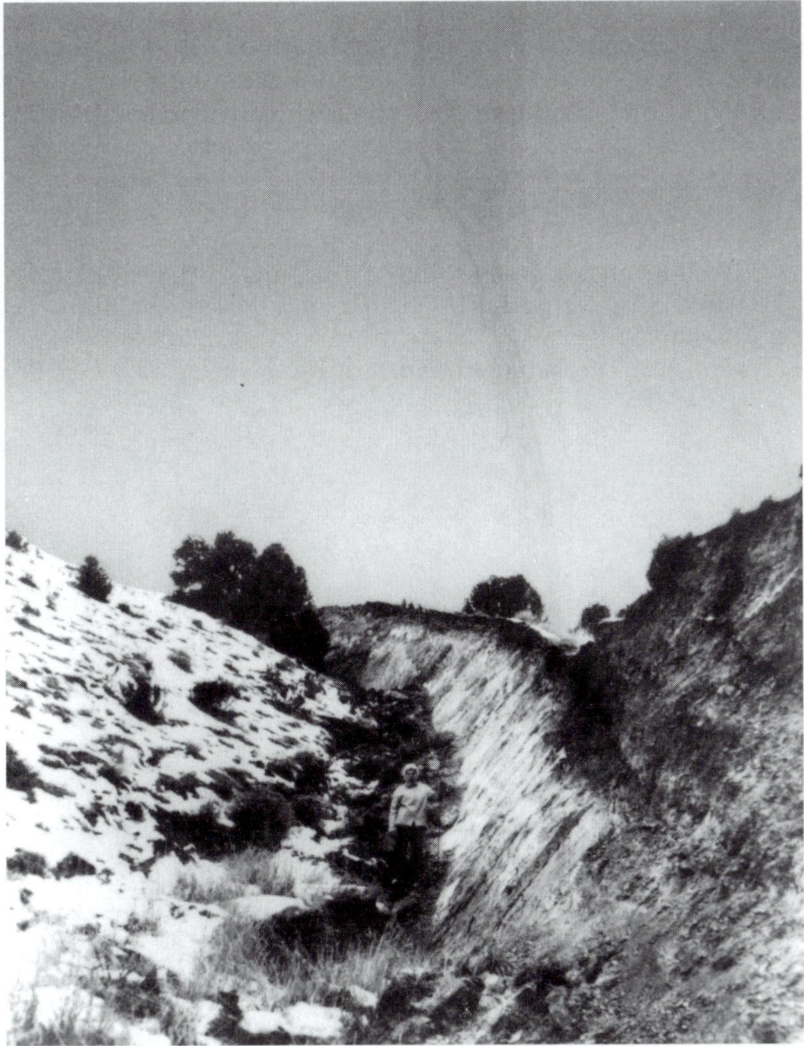

Figure 44 Pleasant Valley, Nevada, earthquake, 1915. Tobin Range, looking east. The white line at the base of the mountains is a fault scarp from the 1915 Pleasant Valley earthquake.

placement eighteen feet. Several northwest-striking segments of the scarps had a right-lateral component of displacement, generally less than three feet.

At Kennedy, two adobe houses were destroyed, mine tunnels collapsed, and concrete mine foundations were cracked. At Winnemucca, adobe buildings generally were damaged, and several multistory brick buildings lost their coping and parts of upper walls; many chimneys were demolished above the rooflines. In addition, water tanks were thrown down at Battle Mountain, Kodiak, Lovelock, and Parran. Damage occurred on several ranches at the southern end of Pleasant Valley. An adobe house was shaken down, a masonry chicken house and a hog pen were destroyed, and houses were displaced from their foundations. There was a large increase in the flow of springs and streams throughout northern Nevada and cracks formed in unconsolidated materials for considerable distances.

References for Further Study

McPhee, J. 1980. *Basin and Range*. New York: Farrar, Straus, Giroux.

Penick, J. L. 1981. *The New Madrid Earthquakes*, rev. ed. Columbia: University of Missouri Press.

Yeats, R., et al. 1993. *The Geology of Earthquakes*. New York: W. H. Freeman.

70

Mattoon, Illinois, tornado

May 26, 1917
Mattoon, southeast of Springfield

Mattoon was responsible for the deaths of 121 people in the town of the same name and the destruction of 2,000 of its homes

The Mattoon tornado of May 26, 1917, which caused 101 deaths, injured 638, and did $55 million in property damage, was one of two worst tornadoes the state ever experienced. The other of these tornados was the deadliest in the United States, the Tri-state tornado of 1925. The 1917 tornado was a powerful F4 and tore Mattoon apart, killing 101 persons, injuring 689, and leaving more than 2,000 homeless. The business section of Mattoon experienced the worst amount of damage. The storm, traveling from east to west, devastated the entire northern half of the town, leaving no building standing in a section several blocks in width. The Mattoon tornado was the world's longest-lasting tornado, lasting for over seven hours and traveling 293 miles, spreading death and destruction along its path from Missouri through Indiana and then to Illinois. It was also the thirteenth deadliest tornado in U.S. history. Charleston and Mattoon are vulnerable to many disasters, including tornadoes and, because of their locations in what has come to be known as tornado alley, they must always live with capricious weather.

At 7 A.M. on May 19, 1917, a trough of low pressure lay west of Illinois. The isobar of 29.60 inches enclosed an elongated area extending from western Lake Superior to eastern Kansas. The center of this area was at St. Paul. Southerly winds and mild temperatures were general in the Mississippi Valley as far north as Minnesota. By 7 P.M. the center of the low-pressure area lay north of Lake Superior. Thunderstorms had occurred over northern and central Illinois, and winds were west at Springfield and northwest in all of western Illinois. At Springfield the wind veered from southeast to southwest and later to west and northwest. It was evident that the tornado developed at the time of the wind shift. In the aftermath of the tornado, Mattoon and Charleston took up the task of recovering dead bodies, nursing the injured, and housing and feeding the homeless.

References for Further Study

Church, Christopher R. 1993. *The Tornado: Its Structure, Dynamics, Prediction, and Hazards*. Washington, DC: American Geophysical Union.

Grazulis, T. P. 2001. *The Tornado: Nature' s Ultimate Windstorm* Norman: University of Oklahoma Press.

Weems, John Edward. 1991. *The Tornado*. College Station: Texas A&M University Press.

71

Halifax, Nova Scotia, Canada, explosion

December 6, 1917

Two ships collided in the narrow entrance to Halifax Harbor

The explosion that ensued was one of the world's greatest prior to the arrival of atomic bombs. It shattered the port of Halifax and surrounding area. The death toll was 1,600, while 9,000 others were injured, and 6,000 homes were destroyed

Two ships were approaching Halifax harbor on the morning of December 6, 1917, one arriving, loaded with ammunition, and the other on its way to Europe with a load of coal. Some confusion existed between the two ships, in spite of the fixed rule about how to pass, over whether to pass on starboard or port sides of the ships, which caused a collision in the narrow entrance to the harbor. The incoming ship, the *Mont Blanc,* had just come from New York and was about to add some coal to its cargo in Halifax before sailing for the war zone in Europe. The usual red warning flag that is always flown on a munitions ship was missing. The captain did not hoist it because he feared it would make his ship a special target for lurking German submarines. The ships collided and set off a gigantic explosion. Within minutes the whole surrounding area was shattered.

There were other reasons for some carelessness on the part of the outgoing skipper. His ship, the *Imo,* had been delayed and he was anxious to leave with his load of coal for Belgium. Traffic was heavy in the narrow channel because this was December and in a northern country like Canada there were only a small number of daylight hours available. Ships and tugs alike always wanted to get out of the channel before dark. Captain Le Medec of the *Mont Blanc* signaled a port passage to the *Imo* as the ships approached

Figure 45 A building damaged by the Halifax explosion, 1917.

each other. The *Imo* captain replied, suggesting a starboard passage, then sailed on without waiting for a reply. One of the sacred rules of navigation is that you do not act, in a case like this, before the other side agrees.

A few minutes later the *Imo'* sprow cut into the *Mont Blanc* ahead of the main hold where all the TNT was stored. Captain Le Medec tried to swing his ship around in a desperate effort to avoid the collision. He knew what could happen if his ship were to be hit but in the narrow channel it was impossible to get away from the other ship. A drum of solvent was broken open in the collision and a spark ignited it. As the liquid ran down into the hold the fire spread to the huge quantities of TNT. The *Imo* captain backed his ship away and beached it.

Years later a man who lived close to the harbor reflected on the event of December 6, 1917. He lived to tell the tale and he remembered wondering at the time why two ships could come so close to each other without trying to avoid a collision. He noticed that the *Mont Blanc* tried to swing away but it was too late. One moment after the collision it was clear that the munitions ship was about to explode. Halifax harbor is only half a mile wide so the amount of space available for altering course was minimal. The tide carried the *Mont Blanc* toward a pier on the south side where a telegraph operator was on duty.

He watched the ship come closer and closer and he knew about its lethal cargo. Instead of running away he stayed at his post, sending out warning signals, and just before the explosion he shouted a goodbye. His body was found later in the evening. The power of the explosion swept away churches, factories, and every other kind of building. Nothing was left standing. Fires broke out all over the place and shells and other ammunition rained down on people with some of it exploding in the process. Terror-stricken men and women and children, all of them covered with black soot and bleeding from numerous cuts from flying pieces of glass, were the common sight everywhere.

When the *Mont Blanc* exploded it just vanished in a cloud of smoke—blast of air and debris rose a mile high. Devastation was everywhere within a one-mile radius. Some bodies were thrown half-a-mile on to the shore. A thirty-foot tsunami erupted and, carrying rocks scooped up from the seabed, destroyed all the piers together with their contents. The tragedy was all the worse because of the war. Large numbers of military personnel and supplies were assembled at the harbor, awaiting transportation to Europe.

Two further complications made circumstances especially difficult for victims. The worst blizzard in living memory had just hit Halifax and temperatures were well below freezing. Many victims who were trapped in buildings froze to death. The second crisis was a forced evacuation because of the danger of fire at the munitions' stores. Out of a total population of 50,000, about 1,600 lost their lives, a further 9,000 were injured, and 6,000 lost their homes. It was the most violent human-made explosion prior to the appearance of atomic weapons. The blast shattered windows one hundred miles away. Damage amounted to $35 million, an enormous sum at that time. Subsequent investigations concluded that the captains of both ships were to blame for what had happened but only minor penalties were given. The city of Halifax had to be completely rebuilt.

Halifax was not the only place in North America where accidents involving munitions occurred both during World War I and in the years immediately afterward. On May 18, 1918, in a suburb of Pittsburgh, an explosion shattered the neighborhood around the factory of the Aetna Chemical Company, a manufacturer of TNT. The accident was triggered by an error in the part of the factory where various chemical components of TNT were being mixed. Workers nearby heard a low popping sound, something that would normally be ignored, but those familiar with the manufacturing process reacted immediately. They knew that in a matter of seconds the whole building would explode. A few managed to escape but most died. By the end of the day 241 were dead or missing and four hundred others were injured. The first building to explode was the one in which chemicals were being assembled.

As the building went up in flames it set off the next building in the complex and so the fires and explosions continued like a series of gigantic firecrackers until, within a few minutes, the whole neighborhood was wrecked. Heavy machinery, walls, roofs, and rafters were shot into the air, to descend minutes later on those trying to escape the inferno. Ambulances were dispatched to the scene from every hospital in the Pittsburgh area while company guards and local police set up a barrier to protect people from the burning factory. A morgue was set up near the factory and a train arrived to supplement the work of the ambulances by bringing the injured to hospitals. This train could only come to a point four miles from the accident scene because tracks had been covered with debris so the injured had to be carried to the train. All telephone and telegraph lines had been severed so there were no means of communication with places beyond the factory area, resulting in delays in getting help for the injured.

Eight years after the TNT explosions at the Aetna Chemical Company, on July 10, 1926, a lightning strike hit the depot at Lake Denmark, New Jersey, where the entire U.S. Navy's store of munitions was kept. Everything was blown sky-high in one gigantic explosion. It all happened during a thunderstorm in the late afternoon of July 10. A lightning bolt struck one of the storage units where TNT was kept and started a fire. It could have been contained but the officer in charge had been assured that the protective system in place would prevent damage from any lightning strike. The result was that the little fire mushroomed quickly into a catastrophe. The lightning-arresting system which had been installed for just such an event, for some reason failed.

Lake Denmark's Naval Ammunition Depot was located about thirty miles west of the Hudson River in New Jersey. The navy's entire supply of munitions was stored here and ships came up the Hudson River for supplies. They were then transferred by rail from the depot to the ships. In those years the fleet was concentrated on the Atlantic Coast so this location was accessible at all times. The army also had a munitions supply depot alongside the navy's depot. In all there was a complex of 180 buildings, including some manufacturing. Because of the huge quantities of explosives kept at this center and because of the frequency of summer thunderstorms in this part of New Jersey, a lightning-arresting system had been installed.

On July 10, 1926, near a storage unit that housed a million pounds of high-intensity TNT, a lightning bolt struck. That should not have been a problem as the lightning rod had been installed within a few feet of that location. For reasons that were never clear, something failed to work because within a few minutes a small fire appeared and almost at once a fire alarm rang out across the whole complex. One officer half a mile away from the fire looked out of his office window in time to see a huge white flash. He ducked down under the window and lay on the floor, knowing that the blast from the explosion would momentarily smash into his building and demolish it. A few seconds later that was what happened.

One after another high-explosive rounds exploded and fires sprang up. The entire area within half a mile of the arsenal including all the buildings was destroyed with all surface objects swept away into the distance. Of the 180 buildings that comprised the arsenal only sixteen survived. For about ten hours, fires and explosions continued unabated and none of the fires went out during that time. Not until the following morning were the flames finally doused. Residents as far as fifty miles away heard and to some extent felt the blasts. When it was all over damage added up to more than $150 million. Thirty lives had been lost and two hundred others injured.

The countryside was all torn up around the arsenal, leaving it like an old-style battlefield. Deep craters were torn out of the sandy soil. Steel girders were thrown a mile from the blast site. A large piece of a charred wooden beam was found on a farm three-and-a-half miles from the blast site. New Jersey's governor together with its two senators requested that the whole arsenal be moved from the state. Both the general public and the media supported the governor. The War Department was so moved by the event that it thought it had been the world's worst explosion. It certainly was the worst explosion in U.S. history up to that time.

The navy was rightly blamed for not taking adequate safety precautions. The lightning-arresting system clearly was inadequate and the high concentration of explosive material in so small a space was, to say the least, unwise. There was severe criticism of the navy from the U.S. government, both for the cost of the tragedy and for the dangerous position in which it placed the navy. Two years after the explosion the Department of Defense Explosives Safety Board was established. It was instructed to provide oversight on all aspects of explosives, including maintenance, transportation, and storage. Never again would so high a concentration of munitions be found in one place. Arsenals were subsequently placed in low population density areas across the country.

References for Further Study

Armstrong, John Griffith. 2002. *The Halifax Explosion and the Royal Canadian Navy: Inquiry and Intrigue*. Vancouver: University of British Columbia Press.

Armstrong, John Griffith. 2005. *Curse of the Narrows: The Halifax Explosion 1917*. New York: Harper-Collins.

Flemming, David B. 2004. *Explosion in Halifax Harbor: The Illustrated Account of a Disaster that Shook the World*. Toronto: Formac Publishing.

Glasner, Joyce. 2003. *The Halifax Explosion: Surviving the Blast that Shook a Nation*. Vancouver: Altitude Press.

Ruffman, Alan. 1994. *Ground Zero: A Reassessment of the 1917 Explosion in Halifax Harbo*r. Halifax: Nimbus Publishing.

72

World-wide flu pandemic

1918–1919

Flu pandemic affected the whole world with first reports coming from Spain

The disease spread from places where there were high concentrations of soldiers. It spread all over the world and took the lives of thirty million people

In the last year of World War I, the world was hit with a flu pandemic, the H1N1 virus. It would prove be the deadliest disease in human history. Far worse in the total number of fatalities than the black death scourges of the Middle Ages or the total number killed in World War I, counting both military and civilian casualties. In less than six months of 1918, thirty million people worldwide died from this flu and most of those who died were young. Many insisted that the total number of deaths was far greater than thirty million. Even worse than the number of deaths was the speed with which it spread and the terrible nature of the illness that people experienced. Common symptoms were severe coughing accompanied with bleeding from different places and the skin turning blue because of the lack of oxygen in the lungs. For large numbers of sufferers the painful end came within a few hours as their lungs became filled with fluid and they suffocated.

Wherever people are crowded together, especially in the terrible conditions of World War I, in frontline trenches or on troop ships from the United States, conditions are ideal for the spread of a flu virus. Because the outbreak occurred at a critical point of the war, when it seemed for a time that German forces might succeed, strict secrecy about the spread of the disease was maintained by American and allied governments. The German government was equally secretive and the post-war publication of documents from that time revealed that the German army was being decimated by flu outbreaks. It was because of this secrecy that the name "Spanish Flu" came to be its popular name. Spain was not involved in the war so they freely reported on their experiences of the flu and, because they were the first to report on it, everyone assumed that it had originated in Spain. Reports of the spread of the disease came in from all over the world. It traveled as quickly as a bushfire to the countries of Europe, to the United States, and to Asia. It is likely that the total number of deaths in Asia, given the high concentrations of people in many regions, was as great as the total number of deaths in Europe and North America combined.

In the United States there were half a million deaths from the flu pandemic, all within a period of six months. Most of these were recorded as deaths from pneumonia, the outcome that in most cases led to death. Another half million of soldiers from service in both Europe and the United States were hospitalized and a large number of these died, as many as had died in combat for the whole period of the war. In Britain 200,000 died from the same pandemic flu and, as happened everywhere else, they all died within the same months of 1918 and the beginning of 1919. The course of the disease, just as had been the experience of others with diseases in earlier centuries, was always the same: because the strain of the destructive virus was new, and people therefore had no existing immunity with which to counter it, death rates were high. As immunity was built up among all the sufferers, the death rate decreased and finally reached the low level that is recognized as normal for any flu. In places around the world where population density was very low, and where because of their isolation there had never been exposures to the kind of flu we experience every year, the impacts were devastating. Whole Inuit villages in Northern Canada were wiped out, and on the Island of Samoa in the South Pacific a quarter of the population died.

By October, across the United States, as the numbers of dead mounted, a near panic atmosphere appeared. Theaters, movies, bars, and a host of other places were closed down. Even schools, churches, and public campaigns to raise money for the war were shut down. Laws were introduced that required everyone to wear a face mask in public. Stiff fines were imposed on those who sneezed or coughed in public without covering their mouths with handkerchiefs. With our current knowledge of viruses we can conclude that these precautions would not have stopped the spread of the 1918 flu but it was all that seemed possible to people of that time. The Catholic Charities of Philadelphia hired several horse-drawn wagons with which they searched alleys and tenements for the bodies of abandoned victims. The city morgue had no space for the bodies so they had to be placed in mass graves, and without caskets too since Philadelphia, like many cities, had run out of them. Police departments suddenly found their work greatly eased. Crime had dropped to half what it was a few months earlier. The problem was quite different for the generals in charge

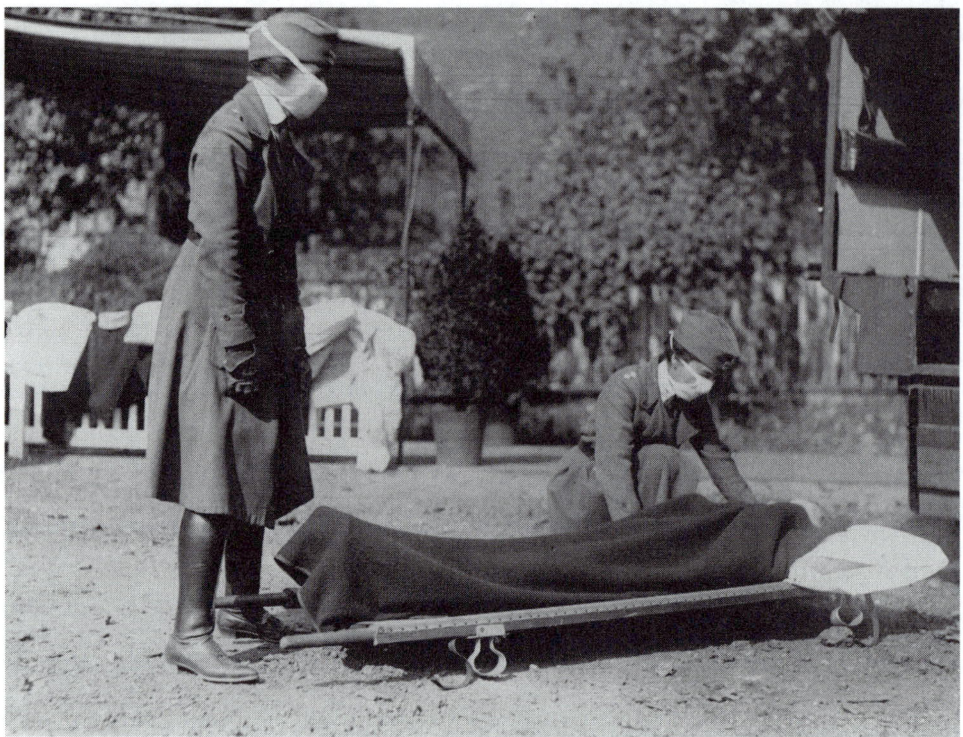

Figure 46 Demonstration at the Red Cross Emergency Ambulance Station in Washington, D.C., during the influenza pandemic of 1918.

of the army. This was a time of conscription, not the volunteer army of today, and those in charge of the draft and preliminary training before going overseas had to decide what to do.

Field Marshall General Crowder, in charge of the draft and training, was aware that crowded conditions in training camps were a recipe for the rapid spread of the flu. He knew what had happened earlier in 1918 at Camp Funston in Kansas, with the members of the Tenth Division, when soldiers in large numbers fell sick and many of them died. The officer in charge on that occasion wrote to the governor of Kansas, telling him that he had 1,440 admissions to hospital a day, that is to say about one a minute, and asking him to realize the strain that all of this was putting on his nursing and medical staff. General Crowder also knew that several other camps had, more recently, experienced a rash of flu infections. Following consultations with both President Wilson and the army leaders in Europe, Crowder decided to defer the training of 142,000 registrants who were due to begin on October 7, and wait for the end of the flu pandemic before bringing them to camp for training. Settling the question of training camps was easier than the one that President Wilson now faced. The army in Europe wanted more troops in order to capitalize on the successes they were experiencing but medical authorities urged him to stop the mass shipment of troops until the flu abated. Death rates on troop ships were running higher than the numbers that died in battle. Wilson accepted the advice of Army Chief of Staff General March, and decided not to suspend troop shipments. Fortunately, the end of the war came in less than a month after the President's decision.

In 1918 little was known about viruses and almost nothing was available to provide an adequate cure. Almost eighty years later, with concerns mounting that another flu pandemic could hit the world, scientists set about recreating the 1918 virus so that it could be tested out on lab animals to measure its strength. First they had to find a human body that had died as a result of the 1918 flu. They found one in Alaska that had been frozen in the Arctic permafrost soon after death so scientists were able to extract samples of lung tissue from it. The overlapping gene sequences were pieced together from this sample to give the full genome sequence and it was at that point that scientists became fairly certain that some ancestor had originally infected birds and the virus had moved from there into humans. A report from 1918, that was only investigated after 1998, confirmed this conviction. A veterinarian who was studying hog cholera in Iowa at that time discovered that the epidemic he was dealing with in pigs had symptoms that were identical to those he observed in the victims of the pandemic flu. He said in his report that whatever was caus-

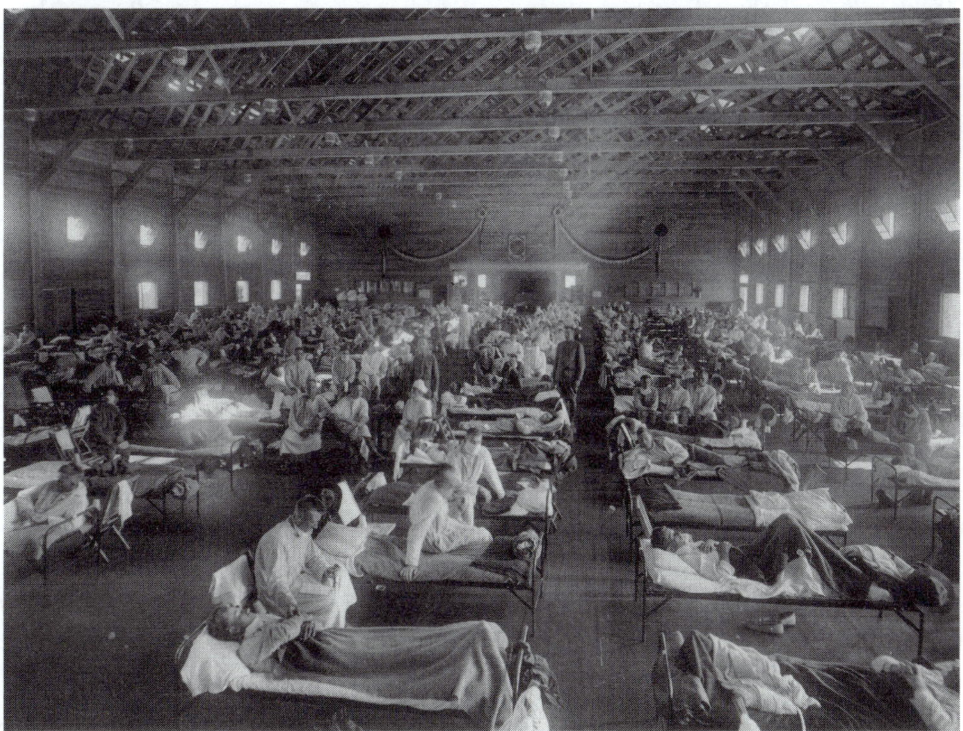

Figure 47 Emergency hospital during influenza epidemic, Camp Funston, Kansas.

ing the flu in pigs must be very similar to the flu affecting humans. Today, with all our understanding of viruses, experts are convinced that the pandemic flu of 1918 was indeed a mutation of one that had been resident in pigs. When the recently-reconstructed 1918 virus was tested in mice it was found to be extremely virulent, creating 40,000 more particles in a lung than happens with ordinary flu. All the mice that were tested with the 1918 virus died within six days. Samples of the virus are now stored in a secure vault at the Center for Diseases in Atlanta, Georgia, but fears exist over the risk of it getting into terrorist hands.

In 2005, the United Nations General Assembly called for immediate international mobilization against an avian flu that had already transferred into humans and, by early 2005, killed sixty-one people in Southeast Asia. There were fears that this virus could become a pandemic and be as destructive as the flu of 1918, a similar bird to human virus and the cause of the deaths of thirty million people worldwide. This new bird to human virus could be worse than the 1918 flu because, while there is much greater knowledge on how to cope with it, there is at the same time far greater and more frequent travel around the world. Finding a vaccine for a new type of virus, one that might change as it moves from bird to human, and then have it available in huge quantities at short notice is a huge challenge. An examination of what happened in Central Africa in the past few years illustrates the problem. Within a year, an outbreak of the deadly Ebola virus took the lives of more than five hundred people in the Congo. The source of the virus was unknown for some time then, in December of 2005, a team of scientists found the virus in three species of fruit bats in the Congo. These bats were part of the human food chain in the Congo and it seemed likely that the transmission from bird to human occurred in this way. The possibility of a similar bird or bat to human transmission in Asia has raised concern everywhere. Especially since the 1918 virus, though unknown at that time, was a transfer from bird to humans.

The United States is not the only country that reconstituted the 1918 virus. The director and staff of the U.S. Federation of American Scientists' Working Group on Biological Weapons are far from being satisfied with the level of security presently provided in Atlanta. They say that the risk of theft by a disgruntled, disturbed, or extremist lab employee at the facility is so great that it comes close to being inevitable. They have proposed raising the level of security to the highest possible. In 2003, they point out, a SARS virus escaped accidentally from a lab in Singapore and a year later there were two escapes of the same virus from labs in Beijing. The avian flu virus was found in thousands of birds in Asia and in smaller numbers in many other countries, presumably carried worldwide by migrating birds. The detailed gene sequences of this virus are well known. It is defined as the virus H5N1 and it is one that has never before been experienced by humans except for those who died from it in Asia. There are therefore no antibodies in humans that could fight off infections from this virus, as is the case year by year when more familiar strains of flu viruses appear.

Dr. Andrew Fauci of the U.S. National Institute of Health is the United States watchdog for tracing the behavior of the H5N1 virus, monitoring it regularly as samples are collected from time to time, to check any mutations that develop and to give warning if any evidence of transfers from human to human are found. To date this has not yet happened. Soon after the first human death from H5N1, Fauci's lab developed a vaccine that would be able to protect humans. It had to be tested out on mice before it was safe to be administered to humans and Fauci discovered that the dosage needed to protect test animals was far greater than required for traditional flu attacks. Thus the various difficulties associated with responding to the United Nations appeal remained: how to produce enough vaccine in a very short time. That is, once the right mutation is present for creating a pandemic, how to cope with breakdowns in social organizations and institutions if large numbers of people die, and how to equip and protect adequately the care givers in hospitals so that the damage can be minimized.

References for Further Study

Barry, John M. 2004. *The Great Influenza: The Epic Story of the Greatest Plague in History*. London: Penguin.

Beatty, W. K. 1976. *Epidemics*. New York: Scribners.

Crosby, Alfred W. 1990. *America' s Forgotten Pandemic: The Influenza of 1918*. Cambridge: Cambridge University Press.

Johnson, Niall. 2006. *Britain and the 1918– 19 Influenza Pandemic: A Dark Epilogue*. London: Routledge.

Rice, Geoffrey W. 2005. *Black November: The 1918 Influenza Pandemic in New Zealand*. Canterbury: Canterbury University Press.

Rosenau, M. J., and Last, J. M. 1980. *Maxcy-Rosenau Preventative Medicine and Public Health*. New York: Appleton-Century-Crofts.

73

Mona Passage, Puerto Rico, earthquake

October 11, 1918
Offshore between Puerto Rica and Dominican Republic

It was wartime. World War I was still being fought. The death toll was 116 and damage costs four million dollars

On the morning of October 11, 1918, Puerto Rico was visited by one of the most severe earthquakes it had ever experienced in modern times. It was later identified as having a magnitude of 7.5. The earthquake was followed, almost immediately, by a tsunami that broke upon the shore, drowning 116 people and destroying native huts. Property loss amounted to $4 million. In the northwestern part of the island, where the damage was greatest, a number of people left their dwellings and went to the hills, partly because of the unusual strength of the earthquake and partly because of the aftershocks that were almost continuous for two days.

The governor of Puerto Rico requested the secretary of war to investigate conditions throughout the island, to assess the damage and to assure everybody that the danger was over. An intensive one-month search of the territory was carried out, including the islands of Vieques and Saint Thomas. The epicenter was finally located deep in the northeast part of the sea passage between the island of Mona and the international border between Dominican Republic and Puerto Rico, a stretch of water known as Mona Passage. Everything that could throw light on the earthquake was carefully examined. The experiences and observations of a large number of persons were collected. Some of them had felt the shock in Santo Domingo and some had experienced the shaking on the Island of Vieques. The meteorologist in charge of the weather bureau at San Juan collected information for the investigating group through his many observers. Information was also gained through correspondence with persons where the shock was felt. The earthquake occurred in daytime. Puerto Rico is accustomed to shocks of mild to moderate intensity and this may explain the close agreement that was discovered in descriptions of the shock. Most observers say that the earthquake began as a pronounced vertical vibration, which was followed by horizontal oscillations. In regard to the directions of movements, they were mainly east to west.

The earthquake began suddenly without warning. There were no preliminary vibrations of any kind. Furthermore, no evidence of earthquakes of any kind had been felt over the previous eight months. The first shock was felt in San Juan shortly after ten in the morning. It lasted for a full two minutes, first as a series of vertical motions, accompanied by creaking of the timbers in wooden building, then latterly as horizontal shakings sufficient to cause nausea and evident in the swinging to and fro of electrical fixtures. A second shock followed about five minutes after the first one and a third one after a further five minutes. Both of these were of short duration, less than a minute each. In some of the churches, as at Arecibo and Mayaguez, places that are one hundred miles apart, columns supporting arches between the nave and the aisles were crushed as though they had been subjected to strong vertical compression. At a house near Mayaguez, wooden columns supporting a porch roof jumped up and down, and after the earthquake a shoe was found between the base of the column and the floor of the porch. The tower of the Arecibo church was badly cracked and tilted toward the east. Nearby, a steel smokestack was bent in an easterly direction. The cracks in the brick roof of the municipal building ran chiefly in a north-south direction and, at a place four miles south of Arecibo, books in a concrete vault were thrown from the shelves on the northwest wall but not from the other shelves. At the southwest corner of Puerto Rico the surface of the ground moved in waves as if it had been part of the ocean.

A great wave from the sea, now understood as a tsunami, following the earthquake of October 11, was highest near the northwestern part of Puerto Rico. It was seen almost immediately after the earthquake. Wherever the wave appeared on Puerto Rico or on its neighboring islands, observers reported that the ocean first withdrew from the land, in places exposing reefs and stretches of sea bottom never before visible during low tides, and then the water returned, reaching heights that were high above normal. At some places the main wave was followed by one or more smaller ones and, especially in shattered bays, the water continued to ebb and flow for some time. At the Boqueron Lighthouse the keeper, who was up in the tower when the earthquake began, immediately started down the stairs, and as he went down he noticed that the water along the shore had already begun to recede. It returned quickly and his measurements show that the height reached by the water, not counting the wash of the wave, was about fourteen feet above sea level. Southwest of the lighthouse, where the land is lower, the water was reported to have reached inland for a distance of three hundred feet into a grove of coconut palms. The lighthouse keeper had the impression that the wave came from the northwest. Near Point Agujereada the limestone cliffs are about 330–400 feet in height, and their base is a narrow strip of beach. Several hundred palms were uprooted by the wave, and the beach was turned into a sandy waste. In this vicinity a few small houses were destroyed and eight people reported to be drowned. People visiting this district soon after the earthquake estimated the height of the wave at eighteen feet.

As the seat of the disturbance was under the ocean it was impossible, in 1918, to determine its exact location, but it was estimated as being near latitude 18° 30′ north and longitude 67° 20′ west, or roughly ten miles west of Boqueron Lighthouse. The sea wave was highest along the northwest coat of Puerto Rico and decreased progressively in all directions. Submarine cables were broken at several places within the area bounded by parallels 18° 25′ and 18° 35′ north and meridians 67° 15′ and 67° 30′ west. The seismographic records of the earthquake do not fix the position of the origin with a high degree of accuracy. This is not to be wondered at when we remember that an error of one second in the record time of arrival of vibrations at the various stations in eastern North America would correspond to a difference of six miles in the distance from the point of origin. The errors seem to have balanced because together they identified the location as being in the northeastern part of the Mona Passage. As has already been mentioned the limitations of the technology in use in 1918 are reflected in the reports that were given by observers. The interpretation of the cause of the earthquake is one example of these limitations: severe earthquakes are the result of the sudden relief of stress that slowly accumulated in the rocks on the sea floor.

The tsunami that accompanied the earthquake had a different origin. Research conducted on the ocean floor around the island of Mona many years after 1918 revealed underwater landslides that dated back to 1918. The small portion of the earth's crust beneath Puerto Rico, in contact with the much bigger North American Tectonic Plate, was seen to have tilted at the point of contact, presumably due to interactions between the two. Gigantic slabs of limestone were released by these interactions, some of them as big as fifty miles wide, and the result of the displacement of water they caused gave rise to the tsunami. The damage it caused was greatest on the low-lying coastal areas and, as has so often been seen in the actions of tsunamis, the retreating wave because it carries so much debris and rocks is often more deadly than the first incoming wave. The Columbus Memorial stood on the western beach. It was demolished and a 2,500 pound limestone block from the wreckage was carried inland for more that three hundred feet. The island of Mona experienced the tsunami in the form of a twelve-foot wave that washed away a pier.

References for Further Study

Bolt, Bruce. A. 1993. *Earthquakes*. New York: W. H. Freeman.

Moores, E. M., ed. 1990. *Shaping the Earth: Tectonics of Continents and Oceans*. New York: W. H. Freeman.

Sieh, Kerry, et al. 1998. *The Earth in Turmoil*. New York: W. H. Freeman.

74

Vancouver Island, Canda, earthquake

December 6, 1918

West Coast of Vancouver Island west of Port Alberni

This one had a magnitude of 7 but its activity was unrelated to the subducting plate. Earthquakes are common in this area and fortunately this one was intra-plate and, while felt over a very large area, caused no casualties and did minor damage to buildings

This earthquake of magnitude 7 occurred on Friday, December 6, 1918. Its epicenter was near the west coast of Vancouver Island at a depth of ten miles, and was felt very strongly at Estevan Point Lighthouse and at Nootka Lighthouse on the southern tip of Nootka Island. There was some damage done to the Estevan Point Lighthouse and to a wharf at Ucluelet. This earthquake awakened people all over Vancouver Island and in the greater Vancouver area. It was felt in northern Washington State and at Kelowna, in the interior of British Columbia. Due to sparse population, no injuries and little damage resulted from this earthquake. Other than broken dishes and some instances of cracked plaster on central Vancouver Island, the only damage reported was to the Estevan Point lighthouse. Its steel reinforced concrete tower cracked for its full length in several places, and parts of the glass lens were smashed.

There is an average of one earthquake in southwest British Columbia every day. Nearly all are too small to be felt, but a damaging earthquake occurs somewhere in the region about once every twenty years. The largest earthquake in this century had a magnitude of 7.3. It hit in 1946 and was centered beneath Vancouver Island. Were this earthquake to occur today under Vancouver, damage would be in the billions of dollars.

Recently, scientists have recognized a history of infrequent, but great earthquakes on the fault separating the subducting Juan de Fuca and North America plates. The last great earthquake in 1700 AD affected the entire coast from northern California to southern British Columbia. The 1918 earthquake appears to be a crustal intraplate event occurring in the lithosphere of the America Plate, resulting from the complicated interaction of the Explorer, Juan de Fuca, and America plates.

The major tectonic boundary separating the Pacific and North American lithospheric plates lies near the west coast of North America. The San Andreas and Queen Charlotte transform faults dominate this boundary. However, in the region between northern Vancouver Island and northern California, the oceanic Juan de Fuca and Explorer plates lie between the major plates and are being subducted beneath North America. These two smaller plates act independently of the two bigger ones, the Juan de Fuca moving under the North American Plate at approximately an inch and a half a year. While major concerns over earthquakes in this region tend to focus on subduction motions, it is important to note that this 1918 one was not of this type. Instead it was a crustal, intraplate earthquake. Rather than being directly associated with the subducting Nootka fault zone, it was linked to the stress in the continental crust as the North American Plate interacts with the Explorer and Juan de Fuca plates.

References for Further Study

Halacy, D. 1974. *Earthquakes: A Natural History*. Indianapolis: Bobbs-Merrill.

Moores, E. M., ed. 1990. *Shaping the Earth: Tectonics of Continents and Oceans*. New York: W. H. Freeman.

Sieh, Kerry, et al. 1998. *The Earth in Turmoil*. New York: W. H. Freeman.

75

Kelud, Indonesia, volcanic eruption

May 1, 1919

Eastern Java, southwest of Surabaja

The eruption expelled a lake on its surface, throwing mud and pyroclastic flows from the heated water all over the surrounding agricultural areas and killing 5,000 people

On May 1, 1919, the volcano Kelud, on the island of Java in Indonesia, erupted. It was its deadliest strike of the twentieth century. The eruption expelled the lake at the summit, approximately 5,000 feet above sea level. Mud and pyroclastic flows from the heated waters of the lake swept over the surrounding agricultural areas of Kediri and Blitar. They traveled as far as twenty-five miles from the volcano, destroying 40,000 acres of farmland. Three million people live within fifteen miles of the volcano and more than 5,000 people were killed on the day of the eruption. A hundred villages were destroyed. Kelud is a small volcano when compared with Indonesia's others but, because of the lake at its summit and the frequency of its eruptions, it has been the source of many of Indonesia's deadliest eruptions.

The 1919 eruption prompted the creation of the Volcano Survey of Indonesia with its first task being how to drain the lake waters from Kelud. There had been earlier attempts because of the known frequency of Kelud's eruptions. In 1905, the local Dutch administration arranged for a dam to be built at the foot of the mountain in order to divert flows into the nearby river Badak. When the 1919 eruption occurred, this dam proved to be ineffective. It was taken away by the heavy mudflows that occurred. After this very destructive eruption, authorities decided to dig a tunnel and so prevent a repeat of the 1919 tragedy. Extensive engineering work started in September 1919 and was finally completed in 1926. A tunnel, a thousand feet in length, had been excavated through the walls of the crater by that time. It lowered the elevation of the water by two hundred feet and thus reduced considerably the volume of water that remained. Unfortunately, successive eruptions in 1951 and 1966, though much weaker than the 1919 event, destroyed the drainage system that was in place and raised both the elevation and the volume of the summit lake. The reconstruction of the drainage system was initiated immediately after the 1966 event and it succeeded in limiting the volume of water in the lake to a manageable level.

Indonesia has a chain of 129 active volcanoes extending eastward for 4,000 miles from the northern end of Sumatra. Several eruptions of these volcanoes have been catastrophic in the past, as in the cases of Tambora in 1815 and Krakatau in 1883, both in terms of the loss of human life and the partial or total destruction of infrastructure and economy. Millions of Indonesians are currently living on volcanoes and civil infrastructures are progressively developing on their slopes. Due to the economic and demographic pressures that exist in Indonesia today, it is clearly not possible to prohibit settlement of population around these active volcanoes. The soil is incredibly good. One of the challenges for Indonesia is how to use and manage this land resource as well as to minimize the risk to humans and long-term economic effects of future eruptions. The relatively inconspicuous 5,000-foot-high Kelud *stratovolcano* contains a lake in its crater at the summit that has been the source of some of Indonesia's most deadly eruptions. More than thirty eruptions have been recorded from it over the past thousand years. In 1556 its mudflow from an eruption was responsible for 10,000 deaths. The ejection of water from its lake during Kelud's typically short, but violent, eruptions creates pyroclastic and mud flows that lead to fatalities and destruction. These events have claimed more than 15,000 lives since 1500 and caused widespread destruction.

References for Further Study

Cas, R. A. F., et al. 1987. *Volcanic Successions Modern and Ancient*. London: Allen and Unwin.

Fisher, R. V., et al. 1984. *Pyroclastic Rocks*. Berlin: Springer-Verlag.

Francis, P. 1976. *Volcanoes*. Harmondsworth: Penguin.

Simkin, T., et al. 1981. *Volcanoes of the World*. Stroudsburg: Hutchinson Ross.

Tazieff, H., et al. 1983. *Forecasting Volcanic Events*. Amsterdam: Elsevier.

76

Florida/Gulf of Mexico hurricane

September 14, 1919
Florida Keys and Corpus Christi, Texas

After causing major damage in the Florida Keys this hurricane devastated Corpus Christi

The hurricane of 1919 was one of the deadliest and perhaps strongest storms of the twentieth century. With winds reaching at least 110 mph and wave heights as high as sixteen feet, the great storm made landfall in the Corpus Christi area on September 14, 1919. Local people were influenced by the widespread belief that the city was protected from severe damage of hurricanes by the barrier islands. Even when stories reached them just ahead of the storm, of incredible damage from a hurricane in the Florida Keys, little was made of the possibility of a Texas landfall. Before September 14 had passed into history the terrible reality was evident to all: debris was piled up as high as sixteen feet in downtown Corpus Christi and the official total of dead was 287. Many believed that the accurate figure was in the range of 600–1,000 because city officials wanted to downplay the severity of the event.

The storm was first detected near the Lesser Antilles on September 2, 1919. It traveled to the west-northwest and hit the Dominican Republic and the Bahamas, where it reached peak strength as a category 4 hurricane. The storm's center grazed the Florida Keys on September 9 as a category 4 hurricane on the Saffir-Simpson Hurricane Scale, killing several hundred people before making its way into the Gulf of Mexico. The barometric pressure of the hurricane after leaving the Keys, as taken by a ship, was 27.37 inches, making this hurricane one of the most intense in U.S. recorded history. It was certainly the most intense to strike Key West in all of the twentieth century. As it moved into the Gulf something strange happened. All indications at the time pointed to the hurricane curving into the Louisiana coastline on September 13. On the basis of that prediction the Weather Bureau seemed to have ignored what was going on for a time. It is difficult to understand what happened subsequently unless this was the explanation.

With the advantages of radar, satellite, and weather balloon reports, it seems to be almost inconceivable today that we have not always had the luxury of tracking hurricanes hour by hour. Inconceivable as it may be, none of these technical resources were available to forecasters in 1919, but what was available, limited though it was, failed them. The Weather Bureau lost the hurricane in the Gulf soon after it had left the Keys. With no ship reports and only sporadic observations along the coastline, the Weather Bureau began a desperate attempt to find the hurricane center. Coastal offices sent special observations by telegraph every two hours to the Washington headquarters. By midnight on September 13 the storm's center was still missing as far as the forecasters were concerned. They sent a message to Corpus Christi urging everyone to take all possible precautions against a hurricane, especially if high winds, high tide, and low barometer readings were observed.

Finally, at 9:30 A.M. on September 14, the Meteorologist-In-Charge of the Corpus Christi Office issued a statement to get people out of low-lying areas at once. Police, city, and Weather Bureau officials began to notify the public. By 10:30 A.M. they knew that the hurricane was near. Shortly thereafter, wires to Port Aransas went down, isolating the city of Corpus Christi. Rockport did receive later advisories, and the last one gave an accurate if not cryptic analysis, this is the worst hurricane in history. The first two deadly effects, the storm surge and wind, weakened and then tore away at buildings close to the coastline. But with the track and strength of the hurricane, a seiche developed along the bay front region of Corpus Christi. A northeast wind developed and, as it veered to the east, it strengthened the seiche. creating an even greater height in the storm surge. Water reached twelve feet in the downtown district, and even higher in the narrow inlet into Nueces Bay.

No one can give a reliable estimate of the strength of the hurricane when it made landfall. Wind data at the Corpus Christi Weather Office was lost when the anemometer was destroyed. One nearby town reported wind gusts of 170 mph. Damage all along the coast was both catastrophic and deadly. In the North Beach area of Corpus Christi only two buildings survived and both of them were severely damaged. Crude oil had been spilled everywhere and despite the harm done it ensured a lower rate of disease than might otherwise have occurred because the oil preserved dead bodies from quick decay. The personal stories of survivors are quite extraordinary. One woman was found exhausted at the beach, tarred and feathered. She had become immersed in oil while drifting on debris. Her head rested on a feathered-down pillow that had come from somewhere. Another woman was washed ashore with her dog. Three times she had slipped off the raft on which she rested and three times her dog pulled her back on to it. One of the people forced to evacuate Corpus Christi was Bob Simpson, who would later become head of the National Hurricane Center and one of the designers of the Saffir-Simpson Hurricane Scale.

References for Further Study

Barnes, Jay. 1998. *Florida' s Hurricane History* Chapel Hill: University of North Carolina Press.

Lee, Sally. 1993. *Hurricanes*. New York: Franklin Watts Publishing.

Tannehill, Ivan Ray. 1956. *Hurricanes: Their Nature and History*. Princeton: Princeton University Press.

Williams, J. M., and Duedall, I. W. 1997. *Florida Hurricanes and Tropical Storms*. Gainesville: University of Florida Press.

77

Humboldt, California, earthquake

January 22, 1923
The coast of California near Humboldt Bay

This whole coastal area experiences greater damage from earthquakes and tsunamis than anywhere else on the Californian coast because of the influence of the Gorda offshore tectonic plate. There was widespread damage of buildings but no casualties

A 7.2 magnitude earthquake struck California off the coast of Humboldt County on January 22, 1923. Houses were severely damaged at Ferndale, Petrolia, and Upper Mattole. Many chimneys were downed and water lines were broken. At Pepperwood, one house was shaken from its foundation and split apart, and another was twisted from its base. Chimneys also were knocked over at a number of places. Several landslides occurred. The impact of the earthquake was felt all the way from Siskiyou County on the Oregon border south to San Francisco, three hundred miles away, and eastward to Nevada County. It was also observed on several ships at sea. Many aftershocks occurred in the Petrolia and Upper Mattole regions. A small tsunami was recorded.

The North Coast of California and adjacent offshore area is the most active seismic region in the continental United States. The size, location, and frequency of past earthquakes give an indication of what to expect in the future. The instrumental record of earthquakes on this coast extends back only into the early 1900s. However, it is possible to learn about older earthquakes from written accounts in newspapers, church logs, and diaries. From these accounts, seismologists can reconstruct the pattern of ground shaking and estimate the location and magnitude of early earthquakes. Since 1853, more than sixty earthquakes have caused some damage to North Coast communities. The majority of these earthquakes have been centered offshore in the southeastern portion of the Gorda Plate offshore from Crescent City and Eureka.

These earthquakes recur frequently, causing some damage to communities, particularly in the Cape Mendocino area, almost every two years. Since the early 1990s there has been the highest level of regional earthquake activity of the twentieth century. Nine earthquakes of magnitude 6 or larger have struck the coastal and offshore areas. Seven earthquakes were close enough to coastal communities to cause at least moderate damage. Damaging earthquake activity was not restricted to the coast. Klamath Falls, Oregon, experienced its strongest earthquake in historic times. West of Eureka an earthquake with a magnitude of 7.3 occurred in 1922. This potentially damaging earthquake was felt from Eugene, Oregon, all the way to San Francisco. In 1994, the area around Eureka experienced its largest earthquake since 1932. It caused an estimated $5 million in property losses. In that same year there was the Mendocino Fault Earthquake, the largest ever recorded along this fault. It was felt as extensively as the Eureka earthquake of 1922.

A major reason for the recurrence of earthquakes in north coastal California right up to the present time is found in the behavior of the Gorda Plate, offshore from the stretch of coast between Crescent City and Eureka. This smaller tectonic plate is gradually breaking apart under the stresses it is experiencing from much larger plates. In 2005, for example, an earthquake of magnitude 7 was recorded in this coastal area and, because of its size, it was feared that tsunamis would be triggered. It turned out that the quake was caused by undersea pieces of the Gorda Plate jerking violently past one another in a sideways motion known as strike-slip, not the kind of motion that would create big tsunamis. A subduction motion of the Gorda Plate beneath the North American Plate would be a much more dangerous event. The fundamental action that is compressing the Gorda Plate is the northward movement of the Pacific Plate as it slides parallel to the San Andreas Fault. A strike-slip movement close to the coast could give rise to a tsunami and places such as Humboldt Bay and Crescent City would be the victims of the waves within half an hour.

References for Further Study

Hansen, R. J., ed. 1970. *Seismic Design for Nuclear Power Plants*. Cambridge: MIT Press.

Jordan, D. S., ed. 1907. *The California Earthquake of 1906*. San Francisco: A. M. Robertson.

McPhee, J. 1980. *Basin and Range*. New York: Farrar, Straus, Giroux.

Yeats, R., et al. 1993. *The Geology of Earthquakes*. New York: W. H. Freeman.

78

Kamchatka, Russia, earthquake

February 3, 1923
The Peninsula of Kamchatka, Russia,
in the Northwest Pacific Ocean

This region of Russia is well known as a source of powerful earthquakes and equally powerful tsunamis. In the case of the 1923 earthquake the tsunami began as a twenty-five-foot wave and within half a day it reached Hawaii and California, causing damage and disruption there

On February 3, 1923, an earthquake of magnitude 8.3 struck the east coast of Kamchatka, Russia, generating a twenty-five-foot tsunami that raced across the Pacific to Japan, Hawaii, and California. Local government documents show that this tsunami, at its origin, flooded low-lying coastal areas that were covered by thick snow. The unusual process of tsunami run-up without loss from ground friction is a result of the smoothing of the ground by ice. It was concluded that the tsunami flooded snowfields and deposited an extensive sheet of sand. A mixture of snow and seawater flooded over the area and caused damage to vegetation. Kamchatka is notorious for triggering earthquake tsunamis, and historical documents show that they have repeatedly caused considerable damage over the past two centuries. The tsunami from the 1923 earthquake caused an eight-inch rise in sea level at San Diego and a four-inch rise at San Francisco.

The Pacific Plate's behavior is the key to the Kamchatkan earthquakes and tsunamis and its history is clearly illustrated in the evolution of the Hawaiian-Emperor Chain, a series of volcanic mountains stretching 4,000 miles across the North Pacific from Hawaii to a subduction zone at Kamchatka. The chain also provides a concrete illustration of sea floor spreading. The Pacific Plate, over millions of years, moved northwards and then northwestwards, first at a rate of three inches per year, then four inches, over the last seventy million years. Volcanic mountains in the chain older than seventy million years were carried down into the Kamchatka subduction zone and, as a subduction zone, every earthquake of the size of the 1823 quake carried the likelihood of a major tsunami.

The Kamchatka Peninsula is one of the most tectonically active regions of the world, and has historically experienced a number of large tsunamis. Assessing tsunami records is important for long-term tsunami prediction and for mapping the likely hazards. In the case of Kamchatka, historical records of tsunamis are too short to develop a predictive chronology of events. The way to obtain long-term data is to study paleotsunamis, that is, to identify, map and date prehistoric tsunami deposits. These deposits also provide a proxy record of large earthquakes. Paleotsunami research became an active field of investigation in the late 1980s. Evidence of strong modern and pre-historic earthquakes and tsunamis has been found and studied in Japan, North America, and a number of other localities. At Kamchatka, studies of tsunami deposits began about 1990. Preliminary results suggest that the period from 0 to 1000 AD was particularly active. The combined record of tsunami deposits and of numerous marker tephra on Kamchatka offers an unprecedented opportunity to study tsunami frequency. It is possible to examine both the average frequency of events as well as the changes in frequency through time.

Some examples since 1923 of major earthquakes at the Kamchatka-Kuril-Islands (KKI) site provide good illustrations of the power of the tsunamis that follow. These outcomes are giving rise to increased efforts by national governments around the Pacific to anticipate and deal with tsunamis. In November of 1952, an unusually big quake occurred at KKI. It had a magnitude of 9 and it triggered Pacific-wide tsunamis in all directions toward the south and east. New Zealand experienced waves three feet high, Peru and Chile had lower wave heights, and Alaska and California had wave heights of four to five feet. The area that suffered most from this tsunami was Hawaii. Altogether there was one million dollars worth of damage. In Oahu, boats and piers were destroyed and at the Big Island a bridge linking an outlying island to Hilo was shattered. The year 1958 saw another major earthquake from KKI, this time one of magnitude 8.3. Five years later there was an earthquake of 8.5 magnitude and, in 2002, another of magnitude 7.5. In November of 2006 there was one of magnitude 8.3 and, this time, the preparations that are described in the following paragraph were in place. The Pacific-wide tsunami alert was received in good time. This time Crescent City of California received the strongest hit. Two docks were damaged and several boats were tossed on to dry land. Waves were three feet above normal and they persisted for twenty minutes.

The U.S. National Tsunami Hazard Mitigation Program has representatives from the National Oceanic and Atmospheric Administration, the Federal Emergency Management Agency, the U.S. Geological Survey, and the states of Alaska, California, Hawaii, Oregon, and Washington. The program addresses three major tasks: hazard assessment, warning guidance, and mitigation. The first two tasks, hazard assessment and warning guidance, are led by physical scientists who, using research and modeling methods, develop products that allow communities to identify their tsunami hazard areas and receive more accurate and timely warning information. The third task, mitigation, is handled by emergency organizations that use their experience and networks to translate science and technology into user-friendly planning and education projects. Their activities focus on assisting federal, state, and local officials as they plan for and respond to disasters. They also provide information for the public that is deeply affected by the impacts of both the disaster and the pre-event planning arrangements that have to be made.

References for Further Study

Ayre, Robert S. 1975. *Earthquake and Tsunami Hazards in the United States*. Boulder, CO: Institute of Behavioral Science.

Claque, D. A., et al. 1973. *Tertiary Pacific Plate Motion Deduced from the Hawaiian-Emperor Chain*. Boulder, CO: Geological Society of America Bulletin.

Cox, D. C., et al. 1877. *Local Tsunamis and Possible Local Tsunamis in Hawaii*. Honolulu: Hawaiian Institute of Geophysics.

Moores, E. M., ed. 1990. *Shaping the Earth: Tectonics of Continents and Oceans*. New York: W. H. Freeman.

Sieh, Kerry, et al. 1998. *The Earth in Turmoil*. New York: W. H. Freeman.

79

Tokyo, Japan, earthquake

September 1, 1923
Close to the city center

An earthquake of magnitude 7.8 with its epicenter close to the city destroyed most of Tokyo and burned down what was left. Death toll was 150,000 and an additional million were left homeless

On the first day of September 1923, Tokyo was hit with a powerful 7.8 strength earthquake. It was centered south of Tokyo, at that time a city of 2.3 million, the world's fifth largest. Many aftershocks followed. As had happened with the San Francisco earthquake, seventeen years earlier, the main destruction came from outbreaks of fire. Open cooking utensils spilled their coals on to wooden kitchen floors. When flames appeared there was no water available to quench them as the piping had been severed when the earth shook. Thousands of fires soon sprang up, rising gradually to a firestorm as they easily jumped over the narrow streets to ignite the next row of wooden homes. When the fires finally died down and conditions in Tokyo and the areas nearby were assessed, about 150,000 had died and a million were left homeless.

Tokyo, the city known as Edo in earlier centuries, became the administrative capital of the country about four hundred years ago under the control of the Tokugawa family who extended the city's territory by reclaiming land at the mouth of the Sumida River. Unconsolidated ground, that is to say the filled land on which new areas of the city were built, is a dangerous place when an earthquake strikes as was seen during the 1906 San Francisco earthquake. The shaking transforms such land, turning it into a kind of jelly that cannot support the buildings standing on it. In 1868, Tokyo came under a new form of government, one that brought the Emperor from Kyoto to Tokyo to take his place as ruler of the whole country. Under this new regime the city flourished, bringing it to its high population. The filled land, however, remained as it had been in earlier years, so liquefaction and destruction of many buildings in this part of the city became additional features of the earthquake.

Rebuilding the Kanto area west and south of Tokyo was a major undertaking. To compound the problem, the Prime Minister of Japan had died suddenly and his successor had not yet taken office, nor identified his cabinet, so various members of the previous government had to take responsibility for the restoration work. The first thing they did was to declare martial law. It was the only way to cope with the widespread destruction and the raging fires. Fortunately there were many individuals and agencies, both locally and in many other countries, able and ready to help. Reconstruction went ahead with remarkable speed, perhaps because Japan is so used to earthquakes that it reacts with predictable speed when a big one hits. Streets were laid out in the same patterns they held before the earthquake, often semi-circular and always narrow in order to provide space for the hundreds of thousands who needed housing. Such an arrangement was bad from the point of view of future earthquakes or outbreaks of fire but the damage done was so great that the needs of people outweighed the advantages of making the city better prepared for the next earthquake.

The Philippine Plate moved about ten feet in a northwestward direction as the fault slippage occurred, and numerous ground fissures, land uplift, and areas of subsistence were seen. Parts of Sagami Bay were uplifted twenty-five feet and then slowly, over a four-week period, sank back to within five feet of their original elevation. At the same time, parts of Sagami Bay subsided by more than six hundred feet. This amount of subsidence could not be explained on the basis of the fault slippage. Following subsequent examination of the sea floor geologists concluded that the earthquake had triggered mudflows and enormous quantities of sedimentary material had been carried out of the bay into deeper water. It was also concluded that the shaking from the earthquake had compacted much of the unconsolidated material on the sea floor. The great depths of six hundred feet could have been formed in such ways. A few minutes after the earthquake occurred, a tsunami that reached heights of forty feet swept across the Boso Peninsula on the east side of Tokyo Bay, causing a large number of deaths.

The earthquake was directly responsible for many of the deaths in and around Tokyo as buildings collapsed on people. However, it was fire that killed the largest number of people. Everything happened at noon when midday meals were being prepared over open charcoal braziers. As thousands of these hibachis were knocked over on to wooden floors a mass of fires broke out and there was no water to extinguish them because the city's water mains had been severed. People poured out on to the streets for safety, taking as much of their personal possessions as they could carry, but safety eluded them. The mushrooming fires, aided by a strong wind, turned into a firestorm and streets became deadly traps. On the east bank of the Sumida River police and firemen designated a park that had been an army clothing store as a safe place for anyone. About 40,000 people crowded into it. At four o'clock in the afternoon this place was hit with a firestorm and most of the 40,000 were killed.

At times in the past Japan has been suspicious of the value of western technology for the construction of earthquake resistant or earthquake proof buildings. On more than one occasion they noted that the simple wooden buildings used by farmers were able to withstand the shaking from an earthquake much better than brick or concrete structures. During this terrible disaster of 1923, one building that had been designed by an American architect stood firm when everything around it collapsed. The architect's name was Frank Lloyd Wright and the building he had designed was the Imperial Hotel, still today a landmark in downtown Tokyo. The interesting thing about this man was his adoption of Japanese ideas in his work, ideas that later would be known as organic architecture. Wright had designed the Imperial by floating it on a bed of piles that had been sunk into the ground. He then reinforced the walls with steel bars and divided the whole structure into sections each of which could move independently during an earthquake. At noon on September 1, 1923, two hundred dignitaries were having lunch in the Imperial to celebrate its opening. The luncheon ended abruptly as the earthquake stuck but the Imperial Hotel stood firm.

Japan has always been prone to earthquakes because it stands on the Eurasian Tectonic Plate, and is subjected to pressure from another two, the Pacific and the Philippine plates, both of which are continually sliding under it. The southern Kanto region has had two shocks of magnitude 7.8 or more during the past one thousand years. One of these was this 1923 earthquake, the other arrived in 1703. Both occurred along the Sagami trough, a northeastern boundary of the Philippine Plate. Although they both occurred in nearly the same region, the 1703 earthquake was significantly different in the distribution of coastal uplift and tsunami height as can be seen at the present time in the height of the marine terraces along the southern Kanto region. Both of these earthquakes are interpreted as the result of low-angle faulting with a thrust component at the plate boundary. The southern Kanto region has been uplifted at different times over the past six thousand years.

Major uplifts have been associated with earthquakes like those of 1703 and 1923. The recurrence rate of these is estimated at between 800 to 1,500 years. Thus it is unlikely that major earthquakes like those in 1923 and 1703 will occur in the future. It is a very different story when we examine the western end of the Philippine Plate. It is located on the other side of the Island of Honshu, to the west of Tokyo, around Suruga Bay, in a segment of the plate known as Tokai. Here there is a record of frequent earthquakes. This segment is subducting beneath the Eurasian segment. The last earthquake happened in 1854 and, prior to that, in 1707. Both of these were of magnitude 8.4. At earlier stages, in both 1605 and 1498 earthquakes of similar magnitude, that is to say around 8, hit the region. All of that amounts to four massive earthquakes within 350 years but at irregular intervals. Because of these statistics Japanese geologists now talk about the coming Tokai twentieth century earthquake. They do not know when it will arrive but they feel the chances of one in this century are very high indeed.

When writing about present activities in the Tokai Segment they title their reports "The Earthquake of 20xx." Japan has been making preparations for it for the past twenty-five years. They know that it will be extremely destructive when it arrives because the subduction zone within which it moves is very long. They also expect it to be stronger than the 1923 quake. They point out that past earthquakes in Tokai occurred every 110 years plus or minus thirty-three years. In the year 2006 it was 152 years since the last earthquake and the region was overdue for another on the basis of past statistics. In 1978, the local legislature adopted a large-scale earthquake countermeasure act and a year later declared the Tokai segment to be "An area under intensified measures against earthquake disaster." There is also persistent public education designed to show the expected effects of the coming Tokai Earthquake. Japanese geologists often refer to it as worse than Kobe, the devastating 1995 quake in the city of that name.

The endless battle with earthquakes in Japan creates an outlook and a pattern of research unmatched in any other country. The Tokai Segment, for example, receives continuous attention. Both its depth and the height of the land above it are measured regularly and more detailed measurements are made of one part of the segment where the two plates are locked. This is the part that will one day give way and cause an earthquake. Historical studies of past Tokai tsunamis enable geologists to assess their impacts from the wave records. Unlike so many western countries, Japan has maintained accurate records of past earthquakes as far back as 1700. One expert made a prediction in 1999 based on the collection of measurements available at that time. He said in 1999 that there is a 40 percent chance of another Tokai earthquake before the year 2010. Other experts have said that, when the Tokai Segment gives way, there is likely to be 6,000 deaths, another 20,000 serious injuries, and one million buildings damaged. He also said that large areas would be shaken at a level of 7, the highest intensity level in the Japanese intensity scale.

One disturbing prediction says that the greatest shaking from the Tokai earthquake will occur close to the site of a major nuclear power station, the Tokai-mura power station. This was not a consideration in 1923 but it soon became one in the years following World War II as Japan greatly expanded its industrial base and needed lots of energy. Japan lacks significant domestic sources of energy except coal and must import substantial amounts of crude oil, natural gas, and other energy resources, including uranium. Japan's nuclear output nearly doubled between 1985 and 1996, as Japan attempted to move away from dependence on oil following the 1973 Arab oil embargo. The Japanese government is committed to nuclear power development, but several accidents in recent years have aroused public concern. During the past few years, public opposition to Japan's nuclear power program has increased because of a series of accidents at Japanese nuclear plants, including a March 1997 fire and explosion at the Tokai-mura reprocessing plant. Other problems for Japan's nuclear power program have included rising costs of nuclear reactors and fuel, the huge investments necessary for fuel enrichment and reprocessing plants, several reactor failures, and the question of nuclear waste disposal. Regardless, Japan plans to increase the proportion of electricity generated from nuclear to 42 percent within the next decade. Japan ranks third worldwide in installed nuclear capacity, behind the United States and France.

Over four decades have passed since Japan's first commercial nuclear power plant began operation in Ibaraki Prefecture in 1966. As of today the nation has fifty-two reactors operating around the country with a total output of 46,000 megawatts. Nuclear power accounts for approximately one-third of the country's total electric power output. As an island country, it is impossible for Japan to exchange energy with neighboring countries through power transmission lines or pipelines. Japan is also energy scarce, depending on foreign countries for about 80 percent of its energy resources. These conditions are completely different from those of Europe or the United States; therefore, the government of Japan concludes that it is rational to continue making the fullest possible use of nuclear power generation as one of the mainstays of the nation's energy supply. Nuclear power generation contributes to improved energy sufficiency and to the stability of the energy supply, in addition to playing an important role in reducing Japan's carbon dioxide emissions.

References for Further Study

Bureau of Social Affairs Home Office, Japan. 1926. *The Great Earthquake of 1923 in Japan*. Tokyo: Bureau of Social Affairs.

Busch, N. F. 1962. *Two Minutes to Noon*. New York: Simon and Schuster.

Cameron, C. 1998. *The 1923 Great Kanto Earthquake and Fire*. Berkeley, CA: National Information Service for Earthquake Engineering (NISEE).

Poole, O. M. 1968. *The Death of Old Yokohama*. London: George Allen and Unwin, Ltd.

80

Charlevoix, Quebec, earthquake

March 1, 1925

Eastern St. Lawrence Valley, Canada, near the city of Quebec

The shock was felt six hundred miles away, including much of New England. Damage to buildings was substantial but there were no casualties

On March 1, 1925, an earthquake of magnitude 6.7 rocked the lives of thousands of people in eastern Canada. The location was Charlevoix-Kamouraska and the depth of the quake was six miles. The shock was felt six hundred miles away. The main quake was followed by a series of aftershocks caused by the readjusting of the earth's crust. The earthquake was widely felt and caused damage, especially to unreinforced masonry buildings, along the St. Lawrence River, near the epicenter, and at Quebec City, Trois-Rivières, and Shawinigan. The St. Lawrence Valley represents an enormous break in the earth's crust. About 350 million years ago an enormous meteorite collided with this fracture zone, in the Charlevoix area, further weakening the earth's crust. In fact, the most seismically active area in eastern Canada is the Charlevoix-Kamouraska area. In 1663 and 1925, the largest earthquakes ever recorded in Quebec were centered in this particularly vulnerable area.

There is a distinctive feature about earthquakes in eastern Canada in that the crystalline rocks of the Canadian Shield transmit seismic waves very effectively. They die out much more slowly than waves produced by earthquakes in areas such as the West Coast. Thus, damage and shaking occur at greater distances from the epicentre. This explains why, on November

25, 1988, an earthquake of magnitude 6 centered in the Saguenay, was strongly felt in Quebec City and as far away as Washington, D.C., six hundred miles from the epicentre. Objects were shaken off shelves, a power failure followed and minor damage was done to some buildings in the Lower Town of Quebec City. For many people who had never experienced an earthquake before, it was an unsettling and even frightening event. Although the earthquake did not cause any direct casualties, uneasy feelings were widespread among the population. Numerous earthquakes have often occurred in eastern Canada. Some of them had significant geological effects such as surface faulting, liquefaction, submarine slumping, rock avalanches, rock falls, landslides, railroad embankment slides, and one tsunami. These earthquakes had a strong psychological and social impact on people, mainly due to their lack of preparedness for them.

The probability of an earthquake being centered precisely below the Quebec City area is low because very few such earthquakes have ever been recorded. But we are not immune to significant damage because if a major earthquake, like the one that occurred in 1925, were to be centered in the Charlevoix area, Quebec City would experience it. Although earthquakes of magnitude less than 5.5 do not generally do any damage, destructive effects are not related solely to the magnitude of the earthquake. The distance between the epicenter and built-up areas, the condition and type of construction in the area, and the nature of the ground are all factors that can have a significant impact on the extent of damage. Buildings constructed on rock are more earthquake resistant. In unconsolidated sediment, earthquakes are much more intensely felt. When earth fill is not well compacted and contains a great deal of water, it behaves like jelly. Some parts of Quebec City would be at greater risk than others. For example, the valley of the Saint-Charles River is filled with clay sediment, which tends to amplify seismic vibrations.

The previous occurrence of large earthquakes suggests that this part of Canada may be the site of a large earthquake in the future. The study of these past quakes helps to calculate a seismic hazard assessment for surrounding urban areas because it is known that the 1925 quake damaged buildings 150 miles from the epicenter. The National Building Code of Canada contains guidelines for the design and construction of new buildings and for the renovation of existing structures. These guidelines are intended to ensure that buildings are more resistant to the shaking that accompanies an earthquake. Throughout Canada, buildings that are constructed in the areas most susceptible to seismic vibrations must adhere to stricter standards. The higher the seismic hazard, the more safety factors must be taken into account. For example, the seismic hazard in the Quebec City area is ranked at four on a scale of 0–6 for ground acceleration.

References for Further Study

Ebel, J. E., et al. 1991. *Earthquake Activity in the Northeastern United States*. Boulder, CO: Geological Society of America.

Jensen, D. E. 1978. *Minerals of New York State*. Rochester, NY: Ward Press.

Jorgensen, Neil. 1977. *A Guide to New England' s Landscape*Chester: Globe Pequot Press.

Yeats, R., et al. 1993. *The Geology of Earthquakes*. New York: W. H. Freeman.

81

Illinois/Indiana/Missouri tornado

March 18, 1925

Three states were affected, Missouri, Illinois, and Indiana

The main locations hit in the course of the three-state rampage were Ellington, Missouri, southern Illinois, and Princeton, Indiana

Widely considered the most devastating and powerful tornado in American history, the Tri-State tornado ripped through Missouri, Illinois, and Indiana on March 18, 1925. In its 219-mile-long wake this tornado left four completely destroyed towns, six severely damaged ones, about 15,000 destroyed homes, and 2,000 injured. Most significantly, 695 people were killed, a record for a single tornado. It left a legacy that is evidenced by ghost towns, lost ancestors, and stories passed from generation to generation. It all began during an afternoon thunderstorm near Ellington in southeast Missouri. From there it crossed the Mississippi River about seventy-five miles southeast of St. Louis and then followed a northeast course as it plowed through southern Illinois and southwestern Indiana.

This tornado from southeastern Missouri was indeed the deadliest tornado in U.S. history, twice as deadly as the second deadliest, the 1840 Great Natchez Tornado. The track left by the tornado was the longest ever recorded in the world. Historians would recognize it as an example of the F5 on the Saffir-Simpson Scale. It formed part of a series of tornadoes that broke out in the spring of 1925—there were tornadoes at that time in Tennessee, Kentucky, and Indiana. In all, at least 747 were killed and 2,298 were injured during this outbreak. The Tri-State exacted its greatest toll on southern Illinois where it reached speeds of 60 mph. Although this part of its journey was over rural land, it tended to follow a string of railroads, placing several towns in its path. Thus 540 people died in southern Illinois in the following towns: Gorham, 37; Murphysboro, 234; DeSoto,

Figure 48 Ruins of the Longfellow School where seventeen children were killed during the Tri-State tornado, the longest-lived and longest path of any recorded tornado. It traveled 300 miles from SE Missouri to Indiana and killed over 600.

69; West Frankfort, 148. In addition, fifty-two people died on farms and small settlements within southern Illinois.

The vortex was first sighted in northwest Ellington, Missouri. It sped from there to the northeast, killing two and causing extensive damage as it passed through several smaller towns, killing eleven and injuring thirty-two in these places. The tornado crossed the Mississippi River into southern Illinois. It was there that the greatest number of deaths were registered, 613, the most ever for a tornado in a single state. Crossing the Wabash River into Indiana, the tornado struck and nearly demolished Griffin, devastated rural areas, impacted Owensville, then roared into Princeton, destroying half the town. It traveled ten more miles to the northeast before finally dissipating three miles southwest of Petersburg. The tornado's unusual appearance, that of a rolling fog, caught many people by surprise and preventing them sensing the danger in time. Additionally, there were downburst winds that widened the damage caused. In summary, over 15,000 homes were destroyed and damages added up to $16.5 million.

References for Further Study

Bradford, Marlene. 2001. *Scanning the Skies: A History of Tornado Forecasting*. Norman: University of Oklahoma Press.

Felknor, Peter S. 1992. *The Tri-State Tornado*. Ames: Iowa State University Press.

Grazulis, T. P. 2001. *The Tornado: Nature' s Ultimate Windstorm* Norman: University of Oklahoma Press.

Weems, John Edward. 1991. *The Tornado*. College Station: Texas A&M University Press.

82

Clarkson Valley, Montana, earthquake

June 27, 1925
Helena in Montana

People fled in panic when the quake struck. They had never experienced anything of this strength before. There were no casualties but damage amounted to $150,000

On June 27, 1925 an earthquake of magnitude 6.6 struck Montana near Helena. It was followed by several aftershocks. People fled in panic into the streets. Prior to the main shock a lightning storm had raged, six persons being knocked to the ground and stunned by bolts that struck in various parts of the city. Many years later everybody was still talking about this earthquake, wondering when and where the next one would hit, or picking up a new story about the last one. The quake on June 27 was really a brand new experience for Montana because it was a real earthquake, not one of the little baby quakes that had occurred in past years. The quake was felt at strengths of 2 to 3 from Seattle to the South Dakota line, from Spokane to Thermopolis and Casper, Wyoming, and as far north as Calgary, Alberta. The most severe damage occurred in the counties of Gallatin, Three Forks, Logan, and Lombard. Because no large cities were near the epicenter, property damage did not exceed $150,000. At Manhattan, the community high school and the grade school were both severely damaged, but reinforced concrete buildings were not affected. Many chimneys were toppled.

At Three Forks, walls of the schoolhouse bulged on all sides, and its foundation and basement were damaged. A church, whose walls were not tied together by an upper floor, also sustained heavy damage. Later shocks demolished the walls. Almost all masonry buildings showed cracks and damage, but because most of the buildings were of frame construction, they sustained only cracks in plaster and some fallen chimneys. At Logan, the poorly designed and constructed schoolhouse was damaged heavily. However, a large brick roundhouse sustained only a few cracks. As at Three Forks, most of the buildings at Logan were of frame construction and therefore sustained only cracks in plaster and destruction of chimneys. At Lombard, where the Chicago, Milwaukee, and St. Paul Railway crosses the Northern Pacific Railway, large boulders were dislodged. A huge rockslide blocked the Deer Park entrance to the Lombard Tunnel on the Chicago, Milwaukee and St. Paul Railway.

Cracks occurred in graded and filled roads but not in cuts or where the natural surface had not been disturbed. Approaches to many bridges settled by as much as one foot. One spring formed near Josephine and began to flow, but other springs and sources of water in the neighborhood ceased to flow. Landslides were reported to have hemmed in passenger trains loaded with vacationers. Pavements and buildings were cracked in many cities and some buildings were demolished. The Olympian, fast train of the Chicago, Milwaukee, and St. Paul railroad between Chicago and Seattle, is believed to have been stalled between two of the avalanches in the vicinity of Three Forks. Two other trains, one a Milwaukee train and the other a Northern Pacific, were hemmed in by the slides.

There were no reports of material damage to Yellowstone Park, and the quake is believed to have no connection with the avalanche in the Gros

Figure 49 Montana earthquake of June 27, 1925. Broken railroad track near Lombard.

Ventre River valley near Jackson, Wyoming early that week. Out of all the reports of panic and minor property damage there were none telling of any loss of life.

An earthquake insurance policy for $115,000 was written a day after the earthquake. It was taken out on behalf of the First National bank building in Missoula. According to Ira C. Watson of the Watson Agency, who wrote the policy, this was the first earthquake insurance policy ever written in Montana. Mr. Watson said there were other business blocks in the city upon which the owners were considering earthquake insurance and that other policies could be written over coming days. The railroad tracks were restored to service within a week. A length of track had to be installed to bypass temporarily the area blocked in Sixteen Mile Canyon near Lombard. Immediately after he returned from a conference, Governor Erickson arranged for some of his staff to form an executive committee to handle subscriptions for restoration work. Montana has a history of large, damaging earthquakes but relatively little is known about the faults that produced those earthquakes. Only the 1959 Hebgen Lake earthquake caused surface rupture and thus revealed the causal fault lines. The faults for other damaging earthquakes, including this 1925 one did not have surface breaks.

References for Further Study

Bolt, Bruce A. 1993. *Earthquakes and Geological Discovery*. New York: W. H. Freeman.

McPhee, J. 1980. *Basin and Range*. New York: Farrar, Straus, Giroux.

Yeats, R., et al. 1993. *The Geology of Earthquakes*. New York: W. H. Freeman.

83

Santa Barbara, California, earthquake

June 29, 1925
Santa Barbara and immediate surroundings

Damage was extensive and fortunately casualties were few, thirteen in all, because people were still at home when the quake struck

The Santa Barbara earthquake of June 29, 1925, hit the city area early in the morning when, fortunately, no one was outside and the railway was stationery at the terminal. Violent movements were registered on the rail cars, first from east to west and then from north to south. The Mission Creek Dam, the main source of water for the railway, was shaken by the initial shock and all the water ran away, effectively putting the railway line out of business. Those Santa Barbara residents who were not already awake survived the earthquake, as did their homes, but almost every chimney in the city crumbled. Several hotels partially collapsed and a few other buildings completely collapsed. Thirteen people were killed, many fewer than would have been had the earthquake occurred several hours later and they had been on their way to work or were traveling.

Commercial buildings did not ride out the earthquake as well as the residences. In the downtown area, along State Street, the rubble was so thick in the middle of the street that travel by car was impossible. In an odd twist of fate, by leveling much of Santa Barbara's commercial district, the earthquake proved a boon to Santa Barbara's businesses. City officials seized the opportunity that the earthquake gave them to enforce a stricter building code, requiring commercial buildings along State Street to conform to a Spanish-Moorish style of architecture. Thus, the 1925 earthquake is responsible for the distinctive architecture in the city that has made Santa Barbara a popular tourist destination for the years that followed. The area between Naples and Santa Barbara, a stretch of sixteen miles, was extensively damaged with a number of minor landslides having occurred, all of them toward the ocean side. The roundhouse at the Santa Barbara Terminal, a ten-foot brick structure with a wooden roof, was knocked down.

References for Further Study

Ayre, Robert S. 1975. *Earthquake and Tsunami Hazards in the United States*. Boulder, CO: Institute of Behavioral Science.

Cas, R. A. F., et al. 1987. *Volcanic Successions Modern and Ancient*. London: Allen and Unwin.

Sieh, Kerry, et al. 1998. *The Earth in Turmoil*. New York: W. H. Freeman.

84

Florida hurricane

September 18, 1926
Miami and Fort Lauderdale and places in between them

This hurricane was sixty miles wide and it reached Florida at 150 mph, causing a death toll between 325 and 800 and a damage cost of more than $100 million

During the night of September 18, 1926, Fort Lauderdale, Miami, and several coastal locations in between were hit by sustained winds of 150 mph from a hurricane that was sixty miles wide as it made landfall in Florida. The death toll was estimated to be from 325 to 800. Several hotels along the coast had their skylights and windows shattered, and the water rose four feet deep in their lobbies. In one instance, fearing that the walls might cave in, a building inspector ordered all women and children to move to another building farther back from the waterfront. The U.S. Weather Bureau in Miami said that no storm in previous history had done as much property damage.

In the early morning of September 17, the Weather Bureau in Washington issued an advisory about a very severe storm that was moving in the direction of Florida. Newspapers ran the advisory, but readers failed to take it seriously. By early evening the Washington Bureau was sending out hurricane warnings but again not many people took them seriously. In 1926 there were few avenues for warning people. Only a few people owned radios and could hear the warnings being broadcast on southern Florida's only radio station. All through the evening and night the barometer kept falling, flood waters were rising, and gale-force winds were being experienced all along the coast. Then, soon after midnight, September 18, the hurricane made landfall with tremendous force, knocking out all electrical power and overturning many buildings. People waited in the darkness.

Figure 50 Miami's new drydock, results of hurricane, Sept. 18, 1926.

Skylights and windows in hotels were shattered, and the water rose four feet deep in the lobbies. In one hotel, fearing the walls would cave in, a building inspector ordered all women and children to move to another building farther back from the waterfront.

The storm had been born near the Cape Verde Islands off Africa on September 6, 1926. It moved across the Atlantic and into the Caribbean and was reported off St. Kitts on September 14. Two days later it had moved into the Bahamas, and by September 17, it began to take aim at southern Florida where it arrived early on September 18, as a category 4 hurricane. As the eye of the hurricane passed over Miami, hundreds of survivors crawled out of their places of refuge, thinking that the storm was over. Thus, when the second half of the storm roared over the town, dozens were washed away. The storm crossed Florida before making a second landfall along the sparsely populated Alabama coast, still a powerful category 3 hurricane. Most of the coastal inhabitants had not evacuated, partly because they had not received the warnings and partly because the city's relatively new population knew little about the danger that a major hurricane posed. Some tried to leave the barrier islands in the lull before the rear of the hurricane arrived, only to be swept off the bridges by the storm. Farther inland, Lake Okeechobee experienced a high storm surge that broke a portion of the dikes, flooded the town of Moore Haven, and killed many. Two years later, in the deadly Lake Okeechobee Hurricane, more than two thousand lives would be lost in this same area.

Most of the 200,000 people living in the storm's projected path were new to Florida, lured here by the easy money of a land boom. Having never seen a hurricane, they had little knowledge of a storm's destructive force. Striking some twenty-five years before hurricanes were named, the 1926 storm became known in southern Florida as The Hurricane or The Big Blow, a title it retained for sixty-six years until Hurricane Andrew arrived.

The lure of the land boom was premature. The wild real-estate boom had collapsed. Millionaires at the end of 1925 had become poor folks by the middle of 1926. Many citizens skipped monthly payments and tax bills and, as a result, lost their homes. Businesses closed down. The sun still shone, but its rays bounced off the bleaching skeletons of unfinished buildings, especially in Miami where damage was far more severe than anywhere else. A storm surge of sixteen feet was experienced there, gutting homes and offices and devastating the harbor. The damage toll soared to over $100 million in 1926 dollars. If a similar hurricane occurred today the damage bill would be more than $100 billion.

References for Further Study

Barnes, Jay. 1998. *Florida' s Hurricane History* Chapel Hill: University of North Carolina Press.

Elsner, J. B., and Kara, A. B. 1999. *Hurricanes of the North Atlantic.* New York: Oxford University Press.

Lee, Sally. 1993. *Hurricanes.* New York: Franklin Watts Publishing.

Williams, J. M., and Duedall, I. W. 1997. *Florida Hurricanes and Tropical Storms.* Gainesville: University of Florida Press.

85

Lompoc, California, earthquake

November 4, 1927
Offshore from Lompoc, west of Santa Barbara

All places within fifty miles of Lompoc suffered damage and a tsunami from the earthquake was recorded on the tidal gauges at San Francisco and San Diego

An area offshore, west of Lompoc, California, experienced an earthquake of magnitude 7.1 on November 4, 1927. The most severe damage occurred north and west of Lompoc. Chimneys were wrecked in several towns in these areas, including Guadalupe and Arroyo Grande, all places within fifty miles of Lompoc. There were sand craters and cracks in numerous buildings where water-soaked soil had weakened foundations. The Southern Pacific Railroad tracks, running close to the coast west of Lompoc and near Vandenberg Air Force Base, were thrown out of alignment. A tsunami from this earthquake was recorded on the tide gages at San Francisco and San Diego.

Late in the morning of November 4, the captain of a ship at sea a few miles west of Point Arguello was startled to discover great quantities of dead or stunned fish floating on the surface of the ocean. He was unaware that he was viewing the aftermath of an earthquake that had struck underneath him a few hours earlier that day. Other signs of trouble had come an hour after midnight on the fourth when residents of a coastal community were awakened. Others soon followed because of the strength of the earthquake, powerful enough to awaken most of the inhabitants of Lompoc. Several other ships at sea were shaken. At the Roberds Ranch southwest of Lompoc ten to twenty sand blows appeared. These sand blows occur when shaking from an earthquake causes the pore pressure of water trapped between sand particles to suddenly increase. The result is a fountain of water and sand coming straight out of the earth. The Lompoc office of the Los Angeles National Trust building had all of its furniture and equipment broken and scattered around the rooms. Hundreds of residents of Lompoc, probably recalling the recent earthquake damage in downtown Santa Barbara, hurried to downtown Lompoc to check on buildings.

This was one of the largest Californian earthquakes of the twentieth century and a great deal of interest persisted about it for a long time, particularly questions concerning its epicenter. The quest for this location was heightened because the earthquake was the third largest occurring offshore of California since 1900 and because, over the years, many questions remained unanswered about the earthquakes and tsunamis that had been reported from areas offshore from coastal locations around Santa Barbara. Some indications of the range of opinions about the Lompoc epicenter were documented in 1977, fifty years after the earthquake, each no doubt influenced by the growing body of information and technological expertise that had accumulated over the years. The earliest estimate had placed the epicenter more than forty miles west of Point Arguello and others had followed with a range of alternatives closer to the coast. Still later reassessments of the epicenter placed them along a fault, defined as the Hosgri Fault, stretching for a hundred miles along the coast but with ruptures that may have triggered earthquakes farther west of the defined fault.

References for Further Study

Adams, W., ed. 1970. *Tsunamis in the Pacific Ocean*. Honolulu: East-West Center Press.

Ritchie, D. 1981. *The Ring of Fire*. New York: The Atheneum.

Wood, H. O., and Heck, N. 1966. *Earthquake History of the United States: Stronger Earthquakes of California and Western Nevada*. Washington, DC: Environmental Science Services Administration.

86

St. Francis Dam failure

March 12, 1928
Part of the Los Angeles aqueduct system

This dam, part of the Los Angeles aqueduct system, was constructed on a fault. The dam failure caused the deaths of five hundred and it also changed the course of the Santa Clara River

Shortly before midnight on March 12, 1928, the St. Francis Dam, part of the Los Angeles aqueduct system, collapsed and released twelve billion gallons of water, destroying a swath of land all the way to the ocean and killing five hundred people in its path. The dam had been constructed on a fault, a common geological feature in that part of the country. Unfortunately no geological investigation was made before the dam was built. The collapse of this dam, built by the city of Los Angeles, is a classic example of the neglect of scientific expertise. At that time engineering projects did not consult geologists prior to selecting dam sites.

The accident that followed, California's second worst, next to the San Francisco earthquake of 1906, became a landmark in the history of dam construction. Some have called it America's greatest civil engineering failure of the twentieth century. Never again, in the multiple-fault, earthquake-prone state of California would a major dam be built without a prior, extensive, geological assessment. The St. Francis Dam was a curved, concrete, gravity dam in San Francisquito Canyon, two hundred feet high, with a span of six hundred feet across the mouth of the canyon, and a dike along one side of the canyon. It was built to provide an additional 38,000 acre-feet of water storage for the Los Angeles aqueduct system. Behind the dam, the second biggest in a chain of storage basins, were twelve billion gallons of water, enough to meet the needs of the city of Los Angeles for more than two months. The catastrophic failure that occurred on March 12, 1928, happened as the dam filled to full capacity for the first time. Only much later, in the light of better knowledge of the geology of the Los Angeles area, was a full explanation provided for the failure of the dam.

The architect of the dam was William Mulholland, chief engineer of the Los Angeles Bureau of Water and Power. He had a history of success in the years before 1928 with a variety of projects that were designed to provide both water and hydroelectricity for Los Angeles. It was he who planned and supervised the construction of a 233-mile-long aqueduct that came through the Sierra Nevadas and brought water and electrical power to Los Angeles. Early in 1928 he was working on a very ambitious plan to bring water from the Colorado River across 250 miles of deserts and a series of tunnels to Los Angeles. Thus, when he proposed building the San Francisquito Dam, his plan was enthusiastically welcomed. He was a trusted man, and he was allowed to go ahead with construction of the dam even in the face of warnings from geologists. He ignored their warnings and the local laws of that time allowed him to do this. What he was told by geologists, however, proved to be the cause of the disaster that followed on March 12: they had pointed out that the type of rock under the dam was too weak to sustain the weight of the dam and, furthermore, the dam site was a major geological fault.

Figure 51 St. Francis Dam flood, March 12–13, 1928, Los Angeles County, California. St. Francis Dam before the 1928 failure.

Figure 52 St. Francis Dam flood, March 12–13, 1928, Los Angeles County, California. Taken from the same location, showing the remains of the dam and reservoir floor. The dam failed at 1:58 P.M. Monday, March 12, 1928, according to the water storage recorder on the dam. Twenty minutes prior to that time, the water was slowly dropping in the reservoir indicating that leakage was increasing. The flood destroyed the power house about one mile below the dam at 12:04 A.M. March 13, 1928. The left (west) abutment of the dam was entirely swept away.

For about a week before the failure of the dam, farmers in the surrounding area reported leaks and their quantity and volume seemed to increase day by day. On the morning of March 12, one man observed an unusual amount of water escaping through cracks at the dam's base. This report was immediately brought to Mulholland's attention. He inspected the location and pronounced it safe. Rain had been falling steadily since March 6 and the level of water in the dam had reached the maximum possible, to the point of overtopping. Either the water release mechanism had failed to operate or it had never been installed. Close to midnight, while most of the residents of the Santa Clara Valley were asleep, billions of gallons of water swept down the Santa Clara River. There was no time for local residents to escape. Houses were crushed, farms turned into seas of mud, and cars tossed around like toys. A wide swath of land, in places as wide as sixty miles, was cleared of everything as the water cascaded along a seventy-five-mile-long path to the ocean. Five hundred people had been killed and damage estimates reached $20 million.

This failure represents but one of a number of important dam failures that occurred in the 1920s and 1930s, when American civil engineers were pushing the limits of a technology that was still in its infancy. Like most major engineering failures, looking back on it one can see that considerable long-term societal benefits resulted from the public outcry that followed the disaster. One immediate action was the establishment of a dam safety agency, the first of its kind anywhere. This new organization required geological assessments of dam sites before the design stage, including a normalization of uniform engineering criteria for testing of compacted earth. Foundation material of this kind is still in use worldwide. All the Los Angeles Department of Water and Power dams and reservoirs were assessed in the light of the St. Francis experience and one of the outcomes was an extensive retrofit of the Mulholland Dam. Mulholland's reputation as an outstanding engineer ended suddenly in the wake of the failure of the St. Francis Dam.

References for Further Study

Cornell, James. 1976. *The Great International Disaster Book*. New York: Charles Scribner's Sons.

FEMA. 1993. *Dam or Levee Break*. Washington, DC: FEMA.

Kingston, Jeremy, and Lambert, David. 1979. *Catastrophe and Crisis*. London: Aldus Books.

87

Lake Okeechobee hurricane

September 16, 1928

Lake Okeechobee, west of West Palm Beach

This deadly hurricane with its 150 mph winds and wall of water caused the deaths of 2,500 in Florida and overall a death toll of 4,075

The hurricane San Felipe Segundo, named after the saint's day on which it did so much damage to Puerto Rico, but better known as the Okeechobee Hurricane, was the first recorded hurricane to reach category 5 status. It remains the only recorded hurricane to strike Puerto Rico at category 5 strength, and one of the ten most intense ever recorded to make landfall in the United States. In South Florida at least 2,500 were killed when storm surge from Lake Okeechobee breached the dike surrounding the lake, flooding an area covering hundreds of square miles. In total, the hurricane killed at least 4,075 people and caused around $100 million in damages.

The Okeechobee Hurricane struck the Leeward Islands, Puerto Rico, and the Bahamas, before reaching Florida on September 16, 1928. In Guadeloupe, about 1,200 people were killed, and in Puerto Rico where the storm hit directly at peak strength, three hundred died and hundreds of thousands were left homeless. The storm was first observed nine hundred miles to the east of Guadeloupe on September 10, by a ship, the most easterly report of a tropical cyclone ever received via ship radio. A ship in the Virgin Islands later reported the pressure of this storm as being at 27.50, a rare low value, and hence the identification of a very powerful storm. After leaving Puerto Rico, the hurricane moved across the Bahamas as a strong category 4 hurricane. It continued to the west-northwest, and made landfall in southern Florida on the evening of September 16 with winds in excess of 150 mph. The eye passed near West Palm Beach and then directly over Lake Okeechobee.

In September 1928, only about 50,000 persons lived in southern Florida. The land and real estate boom was already beginning to fade, although many subdivisions and new communities were still being built. The Great Hurricane of September 1926 had already sounded a loud alarm to the new residents about the vulnerability of their new homes. Lake Okeechobee is about seven hundred square miles in extent, making it the second-biggest body of fresh water that is entirely within U.S. borders. It is quite shallow and, prior to land reclamation around 1910 in the Everglades south of the lake, water drained out of it at its south end. A dike of packed soil, six feet high, was built around the south side of the lake to restrain water in times of heavy rainfall. Draining the Everglades with a view to the development of farmland in it began around 1910, and migrant workers from the Caribbean along with local sharecroppers were employed to work the new land. Several new towns began to appear along the shores of the Lake. On September 16, as the storm approached, residents of these towns heard about it but did not pay much attention to what they heard. Once again, as had happened before, the Weather Bureau forecasters were convinced right up to the afternoon of the sixteenth that the storm was going to move northwards and avoid hitting Florida. Their warnings finally came too late for people to evacuate danger spots.

By September 16, Lake Okeechobee already had a high level of water due to heavy rains over the previous week. By the evening of that day, as the hurricane's eye passed over the lake's southeast corner, accompanied with 120 mph winds and a wall of water that had swept inland with it, the six-foot dike disintegrated and homes were crushed. Waves of debris carried everything before them. Some survived by hanging on to floating remains of homes, most drowned. The aftermath was as difficult as the terror of the storm. Bodies in that hot climate had to be buried quickly but that was not easy in a place where the water table was so close to the surface. People said that they could not keep the coffins in the ground. But something had to be done with the 2,000 bodies that were there. Some were sent to West Palm Beach where a steam shovel dug a mass grave for the white victims. The bodies of hundreds of black farm workers were buried in a cemetery for blacks. Days later a much bigger grave was dug on higher, sandy soil for 1,000 victims, but still there were many more awaiting burial. They were finally burned in a mass cremation.

News of the disaster was slow to reach the outside world. The nearest city of any size to Lake Okeechobee was West Palm Beach, forty-five miles away, and it was busy coping with its own disaster. All communication lines had been severed. Newspapers across the country a couple of days later reported on the terrible tragedy of a storm that had hit Florida's east coast, unaware of the much greater tragedy farther inland. Migrant workers were not included in census records and there was a general callousness toward their welfare. No one seemed to care about the number of blacks who might have died. When the Red Cross reported that more than 2,000 blacks had lost their lives, state officials changed its total, fearing that such a large number might scare off visitors and endanger the tourist industry. The reality was that this was the second-worst hurricane disaster in the nation's history up to that time, second only to the Galveston Hurricane of 1900. For years after 1928 farmers cultivating land south of the lake came across human skeletons.

The hurricane's path turned northeast as it crossed Florida, taking it across northern Florida, eastern Georgia, and the Carolinas on September 19. It then moved inland and merged with a low-pressure system much farther north around Toronto, in Canada, by September 20. Everyone now knows the potential of Lake Okeechobee. Hence, in the three decades after the storm, the U.S. Army Corps of Engineers constructed a 150-mile dike around the lake. In places, the dike was forty-five feet high and 150 feet wide. Built out of mud, sand, grass, rock and concrete, and named after President Herbert Hoover, the dike has withstood a handful of hurricanes, though none as powerful as the 1928 storm. In the event of a powerful hurricane, to take pressure off the dike, water can be pumped in large volume out of the lake through two wide canals into the sea. Many people have concluded that the site is safe no matter how powerful the next hurricane might be and they have built homes close to the lake. Farms and ranches have also appeared. The dike and the flood control structures have encouraged people to develop 700,000 acres of sugarcane and other market crops. The whole area is sometimes called the nation's winter vegetable basket.

References for Further Study

Barnes, Jay. 1998. *North Carolina' s Hurricane History* Chapel Hill: University of North Caroline Press.

Barnes, Jay. 1998. *Florida' s Hurricane History* Chapel Hill: University of North Carolina Press.

Tannehill, Ivan Ray. 1956. *Hurricanes: Their Nature and History*. Princeton: Princeton University Press.

Williams, J. M., and Duedall, I. W. 1997. *Florida Hurricanes and Tropical Storms*. Gainesville: University of Florida Press.

88

Stock Market Collapse

October 24, 1929

Wall Street at the south of Manhattan Island

Black Thursday received its name because it was on that day that the Stock Market began to crash. Investment in the Stock Market was quite small in 1929 compared with the present time but the conditions surrounding the market at that time were the reasons for its collapse

Thursday, October 24, 1929, is remembered as "Black Thursday," the day that the New York stock exchange began to crash. Close to thirteen million shares were traded in the panic selling that took place on that day. It was not the biggest day of volume but the level of trading and the downward trend created fear and confusion, elements that are the greatest enemies of the market. The bigger day of selling came later, on Tuesday, October 29, when more than sixteen million shares were sold. It was the most devastating day in the history of the New York stock market. One story from later in the day, perhaps apocryphal, is that someone offered to buy a large number of shares for a dollar each and because there were no offers he got them all.

Newspapers across the country told the story in their headlines, next day, October 30, in words like the following: stock prices virtually collapsed yesterday; billions of dollars of market value were wiped out; from every point of view it was the most disastrous day in Wall Street's history. New York bankers, the people to whom investors looked for hope in the crisis, like all others, saw little prospect of recovery for the foreseeable future. Black Thursday had indeed been a turning point. Stocks began to lose their value rapidly, beginning on October 24. By the close of business on that day four billion dollars had been lost. It took exchange clerks until five

Figure 53 Crowd of people gather outside the New York Stock Exchange following the crash of 1929.

o'clock next morning to complete the paper work. By the following Monday, the realization of what had happened began to sink in, and a full-blown panic was evident. Thousands of people, many of them ordinary working people, saw their recently acquired wealth disappear. In that last week of October the total value of stocks dropped by $15 billion.

The crash heralded the end of a long period of economic growth, often referred to as the "Roaring Twenties." There was a rapid increase in industrialization coupled with a rash of new technologies. The Ford "Model A" car came out in 1927. Radios were everywhere and sound movies were breaking all records about the same time. Most of all there was a spirit of optimism about the future. Wages were high and consumer spending was also high. The stock market caught the attention of more and more people as its values kept on climbing. One feature that caught the attention of more thoughtful people was the strength of a widespread desire to get rich quickly with a minimum of effort. It was a distorted understanding of the American dream that anyone can get to the top if he or she tries hard enough, and it became very evident in the Florida real estate boom of the mid twenties.

Large tracts of land in Florida were being subdivided into building lots and sold for a 10 percent down payment. The people who bought these lots had no intention of living on them. They had become convinced that Florida's warm climate would attract an endless number of people from the cold northern states and this demand would continue to raise the value of the lots they had bought. Within a few weeks they could sell for a good profit what they had bought with borrowed money. As long as this continued and everyone profited from recurring sales there was no incentive to ask questions about how such a trend could continue indefinitely. The optimism of the time failed to see the risks in the speculative bubble with which they were involved. The first sobering reassessment came with the 1926 hurricane that killed hundreds and tore roofs off thousands of houses. Then, within two years of the first explosion of demand, the number of buyers from the north steadily decreased. By 1928 it was all over and defaults had multiplied.

The boom and bust experience of Florida did not have a lasting influence on the get-rich-quick outlook. The new prospective bubble that appeared on the horizon was the stock market. The familiar Dow-Jones Industrial Index, often known as the Dow, had risen rapidly, from 100 in 1924 to 150 in 1926, then to 200 in 1928. These numbers might seem insignificant when we see more than 10,000 as the Dow's value today, but

STAGE BROADWAY SCREEN

VARIETY

PRICE 25¢.

VOL. XCVII. No. 3 NEW YORK, WEDNESDAY, OCTOBER 30, 1929 88 PAGES

WALL ST. LAYS AN EGG

Going Dumb Is Deadly to Hostess In Her Serious Dance Hall Profesh

A hostess at Roseland has her problems. The paid steppers consider their work a definite profession calling for specialized technique and high-power salesmanship.

"You see, you gotta sell your personality," said one. "Each one of we girls has our own clientele to cater to. It's just like selling dresses in a store—you have to know what to sell each particular customer.

"Some want to dance, some want to kid, some want to get soupy, and others are just 'misunderstood husbands'."

Girls applying for hostess jobs at Roseland must be 21 or older. They must work five nights a week. They

Hunk on Winchell

When the Walter Winchells moved into 204 West 55th street, late last week, June, that's Mrs. Winchell, selected a special room as Walter's exclusive sleep den for his late hour nights. She shushed the Winchell kidlets when her husband dove in at his usual eight o'clock the first morning.

At noon, Walter's midnight, his sound proof room was penetrated by so many high C's he awoke with but four hours of dreams and a grouch.

DROP IN STOCKS ROPES SHOWMEN

Many Weep and Call Off Christmas Orders—Legit Shows Hit

MERGERS HALTED

The most dramatic event in the financial history of America is the collapse of the New York Stock Market. The stage was Wall Street, but the onlookers covered the country. Estimates are that

Kidding Kissers in Talkers Burns Up Fans of Screen's Best Lovers

Talker Crashes Olympus

Paris, Oct. 29.

Fox "Follies" and the Fox Movietone newsreel are running this week in Athens, Greece, the first sound pictures heard in the birthplace of world culture, and in all Greece, for that matter.

Several weeks ago, Variety's Cairo correspondent cabled that a cinema had been wired in Alexandria, Cleopatra's home town.

Boys who used to whistle and girls who used to giggle when love scenes were flashed on the screen are in action again. A couple of years ago they began to take the love stuff seriously and desisted, but the talkers are reviving the ha ha for film osculators.

Heavy loving lovers of silent picture days accustomed to charming audiences into spasms of silent ecstasy when kissing the leading lady are getting the bird instead of the heartbeat. The sound accompaniment is making it tough.

Such a picture romancer as John Gilbert is getting laughs in place

Figure 54 The famous cover of *Variety*: "Wall St. Lays An Egg."

the important thing to note about the 1920s was the rate of growth, doubling in four years. In fact it accelerated rapidly after 1928, jumping from 200 to 350 within a year. That should have given some warning to investors but they failed to see the danger. Buying on margin became the popular activity in these years of rapid growth. It meant that you could buy stock at one tenth of its value using borrowed money. Borrowing money was no easier then than now but people thought that the high gains in the market would justify a high rate of borrowing. You then paid back over time what you borrowed, including interest, but as you did so the increased value of your stock more than paid for the cost of borrowing.

It all looked so perfect that many thousands who never previously paid any attention to the stock market began to invest. They borrowed all they could, withdrew all their savings, even mortgaged their homes, and bought stock. A more useful measure of the times can be gained from the prices of individual stocks rather than the Dow. One mining company had a share value of $50 in 1924. By 1927 it had jumped to $274 and two years later to $575. If one could pick the right place in which to invest, people thought, enormous wealth could be secured. The Marconi Company's shares jumped from $4 in 1927 to $28 a year later but one comment from the president of the company, warning everyone that shares were running too high, should have alerted investors to the volatility of the market. For that one remark the company's shares dropped to $7 within two days.

By the summer of 1929 interest in the stock market was at a fever pitch. The nation had never seen anything like it since the days of the nineteenth century gold rushes. Stock prices had jumped 78 percent since 1928. At lunchtime all traffic came to a standstill as thousands crowded into the New York Stock Exchange. New office blocks appeared almost every week to cope with demand. Anyone could buy stocks even if he had no money. Brokers were glad to loan money because they were sure that the rising value of stocks would more than cover their risk. Ships sailing for Europe were fitted with tickertape and brokerage offices so people could speculate in the course of the voyage. The enormous amount of unsecured consumer debt created by speculation left the stock market fragile. Some economic analysts warned of an impending correction, but their warnings were largely ignored. Banks, eager to increase their profits, speculated dangerously. Finally, in October 1929, the buying craze began to slow down. Many took note of the extremely high rate of growth and pulled back, but for most it was too late to change course.

Before long the Federal Government decided it had to step in to establish control mechanisms such as the Securities Exchange Commission to make sure that fraud, overpriced stocks, and unrealistic levels of risk would never again ruin the stock market. At the same time the loss of so much wealth led to a massive downturn in the national economy and the first signs of the Great Depression surfaced. It lasted for ten years and the causes of this long period of economic stagnation are varied. Production of products had outrun demand. In the enthusiasm of the good times, manufacturing firms and investors had anticipated a certain high demand and designed production levels accordingly. It seems strange that the memories of the late 1920s did not last long. The intensity of the failures of that period should have alerted everyone to the unpredictability of the stock market, but in less than sixty years a similar collapse occurred.

In 1987 there was a crash very much like that in 1929. Again it happened in October and it was a Monday, a "Black Monday," that led the crash.

In some ways, the 1987 crash was much worse than the 1929 one—508 points on the Dow, the biggest drop ever, compared with 124 points in 1929. In percentage terms the market lost 23 percent of its value in 1987 against 25 percent in 1929. The important differences, however, are the effects of the various controls instituted after 1929. There was no worldwide economic crisis in the wake of the 1987 crash, just a temporary slowdown before a rapid rise soon after, one that continued throughout the 1990s.

References for Further Study

Beaudreau, Bernard C. 1996. *Mass production, The Stock Market Crash, and The Great Depression*. Westport, CT: Greenwood Press.

Benedict, Michael, ed. 2000. *In the Face of Disaster*. Toronto: Viking.

Galbraith, John Kenneth. 1988. *The Great Crash of 1929*. Boston: Houghton Mifflin.

Prideaux, Michael, ed. 1976. *World Disasters*. London: Phoebus Company.

89

Grand Banks, Nova Scotia, earthquake

November 18, 1929
At the edge of the continental shelf, three hundred miles southeast of Newfoundland

The slump was triggered by an earthquake of magnitude 7.3, 150 miles south of the Island of Newfoundland, Canada, at the edge of the relatively shallow continental shelf

On November 18, 1929, a major earthquake occurred 150 miles south of Newfoundland, Canada, along the southern edge of the Grand Banks. This magnitude 7.3 event was felt as far away as New York and Montreal. Damage on land was concentrated on Cape Breton Island in the northern part of Nova Scotia where chimneys were overthrown or cracked. Highways in Nova Scotia were blocked by landslides. Aftershocks, some of magnitude 6, were experienced in both Newfoundland and Nova Scotia. A tsunami that was triggered by the earthquake caused extensive destruction on the coast of Newfoundland and killed a number of people.

Dense coastal settlements along the south and east coasts of Newfoundland have long been a feature of this part of Canada because of the fish resources provided by the banks. The Grand Banks is the largest of them. They mark the seaward limit of the continental shelf and they constitute the most extensive area of banks anywhere along the North American coast. Because they are shallow they serve as a rich habitat for fish as they are constantly being enriched by nutrients from both the southward-moving cold Labrador Current and the northward-moving warm Gulf Stream. In recent years, with the increasing use of bigger and bigger fishing vessels and their use of trawl nets with which to scour the sea bottom, over fishing has almost destroyed some stocks of fish and local residents have had to find alternative livelihoods.

The earthquake's epicenter was 6,000 feet below sea level and the landslide it caused was multi-faceted. It constituted a massive submarine slump involving a number of small landslides, adding up in aggregate to more than two hundred cubic miles of debris. The many smaller slides were spread out over a distance of seventy miles along the edge of the continental shelf. As the smaller landslides were coalescing into one big mass they formed into a mixed current hundreds of feet thick. This current as part of the whole overall landslide swept down slope at the edge of the continental shelf at a speed of fifty feet per second, cutting twelve transatlantic cables in numerous places as it moved. About 80,000 square miles of the seafloor was covered with sediment to a depth of ten feet. It was one of the biggest turbidity currents ever identified either historically or in the geological record.

The main story from this earthquake was the tsunami that followed. It was felt along the eastern seaboard as far as South Carolina and across the Atlantic in Portugal. Approximately two and a half hours after the earthquake the tsunami struck the southern part of Newfoundland as three main pulses, causing local sea levels to rise as high as twenty-two feet. At the heads of several long narrow bays the momentum of the tsunami carried water as high as eighty-five feet. This giant mountain of water claimed a total of twenty-eight lives, twenty-seven of them drowned and a young girl never recovered from her injuries and died a few years later. This was Canada's largest documented loss of life directly related to an earthquake, although oral traditions of First Nations people record stories of entire villages being destroyed by tsunamis.

More than forty local villages in southern Newfoundland were affected, where numerous homes, ships, businesses, livestock, and fishing gear were destroyed. Also lost were more than 280,000 pounds of salt cod. Total property losses were estimated at more than $1 million. Many buildings were lifted off their foundations and they floated away. The ferocity of the tsunami was not restricted to the land; it also tore up the seabed. This destruction of the seabed was believed by many to be the dominant factor in poor fish catches during much of the Great Economic Depression that followed in the years of the 1930s. The provincial capital of Newfoundland, St. John's, and the rest of the world did not immediately know of the devastation caused by the tsunami. The only telegraph line from the Burin Peninsula had, coincidentally and unfortunately, gone out of service just prior to the earthquake. When word did finally get out, help came quickly. A relief committee of the government, including doctors and nurses, arrived at communities on the south coast of Newfoundland on the afternoon of November 22. Recovery assistance was also provided by the Red Cross.

References for Further Study

Barton, Robert. 1980. *The Oceans*. London: Aldus Books.

Bolt, Bruce A. 1982. *Inside the Earth*. San Francisco: W. H. Freeman.

Lynch, J. 1940. *Our Trembling Earth*. New York: Dodd.

90

Ukraine catastrophe

November 1932

A terror famine in the old Soviet Union killed more than ten million people in the Ukraine

Stalin's systematic slaughter by famine and control of movement of more than ten million people was the worst mass atrocity in Europe before World War II

In November 1932, Joseph Stalin launched a campaign of terror against the farmers of the Ukraine to force them into joining a system of collective farming. The peasants, especially the owners of small farms, often referred to as the kulaks, opposed the plan for collective farming, so Stalin decided to starve them into submission by taking away their grain, their main source of food. Millions died from starvation in the year that followed.

In the aftermath of the Communist Revolution of 1917, peasants seized land from the owners of the big farms and Lenin allowed them to do this. He saw a period of small-scale free enterprise as a useful intermediate stage on the path to dictatorship. This stage went on for some time and farmers continued to work their land for profit. After Lenin died, Stalin came to power and, by the end of the 1920s, he decided it was time to abolish all private ownership of land and establish collective farms. This decision was part of a much bigger plan to double the nation's industrial output, a plan that was fully realized by 1932 at a time when the Western World's economies were in disarray due to the collapse of the world's stock markets. Stalin's plan required total control of the country's agricultural resources so that he could get adequate food supplies for the busy industrial cities at low prices, not the prices charged by the farmers.

The focus of his plan was the Ukraine where the best agricultural land of the nation was found and where he soon encountered the strongest opposition. The small-scale farmers, the kulaks, were determined to retain possession of their farms, and when they saw that Stalin was determined to create collective farms they decided to resist. They killed off all their stock for food and held back as much of their grain crops as they could. In less than a year these moves began to starve the cities of their food supplies and Stalin's drive for industrialization was threatened. In the two or three years before 1932 about twelve million new workers had joined the industrial enterprises around Moscow and farther east and most of these additional workers came from rural areas. Stalin felt he had to take drastic action.

Tensions between Russia and Ukraine have a long history. Historically, they were separate countries and after the Communist Revolution of 1917, which was a Russian revolution, Lenin was determined to make sure that Ukrainians supported the new dictatorship in Moscow. As early as 1918 a quarrel involving some Ukrainian farmers led to a response along the following lines from Lenin: These kulaks must be mercilessly suppressed. Find a hundred of their richest and hang them. Publish their names as a warning to others. Stalin's campaign took forms far worse than Lenin ever envisaged and it became even more violent after an incident in the Kremlin during the November 1932 anniversary celebration of the 1917 revolution. In the course of the evening his young wife, Nadezhda Alliluyeva, criticized Stalin publicly, an unthinkable act in that society at that time.

The reason for her criticism arose from her contacts with students who had been forcibly sent to the Ukraine to help with collectivization. Stalin had permitted her to study textiles at a technical school and there she met students returning from the Ukraine. She reported what she heard to Stalin—the mass terror, starvation, the bands of orphaned children begging for bread, even cannibalism. One student reported that he had to arrest two men who were selling corpses. Alliluyeva was anxious to do what she could to alleviate the suffering and when she saw that her husband was not interested she criticized him in front of his closest colleagues. She did not know that Stalin was well aware of all that was happening and had deliberately instigated it. He told her she had been collecting gossip, that these stories were all lies. Determined to prevent news of the atrocities reaching the rest of the country he immediately arranged for the execution of all the students who had been working in the Ukraine.

Alliluyeva knew at once that she had violated the code of secrecy surrounding Ukrainian matters when she spoke out in the Kremlin. Shortly afterward she was found dead, shot either by her own hand or that of another's. The evening's celebration ended abruptly. Later, all who had been in attendance were shot except for one young woman who happened to visit the party for a short time on an errand, unknown to Stalin, and who was able to leave quickly after the news of Alliluyeva's death. Many more executions followed. Stalin's whole character seemed to change. He acted in the most violent way against the slightest opposition from anyone. He intensified the campaign against the kulaks in a way that can best be described as extermination.

Stalin's drive to complete collectivization of farms was speeded up. The slightest opposition meant either instant death or banishment to Siberia. The quantity of grain to be given to the government was suddenly doubled at a time when the existing quota was at the starvation level. What was left for the people of the Ukraine was insufficient to sustain life. Any who tried to hold on to grain and hide it were also killed. Military units assisted by the secret police searched homes and the areas around them and shot anyone found guilty. These military units also guarded the government's quota of grain, stored locally in elevators. Within one month of the incident in the Kremlin, Stalin instituted a new passport system in order to keep tight control of everyone living in the Ukraine, especially to prevent starving peasants going elsewhere in search of food. Those who tried to leave without permission were shot.

Other rules accompanied the passport decree. Not only was a Ukrainian unable to leave his territory to look for the essentials of life, he was not permitted to leave the collective farm and seek work in the big industrial enterprises without permission from the local party official. The high death rate and the large numbers that had been banished to Siberia left the collectives with a shortage of labor. No party official would allow a worker to leave for the city. Alongside the needs of labor were the demands from Stalin to maintain secrecy about the devastation that had occurred and these demands were best met by isolating the Ukraine. Both the Ukrainian peasant as well as the former kulak, the owner of a small farm, had become serfs with no rights and no ownership of anything, just like the old days under the czar.

The *New York Times* reporter in Moscow in 1932, Walter Duranty, described the passport laws as popular and valuable in his dispatches to the United States. While he recognized that Westerners would see them as a shocking infringement of individual rights and freedom, in his view the Soviet worker sees them as a vigorous step toward the improvement of living conditions. Duranty, in his reports, stressed the value of the passports for preventing large numbers of agricultural workers leaving their communities. That was exactly why they were introduced by Stalin, but Duranty failed to include the real reason, to prevent starving peasants finding food. In his reports to the *New York Times* he goes so far as to identify some of these people. He lists some as class enemies, such as kulaks who are opposed to the good work being done by the government. This was the kind of reporting that gave him a Pulitzer Prize, yet at that very time he knew that many millions had already lost their lives due to the forced famine.

Duranty blamed the famine stories of 1932 on people who were hostile to the Soviet Union and wanted to prevent the United States from recognizing the new Communist Government. Whatever may have been his motives in falsifying facts the results were very favorable to Stalin and he was duly rewarded with special privileges not granted other correspondents. His reports carried a lot of weight in the United States because of the newspaper he represented. When, a short time later, the United States recognized the Soviet Union as the authentic government of the country, Walter Duranty's news reports were described as enlightening and dispassionate. The worst case of falsification came later, in the 1940s, when Hollywood produced the film "North Star," a Soviet collective farm run by well-fed happy peasants.

In the reality of 1932, village after village saw their infrastructures taken away as part of Stalin's method of total destruction. Churches were set on fire because they were symbols of the old Russia, a relic of the past that might compete with the new Russia if left standing. Bureaucrats from the Communist Party were put in charge of huge farms, deciding what to plant and where, what machinery to buy and how to use it, all without any expertise. The only sources of wisdom for this work were either dead or in Siberia. The inefficiency of the new system and its new managers, especially in the short term while the collectives were being organized, meant less grain for the cities. Hence Stalin demanded higher quotas and the cycle of starvation and death deepened. Cannibalism appeared here and there.

Students from the Soviet School of Mines in Moscow and other colleges like the one attended by Alliluyeva were sent to assist in the collectives because there were no peasants to do the work. Each group was allocated to a particular village but, as they traveled through the Ukraine, they noticed that there were no people anywhere. Sometimes they would arrive at a place that the map said was a village but nothing was there, only some bricks and weeds. At one destination where they were expected to stay a group found only one young girl, the only survivor in the village. She was in a state of dehydration, barely alive, and beyond medical help. She was anxious to tell the students as much as she could. The only regular food they had for some time was a kind of pancake made from beet and cherry leaves. In other villages the students met similar devastation. Here and there they met individuals who were insane through hunger and were attacking anyone and everyone they met. Any student who reported in Moscow what he saw was immediately shot.

As hunger spread the violence increased. Whole villages were wiped out and their inhabitants shot at the slightest provocation. Hundreds of thousands were banished to Siberia to work in mines or forests. The slaughter could almost be termed a genocide because a whole ethnic group was seen as the enemy of the Soviet State. Millions died from starvation. The number is uncertain but many estimates give five million as the likely number, half of that number being children. It was similar to the Nazi Jewish Holocaust as far as numbers of people are concerned. The reason the West knew so little about this holocaust compared with the German one is due to Stalin's effective propaganda. No foreign correspondent was allowed to visit the Ukraine. He arranged special conducted visits for distinguished foreigners who were supportive of socialist ideas and made sure that they only saw what he wanted them to see. George Bernard Shaw, the well-known British playwright, was one of those. He returned to Britain and announced that reports of starvation and forced collectivization were, in his words, "nonsense."

Certain villages with model collective farms were set up for the special visitors where everyone was well fed and well housed. Edouard Herriot, twice premier of France and also a strong socialist, spent five days in the Ukraine and stated that there was no famine there. Sir John Maynard Keynes, one of the world's greatest economists of his time and an expert on Russian agriculture, visited the Ukraine and told everyone in Britain when he returned that reports of famines were totally unfounded. Sidney and Beatrice Webb, British social scientists, spent a lot of time in the Ukraine in 1932 and afterward published a massive volume on their research. In it the peasants are described as greedy and cunning, subject to drunkenness and laziness. They are seen to be hostile toward the good work of a government that only wants to see resources shared equally by all. With allies like these Stalin made sure that the West knew little about the terror-famine, the name given to the catastrophe by Robert Conquest in his book *The Harvest of Sorrow*.

References for Further Study

Conquest, Robert. 1986. *The Harvest of Sorrow: Soviet Collectivization and the Terror Famine*. Edmonton, AB: University of Alberta Press.

Dolot, Miron, 1985. *Execution by Hunger: The Hidden Holocaust*. New York, London: W.W. Norton and Co.

Hryshko, Wasyl, 1983. *The Ukrainian Holocaust of 1933*. Toronto: Bahriany Foundation.

Isajiw, Wsevolod W., ed. 2003. *Famine-Genocide in Ukraine, 1932– 1933: Westem Archives, Testimonies and New Research*. Toronto: The Basilian Press.

91

Nevada earthquake

December 21, 1932

An uninhabited area of Nevada southeast of Reno

There were no casualties from this quake but complicated faulting occurred along a stretch of forty miles

A major earthquake of magnitude 7.2 occurred in an uninhabited area of western Nevada on December 21, 1932, and thereof caused minimal damage to buildings. Two cabins, one of stone and the other of adobe were destroyed, and ore-treating plants and mines were damaged. The main shock was felt in and around the community of Mina where many chimneys were knocked down, walls fell down, and cracks appeared in the ground. Extensive and complicated faulting happened over an area forty miles long and four to eight miles wide with numerous rifts developing, each as long as four miles in length and more than three hundred feet in width. Significant vertical and horizontal displacements were common. Boulders were shaken from cliffs, landslides took place, and ground water fluctuated vertically. The earthquake was felt from San Diego to southern Oregon and several aftershocks followed.

An earthquake of almost identical magnitude occurred a few hundred miles northeast of Mina in 1915, and the results on the ground were quite similar to the 1932 one: scarps as long as forty miles and extensive vertical and horizontal displacements happened. There was also a third major quake prior to 1915, within the twentieth century, and again primary rifts and fault scarps were observed along with significant earth movements. It is of special interest that the horizontal direction of movement of the adjoining mountain masses in the 1932 quake is the same as those observed at Owens Valley along the eastern slopes of the Sierra Nevada Mountains and also the same as on the east side of the San Andreas Fault.

These similarities are reminders of the nature of the underlying geological structures that form the westernmost limits of the North American Tectonic Plate. From Florida to Alaska there are places in the United States that are today found together in one location but geologically they are quite different from one another. They carry the name terranes. Florida, all of it, may well have come from Africa, and several places east of San Francisco certainly came to that location from elsewhere. For example, the Marin Headlands north of San Francisco was recently identified by its fossils as coming from somewhere on the seabed of the Pacific Ocean. Similar stories describe the history of Alcatraz and Angel islands.

These are but a few of the many terranes found across the nation. Parts of Nevada, which is quite some distance inland, came from Asia. All along the west coast, from Baja, California to Alaska, terranes are everywhere. Two hundred separate ones have been discovered, some large and some quite small, some located as far inland as Utah and Colorado. Most of these terranes arrived between 100 and 200 million years ago and as a result of their arrival the continent was extended westward by three hundred miles. The sources of these new lands are unknown. Some came from ocean floors, some from islands, and some from other continents. These terranes now provide valuable clues about ancient rock formations that lie underground beneath more recent formations.

Locating the epicenter for the 1932 earthquake was difficult for the geologists who examined the area in depth in 1934. This can readily be appreciated since their work preceded the knowledge of tectonic plates by more than thirty years. When no clear center became obvious from the various reports collected, an area southeast of Reno was selected as the epicenter region. Years later, with present day technology, the epicenter was located northeast of Reno, a location that is more in keeping with the direction of surface movements that has already been noted. Overall this earthquake was the second most severe ever for Nevada in terms of the available knowledge of that time.

References for Further Study

Moores, E. M., ed. 1990. *Shaping the Earth: Tectonics of Continents and Oceans*. New York: W. H. Freeman.

Sieh, Kerry, et al. 1998. *The Earth in Turmoil*. New York: W. H. Freeman.

Wood, H. O., and Heck, N. 1966. *Earthquake History of the United States: Stronger Earthquakes of California and Western Nevada*. Washington, DC: Environmental Science Services Administration.

92

Sanriku, Japan, earthquake

March 2, 1933

Northeast Honshu, Japan, in the Prefecture of Iwate

The offshore earthquake, though powerful, was barely felt on shore so no one was prepared for the tsunami that followed

The northeast coast of Honshu, Japan, in Iwate Prefecture, was hit with a powerful earthquake of magnitude 8.4 on March 2, 1933. It was followed by a tsunami that reached heights of seventy feet, causing catastrophic destruction to countless homes and ships and taking the lives of more than 6,000 people. An almost identical event occurred in the same location in 1896, causing the deaths of more than 26,000 people. The lower death rate in 1933 reflects, in part, the precautions taken after 1896 earthquake to cope with possible future earthquakes and tsunamis. It is also partially explained by the difference between the two causal earthquakes.

The 1896 event with the same name and a greater magnitude, 8.5, occurred on a reverse fault, as an interplate event, instead of the normal pattern, and this resulted in less shaking and slower initial speed. Its epicenter was ninety miles offshore, near an area of very deep water known as the Japan Trench, where the Pacific Plate subducts beneath the Asian Plate. Because of the nature of the fault, the impact on shore was much weaker than would normally be expected from such a powerful earthquake. Hence, people on shore paid little attention to the mild shaking they experienced so there was little expectation of a tsunami, even though this part of the Japanese coast experiences earthquakes frequently. Thirty-five minutes after the earthquake, the most devastating tsunami in Japan's history reached the shore at the same time as high tide. In some places the tsunami's wave reached a height of 125 feet. Everything in its path was totally devastated.

It was quite a different story with the 1933 event. The ground shaking was much more violent as the tsunami reached the shore about forty minutes after the earthquake. There were widespread cracking of walls and numerous landslides. Aftershocks followed, with the largest, occurring three hours after the main earthquake, having a magnitude of 6.8. These aftershocks continued intermittingly for about six months. Many different studies have been conducted on this tsunami. The results indicate that tsunamis became much larger in areas with a V-shaped bay, such as those on a ria coast. Later studies found that tsunamis in general become larger in V-shaped bays when the earthquake occurs relatively close to shore.

References for Further Study

Bryant, Edward. 2001. *Tsunamis: The Underrated Hazards*. Cambridge: Cambridge University Press.

Fuchs, Sir Vivian. 1977. *Forces of Nature*. London: Thames and Hudson.

Prager, Ellen J. 1999. *Furious Earth: The Science and Nature of Earthquakes, Volcanoes, and Tsunamis*. New York: McGraw-Hill.

93

Baffin Bay, Canada, earthquake

November 20, 1933

Off the east coast of Canada in Baffin Bay north of Iwate

This earthquake had a magnitude of 7.4 but the outstanding point about it is that this part of Canada's offshore in Baffin Bay is rarely hit with strong earthquakes

On November 20, 1933, the largest instrumentally recorded earthquake to have occurred along the passive margin of North America occurred in Baffin Bay. Coincidentally, it also was the largest known earthquake north of the Arctic Circle. In spite of its size, the 1933 earthquake did not result in any damage because of its offshore location and the sparse population of the adjacent onshore regions. The only known location that felt the earthquake was in Upernavik, Greenland. It was not felt in Thule to the north or in Disko Fjord to the south. One would have expected the earthquake to be felt in the closer northeastern coastal communities of Baffin Island but no reports were ever received.

The Baffin Island region continues to be active. In fact it is one of the most active regions in eastern Canada. Five magnitude 6 earthquakes have occurred here since 1933. The latest moderate-sized earthquake had a magnitude 4.8 and occurred on July 5, 2004. Analysis of seismograms of this earthquake shows strong evidence for strike-slip faulting, a condition that contrasts with the generally accepted belief that Baffin Bay is dominated by thrust faulting. The best-fitting solution consists of a large strike-slip sub event followed by two smaller oblique-thrust sub events. All of these occur at a depth of about six miles. An instrumental magnitude of 7.4 was determined for this earthquake. Preliminary analysis of subsequent large earthquakes in Baffin Bay finds additional evidence for strike-slip faulting in the region. The results for Baffin Bay, together with those for other passive margin earthquakes, suggest strike-slip faulting may be more prevalent in these regions than was previously believed.

It was believed that Baffin Bay was formed by seafloor spreading between sixty and forty million years ago, but more recent evidence suggests that the seafloor spreading began much earlier, around sixty-nine million years ago. It has been difficult to define the ocean-continent boundary owing to the thick sediments in Baffin Bay. There is evidence for faulting in the basement rocks and older sediments in Baffin Bay and for slumping, which could be seismically related, in the younger sediments. Although Baffin Bay is now known to be a very active seismic zone, considerably less was known about the 1933 event for a long time. Prior to the 1933 earthquake, the region was believed to be aseismic. Earthquakes of magnitude 6 and greater subsequent to1933 are noted in the International Seismological Summary and similar summaries, but it was only with the expansion of the Canadian seismograph network in the north during the 1950s and 1960s that these earthquakes could be put into any kind of regional context.

Estimates suggest that the earthquake catalogue for Baffin Bay has been complete above the magnitude 7.0 level since 1920, magnitude 5.5 since 1950, magnitude 4.0 since 1968 and is incomplete for magnitudes less than 4.0 for all time periods.

This contrasts sharply with the Charlevoix seismic zone in the long settled St. Lawrence Valley where the completeness years for the same magnitude levels are estimated to be 1660, 1900, and 1937, respectively, and where earthquakes of magnitude less than 0.0 can now be routinely located by a dense local seismograph network. Historical seismic activity is not uniformly distributed throughout Baffin Bay but is concentrated in northwestern Baffin Bay on the Baffin Island side of the 6,000 feet bathymetric contour. To date no one has been able to correlate the seismicity with particular geological structures or geophysical anomalies. It has been suggested that it is related to the stresses associated with post-glacial rebound.

References for Further Study

Andrews, A. 1963. *Earthquake.* London: Angus and Robertson.

Ebel, J. E., et al. 1991. *Earthquake Activity in the Northeastern United States.* Boulder, CO: Geological Society of America.

Jeffreys, H. 1950. *Earthquakes and Mountains.* London: Methuen.

94

Bihar, India, earthquake

January 15, 1934

Nepal, six miles south of Mount Everest

This magnitude 8.1 earthquake ruptured the earth for a distance of 1,200 miles and killed 12,000 people

The 1934 Bihar-Nepal earthquake had a magnitude of 8.1 and caused 12,000 deaths in Nepal and India combined. The epicenter of the earthquake was in Nepal six miles south of Mt. Everest. It was the worst that ever occurred in that country. Its rupture length was estimated to be 1,200 miles. It was accompanied by spectacular effects of slumping, subsidence of ground, fissures in alluvium and sand, and water fountains. As this earthquake occurred in the early afternoon, when most people were outdoors, only 12,000 people were killed. Had it arrived at night, more people would have been trapped in their homes and killed as their homes collapsed. Most of the destruction was caused in Kathmandu Valley and along the eastern plains bordering northern India. More than 80,000 houses were damaged.

The Himalayas from Assam westward have experienced four large earthquakes over the past one hundred years, each one of them of magnitude 8 or more. There is evidence that even larger events have occurred in the past, and geodetic and seismic monitoring show that stress is accumulating now. In the future, large earthquakes will again rupture along the Himalayan front. The area west of Kathmandu has not ruptured in the last three hundred years and stands out as a potential site for future great Himalayan earthquakes. The Indian Department of Mines and Geology is collaboratying with many scientists from all over the world to understand the causes and effects of these devastating earthquakes, and to help mitigate the ensuing destruction.

About two hundred million years ago an ocean separated India from the rest of Eurasia. This sea was gradually consumed through the subduction of the oceanic floor beneath Tibet. Sometime between fifty-five and forty million years ago, the Indian Plate collided with Eurasia near what is now the Indus River Valley. Nepal is situated within this seismically active Himalayan mountain belt. The continuing northward motion of India at the rate of about four centimeters per year has created wide-spread deformation, giving rise to the world's highest mountains. Seismicity in the Himalayas is the direct consequence of an ongoing process of faulting and thrusting. Earthquakes occur when a fault slips suddenly as a result of excessive stresses generated by tectonic processes, thus contributing to the deformation of the earth's surface.

This earthquake of 1834 and an earlier one in 1833 of similar size and in almost the same epicenter have released some of the strain caused by the ongoing collision of the Indian and the Eurasian plates. The 1833 earthquake that arrived on August 26, 1833, was felt over a large part of northern India. It shook an area half a million square miles in extent in Nepal and Tibet. Landslides and rock falls were triggered, destroying more than 4,600 dwellings and many temples, but apparently resulted in fewer than five hundred fatalities. It is certain that the loss of life would have been far more severe had not the main shock been preceded by two large foreshocks five hours before the main shock so that people went outdoors in alarm. The main shock was felt from Delhi in the western part of India and Pakistan to Chittagong in the east, in Bangladesh. Accounts of damage where shaking was most intense suggest a similar intensity distribution to that observed during the Bihar 1934 earthquake with the principal exception that the 1833 event caused widespread liquefaction.

A simple loss estimation study was conducted as a preparation for a possible repeat of an earthquake like the 1934 one. Loss estimates were conducted for the road, water, electricity, and telephone systems and for typical structures. In addition, possible death and injury figures were estimated by looking at statistics from previous comparable earthquakes in other parts of the world. Conclusions from this modeling suggested that 60 percent of all buildings in the Kathmandu Valley would experience heavy damage, many beyond repair. Almost half of the bridges in the valley would be impassible, and 10 percent of all paved roads would have moderate damage, such as deep cracks or subsidence. Nepal's only international airport would be inaccessible. Ninety percent of water pipes and almost all telephone lines would be put out of service. Half of all electric lines would be knocked out. In the light of the increased population today, compared with 1934, the death toll would likely be 22,000 and the number of injured 25,000.

References for Further Study

Bolt, Bruce A. 1993. *Earthquakes and Geological Discovery*. New York: Scientific American Library.
Fuchs, Sir Vivian. 1977. *Forces of Nature*. London: Thames and Hudson.
Jeffreys, H. 1950. *Earthquakes and Mountains*. London: Methuen.
Ritchie, D. 1988. *Superquake*. New York: Crown.

95

Quetta earthquake

May 31, 1935

The city of Quetta in what is now Pakistan

Quetta is 5,500 feet above sea level and is located in a very mountainous area about fifty miles from the Afghanistan border

At 3 A.M. on May 31, 1935, the city of Quetta was devastated by a severe earthquake of magnitude 7.7, lasting about thirty seconds, followed by many aftershocks. This city, at 5,500 feet above sea level, is in Southwest Pakistan, about fifty miles from the Afghanistan border. It was razed to the ground by the earthquake and more than 30,000 people lost their lives. Quetta, in 1935, was part of India and was ruled by Britain. British military officials immediately arranged to clear away the debris of the earthquake so that ambulance convoys could transport the injured to local dressing stations. At the same time groups of soldiers began to dig out the victims who lay under the ruins of their homes. There was little contact with the outside world as the telegraph center had been destroyed so Quetta had to cope on its own with the disaster.

Before the earthquake, Quetta had been a British military garrison since 1876 in the area that was called Northwest Frontier. Twelve thousand soldiers were stationed there to cope with the conflicts that emerged from time to time with local warlords. Its name comes from a local dialect meaning "fort." In order to accommodate the soldiers their residences were constructed in a multi-storied fashion. When the earthquake struck, these buildings collapsed and many lost their lives as they came down.

When reconstruction began after the earthquake all buildings were single-storied. The officer in charge of the garrison was Lieutenant-General Sir Henry Karslake, an experienced frontier specialist. His quick action both in rescue work and in reconstruction prevented an outbreak of disease. May is a hot month in Quetta and bodies had to be buried before decomposition set in.

Within three hours of the earthquake, that is to say between 3 A.M. and 6 A.M. on May 31, Karslake had divided up the devastated area into sections, allocated a group of soldiers to each section and told them to do everything possible to save lives and help the injured. They rescued people from the debris, moved in supplies, kept law and order, ran medical services, and set up a refugee camp on the open ground. Much of the work was done before breakfast! Only a military organization could have done it. The dead were laid out on the side of the road and collected in carts for burial and a separate group of soldiers had earlier been given the task of digging graves. Rescue work went on steadily throughout the day. By 8 P.M. it was dark and everything stopped.

Long before the evening the men were totally exhausted. It had been a very hot day and they had worked continuously since early morning, for the most part with nothing to eat. They had to wear medicated pads over their mouths and noses owing to the danger of disease from dead bodies and the odor hourly became worse. The pitiful requests of the survivors, who could do nothing to help themselves, and the sight of the dead bodies added to the strain of the day's work. Christians were buried in one place, Muslims in another, and Hindus burned their dead at any convenient location. A major problem was the question of what to do with animals. The city was full of cows and water buffaloes, and most of them had calves. Karslake had the injured shot.

During the first day or two, when everything was disorganized, young people from local tribal areas came to Quetta. They knew that beneath all those bricks thousands and thousands of rupees and valuables were buried. The large majority of native people kept their money in a box under their beds rather than trust the banks. Martial law was declared, which meant looters could be shot on sight, and soldiers were posted on the outskirts of Quetta to stop thieves from coming in. By June 12 all British women and children had been moved to temporary accommodation elsewhere along with thousands of refugees and over ten thousand injured men, women, and children. Some were taken by air but most went by rail. In retrospect, the Quetta earthquake of 1935 represented a landmark in India's history. For the first time, serious and systematic efforts were made in the design of earthquake-resistant methods of construction. The use of reinforced concrete at different levels in buildings dates from the experience of the Quetta earthquake. This and other actions taken in 1935 became the model for earthquake response in all the other earthquake-prone regions of India.

References for Further Study

Jeffreys, H. 1950. *Earthquakes and Mountains*. London: Methuen.
Moores, E. M., ed. 1990. *Shaping the Earth: Tectonics of Continents and Oceans*. New York: W. H. Freeman.
Ritchie, D. 1988. *Superquake*. New York: Crown.
Sullivan, Walter. 1974. *Continents in Motion*. New York: McGraw-Hill.

96

Labor Day hurricane

September 2, 1935
The Florida Keys

This storm's extremely high winds, high storm surge, record low pressure, and high fatalities earned it the name of the most powerful ever to strike the United States

The 1935 Labor Day Hurricane was the most powerful ever to strike the United States. It was not the most deadly in terms of fatalities but its extraordinary high winds, huge storm surge, and lowest barometric pressure ever recorded in the United States up to that time rank it as number one in intensity and destructive power. It was appropriately named "Storm of the Century." This category 5 event made landfall along the Florida Keys on Labor Day, September 2, 1935. People on the Keys were hit with 200 mph wind gusts, a storm surge of fifteen feet, and waves that carried everything before them.

It formed over the Atlantic and, after striking the Bahamas, it headed for Florida, reaching the Keys with sustained winds of 185 mph. Its central pressure was 26.35 of mercury, a level that was not surpassed until Hurricane Gilbert arrived in 1988. The population of Florida, including the Keys, was growing very fast in the mid-thirties. The disastrous outcome of the land grab of the 1926s had been forgotten. A railway line had been built at a cost of almost $50 million to link the Keys with the rest of the state. Large numbers of settlers and tourists kept arriving every year. By the summer of 1935 there were more than 12,000 residents there plus another 750 who were veterans, hired by the Federal Government to build a road linking the islands of the Keys.

Early on Sunday morning, September 1, the weather bureau, having noted that this storm had reached hurricane status, issued an advisory that it was going to move through the Straits of Florida and pass on into the

Gulf. Given the level of skills in meteorology at the time, and the limited number of stations relaying data to the bureau, this forecast was a reasonably estimate. By the evening of the day the advisory was extended to include all of southern Florida as well as areas along the west coast of the state. Very few people received this information. Those who did were the residents who had lived in the area for some years and were familiar with hurricanes. They were the ones who called the weather bureau frequently to get the latest information and shared it with others. They were also the ones who made all possible preparations to protect themselves from a strike. More recent arrivals, including the administrators of the veterans' road-construction project, decided to go with the earlier advisory that the storm would pass west south of the Keys.

The Bureau's estimate of the storm's location on Labor Day morning was out by almost three hundred miles. Furthermore, because they did not know at that time that it was a very narrow hurricane, less than ten miles across, they had little advance warning of the nature or direction of its forward winds. Before 11 A.M. the bureau decided to include the Keys as a place that might be hit. The Administrator of the veterans' project decided at that time to get a train backed down to the Keys on the one-track line to bring veterans away from the danger area. There were extended delays in getting this done. Because of the holiday no train was waiting and ready at the town of Homestead. It was after 5 P.M. before the needed train began to back down into the Keys. By 8 P.M. on Labor Day the storm struck. The train had not yet reached the middle Keys. Ten cars were tossed off the train by powerful waves that were surging over the islands. More than four hundred lost their lives.

Even today, with all the advances made in weather forecasting, a storm of the intensity of this Labor Day one would destroy every building in the keys. Few would survive. The only remedy in the face of an approaching hurricane is evacuation and this is the course consistently taken now especially since the total population of the Keys has risen to well over 100,000 when tourists are included in the total number. After striking the Keys, the hurricane continued up the west coast of Florida and landed again on the Florida Panhandle as a category 2 hurricane on September 4. It then passed over Georgia and South Carolina and back into the Atlantic Ocean off the coast of Virginia.

References for Further Study

Barnes, Jay. 1998. *Florida' s Hurricane History* Chapel Hill: University of North Carolina Press.

Lee, Sally. 1993. *Hurricanes*. New York: Franklin Watts Publishing.

Simpson, R., ed. 2003. *Hurricane: Coping with Disaster*. Washington, DC: American Geophysical Union.

Tannehill, Ivan Ray. 1956. *Hurricanes: Their Nature and History*. Princeton: Princeton University Press.

97

Gainesville tornado

April 6, 1936

Hall County, Georgia, southwest of Gainesville

This tornado reached downtown Gainesville as a double-funnel storm that caused 203 deaths and $13 million worth of damage

Early in the morning of April 6, 1936, an F4 tornado landed in Hall County southwest of Gainesville, Georgia, destroying homes and infrastructure as it moved toward downtown Gainesville. A second funnel from west of the city joined it and together they hit the square in downtown Gainesville. Memories linger long in situations like these. One lady recalled, sixty years later, how dark the city had suddenly become in the middle of the day. She had never seen anything like it before and all she heard from the people around her was to take cover as quickly as possible. She had no idea what they meant. The tornado destroyed almost everything in the downtown area, killing 203, injuring another 1,600, and causing $13 million worth of damage.

President Franklin Delano Roosevelt, who was on his way from Washington, D.C., to Warm Springs, Georgia, stopped in Gainesville three days after the storm and witnessed the destruction. This city was a struggling community in 1936. Its economic base had been weakened as a result of the depression of the 1930s. The boll weevil, drought, and crop failure had destroyed so much farmland that many farmers sought jobs away from the farms. Unemployment levels were high. Weather was not on many people's minds. In the downtown area on the morning of April 6, 1936, about two hundred people reported for work at the Cooper Pants factory. People on the way to the courthouse and kids on the way to school began to fill the square. Had there been better warning systems in place, the people of Gainesville would have been more prepared for what happened because, on the evening of the previous day, an F5 tornado passed through Tupelo, Mississippi, one of many tornadoes that were moving in the direction of Gainesville, about two hundred miles farther east.

References for Further Study

Bradford, Marlene. 2001. *Scanning the Skies: A History of Tornado Forecasting*. Norman: University of Oklahoma Press.

Grazulis, T. P. 1993. *Significant Tornadoes, 1680– 1991* St. Johnsbury,VT: Environmental Films.

Riehl, Herbert. 1954. *Tropical Meteorology*. New York: McGraw-Hill.

98

Hindenburg crash

May 6, 1937
Lakehurst, New Jersey

As the Hindenburg came in to land at Lakehurst, New Jersey, it caught fire and, with hydrogen tanks in use, a huge explosion followed

In the evening of May 6, 1937, the German airship Hindenburg was approaching Lakehurst, New Jersey, preparing to land. The ground crew stood ready as the ship reduced its speed, dropped its landing ropes, and prepared to connect with the mooring mast. Suddenly there was a flash of light and before anyone could assess what was happening a gigantic fireball erupted and the whole ship was engulfed in flames. In a few minutes the Hindenburg was reduced to a smoking mass of flames and molten metal.

In 1937, Hitler was at the height of his power in Germany and the zeppelin *Hindenburg* was the biggest airship in the world. As flagship of Germany's lighter-than-air fleet Hitler wanted to use it in a regular service to the United States to demonstrate the benefits of this new mode of travel. The *Hindenburg* had made the Atlantic crossing several times in the previous year and this was its first trip in 1937. With its huge size, almost as long as the *Titanic*, and with enough width and height to provide lounges and dining rooms, it offered a new and luxurious style of air travel. Everyone knew that the gas used to hold the airship aloft was hydrogen, inexpensive to produce and very effective, except that it was highly flammable. A single match or a bullet could easily set off the kind of explosion that occurred at Lakehurst.

This may have been the reason for premonitions of doom that were expressed before the flight left Frankfurt. These concerns affected some people so much that they cancelled their plans to travel. Seven million

Figure 55 This photo, taken at almost the split second that the *Hindenburg* exploded, shows the 804-foot German zeppelin just before the second and third explosions send the ship crashing to the earth over the Lakehurst Naval Air Station in Lakehurst, New Jersey, on May 6, 1937. The roaring flames silhouette two men, at right atop the mooring mast, dangerously close to the explosions.

cubic feet of hydrogen was needed to hold the 242-ton ship in the air and the presence of this huge quantity of a flammable gas might also have caused fears. The much safer gas to use in zeppelins was helium, more expensive to produce than hydrogen but not flammable. Germany would probably have used helium had it been available. In the 1930s the United States had control of the world's supply of helium and was not willing to let a country like Germany have access to it because of all the military buildups taking place in Europe.

The debate over helium versus hydrogen was not an easy one to settle and most German authorities finally relied on years of experience with hydrogen-filled airships to support sticking to this gas. It was sixty times cheaper than helium to produce so that was a big factor even if there had been no problem with supply. Helium had only 90 percent of the lifting power of hydrogen, because it was a slightly heavier gas, and Germany was anxious to mount the biggest cargo possible. It even changed the passenger terminal city for the *Hindenburg* from Friedrichshafen to Frankfurt because the latter was a thousand feet lower in elevation. At the higher air pressure that this change provided the airship could carry an additional seven tons of payload. To avoid the risk of an explosion when releasing gas to allow descent, which had previously led to two explosions, stored water was used instead.

The *Hindenburg* was a new airship. Its first flight took place in 1936. It was a luxury, air-conditioned vessel with twenty-five two-berth cabins to accommodate its fifty passengers. Passengers could live aboard in a style of luxury unmatched in all earlier airships. It was like living in a first-class hotel. Along both sides of the passenger deck was the promenade with seats and with slanted windows that gave clear views of the landscape below. It was always a spectacular scene as the vessel was only 650 feet above the ground or sea level. Passengers boarded the ship via a retractable set of stairs as far as the lower deck, then by a staircase to the top deck. The *Hindenburg* could travel 8,000 miles without refueling at a speed of 80 mph.

The material used for the sides was cotton or linen as these were found to have better resistance to wind and rain than any other materials. A varnish and several coats of aluminum paint completed the outer shell. Everywhere inside the ship the lightest materials were used for framing, usually aluminum. The ship's brain was the control car, located on the bottom of the vessel close to the front. Two of the key officers always on duty were the rudder and elevator men. The former kept the ship on a fixed course while the elevator man watched four instruments dealing with horizontal and vertical shifts, elevation, and hydrogen pressure.

Hindenburg was the first of the zeppelins to allow smoking but the rules for smokers were strict. There was a revolving door that served as an airlock through which people passed to reach the smoking-room. Asbestos lined the walls of this room and no passenger could leave until the cigarette was extinguished in a water-filled ashtray. No one was ever seasick on this airship; its motion was so smooth that often passengers refused to believe it was in the air, quite a contrast to today's big planes. One popular game that related to the airship's stability saw people competing to see how long a pen or pencil could be stood on end without falling over. Ernst Lehmann was the captain, a man with long years of experience on zeppelins stretching back to World War I days. As the airship traveled across the Atlantic on its fateful final voyage everything seemed to go well. The weather was good so speed was maintained at 60 mph. This meant crossing the Atlantic in three days. At Lakehurst, New Jersey, there was some delay due to bad weather but the rain and wind had gone by the time the *Hindenburg* touched down.

No one was prepared for the chaos and destruction that followed the spark from somewhere as the nose of the *Hindenburg* approached the mooring mast. The landing ropes had been thrown down and ground crew was steadily drawing the ship to the ground. Suddenly the whole structure collapsed and fire was everywhere. Some jumped to the ground, others waited until the ship dropped farther down, risking getting incinerated in the process. One passenger called it a medieval picture of hell. Some had no chance of escape and were caught in the flames. The whole conflagration started and was all over in half a minute. Captain Lehmann, who ran back into the flaming fuselage more than once to rescue people, was so badly burned that he died soon after being taken to hospital. Thirty-six people lost their lives and many were injured.

The fire burned on long after the airship was a mass of tangled wreckage. Diesel oil from the engines kept it going. An attempt was made to rescue some of the mail and there was some success. People in Germany and across the United States received badly charred letters a few days later. Some looting occurred because the police did not cordon off the area for a few hours. The conclusion as to cause was simple, the ship was destroyed because it had hydrogen. Suggestions of sabotage were given serious consideration but were later dismissed. The fact that a storm had passed over the area just before the ship arrived gave confirmation to the idea that a static electrical charge had built up between the outside of the airship and any metal structures within.

It was discovered that the fabric cover, unique to the *Hindenburg*, was a poor conductor, thus allowing an electrical charge to build up. Immediately after this tragedy, the fabric of other airships was checked and, where necessary, changed to ensure good conduction. Other changes in the aftermath of the *Hindenburg* explosion saw hydrogen being removed and helium put in its place on all airships. At the same time, new regulations were put in place to anticipate electrical discharges. The electrical gradient between ship and ground was always thereafter measured at landing time. Perhaps if the *Hindenburg* had decided to get to ground first instead of the mooring mast the story might have been quite different because the size of the electrical charge would have been less. In any case, this one event changed the history of aviation. The zeppelin never regained an important role in air travel and production of new airships was stopped soon after 1937. Sixty-four years later, Friedrichshafen was once again in the news as a new eight million dollar, helium powered, zeppelin was built there for low altitude tourist trips around central and southern Europe.

Germany's alternative to the growing demand for luxury travel across the Atlantic in bigger and more luxurious liners came to a sudden end when the *Hindenburg* caught fire. A comparable shock had come twenty-five years earlier with the sinking of the *Titanic* and, as a result, new rules about safety were introduced at that time for all ocean liners. The demand for ways of moving from place to place greatly increased after World War II and, because there were large numbers of people leaving Europe for short or long stays at countries around the world, faster ways of traveling were demanded. In the final years of World War II, jet fighter planes came into use. Immediately after the war this type of plane was seen as the answer to faster modes of travel. By the early 1950s commercial travel by jet planes had started. Like all new developments in the technology of air travel there were risks of failures. To use jets in warfare was quite different from long distance usage with large numbers of people. The wartime machines were light and their length of time in the air on any one sortie was only a few hours.

It was a very different challenge to fly a big airliner on jet engines halfway around the world. Britain was a pioneer in this new way of air travel and in 1952 the De Havilland Company launched the first turbo-jet airliner, the comet. It was a thirty-six-seat jet and it could fly from London to Johannesburg, South Africa, at speeds of 500 mph. The British Overseas Airways Corporation (BOAC) adopted it at once and in less than a year comets were flying around the world. Other airlines were equally eager to buy these new jets and De Havilland soon had a waiting list of five for every comet that came off the assembly line. The trip from London to Singapore was one of BOAC's longest routes and comets were particularly welcome on it because they cut back substantially on the time taken. One comet was flying that route in 1953 and had stopped over in Calcutta en route. As it took off on May 2, 1953, to continue its flight to London everything seemed normal. Six minutes later communication with the control tower was lost. The plane had gone down less than ten miles from the airport and all forty-three on board were killed. This was BOAC's first fatal crash in five years and the fact that it happened to one of its newest planes was a big shock. Commentators insisted that some unusual weather much have caused the accident. One newspaper concocted a story of a downdraft meeting an updraft of air just where the comet was flying. Many believed it.

Another long-distance route flown by BOAC was London to Johannesburg so comets were popular there too. For eight months after the tragedy near Calcutta, nothing occurred to make BOAC change its activities. The comet continued to be enormously popular. Then, on January 10, 1954, a comet from London, one that had stopped over in Rome, took off from there to continue its journey to Johannesburg. There were thirty-five people aboard. These numbers seem small by today's standards but the 1950s were years that knew nothing about the jumbo plane or even smaller jets of the kind we know now. Jets were still quite new ways of traveling. An Italian fisherman saw this jet shortly after its takeoff while it was high in the sky, then watched it plummet down into the sea near the Island of Elba, about one hundred miles from Rome. BOAC immediately grounded all of its comets and proceeded to conduct a full scale inspection of its entire fleet.

Following a meticulous series of examinations, flights resumed in March of 1954 but within a few days another comet went down, this time on the London–Johannesburg route. Commentators and officials now began to ask big questions. Newspaper reports wondered about the basic safety of the comet, asking whether there might be something wrong in the design that no one had yet recognized. A major salvage operation was launched to recover the wreckage of the jet that went down off the Island of Elba and the results were very surprising. There was no evidence of fire, explosion, or engine failure. The only possible explanation for the crash was the condition of the fuselage. It had been ripped apart in several places.

Intensive tension and pressure tests on the materials being used in the comet's fuselage finally revealed what was wrong. The materials were inadequate for long distance travel at high altitudes. The jet's fuselage was fine for short-range military fighters at low altitudes but it could not cope with repeated pressurization, speed, and high altitude over long distances. The career of the comet came to an abrupt end two years after its debut. Some time later it was redesigned with better materials but by then other manufacturers like Boeing had captured the jet plane market and the comet was no longer the only choice available.

References for Further Study

Archbold, Rick. 1994. *Hindenburg: An Illustrated History*. Toronto: Penguin Books.

Cornell, James. 1976. *The Great International Disaster Book*. New York: Charles Scribner's Sons.

Dick, Harold G., and Robinson, Douglass H. 1985. *The Golden Age of the Great Passenger Airships: Graf Zeppelin and Hindenburg*. Washington, DC: Smithsonian Institution.

Prideaux, Michael, ed. 1976. *World Disasters*. London: Phoebus Publishing Company.

Ward, Kaari, ed. 1989. *Great Disasters*. Pleasantville, NY: Readers Digest Association.

99

Nanking massacre

December 13, 1937

Nanking, the capital of China at the time of the massacre

In violation of international agreements that Japan had signed Japanese soldiers assaulted China. Nanking, the capital of China at that time, was the scene of their greatest and most brutal actions

On December 13, 1937, the Japanese Army, as it continued it's assault against China, in knowing violation of an international agreement, reached Nanking, the Chinese capital, and began to loot, rape, torture, and murder all over the city. Soldiers who surrendered were shot or bayoneted and homes were looted, often in full view of the commanding officers. The atrocities committed were so barbaric that they rank among the worst of the twentieth century.

In the years before World War II, Japan began its series of military conquests in China. It was led by a group of officers who had either forced or persuaded the rest of Japan's leaders to take these steps. Some who opposed their plans were killed. It was a reckless venture and a violation of an agreement that Japan had signed regarding international relations. The militarists responsible for all that happened subsequently were completely indifferent to this agreement. They not only attacked China, beginning with the conquest of Manchuria in 1931, but they ignored virtually every known rule of law for dealing with civilians and prisoners during war.

The Tokyo War Crimes trials, the Asian equivalent of the Nuremberg trials of the Nazi war criminals, began in 1946 and exposed the details of what had gone on over the previous years. Its rationale for the indictments it handed down was the UN War Crimes Commission Report of a year earlier. In this report blame for all the atrocities was laid on both the government in Tokyo as much as on the commanders in the field. The following are a few extracts from the damning indictments that were listed: "Inhabitants of countries which were overrun by the Japanese were ruthlessly tortured, murdered, and massacred in cold blood. Torture, rape, pillage, and other barbarities occurred. Despite the laws and customs of war as well as their own assurances, prisoners-of-war and civilians were systematically subjected to brutal treatment and horrible outrages, all calculated to exterminate them."

Nowhere were these acts of bestiality more violently executed than in Nanking. On December 13, 1937, advance units of Japanese soldiers captured the city, China's capital. The defenders, against the advice of General Chiang Kai-shek who commanded the Chinese Army, tried hard to hold out against the invaders but lost. As soon as they entered the city the Japanese launched an orgy of cruelty and destruction. Women of all ages were raped, by individuals and by groups, then killed, as many as 20,000 in all. Soldiers who surrendered were shot, beheaded, or bayoneted. Others were mutilated and killed in other ways, often in the most bestial ways imaginable. Altogether about 300,000 died in these ways.

For the weeks following December 13, 1937, Japanese rapes and massacres continued. There were atrocities against civilians and mass executions. The enormity of the scale and nature of these crimes was documented by survivors and recorded in the diaries of Japanese soldiers. Nanking had been a city of 250,000 but as people retreated westward from the Japanese advance the city's population swelled to a million by December of 1937. On December 13, as the city fell, a large number of refugees tried to escape across the Yangtze River but were unable to get away because all the boats were missing. Some tried to swim but they were all shot by Japanese soldiers, some in the water, most at the river's bank. Altogether 50,000 died at that location in a few hours.

In the streets, about 100,000 refugees or wounded soldiers were huddled, and they became targets for tank and artillery gunners. Dead bodies covered the streets. They became "streets of blood" in the course of a two-day massacre. Many Chinese soldiers moved around inside the city and changed into civilian clothes but that made little difference to their fate. Anyone who was suspected of being a soldier was arrested. They were all sent outside the city in groups numbering from several thousand to tens of thousands and shot by machine guns. Any who were still alive were bayoneted. Gasoline was poured on some and they were burned alive. Numerous atrocities occurred all over the city, mainly on civilians. Japanese soldiers invented and exercised inhumane and barbaric methods of killing, including stabbing, striking off the head, and drowning.

A group of concerned foreigners formed an international rescue committee and established a safety zone for refugees within the city. Japanese soldiers ignored the rights of the foreigners and frequently entered the safety zone where they arrested young men. Every time they did so, the men they arrested were executed on the site. All the storehouses were emptied and everything else of value was seized, including jewelry, coins, and antiques. There was an organized burning of buildings throughout the city. Nanking, once a beautiful historical center, was burned to ashes. The best that can be said about all this horror is that it conforms to some of the worst practices in wars from the ancient past. Citizens and soldiers alike were often terrorized by successive acts of such brutality and cruelty that they remained passive and submissive. The conquering army could thus proceed with its mission without having to worry about resistance from the conquered.

Women who did not readily submit to their rapists were tortured afterwards before being killed. The only ones who were allowed to live were the so-called "comfort women," prostitutes who were forced to accompany the soldiers on their campaigns. After World War II, some survivors from this group successfully sued the military authorities. The brutal rape scenes of Nanking are matched by others since that time. Gang sexual assault and rape with murder was commonplace during the Bangladesh war of independence in 1971 and is described by Susan Brownmiller in her book, *Against our will: Men, women and rape*. Some aspects of the rapes of Nanking left scars for a long time. No Chinese woman from that time ever admitted that her child was the result of rape. The whole subject of Chinese women being impregnated by Japanese rapists remained so sensitive that it has never been thoroughly studied.

Rape victims finally received the recognition they deserved in the Bosnia Civil War of the 1990s. In that conflict Serbian soldiers singled out Muslim women and girls and raped them as violently as did the Japanese in China. For the first time in history there was a declaration by an international tribunal that these sexual crimes alone constituted a crime against humanity. Three former Serbian soldiers were indicted on this charge in March of 2000. The things they did were just the same as those committed in Nanking, but fortunately their evils were raised to the highest level of international crime. Information about the Japanese activities was poorly circulated at the time but sufficient was known in western countries, especially in the United States, and thus strong condemnations were sent to Japan.

On one occasion, the Japanese officer in charge invited sailors from a Japanese boat that was anchored on the Yangtze River to witness the mass executions. A memorial building now stands on the spot where many of these mass executions took place. For decades, Japanese authorities denied that anything extraordinary had happened. One eyewitness account did reach the Western World and was published in the *New York Times* in December of 1937 but the details were few. Not until the War Crimes Trials were held in Tokyo in 1946 was the full account recorded. Many who witnessed the terrible events told their story at that time.

There is one puzzling aspect of Japanese activities at Nanking that may relate to a friendship from an earlier time between Sun Yat-sen, the Chinese revolutionary, whose memorial is in Nanking, and General Matsui who commanded Japanese forces when they captured the city. Sun Yat-sen had previously visited Japan on more than one occasion and met with General Matsui. They became good friends and shared the same ideals for many of the problems of East Asia. Japanese Emperor Hirohito took a detailed interest in all aspects of the country's military exploits but his focus on Nanking was intense. Could it be that he knew of the friendship between Matsui and Sun Yat-sen and was afraid that it might prevent his orders from being carried out?

Whatever the reason might have been for the Emperor Hirohito's involvement in the fighting at Nanking, the records of the war show that he decided to interfere by appointing his uncle, Prince Asaka, as commander of all forces at Nanking. Matsui was not replaced but his authority was taken away because Prince Asaka had greater status. The first thing Asaka did was to send sealed orders to all the officers under his new command ordering them to execute all captives. A note accompanying his orders told the officers to destroy the orders after reading them. Asaka knew that what he had commanded was wrong and that it was a flagrant violation of all international agreements for dealing with captured soldiers. He stayed on in Nanking until February 10, 1938. Matsui left the city soon after Asaka arrived.

The Rape of Nanking was the phrase used at the Tokyo trials to describe the atrocities that occurred there and the witnesses to what happened were many. Dr. Wilson, a native of Nanking who had been educated in the United States, saw his hospital filled to overflowing with patients who had received bullet or bayonet wounds, and women who had been sexually molested the morning after the Japanese captured the city. This scene was repeated every day for the following several weeks. An older official from the Chinese Ministry of Railways described the scene in street after street. There were bodies lying everywhere, some badly mutilated. It was no use counting them. There were far too many. All of these personal reports were given to the prosecutors in the presence of the Japanese officers who were on trial.

Hsu, a member of the Chinese Red Cross, gave help in burying the corpses to avoid an epidemic. He counted as many as 43,000 then left off counting. The bodies had their hands tied with either rope or wire so he could not follow the Chinese custom of loosening anything that was tied before burial. Several survivors of mass killings testified how they were able to feign death by falling and getting covered with those beside them who were just shot. Many of those had to endure thrusts from bayonets, a common Japanese practice to make sure that there would be no witnesses to their atrocities. An American professor of history, Miner Bates, at the University of Nanking told of numerous killings for each of which there was no provocation or apparent reason.

Bates also told of thirty college girls at his university being raped two days after the Japanese entered the city and a further eighteen three days later in different parts of the campus. All the other women were in a state of hysteria. Furthermore, his campus was next door to the Japanese Embassy so Japanese officials in the embassy must also have been aware of what was happening. Prosecutors asked Bates for the name of the officer in command of the Japanese troops at that time. General Matsui was the answer, the man now standing in the court along with Koki Hirota, Japan's foreign minister at that time. For most of the time during the Tokyo trials defense lawyers were silent in the face of damning personal testimonies but this time, because Matsui and Hirota were importance defendants it was different.

When Bates told the prosecution that he had sent reports of the atrocities to the Japanese Embassy, William Logan, who was defending the accused, immediately inquired if Bates' reports had been sent to Tokyo. Bates assured him that they were sent but he was then asked how he knew. Bates informed him that he had received detailed accounts from the U.S. Ambassador in Tokyo, describing discussions he had had with Hirota over these very reports. There were numerous additional personal testimonies added to these, many of them so gruesome that only the barest details should be recorded. The randomness and the cruelty of the ways that people were tortured before being killed all pointed to a deliberate policy, not just the actions of a few depraved individuals.

On the basis of massive amounts of evidence, twenty-eight Japanese officers were prosecuted for mass murder, rape, pillage, brigandage, torture and other barbaric cruelties upon a helpless civilian population. Eyewitnesses gave testimonies of the atrocities. Of the twenty-eight men, twenty-five were found guilty. Of the other three, two died during the trials, and one had a mental breakdown. Seven criminals were put to death by hanging, sixteen were sentenced to life imprisonment, and two had lesser sentences. Of the seven who were hanged, four were executed for their involvement in the Rape of Nanking. Quite apart from the decisions at the trials, about one thousand officers committed hara-kiri suicide, in the days following Japan's defeat. This form of suicide was a Japanese national tradition in the wake of failure.

Matsui pretended all through the trials that nothing more than a few incidents had happened. When asked if Prince Asaka, uncle of the Emperor Hirohito, had anything to do with all the crimes he strongly defended him. In fact, all of the emperor's household was exempted from prosecution, despite extensive evidence of their involvement. This was a firm policy of the countries conducting the trials. On the night before he was hanged, Matsui changed his mind about Nanking. In his words it was a "national disgrace." He went further and said that the real culprit for all of it was Prince Asaka. Over the years that followed the trials, Japanese citizens maintained a denial of the massacre. During the war, because of the strict control of news, civilians knew almost nothing about atrocities. They heard only about heroic war figures.

The facts released during the Tokyo War Trials shocked the whole country. Many books were written on the subject. At that time, there was no public government denial of the massacre, but there was not any official public acceptance of responsibility either. From the 1960s to the 1980s deliberate efforts were made to deny the horrors of Nanking. A highly controversial history textbook for schools was published in 1982. The Rape of Nanking was described as action in response to resistance from the Chinese Army. The nations of Asia were enraged and their anger made Japanese authorities reconsider the contents of the book.

By the 1990s, a different version of history made its way into school texts. These books now refer to the "Great Nanking Massacre," in which Japanese soldiers conducted a rampage of looting, burning, and raping against international condemnation, and killed those who surrendered. Media sensitivity in North America has also changed since the 1930s. The reports that were published by the press and in magazines in 1937 would not be acceptable today because they might generate destructive hatred against the perpetrators. Press reports on Rwanda, a similar event of mass murder, toned down the horror of the actual event. By contrast, the following are the kinds of reports carried in the Western press and journals in 1937 regarding Nanking: it was his job to complete the butchery of the Chinese defenders. He lined them up in batches and shot them all. It was a tiresome business killing them. Japanese sailors watched the executions.

References for Further Study

Brackman, Arnold C. 1987. *The Other Nuremberg: The Untold Story of the Tokyo War Crimes*. New York: William Morrow and Company.

Chang, Iris. 1997. *The Rape of Nanking*. New York: Basic Books.

Hoehling, A. A. 1973. *Disaster: Major American Catastrophes*. New York: Hawthorn Books.

Katsuichi, Honda. 1999. *The Nanjing Massacre*. New York: Pacific Basin Institute.

Yin, James, and Young, Shi. 1996. *The Rape of Nanking*. Chicago: Innovative Publishing.